The Office Book

IDEAS AND DESIGNS FOR CONTEMPORARY WORK SPACES

Judy Graf Klein

Consulting Editors: Francis Duffy & John Pile

Facts On File, Inc.
460 Park Avenue South
New York, New York 10016

Editor: John Smallwood

Project Editor and Caption Writer: Linda Sunshine

Consulting Editors: Francis Duffy (UK) and John Pile

Contributing Editors: Pamela Ferguson, Richard Horn,

Kathy Matthews, Melissa Sutphen

Photo Research: Martina D'Alton and Sylvia Katz (UK)

Copy Editors: Linda Calabro and Wendy L. Ruoff

Design: M & Co.

Associate Designer: Larry Kazal

Mechanical Production: Deborah DeStaffan

Typeset by BPE Graphics, Inc.

Printed in Japan.

Library of Congress Cataloging in Publication Data

Klein, Judy Graf.
The office book.

Bibliography: p. 281
Includes index.
1.   Office layout.
I.   Facts On File, Inc.   II.   Title.
HF5547.2.K55   725'.23   81-12559
ISBN 0-87196-499-6   AACR2

A Quarto Book

Copyright © 1982 by Quarto Marketing Ltd.

First published in 1982 by Facts On File, Inc.
460 Park Avenue South, New York, N.Y. 10016

Every effort has been made to locate the copyright owners
of the photographs in this book. Omissions brought to our attention will
be corrected in subsequent editions.

The Office Book
was produced and prepared by
Quarto Marketing Ltd.
32-33 Kingly Court
London W.1., England

Dedicated to Adina, Oleanna, and Stephan Klein

CONTENTS

Introduction
By Frank Duffy

1

History
Page 9

The Earliest Offices
The Industrial Revolution
Office Industries
The Office Building
The Office in the Cityscape
Office Interiors
Office Technology
Office Management
Refining the Office
Famous Offices in Film
Offices of Famous People
Recent Developments
The Open Office
Office Automation
Humanizing the Office
Economic Issues
Future Trends

2

Designer's Choice
Page 46

Ward Bennett
Vignelli Associates
Doris La Porte
Gwathmey/Siegel and Associates
John Saladino Associates
Pentagram
David Hicks
Terence Conran

3

Elements of Design
Page 65

Ceilings
Lighting
Walls
Floors
Windows
Doors
Desks
Chairs
Machines in the Private Office
Accessories
Lamps
Plants in the Office
Art in the Office

4

Designing Office Space
Page 125

Entrance Doors

Reception Area

Executive Suites

Executive Secretary Area

Board Rooms
& Dining Rooms

Cafeterias & Bars and Baths

Clerical & Operational Areas

Corridors & Coat Closets

Libraries & Conference
Rooms

Files & Storage

Coffee-Breaks & Kitchens

Mail Rooms

Spaces for Machines

Stairs

Open Office

Non-Traditional Approaches:
Johnson's Wax; Ford Foundation;
Best Products; Central Beheer;
Willis Faber & Dumas; Ferryboat;
Victorian Residence; Industrial
Loft; Townhouses.

5

Adapting Spaces
Page 187

Advertising Agencies

Architects and Designers

Consulates

Dentists

Doctors

Fashion Designers

Lawyers

Producers

Publishers

Traders

Working at Home

The Moving Office

The Portable Office

6

Office Planning
Page 233

Planning Office Spaces

Planning the Total Image

Getting Advice from
Design Professionals

Warren Platner
Associates, Architects

Kevin Roche, John Dinkleoo
& Associates

Karen Daroff

George Nelson

DEGW

A

Appendix
Page 253

Useful Addresses
page 268

Bibliography
page 281

Index
page 282

C O N T E N T S

Introduction

Working to Live: The work ethic has a lot to answer for. Until now, office design has never had the attention it deserves because for generations we have been schooled to live for work rather than work to live. The idea that the working environment can be enjoyed, rather than suffered, is new.

Perhaps it is as well that a massive change in office expectations is happening now. Office work is well on the way to absorbing us all in one way or another. Downtown, in the suburbs, at home, if we work at all, more than likely we work in an office. If office work is becoming so important to so many people then perhaps the office environment can be allowed to become important too.

The Office Book also demonstrates another point. Designers experience two kinds of tension: one a struggle between themselves and the materials—the colors, fabrics, furniture—they are working with and the other between themselves and their audience.

In recent years the material for office design has been enormously enriched. For example, it was not so long ago that carpeting in offices implied rare and unapproachably high status; systems furniture and adjustable chairs were unheard of. If you don't believe this, look back at old interior design magazines and see how bleak the 1960s office actually was. Since then, the office designer's audience has become sophisticated and vocal to a previously unimaginable extent. A book like this couldn't have been written ten years ago. More options, more demands: this is a critical moment for office design.

Gloss versus Grain: Take one example of the changing mood—not necessarily the most important, but an obvious one in *The Office Book*. Two styles of photography are evident here: the timeless, unpeopled and entirely immaculate shots, typical of some high style projects, and the grainier, more human pictures which often come from Europe. It is not only chic to show ordinary not particularly beautiful people, warts and all, in architectural photography; it is evidence of a change of heart. Some designers have begun to think that gloss is not everything, that life matters as well.

But where did the gloss come from in the first place? The modern office is largely an American invention. The United States created not only the technology of the office but also its aesthetic. Scientific management and work studies pioneered by Taylor and the Gilbreths was combined with the architecture of the skyscraper, pioneered in the 1880s in Chicago and sophisticated later in New York. What a reality, what an image—no wonder the world was dazzled. The problem of designing office interiors was solved with the same effortless resource. In the 1930s came the elevation of the decorator and then in the 1960s the apotheosis of the interior designer into the space planner. High standards of design were combined with an efficiency which amazed most European architects. Space planners understood large organizations, the corporate mind, and the transience of design and organizational decisions better than their clients.

Corporate Gods: That's the good side of the glossy image. The darker side of this achievement in office design is the less acceptable face of management: a certain absence of humanity despite the high technical standards, a tendency to pay more reverence to the corporation than to the individual, too much faith in routinized procedures and systems despite the initial freedom of invention.

You will find some of these characteristics in projects described in this book. Look, for example, how common are internal, windowless office rooms (which, incidentally, few Europeans would tolerate). See how much lip service is still paid to formal space standards which are rarely achieved in practice, especially in rapidly growing organizations. Listen to the honeyed words whispered by designers in the ears of corporate moguls about success, gracious living and executive washrooms. Above all, observe the pervasive faith in solving problems by buying systems furniture, a technological talisman if ever there was one, and no substitute for creative design.

Nevertheless, the glossy image at its best, and you will find many examples in these pages, is a considerable feat in organizational and aesthetic terms. You have to see a new, good quality American office with European eyes to realize how high the standard is, how great the achievement.

Evidence of Change: The grainy style is also evident in this book. It is often the result of direct user involvement in the design process. The offices for Central Beheer in Apeldoorn, Holland are an example where office workers are expected to arrange and decorate their own workplaces as they would look after their living rooms at home. Look at the new, highly cellular Swedish and German office buildings which are the direct consequence of worker's councils reacting against the open plan and demanding, in effect, the right for every office worker to have his own room with a view. In America signs to watch are talk about involving social scientists and especially about post-occupancy evaluation: incipient consumerism at work. American pioneers like Robert Sommer, Fritz Steele and Franklin Becker have shown how social science can be employed to help the user get what he wants.

The Designer's Dilemma: The key question for designers is whether involving users in design is going to drag design standards down to a market research or trades-union backed mediocrity, or even lower. Consumerism has vices as well as virtues. One danger visible in European union negotiations about the working environment is an exaggerated conservatism. Because each aspect of the office is discussed in such detail with so many people, only the safest options are chosen. Doubts and fears are easier to express than new ideas. Novelty and creativity are strangled at birth.

This can be incredibly frustrating. Not only is the designer faced with a nightmare multiplication of the old story about the chairman's wife dictating the color scheme, but the range of available options is diminishing all the time. Why bother? What can the designers contribute in participative design?

This is where *The Office Book* is intended to come in. The theory on which it is based is that the more the audience knows, the better the performers will play. Most design books are written by a professional for a closed circle of other professionals. A not so subtle form of censorship excludes styles which aren't approved. *The Office Book* is written not just for professionals or for connoiseurs but for the ordinary consumer of office design.

One thing is certain: no one style, glossy or grainy, will satisfy everyone. What *The Office Book* does is to show as many examples as possible of the more interesting new offices in North America and Europe. Trends are visible: sometimes complementary, sometimes contradictory. The variety is meant to generate more ideas about newer, better and cleverer ways of doing things.

The New Interior and its Significance: Why should so much be happening today? A number of factors are involved. Never has the office been so central to society. Because of information technology, office workers are more likely to be professionals or managers rather than humble clerks. Because office workers have status and

power, they are unlikely to accept meekly what they are given. They want more and there is no obvious ceiling to their wants. Information technology itself is helping to make the office more stressful because expensive equipment means that more is at stake. Equipment—and we haven't seen anything yet—has introduced a new dimension of ergonomic complexity. Making the office comfortable is no longer simply a nice option for rich, philanthropic multi-nationals. It is an economic, social and functional imperative for firms of every size and every management style.

It is significant that furniture manufacturers in both the United States and Europe have responded to this problem faster and in some cases more imaginatively than architects and interior designers. The last ten or fifteen years has been a golden age in office furniture design. Partly this has been intelligent opportunism. But, it also reveals a fundamental change—a shift from a period in which architecture was not only dominant but also permanent to a new era in which interior design has become important visually and economically because it can respond to change. The age of the pyramids has gone. Because organizations are changing so fast, interiors and office furniture, in particular, have become more flexible, more responsive, more functional.

Opening Pandora's Box: *The Office Book* is not alone in opening up design to the consumer. Terence Conran's *House Book* set the style. *High Tech* showed how apparently esoteric design debates can be opened up to a wide and interested public. Conversely, Tom Wolfe's *From Bauhaus To Our House* shows what happens when designers are left to talk only among themselves.

Even if they wanted, designers would have no better chance than King Canute in stemming the tide. The issues involved are too compelling. Paradoxically, this doesn't mean that designers are likely to lose face or sell out. The tougher the struggle with material and audience, the greater is the challenge and potential for invention.

Designers can avoid the challenge or open up their studios and let the users crowd behind them as they draw, jostling and shouting out new ideas. Better to educate the client and face the issue of whose vision matters most and whose style will win, than to hide behind a smoke screen of professional exclusivity.

This book faces two ways—towards the designers and towards the consumer. The designer is challenged, the user told how wide his options could be. This is why I welcome *The Office Book* with open arms.

Francis Duffy
London

History

Chapter 1

The earliest "offices" can be dated to the moment one person crouched down and bartered with another for goods or services and some kind of record was made of the exchange. During the days of agrarian economies, the office could have been a corner of the kitchen, where workers were paid or goods bartered and the farmer made notes in his own form of shorthand. The

The Earliest Offices

first offices were at home, a shelf in the kitchen, a desk in the front room.

Government Offices: Of all offices, those of government have been most often documented. One of the earliest office buildings, according to Nikolaus Pevsner in *A History of Building Types*, was the Uffizi, designed by Giorgio Vasari. Built in Florence in 1560–1571 for Cosimo 1 de Medici,

it reflected the Medici enterprises. The Uffizi was the administrative offices for the grand duchy and later housed the famous Medici art collections. Other early government offices were similarly multifunctional. Some medieval town halls had law courts and chancelleries in the upper floors, while the lower floors functioned as an extension of the marketplace.

Commercial Offices: Regular meetings, interaction, and the formal keeping of records, can be dated back to the earliest administrative offices. The Medicis were innovators. The first documented offices of a banker was the Banco Mediceo in Milan. Pevsner writes, "One must imagine negotiations taking place in any room of the palace, but some space set aside for the storing of money and probably of certain goods and also some space for clerks keeping the books .... for bookkeeping during the 15th century had become a technique requiring considerable skills." Double-entry bookkeeping existed in Venice in the early 15th century and even earlier in Genoa. It revolutionized commerce, the growth of mercantilism in Europe, and eventually the rooms and buildings in which such transactions took place.

The earliest definable "commercial" offices were also part of

a home or store. According to Lewis Mumford in *The Culture of Cities*, a typical late medieval burgher house in Lubeck doubled as office and residence. The family lived on the upper levels, with the commercial space on the lower levels.

Throughout the Georgian and early Victorian era in Britain, banks were housed on the ground floors of private homes. The early colonial trading and shipping companies also operated from private homes until expansion required a separate building.

Professional Offices: The Inns of Court in London, where barristers train, dine, and practice, give perhaps the best example of early professional offices. Dating in origin to the 14th century, the Inns—Gray's Inn, Lincoln's Inn, Inner Temple, and Middle Temple —still control the training and practice of barristers. Imbued with history and legend, the quiet qandrangles, labyrinthlike chambers, chapels, libraries, and stone archways preserve a hallowed air. In the 17th century, the Inns were described as suitable colleges for sons of knights, barons, and nobility to preserve them from the "contagion of vice." Barristers who remain in London are required to occupy chambers in the Inns, preserving the continuity of an upper-middle-class profession.

①

②

③

④

❶ *This Egyptian funerary model of a granary from the tomb of Meket-Ré, Thebes, Dynasty XI shows an office where scribes are keeping accounts of grain being stored. From the Metropolitan Museum of Art.*

❷ *The Ufizzi in Florence, designed by Giorgio Vasari, is the first known office building. ("Ufizzi" means "office" in Italian.) Used for government administrative offices, it adjoined the Medici Palace and dates back to the 1560s. Courtesy: The Italian Government Tourist Office.*

❸ *The conference room in the government offices at Somerset House in England was painted by M. Gheeraeds in 1604.*

❹ *This early 16th-century engraving by Albrecht Durer depicts St. Jerome in his study. Courtesy of The Metropolitan Museum of Art, Fletcher Fund, 1919.*

Impact of the Industrial Revolution

Nurtured by the administrative and commercial needs of palaces, farms, stores, private houses, and family enterprises, offices finally left home during the Industrial Revolution of the late 18th and 19th centuries. The transformation from agrarian to industrial economies started in Britain with innovations in spinning and weaving. The revolution also expanded the use of iron and steel, developed new energy and machines and brought new developments in transportation and communication and expansion in commerce, banking, and management.

Industrial growth required more and more offices. New machines required new paperwork, which created a clerical industry. According to W. H. Leffingwell, in his book *Office Management, Principles and Practice*, the number of clerks in America increased tenfold between 1880 and 1920.

The era also created office machines to cope with increased paperwork. The development of post, trains, and telegraph facilitated transactions. In *The Culture of Cities*, Lewis Mumford writes, "Food chains and production chains of an extremely complicated nature were being formed throughout the planet: ice travelled from Boston to Calcutta and tea journeyed from China to Ireland, whilst machinery from Birmingham and Manchester found its way to the remotest corners of the earth." The office became the hub of expanding trade and the development of new machinery.

With the first public use of the Morse telegraph in 1844 and the invention of the telephone in 1876, the factory and business office could be separated. As enterprises grew in complexity, so did the office function. Offices grew when cottage industries became factories geared to large-scale production. The evolution of an idea into an invention and an invention into a factory, required paperwork, processing, order books, and improved accounting.

The inventions of Bell, Morse, and Remington developed the office into a center of operations and communication. The pace of office work quickened. When E. Remington & Sons developed a practical typewriter, the chief problem was a lack of operators, which led to the birth of commercial schools. By the end of the 19th century, the telephone was used for short-distance communication, and the telegraph was used for long distance. The exchange of information was faster: contact between buyers and suppliers was speeded up not only locally but nationally and internationally.

Yet, in spite of the expansion of offices during the Industrial Revolution, more people were involved in manufacturing than in office functions.

①

②

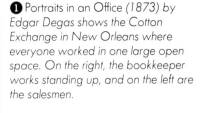

1 Portraits in an Office (1873) by Edgar Degas shows the Cotton Exchange in New Orleans where everyone worked in one large open space. On the right, the bookkeeper works standing up, and on the left are the salesmen.

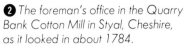

2 The foreman's office in the Quarry Bank Cotton Mill in Styal, Cheshire, as it looked in about 1784.

3 A different view of the same office as in photograph number 2. The entrepreneur and a clerk or two kept track of the orders for the factory. It wasn't until business enterprises expanded that the job of management included administration of the office itself.

4 The Consol's Room in the Bank of England, designed by John Soane in 1798. The rise of industrialism increased the role of banks and other financial institutions. These tables, with individual task lights, functioned as work stations for large groups of clerks.

5 The library in the Pall Mall Reform Club, London, was a place where businessmen met to exchange information. Designed by Sir Charles Barry in 1837–1841.

Emergence of Office Industries

In any study of the history of the office, insurance companies figure prominently. In nearly every respect they epitomize an office industry—a business whose business is paper. Originating in the 18th century in England, and in the 19th century in the United States, the growth and development of insurance was closely linked with the Industrial Revolution. The first factory workers were able to buy industrial insurance, while the owners could insure their property from the same firm. Since that time, insurance companies have continued to be at the forefront of the architectural, design and organizational developments in the office. As businesses which manipulate information only, and never handle goods, they exemplify the "knowledge industries" of the modern Information Age.

Insurance, and its counterparts, banking and finance, is labor-intensive: many people work together, performing numerous small transactions. The "Back Room" in an office is a euphemism for the vast acreage and thousands of people who do the paperwork, essentially recording, storing and retrieving information, that keeps such industries viable. Yet any business, even the smallest, has to maintain careful records; it is the scale and scope of record-keeping in insurance and allied industries that makes a difference. Consequently, through the years the most current theories about design, technology and planning were embodied in their offices.

①

The evolution of the modern office: The English architect Francis Duffy has charted three phases in the development of office technology and the characteristic buildings that house it. The first phase reached its height in the mid-19th century. The only technology was pen and ink, supplemented by skilled clerks, especially those with good penmanship, who were in great demand by insurance companies to write attractive-looking policies. Loyal clerks, all male, worked at wooden desks side by side with owners. Daylight, supplemented with oil or gas lamps, was the primary source of illumination; stoves and fireplaces provided heat. Duffy cites London's Sun Life Insurance Office designed by

C.R. Cockerell, as the prototypical building of this phase. With eighty employees in the 1860s, it was the largest office employer of the day.

The second phase was characterized by offices with hundreds of "deskilled" clerks, each performing specialized, though routine tasks. Their desks were lined up on open office floors, and the factory was the model for efficiency and control. The Larkin Building in Buffalo, New York, designed by Frank Lloyd Wright in 1904 was the building prototype—not an insurance company, but a similar office industry, a mail order company.

During this phase, office organizations grew. Numerical and alphabetical files were introduced to keep track of increasing paper-

②

work. Office machines appeared in great numbers. Women entered the office work force in large numbers, hired to operate the new typewriters, telephones and other equipment. Office management became a science around 1919. Around that time "efficiency experts" began studying office procedures; insurance company workers performing repetitive office tasks were perfect subjects for "time and motion studies", which had been first used in factories.

Although electric lights were commonly used since the early 1900s, daylight was still the major source of illumination for office work. Buildings were built with high floor-to-floor heights, to let in as much light as possible. For the same reason, buildings were relatively narrow—24 feet was considered the maximum distance from a window to any desk. All the windows were operable; they were the source of fresh air and ventilation. It wasn't until after World War II that the requisite technologies for heating, ventilating, air conditioning and lighting vast interior spaces were economically feasible. Only then did the square plan of block-long and wide office buildings become possible. Also, mass produced metal office furniture was ubiquitous.

In Duffy's opinion the third phase began in the 1970s. In this phase, thousands of office workers are still necessary to perform numerous small transactions, now using increasingly sophisticated machinery. Architecture and interior design have become sophisticated as well, integrating the office building with the furniture it contains. The building design is user-oriented, consistent with a management style which allows for individual self-expression. Central Beheer, an insurance company in The Netherlands is the prototype. This latest phase will be discussed in greater detail in Chapter 6 of The Office Book.

③

❶ The Sun Fire Insurance Office (later Sun Life), built in 1842, still stands on London's Threadneedle Street. As originally designed by C. R. Cockerell, the top two floors had apartments that were rented out to resident managers and clerks.

❷ An insurance office in Chicago in 1900. Ornamented, cast-iron columns make possible wide open work spaces—the bullpen. High windows are for light and ventilation (views were considered too distracting). Brass fittings on the gas lighting fixtures and ornamental railings are the only highlights among dark wood furniture and files. One telephone and one woman are visible. Courtesy The Continental Corporation.

❸ In 1920, the open space in this New Jersey headquarters for Prudential is grandiose—and electrified: each desk has a lamp. The fireproofed steel columns perpetuate a neoclassic style evident in much of early office architecture. Otherwise, the layout and technology are surprisingly unchanged compared with offices of 50 years earlier: large windows are still above eye level, but there is a slight intrusion of metal file cabinets and less clutter.

The Office Building:

THE SKYSCRAPER

THE CHICAGO BUILDING OF THE HOME INSURANCE CO.

OF NEW YORK

①

The rapid expansion of business and the growth of offices led to the development of office buildings. There were two traditions: the custom-, or purpose-, built corporate headquarters and the speculative building to rent to anonymous tenants. English architect Francis Duffy points out that since the early 19th century the former were conceived as "palaces," constructed to glorify the company that built them: London's Sun Life, designed by Cockerell is an example. At first, speculative buildings tended to be utilitarian, designed like the warehouses they most resembled. Oriel Chambers in Liverpool, designed by Peter Ellis in 1864, is an example. At first, speculative office buildings were not prestige commissions.

The need for more offices and new construction techniques combined to revolutionize office design. The steel skeleton frame created a distinctly new form of commercial architecture—the skyscraper. In *The Culture of Cities,* Lewis Mumford described the modern skyscraper as "a sort of human filing case, where occupants spend their day in the circumspect care of paper."

In 1871, the Chicago fire destroyed the entire business district and prompted the need for fireproof construction. This thriving transportation center required rebuilding for future office growth. By applying the steel frame originally used in factory buildings, for interior structure and on the exterior wall, architect William le Baron Jenny designed in 1884 the Home Insurance Building. It is generally credited to be the first skyscraper. Skeletal construction reduced the amount of masonry required. Structures were more economic. Interior partitions could be relocated because they were not load bearing. The strength of steel enabled the building to go very high. The invention of the elevator in 1853 made this practical. The upper-

SINGER BUILDING
THE SINGER MANUFACTURING COMPANY

②

most stories, with the most light and best views, became the more desirable.

Skyscrapers as Advertising:
The skyscraper made a dramatic impact on the city skyline. There was a rush to build the tallest building in the world. Three skyscrapers soared into the Manhattan skyline within five years of one another. The 47-story Singer Building, designed by Ernest Flagg, appeared in 1908; the 50-story Metropolitan Life Building, designed by Napoleon Le Brun

③

④

and Sons, in 1909. The 51-story Woolworth tower, designed by Cass Gilbert, in Gothic-revival style in 1913, quickly earned the name Cathedral of Commerce.

Both Singer and Woolworth were consumer companies. The buildings became a part of their promotion. Cardboard cutouts of the Singer building were distributed by the million, and every Singer sewing machine was sold with a picture of the building. Bon Voyage or Welcome Home pennants fluttered from the tower to greet traveling executives.

❶ *The Home Insurance Company in Chicago, completed in 1884 and designed by William LeBaron Jenney, is considered to be the first office building with a steel skeleton. It incorporated an earlier innovation, the safety elevator. The structural system, borrowed from factory buildings, paved the way for tall buildings that could efficiently exploit their sites through additional height. Lithograph by L. Prang, 1884.*

❷ *Manhattan's Singer Building, designed by Ernest Flagg and erected in 1908 is 600 feet (180 m) high and represented a quantum leap in height over any existing New York City structure. The building was visible from all over town and it started the notion of "the tallest building in the world."*

❸ *Five years later, in 1913, the Woolworth Building eclipsed the Singer Building by three floors. Built by another merchant, the Woolworth Building soon became known as the Cathedral of Commerce. Designed*

by architect Cass Gilbert, the Gothic style emphasized the verticality of the structure.

❹ *The first rental brochure for the Philadelphia Savings Fund Society (PSFS) Building was entitled "Nothing More Modern." Completed in 1932, the PSFS Building displayed a structural logic and incorporated street-level shops, banking facilities, and commercial office space. George Howe and William Lescaze were the architects.*

The Office in the Cityscape

During the 19th century, the number of people employed in offices was smaller than those employed in manufacturing, but the 20th century reversed that. Fewer people produce goods. More people process information. New York's skyscraper skyline symbolizes this trend. Without the traditional city background of palaces, courts, and medieval cathedrals, offices are a symbol of trade, finance, banks, and transportation. According to *New York* Magazine (February 9, 1981), the "Regional Plan estimates that more than half of New York City's $100 billion gross city product (the total value of goods and services produced) is generated by people who process information." Most of them work in offices.

According to Peter Cowan in *The Office, a Facet of Urban Growth*, the office function alone does not account for the whole of urban growth, but it is a counterpart of other aspects, which are generally accepted to do so: transportation, housing, and manufacturing. In 1800 no western city had a population of over a million. By 1900 some eleven cities exceeded the million mark. "Thirty years later," writes Lewis Mumford in *The Culture of Cities*, "as a result of this feverish concentration of capital and military and mechanical means of exploitation, there were twenty seven cities with more than a million population, headed by New York and grading down to Birmingham, including metropolises on every continent, even Australia."

The growth of large organizations with their networks of customers, suppliers, and investors required secretaries, filing clerks, bookkeepers, and office managers. They, in turn, contributed to the growth of office space, to housing within commuting distance of business areas, and to transportation facilities.

Certain cities are characterized by their financial areas—Wall Street in New York, La Salle Street in Chicago, and the square mile known as The City in London —because banks, insurance companies, and commodity traders wanted to be close to one another. This concentration increases the possibility for face-to-face communications but can also present urban problems: pollution, crowded sidewalks, blocked sunlight, and strained transportation facilities. In an attempt to prevent overcrowding, New York City passed in 1916 the first United States zoning law. Most municipalities adopted zoning laws as instruments of control: they regulate density, usage, and a building's height and volume. Surprisingly, some cities—Houston, Texas, for example—have never adopted such zoning laws.

The spread of companies and offices from downtown areas or traditional financial centers presents problems to urban planners and transportation experts. The combination of urban congestion, high rent, and the growth of electronic communication is bringing about an interesting dichotomy: more and more professional people are setting up offices in their own homes or converting buildings away from downtown areas for group practices. Yet in cities, office space continues to expand. The net result: more offices.

❶ Two panels from a five-panel photograph entitled "Beale's New York Harbor Panorama." Photographed in 1876, Joshua Beal took this shot while standing on a tower from the Brooklyn Bridge, then under construction in the harbor. The view is looking north and shows that, at the time, shipping was the primary means of transportation into Manhattan; the active harbor is crowded with packet boats, schooners, ferries, and tugs. Docks, warehouses, and shipping offices line the shore. The tallest structures are (from right to left) the spire from St. Paul's Church, the Western Union Telegraph Building, and the Trinity Church spire. Office buildings were just beginning to eclipse church steeples in the urban landscape.

❷ The same view, 100 years later. Church towers are all but obliterated by office buildings and shipping is no longer active in the harbor. The dominance of the office buildings marks the arrival of the information age; the economy of the city is dependent on what's happening in its offices instead of what's being shipped into its harbors. The tallest buildings here, in 1978, are the Twin Towers of the World Trade Center in lower Manhattan. The photograph by Ted Spiegel was taken from a helicopter.

Office Interiors

Basically there are two types of offices: the ceremonial and the functional. Most offices, however, function in both these capacities.

The elaborate offices in the homes of bankers and merchants were the forerunners of the ceremonial offices, fine examples being those of the Medici family. As Francis Duffy points out, Sun Life and London's Reform Club have similar formats. Visitors felt comfortable and relaxed in rooms furnished in silks, with deep leather chairs and roaring fires and tea or coffee served in delicate porcelain on silver trays.

Traditional businesses, mer-chant bankers and professional offices, still convey something of this. Some are housed in older buildings: others strive to create the same ambiance in the sky-scraper executive suites and board rooms of the multina-tionals.

Board rooms are slower to change. The large table formally flanked by rows of upright chairs dominates. Oil paintings and por-traits of founding directors adorn the walls, reminding the board of the past. Murals reinforce corpo-rate identity.

Functional Offices: Even functional offices had something of a personal feeling. The rolltop desk with its bottles of ink, papers, and cubby holes was a symbol of the office. There was nothing grand or ceremonial about it. People sat in swivel chairs to greet visitors and give dictation without having to twist and turn.

For convenience, large rooms were divided by glass partitions. Interior windows provided day-light and were capable of being raised and lowered to help venti-lation. For privacy, partitions were frosted or made of elaborately stained glass.

By 1920, offices were less cozy. The double-pedestal desk re-placed the rolltop because the former was more practical, easier to mass produce, and facilitated the supervision of communication with other office workers.

Additional files were required, and the filing cabinet came into being. Offices were also character-ized by their high ceilings, neces-sary for the proper ventilation of a crowded floor. Today, high ceil-ings are a rarity because air conditioning provides ventilation and lower ceilings reduce air-conditioning loads. The Wool-worth building in 1913 had 51 floors with 792 feet (242 m). Many years later, some 70 stories could be squeezed into the same height if the zoning laws would allow it.

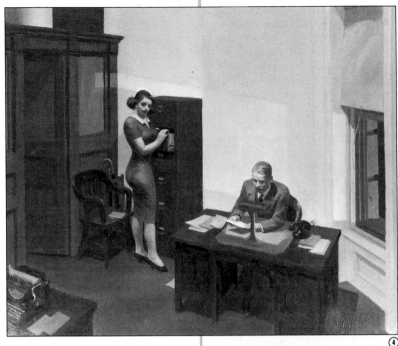

❶ *This vice president's office of the Prudential Insurance Company of America shows the residential style of offices in the late 1880s. Except for its rolltop desk, the stained-glass panels, patterned rug, and formal paintings could have been the parlor room furnishings in any home of this decade.*

❷ *Mail rooms haven't changed very much since the 1880s. Radical change in mail-room design will only occur when the job of hand sorting pieces of paper and stamping letters becomes completely automated or is replaced by other means of communication.*

❸ *Because precedent-setting policies are hammered out in board rooms, they usually reflect the prestige of both the organization and the board members themselves. This corner of the board room at 21 Lombard Street, London, is no exception. The neoclassic details include an elaborately molded plaster ceiling and carved wood panels with pilasters.*

❹ *Edward Hopper's 1940 painting* The Office at Night *reflects the change in office environments in the 55 years since the photograph at far left (number 1) was taken. Although the basic elements of desk, chair, and door remain the same, the office has been denuded of any personal or friendly touches.*

❺ *Another board room that was designed to be impressive. The eclectic style of this 1916 Prudential board room includes murals depicting the "glory of work and battle," a portrait of a founding father, a formal table, overstuffed chairs, and a fireplace mantel with cherubs.*

④

⑤

Office Technology

The development of office technology directly affected two aspects of the office functions: communications (receiving information) and processing (storing and retrieving it).

Communications: The Industrial Revolution introduced communications that were refined to be less noisy and obtrusive.

The Morse telegraph (first used publicly in 1844) made it easier for administrative offices to be separated from the factory but also increased the amount of paper to be handled. Messages came in and were sent out at a faster rate than the postal service could provide, requiring more efficient processing, recording, and filing. Transoceanic cables followed with the first Dover-Calais cable in 1851 and the first transatlantic cable in 1856. The development of speedy international communications made trading between continents more efficient.

Alexander Graham Bell's telephone appeared in 1876. A Massachusetts banker was the first to use a commercial telephone service. He leased two instruments and a line to connect his Boston office with his home in Sommerville. Office activities changed again as communication with customers, suppliers, bankers, and trading partners was even more immediate. Orders had to be made and confirmed, instructions given, and appointments made. Paperwork continued to swell.

The solution to time-consuming handwritten communications was in Remington's first typewriters in 1868, but Marshall McLuhan in *Understanding Media* reminds us that "it was the telephone paradoxically that sped the commercial adoption of the typewriter. The phrase 'send me a memo on that' repeated into millions of phones daily helped create the huge expansion of the typist function." The introduction of the typewriter in the office also encouraged the employment of women away from the factories and domestic service. According to C. W. Mills in *White Collar*, an office full of women became the stereotype of the office world. Women performed routine office work formerly done by men, especially during World War I when men left offices by the hundreds of thousands to enlist. Mills cites a report by the War Manpower Commission that stated, "Finger dexterity is often more important than creative thinking." Such philosophies kept women in low-level clerical jobs.

Processing: The paper load generated by the introduction of the telegraph, telephone, and typewriter inspired numerous inventions for various office machines. According to Mills, office workers became machine operators. Other job categories disappeared (for example, the skilled clerks). The office became more factorylike, inspired by the principles of scientific management first proposed for the factory by F. W. Taylor. As more office machinery was introduced, so were methods to increase their efficiency. According to Mills, placing the office manager in an executive role indicates the enlargement of the office function and signifies the rise of the office as a centralized service.

The Electronic Age: Some routine office functions have been made obsolete by the spread of electronics. The calculations of the statistician in the actuary department are now done by the computer; stenography has largely been replaced by the dictating machines, which will soon defer to the voice-activated computer. Posting ledgers have been replaced by data processing. Telephones now link computers with the head office, national and worldwide subsidiaries, and the organizations that serve them.

The Industrial Revolution heralded the clerk, a skilled employee.

①

But the rapid evolution of office machinery resulted in a proportionate increase of deskilled clerks and an increase of specialized operators performing routine tasks. The electronic age has produced a whole new group of office professionals. Programmers and analysts, experts in the use of electronic information processing, are the new office elite. The introduction of new office technologies has reduced some boring repetitive tasks but not reduced the total number of office workers. Electronics has redistributed the type of work.

②

❶ These women are computing statistics in the actuary department of an insurance company in the late 1890s. Technology has made these jobs obsolete, statistics are now computed electronically.

❷ Women in white, starched blouses and black, bustled skirts entered business offices in the 1880s. This line drawing shows one of the earliest stenographic machines. Courtesy: The Continental Corporation.

❸ The skilled clerk job declined with the advent of the typewriter. Semi-skilled workers were needed to perform specialized tasks, such as operating the machines. Good handwriting was no longer a prerequisite; the typewriter made legible drafts and carbon paper reduced the work load. Business schools taught women the skills they needed to enter typing pools like this one.

❹ In this 1920s office, the man in the background takes orders over the phone and the women process the orders on their typewriters. The company motto, Everybody Hustle, is clearly displayed on the blackboard.

❺ Telephone wires hang from the ceiling in this White House office in the early 1890s. Improved long distance transmission and desk models made telephones more useful in the office at this time.

As office functions became more specialized, they required their own administration. As office work evolved, so did the division of labor.

Philosophy of the Desk and Chair: The desk, no longer the rolltop but a simplified and more appropriate version for office needs, soon reflected the new office hierarchy. In 1925, W. H. Leffingwell's *Office Management,*

Introduction of Office Management

Principles and Practice was considered the definitive work on the subject. He contrasts the executive desk (size, number of drawers, and attachments) with the no-nonsense versions supplied to office clerks. In some ways, things haven't changed. Office-furniture salespeople are still talking about the same things Leffingwell suggested in the 1920s. His suggestions for desks and chairs, to integrate design with human physiology, psychology, and work requirements, are still a sales point.

A swinging telephone arm swung this office into efficiency.

Pencil sharpeners, adding machines, duplicators, etc., all add to efficiency.

Dad's desk can be willed to son—if of steel.

An auxiliary desk is sometimes a necessity for efficiency.

②

He even advises office managers to wander around and observe the posture of clerks and typists as a lesson in the inadequate design of tables and chairs. The typist's chair with its adjustable support for the back and height is considered a prototype of the most comfortable office chair.

Leffingwell suggested that the desk should be simple and light, the surface should not be too highly polished because that causes a glare; nor too dark because the contrast with white paper is too strong, causing eye fatigue. He maintains that an abundance of drawers is unnecessary, and the front of the desk should be equipped to store pens, pencils, and paperclips. (The Quickborner Team, German management consultant group, was to say the same thing 50 years later.) He believed the linoleum top was

a good idea, serviceable, and a sound selling point.

Leffingwell designed a table for clerks based on ergonomic principles: the height was adjustable, there were foot rests and interchangeable drawers. But, he adds sadly, "it will not be found in use in any office though many of my clients have desired to possess them, because no manufacturer made it a standard." Perhaps his time will come.

Yet More Efficiency: In 1919, the National Association of Office Managers was formed under the aegis of Frederick Taylor. A keen awareness of cost-efficiency and time-saving devices in terms of design and the materials used made office planning scientific. Office machines were placed where their noise would be least distracting. Central file rooms

①

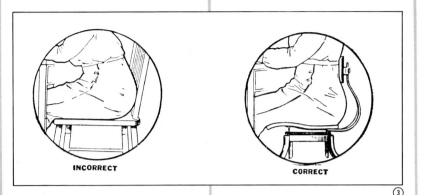

INCORRECT   CORRECT

③

④

were situated where they could be accessible to management and to the offices serving them and the rest of the organization.

Office managers costed the time it took to sharpen a pencil and dictate and type a letter and compared this with the hourly wage. No element of the office function, no matter how tiny, was overlooked in the view of office planning and economics. Such advice is given in *The Optimism Book for Offices* (1918) by Alex F. Osborn and Robert E. Ramsey on details such as the correct moist-ener for the cashier's cage to aid the "speedy counting of notes" and a combination paperweight and memorandum pad by the telephone. The need for neatness is stressed. Desks should not be used as filing systems; there had to be specific places for specific objects, files, and papers.

The switch from wood to steel, hastened by the Industrial Revolution, became a practical solution to office furniture. The vertical steel file took the fatigue out of filing, it didn't swell on humid days as did wood, and it was fireproof.

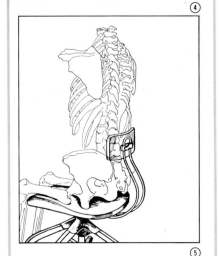

⑤

❶ *Efficiency and productivity was as much an issue in 1924 as they are today. This illustration reflects one of the solutions to fatigue offered in Organizing the Stenographic Department. The adjustable desk was designed to allow the stenographer the choice of standing or sitting, without stopping her work.*

❷ *Four illustrations from The Optimism Book for Offices by Alex Osborn and Robert Ramsey, published in 1918 by Art-Metre, which gave hints for efficiency as it promoted a new line of steel office equipment.*

❸ *Illustration from W. H. Leffingwell's Office Management, Principles and Practice, 1924.*

❹ *For greater control and supervision over employees, the office floor was laid out like a factory. In this photograph of the Bristol United Press office, the only cluttered desk is also the most visible.*

❺ *Another illustration from Leffingwell's book. The book was very popular because Leffingwell was incredibly thorough in his discussions about efficiency for clerical and secretarial workers. He wrote a lot about relieving fatigue with proper support. Although Leffingwell's research wasn't based on scientific data, many of his theories are similar to the modern principles of ergonomics.*

Refining the Office

After World War II, multinational corporations tended to consolidate and centralize their operations. A good number of them commissioned high-rise office buildings to be built in large urban centers. One example is the Union Carbide Building in New York, designed by Skidmore, Owings and Merrill. Finished in 1959, it is known as the "Rolls Royce" of buildings. Its high-quality construction includes stainless steel extrusions on its exterior curtain wall and totally integrated interiors designed by the architects. To some, Union Carbide was a symbol of postwar optimism; to others, in retrospect, a symbol of the exclusion of humanity from office design.

Throughout the world, enormous blocks of offices were built both for corporate headquarters and for speculation. It was the time of the glass box. For the most part, interiors were standardized and systematized according to status in the corporation; hierarchy was reflected in spatial layout.

City-block-long buildings, 50-, 60-, and 100-feet (15-, 18-, and 30-m) deep were built. For economic reasons, square buildings were favored because there was less perimeter per floor, thus cutting down on the most expensive part of the building.

The postwar years marked the conscious beginning of systematized office interiors. In her book *Space Planning*, Lila Shoskes suggests a reason: "Now an entire office building was being used to house just one company. This made it possible for the company to control its construction to suit the company's needs. They began

to be concerned and aware of the office as a work environment."

By 1949, Eero Saarinen had designed a flexible, integrated interior system for General Motors Research Center in Michigan. Shoskes points out that in the 1940s, there were only two manufacturers of contemporary furniture in the United States—Knoll Associates and the Herman Miller Company. Jack Dunbar, an associate partner in Interior Design at Skidmore, Owings and Merrill and

now a partner in the firm de Polo/Dunbar, designed all the Herman Miller Showrooms in the mid-50s. At S.O.M. he worked on Union Carbide. In 1944, the Knoll Planning Unit was formed, headed by Florence Schust Knoll. The Knoll Planning Unit often collaborated with S.O.M. in corporate design. Among the first design firms to specialize in office interiors was Designs for Business, Inc. Maurice Mogelescu was its head. He was joined in 1948 by Geral Luss. Designs for Business' interiors for Time, Inc. and S.O.M.'s interiors for Union Carbide are prime examples of the new field of space planning.

With space planning, nothing was left to chance: ceiling, walls, furniture, lighting, and air conditioning were designed to work

together for flexibility and efficiency. In the Union Carbide Building, for example, the luminous ceiling not only meant the lighting was constant throughout the floors but there was also a visual harmony between the ceilings, partitions, and filing cabinets. All came from the same drawing board. The building was built on a module so that the partitions lined up with the exterior window mullions. The effect was crisp and precise, with the building system taking priority over the employees. The building was used to express the complex corporate hierarchy where top executives had the top floors. Office sizes reflected rank, so a promotion meant a larger office. Windows became status symbols. Desks and chairs were sized and ranked, and

①

office sizes were codified to reflect corporate ranking. Executives were placed on the perimeter of the building beside a window, with the secretaries on the interior.

Times are changing. Union Carbide has moved to a new building in Danbury, Connecticut, with 2,200 private offices all the same size. (Designed by Kevin Roche John Dinkeloo Associates, the new building will be discussed in Section 6.) In the renovations by S.O.M. of Union Carbide's old building for the new owner, Manufacturer's Hanover Trust, the executives are on the interior with glass partitions and secretaries along the perimeter.

The development of efficient fluorescent lighting made it possible to have deep interior spaces. Improved systems of air condi-

tioning and the use of acoustic materials added to the daily comfort of the new offices. In the Union Carbide Building, carpeting was used throughout for the first time. There were new furniture ideas as well. George Nelson claims that he designed the first work station in 1947 for the Herman Miller Company: an L-shaped desk. The Herman Miller Company published a catalog of their best-selling modular desks, which was soon imitated by others. Several conscious space-saving designs came into being as the pressure on space became more acute with office growth. Office components were standardized, from freestanding to built-in files, to files with coordinated sections for hanging coats and storing paper.

❶ *In the 1880s, offices were not preplanned as total environments. The office grew as additional functions were required. In this policy-department office, wood predominates on the floors, walls, ceiling, and furniture. Pendant fixtures hang from the ceiling. Although this particular office is relatively well organized, most offices at the time were less logically laid out. Neither the impetus nor the technology to totally control interior elements was present. Courtesy: The Prudential Company of America.*

❷ *Considered a marvel when it was constructed in 1959, The Union Carbide Headquarters in New York City, designed by Skidmore, Owings and Merrill, reflected the prevailing corporate values. It was one of the first high-rise office buildings conceived as a total system of coordinated parts. The lighting, layout, furniture, and storage cabinets were designed in conjunction with the building architecture. Modules of space were sized to reflect corporate hierarchies, and they could be easily rearranged to reflect changes in status. Although the work environment has been criticized in retrospect as being too controlling, at the time it was considered the "Rolls Royce of office buildings."*

②

Famous Offices in Film

①

The movie industry flourished during the Depression. People craved escapism and Hollywood was quick to provide it. In particular, the executive office with its plate-glass windows offering a panoramic view of office towers symbolised status, glamor, and power. This had more to do with Hollywood than with the reality out on the streets.

The image has pervaded, but it is not the only one. The office has also evolved in film as a new political and sociological metaphor.

There is little glamor in *The Crowd* (1928) by King Vidor, only the lot of anonymous office workers and the generally unhappy lives of a hard-luck couple. The movie was prophetic: the office interiors were more organized and austere than they had actually become in real life where spaces were much more chaotic and personal. Equally prophetic was *Metropolis* (1926), Fritz Lang's classic silent film fantasy of a futuristic society, with an upper-class young man abandoning his comfortable life to join a workers' revolt.

Quite a different image of the office emerged with Clark Gable and Carole Lombard in *Wife vs Secretary* in 1936. Not only was the office high gloss, but the name of the movie was indicative of the impact of the office on home life and marriage, and the emergence of the term "the office marriage."

In *The Maltese Falcon* (1941), with Humphrey Bogart and Mary Astor, the office of the private eye was strictly utilitarian. In later movies, something of a certain mood was set by the detective's office. He frequented it day and night, often slept there, met his cronies there, and did his philosophizing there. The late night silhouette of the detective slouched back with his feet on the desk and a neon light flashing behind his head was very evocative of such movies in the 1940s and 1950s. A more sophisticated version of the detective office appeared in *Chinatown* (1974) with Jack Nicholson and Faye Dunaway.

Room at the Top (1959) with Lawrence Harvey and Simone Signoret as the fated lovers, was the story of a working-class man who marries the boss' daughter and pulls his way to the top in spite of lacking the required social graces and contacts. The office provides a useful backdrop to a classic study of ambition and drive. A less biting and more amusing variation of the same theme came in *How to Succeed in Business* in 1967 with Robert Morse, the story of an ambitious window washer who uses his wiles and a handbook to rise to prominence in the company.

The American version of Kafka's *The Trial* (1962) with Anthony Perkins and Orson Welles dramatized the paranoic fear of every office worker. The organization is mammoth, soulless, with people arranged in countless rows behind desks in a palatial room that is filled and cleared at precisely the same time each morning and evening. It is the perfect backdrop for the story of a young man accused of a crime but never informed of what he is supposed to have done.

The office presents different metaphors in movies ranging from the background of boardroom dramas to the dehumanization of the office clerk, the archetypal small man. A new metaphor was presented in *9 to 5*, released in 1981, starring Dolly Parton, Lily Tomlin, and Jane Fonda. This box-office hit shows the secretary as hero.

②

③

❶ *In his 1928 movie The Crowd King Vidor deliberately exaggerated the impersonal office environment. In this huge, scaleless space, the middle-class hero is just one more face in the office crowd.*

❷ *In the height of a worldwide Depression, the movies portrayed the glamorous aspect of offices. In 1933, Female went so far as to show a woman executive, Ruth Chatterton, as the high-powered president of a motor car company. This production still shows how her chair was propped on blocks so that she could see above her desk.*

❸ *Clark Gable's office in Wife vs. Secretary, 1936, included the Holly-wood version of big-time offices: huge windows overlooking a cityscape and a fully accessorized desk with inkwell, photographs, and lamp. The storyline revolved around the duality of work and homelife, with Carole Lombard playing Gable's secretary.*

❹ *Humphrey Bogart's utilitarian office in The Maltese Falcon, 1941, was the embodiment of the no-nonsense private detective, Sam Spade. Spade wasn't concerned with traditional trappings of power, and his office was not meant to impress clients like Mary Astor.*

❺ *Fritz Lang's vision of the futuristic society in his 1926 silent film Metro-polis proved to be prophetic. The awesome scale of the office, the built-in gadgetry, and the massive glass walls predate some elements of office design in the 1980s.*

④

⑤

Offices associated with the famous and the notorious summarize personality more succinctly than a private home.

There is a difference between the office that is designed to stand out and an office that is famous as a result of who worked there and what he or she did.

Zeckendorf's office is a command post for an entrepreneur, a

Offices of Famous People

①

space-age penthouse room dominated by a huge desk, the ultimate in status symbols. The traditional office in the American financier J. P. Morgan's library was designed to impress. Freud's office in Vienna, characterized by reclining couch and heavy velvet curtains, is a prototype for the analyst. The meaningful clutter of Einstein's office has comforted thousands of lesser geniuses unable to keep their own work space tidy.

Margaret Mead's office was in three rooms at a corner where two sections joined over the anthropology department at the Museum of Natural History in New York. It was lined with books and boxes of films and photographs, with assistants and secretaries spilling into the hallway.

For Mussolini, the office was his political image. Marble columned in the classical style, it was intimidatingly huge, *Il Duce* sat behind raised desk at the far end, requiring the visitor to cross a vast expanse of floor to see him.

The office of more democratic political leaders at 10 Downing Street in London and the Oval

②

❶ *Victoria Sackville-West's study on the first floor of the Elizabethan tower at Sissinghurt Castle. For 32 years, the author worked in this room without changing the wall paper, velvet tassles, or mementos of her youth. To this day the room remains as she designed it.*

❷ *Queen Victoria's writing table at Osborne House on the Isle of Wight.*

❸ *Rudyard Kipling's study in Burwash, England, displays the tools of the writer's trade: a portable typewriter, a globe, and walls of books.*

❹ *The prime minister's office at Number Ten Downing Street in London is surprisingly unpretentious.*

❺ *John Pierpont Morgan's private sanctum in his library was designed by McKim, Mead and White in 1902 and based on a 16th-century Roman Villa. Although Morgan had an office on Wall Street, he sometimes held meetings in this room. (The Panic of 1907 was supposedly resolved here in a meeting with other bankers.) Arnold Genthe, who photographed the office in 1912, called it "the greatest room in America." The photographer was particularly impressed with the masterpieces, the Florentine wall coverings, and the fine antiques.*

③

④

⑤

Office in Washington seem more closely associated with the image of prime minister and president than with specific personalities and eccentricities. The "office" transcends the occupant.

Some companies preserve a certain office image for decades with the loving care of a curator. Scribner's publishers in New York have maintained their original 1920s style office with the dark wood and glass partitions, no different now than from the days when the writer F. Scott Fitzgerald visited for his editorial sessions. Original artwork for Fitzgerald's *The Great Gatsby* and similar best sellers adorn the walls.

Offices of people such as writer Ernest Hemingway's in Key West, Florida, designer Raymond Loewy's art deco style in New York, and 19th-century writer and craftsman William Morris' in London, furnished and wallpapered with his own designs, are associated with arduous hours spent in creative work. They evoke a thrill, like the instrument of a great musician or the studio of a great painter.

Something in an office sums up personality. It may be the cats that used to curl up on Hemingway's desk; or Frank Woolworth's replica of Napoleon's imperial marble office at the top of the Woolworth building; or the small, bare office of Mother Teresa of Calcutta, with nothing on the desk but a telephone.

①

②

❶ Frank Lloyd Wright designed this office in 1937 for Edgar Kaufmann, Jr., owner of the Kaufmann Department Store in Pittsburgh and a patron of architecture. The room is now part of the 20th-century Primary Collection in the Victoria and Albert Museum in London.

❷ In 1934, Raymond Loewy's "Corner of an Industrial Designer's Office and Studio" was installed in the Contemporary American Industrial Arts Exposition at the Metropolitan Museum of Art in Manhattan. Loewy's art deco office used new materials and the streamlined forms he was famous for. The walls are ivory plastic-laminate and the floor is cadet-blue linoleum. The chairs are yellow leather with gun-metal blue tubing.

❸ Mussolini's office in Rome's Palazzo Venezia was two stories high. The huge hall was furnished only with a desk, a chair for himself, and two chairs for visitors. Many visitors have described the awe they experienced walking from the massive entrance door to Mussolini's desk in the distant corner, 66 feet (20m) away. It was perfect staging. The architectonic effect of the columns and decorations painted on the walls makes it seem more enormous than it is.

❹ The Oval Office embodies the authority of United States's presidents and is perhaps better known than some of its occupants. Designed in 1815 by Benjamin Latrobe, it is the focal point of the White House, a combined work place and residence. It looked like this during Benjamin Harrison's administration, circa 1890.

❺ William Zeckendorf's penthouse office at Webb and Knapp was designed in 1952 by I. M. Pei. The private office stands free in a reception area; its cylinder shape is teakwood topped by a glass transom. The real estate tycoon's office resembles some of the futuristic offices from the movies, but it is dated by the telephone equipment built into the desk.

③

④

⑤

Recent Developments

Developments in technology have continued to be the main force behind changes in office design.

Although it was invented later than the computer, the copier was in general office use much earlier than the computer. Xerox made in 1959 the first convenient copier. The copier produced even more paper, which in turn required further office management: paper-flow and paper-storage systems.

In the early 1950s, Remington put the first computer on the market, a UNIVAC, used by the U.S Bureau of Census. Remington was a pioneer in office technology. They developed the first practical typewriter in 1868. IBM's first large-scale computer system was introduced in 1952 and was used by scientists and engineers on a limited basis.

The great expense of these early computers limited their use. Only wealthy corporations could afford them. The first computers were the ultimate in status symbols and were treated like office gods. They were placed in their own controlled environment (often on view through glass), and their ability to process, store, and retrieve information quickly absorbed entire areas of office work.

The introduction of **silicon chips** (semiconductors, tiny integrated circuits) to computers converted the room-sized beast into a more manageable desk-sized machine. Chips carry the wiring and do the same work as the transistors, diodes, and resistors of old fashioned electronic devices.

The chips are tiny. IBM has a quarter-inch chip that can store 72,000 bits of information, thus making it the densest commercially available chip on the market. Chips increase the possibility for information storing and calculation, and they can be programmed to do various things in different office machines.

Chips have helped simplify the manufacturing process and drastically reduced the cost of processing information. As a result, micro- and minicomputers are available to smaller firms that could not afford them 10 to 20 years ago.

More and more people use the computer to streamline bookkeeping; to do advanced calculations; and to speed up mailing, record keeping, and the storing of and retrieval of information. **Word processors** (typewriters with memories) are used in the more sophisticated offices and newspaper offices. There is a computer for everyone from the aerospace engineer to the warehouse supervisor.

A gloomy view of this situation comes from Randy J. Goldfield, president of Gibbs Consulting Group, in *Office Today,* a 1981 *New York Times* advertising supplement: "American offices spew out nearly 600 million pages of computer printouts, 234 million photocopies and 76 million letters *daily.* This deluge of paper (about 45 new sheets of paper per day per office worker) is threatening to overwhelm us in a flood of information which cannot be generated, processed, used or stored effectively." Yet more disciplines in handling paper have to be introduced, and not merely a more efficient filing cabinet for storing electronic data.

(4)

(5)

❶ Tiny silicon chips contain thousands of circuits that govern the operation and memory of computer systems. This wafer, one small part of a system, contains 159 chips, each of which can store about 72,000 bits of information. The chip technology, developed in the 1970s, increased the capacity of large mainframe computer systems and led to the use of small micro- and minicomputers throughout the office. Courtesy IBM.

❷ The IBM 705, announced in 1954, was the first large computer used in commercial installations.

❸ The Xerox 914 Copier was the first xerographic automatic office copier. Released in September, 1959, it reproduced at the rate of seven copies per minute. The machine could make perfect copies on plain paper of anything printed, written, typed, or drawn. The copier revolutionized office procedures and, ultimately, office design.

❹ The copying machine generated reams of paper, creating major problems in storing and handling the paperwork. One solution from Steelcase is this organizer, appropriately called Paper-flow. The slanted cubicles keep work in progress off the desk top yet visible and accessible.

❺ The IBM 701, announced in 1952, was the first production computer. It was designed primarily for scientific calculations, using a technology based on vacuum tubes. It was soon superseded by faster, more powerful systems.

The Open Office

The open office was designed by a management consulting group—the Quickborner Team (named after its German hometown). The Quickborner Team felt that the office layout should reflect the work process. American companies were used to the bull-pen concept, but European companies weren't (except in specific areas like drafting rooms or newsrooms). For the most part, six people sitting together in one partitioned space was the maximum: anything above that was quite alien to the European.

The Quickborner Team considered fixed walls too static and isolating and, therefore, abolished them. Everyone sat out on the open office floor, including the chief executive. Traditional desks, bulky and difficult to move, were replaced with lightweight tables. Files were banished to remote file rooms, and only active files, stored in mobile carts, were allowed on the floor.

The team ignored building geometry and designed according to traffic flow. Plants softened the open work vista and inspired the name *Burolandschaft*, office landscaping. They tried to improve relations in the office and get away from schoolroom supervision.

The result of the open plan was startling and unsettling; not only to the Europeans who had never experienced the like before but even to those Americans accustomed to a more formal layout of desks lined up in rows in their bull pens. Few people refuted the fact that office layout could compliment management goals. But in practice, management could not overlook the fact that many people were upset by the loss of the private office and the appearance of the open plan.

Robert Propst of the Herman Miller Company in the United States studied office function from a designer's viewpoint and agreed with the Quickborner Team that office environments should be dynamic and responsive. He introduced his furniture system, called the Action Office, in 1968. This system was flexible, practical, and based on the concept of the individualized work station. Propst also eliminated the bulky ceremonial desk, calling it wasteful and inefficient. Instead, he designed height-adjustable work tops hung from panels, which also supported eye-level files and storage cabinets.

Panels were covered with fabric to absorb sound and provide surfaces for messages, reminders, memos, and personal nicknacks. At first, the Action Office was designed to be installed within the walls of an existing private office but could be applied equally to the open plan.

The concept of the office-furniture system caught on. Components were adapted to house electronic equipment, the key to future use, and something of a model for dozens of different systems manufactured to adapt to new technology. The merger of flexible planning principles and office technology brought about the biggest changes in office design in 100 years.

The open office has been the most controversial feature of office planning in the last two decades. Many executives don't like it because the loss of a private office implies a loss of status. But because of its flexibility, most executives in the United States seem resigned to the open plan as the office of the future (according to a Lou Harris Poll, commissioned by Steelcase, the largest office-furniture manufacturer in the Unites States). It is estimated that more than 50 percent of American office workers work in open plan; the number of installations increases yearly.

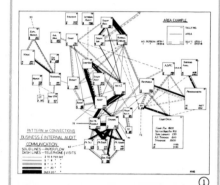

①

②

③

The controversy is ongoing and prompts a psychological study of space and what it means to the individual office worker. The open plan was initially designed for the convenience of management, not for office workers. It seemed like a revolutionary solution, but now people think its success depends on the attitudes of the organization.

Architect Michael Brill of the Buffalo Organization for Technological and Social Innovation (BOSTI), has recently completed such a study, to be published at the end of 1982. "The Impact of Office Environment on Productivity and Quality of Working Life" surveyed 5,000 office workers in 50 offices before they moved, a month after they'd relocated, and a third time 6 or 7 months later. The survey discovered that among office workers there was a strong desire to be with others. Given a choice, only 34 percent of those surveyed preferred to work in an office alone; 44 percent preferred to work with 1 to 8 others. Only 22 percent opted to work with 8 or more. This supports the contention that an open office is desirable for increased communications.

For some companies, the high initial cost of furnishing such work stations can be offset year by year in tax credits and depreciation allowances.

In light of the BOSTI study, claims of the financial advantage of systems because of their flexibility are less easy to support. The study showed that 63 percent of all those surveyed do not relocate; 27 percent do, about twice; and 10 percent move 3 to 6 times a year. (In particular, managers and supervisors don't change much; others do, says Brill.)

Privacy remains the biggest issue. According to Brill, privacy affects environmental satisfaction, job performance, and job satisfaction. The use of more and more voice-activated computers will compound the problems of noise in the open office, where acoustic privacy is considered more important than visual privacy.

And there are practical problems, especially when an organization moves into a new building. Speculative office buildings are designed as shells: there are exterior walls with windows and air-handling units—usually a continuous convector. There are floors and ceilings. Interior walls are never supplied with the raw space because it is assumed the layout will be designed to suit the organization's specific needs. However, details of how a wall will butt into—or connect with—the exterior wall have to be planned in advance.

Some buildings, designed solely for open-planning layouts, are not suitable for subdivision into cellular offices and require extensive work to accommodate them. This is an increasing problem in Europe.

The bald, theoretical advantages of open planning need to be weighed more carefully against the results. When partitions are involved for reasons of privacy or acoustics, the original space-saving advantages of the open plan no longer apply. So the open plan is not a panacea. It is not suitable for all organizations and not suitable for all buildings. It is simply one of many tools available for solving the spatial requirements of the corporation.

⑤

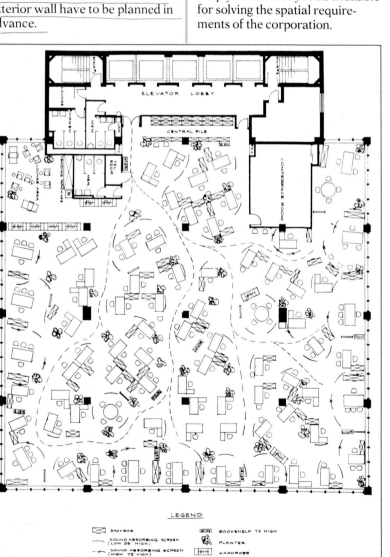

④

LEGEND

❶ A communication survey among 77 tally groups showed how a department was connected according to the work process rather than an organizational chart. This survey was the basis for the Quickborner's Buro-landschaft—office landscaping—system that revolutionized office planning.

❷ In 1973, Weyerhaeuser was one of the first large United States corporations to endorse open-office planning. This is the president's office in their Tacoma headquarters; it has no walls. Skidmore, Owings and Merrill Architects.

❸ A view of an open office floor laid out according to the principles of office landscaping, Burolandschaft, by the Quickborner Team. The new approach, developed in Germany in the 1950's, emphasized the office as an information system.

❹ In 1967, the first office landscape was constructed for the Freon Division of E. I. duPont de Nemours & Company. It was intended as a general test of the concept of open planning. Other floors in the same building had conventional offices. The test proved inconclusive.

❺ In open-office plans, the work stations have to be serviced with computer cables, electricity, and telephones. Here the wires descend from the ceiling.

Office Automation

As mentioned earlier in this chapter, the telegraph, telephone, and typewriter revolutionized the late-19th-century office and created mounds of paper. The automated office is revolutionizing the late-20th-century office. Along with extra paper, wires and cables are requiring their own management as increasing automation integrates the existing office function into an electronic network.

The basic electronic armory of dictaphones, calculators, word processors, computers, copiers, printers, telephones, and telex generates information, stores it, reproduces it, and transmits it. Increased automation will link these activities, speeding up communications and access to information. Eventually, the electronic office may be paperless.

The purpose of automation is to increase productivity among white-collar workers, from clerical staff to executive levels. According to the management consultants Booz Allen & Hamilton, an office is automated when 50 percent of the people get 50 percent of their information electronically, requiring their own devices or having the ability to share them. We're not there yet.

In the meantime, there are several categories of office equipment. In the next generation of their development—a short time in this fiercely competitive industry—separate functions will be combined. In an article in *Architect's Journal* (November 18, 1981), Patrick Hannay called this "the convergence factor, i.e., more tasks being undertaken by fewer machines." Hannay points out that machines are not always smaller, nor does convergence mean that

fewer machines will be used because "ever-reducing costs will mean we can all have one."

According to Hannay, the integrated electronic office will ultimately be reduced to three major components: an intelligent processor, electronic mail, and video conferences. The **intelligent processor** will perform the function of generating, gathering, and processing information. Present technologies to be integrated are dictaphones, typewriters, copiers, drawing boards, typesetters, and calculators. The functions of storing, reorganizing, and retrieving information, now embodied in paper or electronic file systems, will also be performed in part by the intelligent processor as well as by **electronic mail.** Electronic mail will also incorporate the written communications, now present in the postal system, telex, facsimile transmission, and satellite. Speech communication—telephones, meetings, and dictaphones—will eventually be handled by **video conferences.**

The pieces presently exist; what doesn't exist are the means to link them in a single compatible system. Presently, three computer systems exist in the automated office: a central processor system connected by cables to all parts of the office; distributed processing via smaller processors located near the users; and local networks —devices connected by coaxial broadband cable installed like phone wires.

Wiring presents the major design problem, but experts like Mary K. Fenwick, manager of systems marketing, Xerox Corporation, says in *Interior Design* (October 1981): "The trend in electronics is to get smaller, more

powerful and cheaper, so I think we can expect devices that will follow that pattern." Raceways located in the floor, raised flooring systems, flat wiring, and certain furniture designs provide some solutions. Richard Satherly, who designs electronic equipment in Britain, predicts that laser technology will replace complex cable requirements within a decade.

Office interiors will continue to be modified. As video display

terminals (VDTs) replace paper, they'll become the brightest surfaces in the room. "Visual display terminal" is the American term for this machine; the British call it a "visual display unit"—VDU; and other Europeans call it a "cathode ray terminal"—CRT. In any event, lighting with respect to VDTs is the most critical lighting problem in the office. When VDTs are replaced by flat screens, as is now predicted, lighting designs will

①

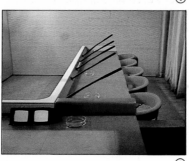

②

③

have to be modified again.

Many areas of the office will continue to change. Television will transmit any sort of printed, electronic, or visual matter. This not only has advantages of speed and immediacy within the corporation but via microdish transmitters and receivers on the roofs of office buildings, can also be beamed to another rooftop receiver machine anywhere in the world via satellite. This technology now exists in selected centers. In a few years, any office in a building with a microdish on the roof and internal cable television can have video-conferencing facilities. This instant conference will save time, travel, and money.

In the future, two types of firms will be the first to be fully automated: the large, progressive, and wealthy corporation and the small, wealthy service organization, such as law or accounting.

Many believe the voice-activated computer will give the biggest impetus to full automation because it will encourage executives who are now reluctant to use keyboards to operate terminals. That will change the function of secretaries and other traditional keyboard operators. The nature of office work and the functions of office workers will be affected.

When the computer became an office tool, it introduced a new breed of office prima donnas—programmers. They control the access to the information and have an advantage over anyone with a disk terminal with access to only as much information as the program allows. These relatively powerful positions are increasing; low-level jobs for routine work will gradually disappear. For not only will electronics reduce filing but will also cut the unnecessary duplication and repetition, retyping, repetitive phone calls, and transcribing that clog the speed of

the modern office. Some predict that the office will become less a place for routine work and more a place where ideas are exchanged.

Offices can be decentralized because the interlocking electronic networks will be accessible from remote locations. In the *Third Wave*, Alvin Toffler talks about the ways in which people can work from home using computer terminals. Certainly the image of future automation splits at this point—between the heavily automated office at central HQ and Toffler's "electronic cottage."

Either way, one is reminded that the future is not simply one of accommodating buildings to machines or machines to buildings. According to Lydia de Polo of New York's de Polo/Dunbar, "It's not a question of the electronic office, but one of the human office, with machines to help. Electronics should always be in the servant position."

❶ *Word processors are specialized microcomputers with text editing capabilities and extensive memories. Because the operators of these machines don't have to be experts, powerful microcomputers can increase job performance throughout the office. When 50 percent of the people get 50 percent of their text or data information electronically, the office will be fully automated. We're not there yet, but the proliferation of electronic equipment is affecting all aspects of office design, from the furniture that supports the equipment to office layout and lighting. Courtesy: The Herman Miller Company.*

❷ *Another aspect of electronics communication in the office is teleconferencing—televised conferences. These stay-at-home meetings save time, travel costs, and wear and tear on busy executives. Applications range from vast national hookups resembling press conferences to intimate one-to-one conversations—telephone calls with pictures. Once available only at central locations in major cities (this is a British Post Office Confravision System), inhouse video conference systems are becoming more common for large corporations. Designed by Pentagram.*

❸ *Traditional machine distinctions are blurring. Advanced office technologies are moving inexorably toward integration. Eventually, networks of machines, interconnected through telecommunications, will be used to obtain, process, and communicate information. It won't matter whether the information is in the form of data, text, image, or human speech. This showroom for Wang Laboratory equipment was designed by SCR Design Organization.*

Humanizing the Office

In the 1950s, the building as a machine reigned supreme. Organization came first; people came second. Very often, this was the unstated but underlying corporate goal, and designers take their cues from their clients.

Today the key word is **productivity.** Over the life cycle of an office building, construction costs, furniture, and equipment account for 2 percent of the total cost. Operating expenses account for 6 percent and the remaining 92 percent is people. Therefore, if the office environment affects people enough to increase their productivity, the leverage is about 12 to 1. Attention to the needs of people pays off. As higher-salaried technical and professional personnel are replacing lower-paid clerical workers as the backbone of the office, personnel costs will increase. Likewise, the investment for expensive office equipment makes sense only when the people using it are more productive.

In the BOSTI study, which was mentioned earlier in this chapter, Michael Brill was able to show that satisfaction with the working environment has a direct relationship with job performance for some office workers and job satisfaction for all. His findings show that as environmental satisfaction increases, so does job performance; as environmental satisfaction remains the same or decreases, job performance decreases. "The environment counts," said Brill at a design management conference, jointly sponsored by *Interiors* Magazine and the Design Management

Institute, where he presented some preliminary findings of his study.

Performance was measured by several factors: how much work was done, its quality, meeting deadlines, frequency of errors, taking responsibility, creativity, getting along with others, and dependability. These all have cost implications. One important finding was that professional/technical people have the lowest environmental satisfaction.

When this study is published, architects, designers, and organizations will have a common understanding of which problems are critical and why. Some of the key issues are privacy and how people interface with technology.

Obviously, the design of the work environment—specifically, office furniture and equipment as it affects the individual worker—is critical. Comfort, task motivation, accommodation to individual needs, and health are the scope of ergonomics. Until now, Europeans have set the standard. Their flexible electronic work-station equipment is better than that made in the United States. Most equipment is designed in Sweden and West Germany, where office-worker protection laws have led to high standards. The work-station equipment includes: limited contrast differential between the working document and work surfaces, adjustable table heights and adjustable chairs.

Amber or orange characters on CRT screens are reported to be more readable than white or green or grey characters. The character size depends on the viewing distance. Chairs should have good backrests to maintain the inward curve of the lower spine. Footrests may be needed. Detached keyboards allow flexible layout of work and equipment. Consider keyboards, CRT screen,

the source documents, writing surface, wrist support, and arm support; each may vary with the tasks.

The critical nature of keyboard tasks requires frequent breaks to maintain quality work and operators' health. More informal spaces should be included in office programs. *Burolandschaft* anticipated this in calling for *pauserums,* or lounges, which had snack dispensers and coffee machines, subdued lighting, and low seating. Central Beheer, designed by Herman Hertzberger in Alpendoorn, Netherlands, provides many such alternate spaces within the building.

German safety requirements for office chairs have raised consciousness of this issue. All chairs on casters must have five legs for stability. The casters must lock in place once the seat is vacated. Open-ended arms are forbidden and all arms must be designed so that it's impossible to catch one's clothing on it.

According to architect James E. Rappoport, former director of interior design at Haines Lundberg Wahler, New York City, so many advances in safety have been made in the past 20 years that it's unconscionable to reuse

furniture that was bought in the 1960s.

The long-term effects of sophisticated office technologies are being studied. We don't really know what effects working with cathode ray tubes, "white noise" (electronic background noise), and stressful moments of waiting while a microprocessor performs a data search will have.

The element of choice for office workers is becoming increasingly important. At a seminar sponsored by British furniture manufacturer Hille International in the fall of 1981, Deiter Jager of the Quickborner Team pointed out that people are not content with the perfectly controlled environment, especially when it comes to air conditioning. He describes it as "the monotony of perfection." His research shows that people would rather have an imperfect environment with the option of opening a window in nice weather. Individual air-handling units, like those in airplanes, might be part of every work station, Jager predicted. This seminar concluded that office workers can no longer be regarded as passive agents without a role in office decisions and technology. Participation in the planning at every level is vitally important.

signed system accomodates electronic equipment and there is a choice of work-station heights and widths.

4 In the sales department of SuCrest Corp., the cloud panels extend the height of the open-office system, adding privacy to each work station. Designed by Wayne Marcus Design, Inc.

5 A sculpture by Karl Rosenberg graces the ceiling of a brown-bag lunchroom at AT&T Longlines and brings down the scale of this large space. Architect: Kohn Pederson Fox. Interior design: dePolo/Dunbar.

6 Glass partitions provide access to windows for people who work in interior spaces. A nice ammenity in the United States, many European countries have laws that require window access for all employees.

1 Padded acoustic walls give this work station a sense of enclosure. Its task light and surfaces for display give individuals a sense of control over their environment. Courtesy: The E. F. Hauserman Company.

2 The work station above attempts to provide some of the advantages of a private office—defined limits, the control of access, opportunities for personalization, and acoustic privacy. This executive office at the Coca-Cola Company headquarters is designed by John Chaloner.

3 John Sayer uses natural-oak timber and conceals the hardware in his Lucas Programme 2 furniture system. He wanted this work station to "look like furniture." The ergonomically de-

Economic Issues

Salaries are an office organization's biggest single outlay—accounting for 90 percent of a building's costs over its lifetime. So there is a sound investment in keeping employees content and productive.

Building design can cut operating costs. This is especially true in energy. Lighting is the largest single user of energy in an office building. It can account for 40 percent of the electricity costs of a building. This is compounded during the summer months when each watt of lighting generates heat that requires a third as many (.314) watts of air conditioning to cool. Space heating, space cooling, fan motors, elevators and building equipment, domestic hot-water heaters, and office equipment are the other energy users. Energy became a critical issue when costs soared in 1973 and people became concerned about future supplies of fuel. A typical office building, built prior to the oil embargo, consumes from 50,000 to 150,000 BTUs of energy per square foot of office space per year. Current United States energy codes limit the use of energy to 70,000 BTUs per square foot per year. The high costs of heating are also encouraging research into insulation, atriums, daylight penetration, and active and passive solar systems. Buildings are being designed that consume less than 25,000 BTUs per square foot per year.

In a two-building project called Enerplex, commissioned by the Prudential Insurance Company, two exciting prototype solutions in conserving energy in office buildings are the result of an unusual collaboration between Skidmore Owings and Merrill, New York, and the Princeton University School of Architecture and Urban Planning. These two distinct architectural expressions have common energy-related objectives: To maximize the efficient use of daylight to reduce electrical demand and to reduce cooling loads; to control solar radiation into the building to offset conduction heat losses in winter and to reduce cooling load in summer; and to minimize conduction heat losses to the outside in winter.

Enerplex, located in Princeton, New Jersey, is comprised of two 3-story multitenant office buildings of 130,000 square feet each and parking for 1,000 cars. Each building has an enclosed atrium facing a central mall—the entrance for the two buildings. The north building is enclosed with a double-layer glass wall. Large windows permit a maximum amount of daylight to enter the space. The enormous amount of solar energy that can be collected in the atrium offsets conduction losses through the large windows. Enerplex South has a limestone exterior with windows sized and designed to respond to the different solar conditions on each exposure. Interior corridors are skylighted with 3-story "light slots." A heat pump linked to a natural aquifer below the project helps heat and cool the buildings. An "ice pond," or ice storage

①

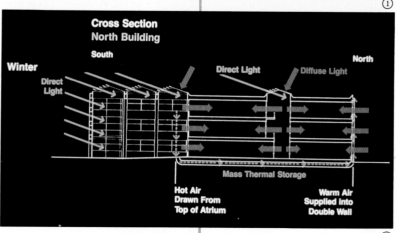

Cross Section
North Building

Winter   South   North

Direct Light   Direct Light   Diffuse Light

Mass Thermal Storage

Hot Air
Drawn From
Top of Atrium

Warm Air
Supplied into
Double Wall

②

facility, is used to cool the North building in summer.

In existing buildings, upgrading the quality of light and reducing its quantity are being considered as two aspects of a common problem. One solution is a combination of task lighting and ambient lighting. **Ambient light** is low-level general illumination for safety and background light. **Task light** is high-intensity light at the work surface.

This solution hadn't been applied to offices before, although we are familiar with it in our homes. In an open plan, high-intensity discharge lamps are often aimed at the ceiling, while other fixtures provide desk lights. Task/ambient lighting can consume only one watt per square foot. Previously, five watts were common.

Individual desk lights humanize the office environment. There are obvious cost advantages here, too. Whole floors of lights controlled by a single switch are, it is hoped, past horrors. When such systems were designed, the initial costs of wiring the lamps and switches were higher than the operating costs. Centralized control by computers that integrates heating, cooling, lighting, and sun-control will be more energy efficient at the expense of individual control.

Collaboratives and Condominiums:
New office buildings in central business districts are being tucked into available sites and they are, therefore, more particular than the anonymous facades of the 1950s. Some companies are recycling buildings or moving into old factories and warehouses, gutting interiors and converting them to office spaces. This was once the way for architecture and design firms; now other companies are following suit. Some small firms who cannot afford the cost of their own office space have created working communities. There is a slowly increasing number of cooperatives,

collectives, or associations of firms who commit themselves to the amount of space they require and share otherwise expensive support facilities: receptionist, conference rooms, and secretarial and telex services. Barley Mow Workspaces, a converted wallpaper factory at Chiswick, West London, is a collection of 120 small independent studio and workshop firms employing some 350 people. The building opened in 1976, but the idea for it began in 1974 following the success of a similar venture known as 5 Dryden Street in Covent Garden. Both projects were initiated and designed by the architectural firm Rock Townsend. Furniture designer-manufacturer John Morton joined them in Barley Mow Workspaces. Similar proposals for building with shared support facilities range from Times Square law office condominiums (in the hopes that the presence of a distinguished profession wil speed the rehabilitation of a blighted neighborhood in New York City) to an office condominium in Denver, Colorado, a landmark tower, formerly part of a department store. Such projects benefit small to medium firms and represent a new attitude toward work places. They are possible only with the cooperation of municipal authorities and financial institutions.

Interiors:
The cost of office interiors can equal the cost of the shell, and interiors are replaced on the average of every seven years. Fred Smith, Jr. a marketing consultant with Smith Stanley, Inc. in Darien, Connecticut, sees a trend toward furniture systems that are built to the client's specifications. "They're so expensive, the people who buy them have to know exactly what they need." James E. Rappoport predicts that "systems" will expand to include prefabricated components that will include all mechanical services. Ceiling tiles, complete with sprinkler lines and air-handling

③

④

ducts; moveable full-height walls that include storage units; raised floor systems that deliver air and power to work stations; as well as work stations themselves are the next step. "Superalfa," a furniture system manufactured by Faram in Italy, is the trend of the future. When organizations move, they'll be able to take their interiors with them. Rappoport predicts the initial costs as well as tax advantages will make these systems increasingly attractive.

❶ *A unique collaboration between the Prudential Insurance Company; architects Skidmore, Owings and Merrill; engineers Flack & Kurtz; and the Princeton University School of Architect produced Enerplex, a speculative, multiuse building complex designed to be energy efficient. One building faces north, the other faces south; both employ different principles to reduce energy consumption.*

❷ *Cross-section drawing by Donovan and Green of the north building at Enerplex; displaying one aspect of the multifaceted energy-consumption system used throughout the building.*

❸ *Cooperative work spaces, such as Barley Mow in West London, represent new real estate strategies to cope with rising rental costs. Here, 100 different firms (employing over 300 people) share costly common facilities such as the reception area, telex machines, and conference rooms Architect: Rock Townsend.*

❹ *The Daniels and Fisher Tower, a Denver landmark built in 1910, is being renovated by Gensler and Associates into office condominiums, with 14 floors of offices and one common conference floor. Once the tallest structure outside of New York City, this renovated building is an example of one of the newest trends.*

Future Trends

Organizational shifts show a trend toward the disintegration of large corporations into smaller, more manageable working units with greater autonomy and identity. The central business district will expand to new areas. The adaptive reuse of existing buildings, houses, warehouses, and factories is on the increase in both the United States and Europe. And people provided with computer terminals that are linked to a central office can perform work at home that before they would have to have done at an office.

The trend underlines the preference for smaller, more controllable working environments in which identity is not lost or smothered by the corporation. Privacy will always remain an issue, especially in open-plan offices.

The smaller environment concept can, if necessary, be incorporated into a large building by designing various self-contained sections. In a seminar organized by Hille International, a British furniture manufacturer, British architect Norman Foster suggested that this could be done by providing several elevators instead of one central shaft. This may provide a more intimate and relaxed atmosphere. People get accustomed to seeing the same faces instead of being one of many in an impersonal group waiting for the main elevators each morning.

The nature of employment will also change in the future. Unemployment and redundancies have

①

②

③

caused many people to retrain, start their own companies, or group with others to make themselves less dependent on the corporation. This also encourages the growth of less orthodox office spaces. Professor Charles Handy of the London Business School points out that we may be moving from an employment economy, in which people sell their time in blocks of hours, to a contractual economy, where service rather than time is sold. The individuals or groups supplying such services would also be dispersed throughout the country and the city.

When the tie between productivity and time is dissolved, organizations can provide more "down time" amenities for their employees, such as lounges, gyms, yoga and exercise classes, and swimming pools. Such bonuses are used to help maintain a level of

employee satisfaction and fitness that benefits the whole corporation. Amenities are used to attract top personnel, such as electronics engineers and programmers, to work for various firms in "Silicon Valley" outside Stanford, California.

When the day-in-day-out routine tasks of office life are replaced by electronics, planners predict that offices will eventually be meeting places, not places to process information transactions. With the increasing need to accommodate technological advances and the needs of the individual, office planning requires a more comprehensive range of skills than was ever imagined in the 1950s. Architects and designers are returning to graduate school to study subjects such as environmental psychology, advanced ergonomics, and ecology.

(4)

(6)

(5)

❶ Communications technology has made it possible for more and more people to work at home and still be in contact with their office headquarters.

❷ Ammenities for employees include providing a kitchen area for coffee and hot lunches. Dexter Design.

❸ Many organizations are seeking unique office space. A skylight enhances the work area at the Farrell/Grimshaw Partnership offices.

❹ Many companies have established their offices in nontraditional office buildings. For example, Hanover Acceptances is located in a turn-of-the-century Voysey townhouse where tiled fireplaces and wood-paneled walls recreate a residential atmosphere. Designer: David Hicks.

❺ Vicars like Patrick Tuft have traditionally enjoyed the flexibility of living and working in the same building. The Reverend Tuft's home office in London is a forerunner of the current trend toward the creation of smaller, more manageable working units with greater autonomy and identity.

❻ Illustration from Environetics International, Inc. showing a fully automated office of the future. Environetics predicts that light, heating, air movement, and sound levels will all be computerized as will each employee's individual biosensitivities and each work station will be tailored to personal comfort. Also, filing will be performed electronically; telephones superseded by voice-activated connection and transmission; video conferencing will be commonplace; and writing will be replaced by new techniques of voice-activated memorializing, text creating, and editing. This illustration incorporates the technology for all these new features.

Designer's Choice

Committed to quality and the pursuit of excellence, Ward Bennett is an accomplished designer, artist, and sculptor. He designs furniture for Brickel Associates and also designs jewelry, silverware, clothes, and fabrics and claims there "isn't a minute of the day that my life is not my work."

Ward Bennett

Ward Bennett's private space radiates all this. He lives and works in the same building—the landmark New York building, the Dakota. In his country residence, he has a studio for ceramics and collages, and "a wonderful work table in the main house." Bennett is something of a Renaissance man, as much at home crouched on the factory floor where his furniture designs are produced as he is working with students, designing offices for multinational corporations, or sitting at his potter's wheel. His love of detail and precision is summed up by his own designs, like a clean-limbed chair adaptable for home and office use. Although he has very specific ideas about his own space… "I like light and air. I like mobile furniture. I like solitude and *don't* like a lot of interference…" Bennett doesn't believe in imposing his tastes on others. "When I design for others I design for *their* needs," he says. "You have to create for your client, and that doesn't happen if you leaf through interior design magazines." He is bitingly critical of much of office design and says, "you're not sure if it's a boutique or a restaurant or an office." During the 1960s he was design consultant to the Chase Manhattan Bank, where he was able to

①

put the intracacies of his design philosophy into practice.

He tried to make the Chase offices very personal. The choice of desks and accessories had to relate to the executives as "they might have been involved with Peru or with the Vatican." He admitted it was hard to discover their real hobbies beyond "golf and grandchildren" but kept on asking them because the information was basic to designing for their work and specific needs.

Bennett also collected a whole range of beautiful objects from which the executives were asked to make personal selections. This included folk art, weather vanes, pre-Columbian sculpture, ship models, chronometers, and sextants. He even ordered special

②

pencil pots, desk sets, and paperweights.

Ward Bennett's own apartment and office is something of an aerie itself with a breathtaking view through windows and skylights. Pyramid shaped, by space reclaimed from the roof, it is constructed around the building's flagpole and has a simplicity and vitality that is characteristically Bennett.

"There are three things necessary in life," he says philosophically, "a table, a chair, and a bed. That's all that matters to me," adding, "I hate to buy other people's things if I can help it, because I love to design. I tell my students to try and design at least **one** thing on every job themselves ….even if it's only a doorknob."

❶ Ward Bennett has said "there isn't a minute of the day that my life is not my work." One of his work places is a factory where the wood frames are made for the furniture he designs for Brickell Associates. Here, tracing a template, he alters the curve of his Turtleback chair.

❷ Bennett lives with his furniture designs in his apartment in the gable of the Dakota before he sends them out in the world. He set his Capsule Conference desk/table on casters so that the table can be brought to the work at hand rather than the reverse. Its' tubular foot railing is an aid to posture. Bennett himself likes to work in solitude, without interference. For his clients, he designs to their work habits.

❸ The Dakota's flagpole forms a central support for the dining/work table in his upper-level study. Seats are Bennett's University armchairs— solid ash and "strong as an ax handle." Not shown in this photograph are extensive, built-in storage cabinets.

❹ Bennett is fond of the work table he designed for his East Hampton residence. Because it has no legs, it seems to float between two columns. The carved-wood frame armchairs are part of a series.

④

❺ Another work place is his East Hampton garage. Here, Bennett makes collages and works rich clays into pottery shapes suggesting spare, pure forms. Like his furniture, his unglazed pottery celebrates natural materials.

③

⑤

Vignelli Associates

The Vignellis combine elegance with a certain romanticism, and they've had an office in New York's east sixties near the East River since 1965. They belong to a European tradition that believes the architect should do more, much more for a client than merely design the office. So they design furniture and products, and they like to control each part of the corporate identity including logo and graphics.

They did this recently for Xoil Energy Resources Inc. Lella Vignelli: "We approached the job by solving their space problems in the simplest, least costly, and most dignified way. We weren't really interested in making a 'design statement'." Although she talks about the job in strictly practical terms and how they took a "lot of short cuts," it is very much a statement of their style and approach.

In the Xoil offices, spaces are unified by the use of finish material and consistent colors. A rust-colored carpet is used throughout. The same warm red is used in the seating in the form of a lounge chair in the reception area and a side chair in the conference room and private office. "The form is not new," says Lella Vignelli, "it's a sort of bucket chair, but we're proud of how it's made and manufactured. It's an intelligent product, very simple, so it's relatively inexpensive. Yet it's dignified and comfortable. It has presence."

Throughout the offices, the vertical surfaces are covered with natural linen, something of a Vignelli signature. This creates a soothing effect and sense of uniformity. "We use it a lot in our own home and in various interiors," says Lella Vignelli.

The reasons for this are both aesthetic and practical. Linen doesn't absorb dirt and dust, not even in New York City. The color is neutral and warm, and the walls are upholstered. The linen is soft-stretched, not glued. "If you take linen, back it with paper and glue it to the walls, you lose the quality of the fabric," she stresses.

Linen is used in the reception area, the private offices, and two conference rooms, and it is stretched over full-height doors and custom cabinet doors. The conference rooms have extensive built-in storage, and the fabric covers their doors as well. Vertical blinds used throughout are also made of the same natural linen.

The conference rooms have flexible interiors, and the larger of the two rooms can be converted into a lecture room. They are also appropriate settings for business lunches and are linked by a conveniently designed service counter. This has doors on each side so that food can be prepared and set up on one side of the pass-through without disturbing a meeting in progress. At the proper time, the doors open, and the food is served.

Vignelli designs also adorn the table, in glassware and simple,

geometric cutlery. Control over each aspect of the corporate image goes beyond conference room and lunch table to extend as far as desk accessories, logo, stationery, and business forms. The sense of Vignelli control exists in such minutae as a dot on the letterhead to indicate where the letter should begin.

The Vignellis are quick to comment on the ways in which their own designs have changed in the last 15 years. In the 1960s they sought more of an architectural look, a geometric effect, but now, "our forms are getting softer, and so are the materials." Their famous Saratoga sofa, which was finished like a grand piano with spirit lacquer and "started a renaissance in Italian designed furniture for lacquer," is very different from the softer, more playful curves they are designing now.

Famous designs associated with

①

②

③

their name, like Bloomingdale's logo, and St. Peter's Lutheran Church interior in New York's Citicorp center, have a geometric, tightly sculpted effect. But one senses their whole approach to design is softening. "I think in the future people will be paying more attention to the *meaning* of spaces," adds Lella Vignelli, and even "passages will become more important."

The Vignelli's own offices re-flect something of their philoso-phy. The building was designed for showroom purposes, and their conversion, in monochromatic grey thoughout, is basic.

❶ *Vignelli Associates' good sense of detail is evident in Xoil Energy Resources, New York offices, in their furniture, in the flexibility they program quietly into conference rooms, and in the goblets and silver they designed to be very much in view. Xoil's offices are on two octagonal-shaped floors and the reception-area walls are positioned to suggest that angling. The company logo lettering is readable, unflashy Century-expanded type.*

❷ *Sections of the segmented conference table top can be stored in adjacent closets that hold 40 stack chairs for larger meetings. Metal sheeting is layered behind the linen panels so that business charts can be put up with small magnets.*

❸ *Vignelli Associates designed the silverplate flatware.*

❹ *The second conference room is joined to the first by a shared food-serving counter.*

❺ *Xoil's previous offices had an abundance of dark-wood panelling and reproduction antiques. In the young president's new office, the Vignelli's set their new desk-table and classic lacquer-framed and leather Saratoga sofa on a vividly authentic Persian carpet.*

❻ *The glass pitchers and goblets they ribbed to match the silver and catch the light.*

❼ *Their "Euclid" glass-topped table is basic geometric shapes—a cube, a cylinder, a pyramid, a ball—each in marble and all to rearrange and play mathematically in almost limitless numbers of ways.*

(4)

(5)

(6)

(7)

Doris La Porte

Doris La Porte concentrates on traditional designs for her clients as they find them "more comfortable, more liveable for themselves and their visitors. My clients like a sense of graciousness."

She chose the New York offices of an international corporation to illustrate her philosophy: "executives come from all over the world, so I want them to find an atmosphere in New York where they will feel comfortable. I try to provide a relaxing mood. That is typical of my approach to design," she says, "Throughout my work there is a certain thread that comes through. I strive for understated and, hopefully, timeless interiors." Although these interiors are fairly luxurious, La Porte says that she avoids a monied, overpowering look. Even if her clients have beautiful things, she tries to place them quietly. "I could never design anything flamboyant. I wouldn't know how to go about it."

The personality of the executive is far more a feature of modern office design that it was 20 years ago. Executives used to tell her "do what you think best." Things are very different now. La Porte finds this exciting as it results in more personalized interiors. She has always encouraged people to bring the paintings and objects that are important to them and finds that over the years executives have moved them to bigger and better offices. La Porte believes in creating a certain hominess in her offices and finds this takes a lot of work in new buildings. "It's difficult to make things look like they've always been there," she says. "It's difficult to make spaces look right. But if you don't, they just look commercial."

A hallmark of her design is her use of antique and fine reproduction furniture. But she strives to make the interior look natural, as though furniture and art have been chosen over the experiences of a number of years, not conveniently selected from one manufacturer for instant delivery. "I don't slavishly reproduce period rooms," she stresses. "I use fabrics, colors, wallcoverings, fine accessories, and fine furniture to interpret the best of the past. My clients prefer their office to look like a living room. But I also provide them with lots of files and work surfaces: those requirements differ from executive to executive."

Her sense of "home" in office design made her an appropriate designer for the interiors of an apartment in the same building as her corporate client. The firm had previously rented hotel space for visiting executives. "The idea of office and living quarters in the same building was very appealing," she admits, "and it also added to the possibility of gracious entertaining."

La Porte believes this is a sign of the future, that mixed-use office buildings will become increasingly desirable. Her projection recalls something of the 16th-, 17th-, and 18th-century offices that were in lavish homes and courts and that were places where business could be conducted with a certain style and elegance.

(4)

(5)

(6)

❶ The offices and residential apartment Doris La Porte designed for executives of ICI Americas, an international chemical and pharmaceutical company, are ten floors apart in New York's Olympic Towers. But the rooms share richly detailed visual affinities. Colors are conspicuously nonprimary, nonjarring, with similar hues looking very different. Antiques are placed to be noticed but not to overwhelm. Though in a "tower," ceilings are a standard eight feet, so gracefully scaled table-desks were chosen for the offices, and credenzas hold dictating machines and papers.

❷ The boardroom did not need audiovisual equipment but did need flexible seating, so extra armchairs flank the Coromandel screen.

❸ The taste of ICI's president was key to all the interiors. He wanted his office to have "a light, library look." Researching 1850-era moldings, La Porte's firm gave his office a subtle architectural shell—baseboards, the window valance, and doors panelled in antiqued pine.

❹ The octagonal dining table in the residential apartment expands to seat ten. The floor is polished marble.

❺ La Porte uses art and fine accessories to make individual statements for each executive.

❻ The anteroom to the board room is a place to wait or socialize. The wall scroll is Japanese 18th century. The Paul Jones glass-and-brass coffee tables are deliberate 20th-century choices.

Gwathmey/Siegel and Associates

Architecture is an education, too, you know," says Charles Gwathmey of Gwathmey/Siegel and Associates, New York. "It's no fun if you don't expand people."

The partnership designed headquarters in New Jersey for the Evans Partnership, builder/developers, and it would be impossible for the client or anyone else to react indifferently to the end result. Evans commissioned Gwathmey/Siegel to design a speculative building, partly for its own use for a staff of under 20 and partly to rent to other companies.

The bulding is unique because there is limited natural light. Except for the reception area, the conference room, and one private office, all the spaces are interior. "Yet," Gwathmey explains, "because of our design solution, you get a sense of transparency, even

from the back office. You can get back to the facade and even see a reflection of the reflecting pool we designed." This was accomplished by a design feature known as "vertical layering." The total ceil-

ing height is 15 feet (5 m), which related to the height of the building's arcade. Office walls were built to 9 feet (3 m), leaving a transom space, a "perceptual space" under the skylights. The standard of their design is consistently high and their use of materials is elegant. The Evans offices have curved glass-block walls, and the ceilings are panels of polished aluminium. An integral part of the design is the flooring, carpeting, and custom cabinetwork of oak and black plastic laminate. They use oak for the furniture and trim. The rest of the materials are painted gypsum wallboard.

Each office is custom-designed

to client needs. "We've developed two sets of forms," says Gwathmey. "One develops spatial adjacencies," and the other assesses the particular and peculiar needs of every office and work station, along with storage needs. "When we finish, we have a whole book of every single person, by title or area," says Gwathmey. "It's so detailed we even know if a person is right-or left-handed so we can get the ideal phone situation." By asking people to fill out questionnaires, Gwathmey is able to see which people are aware of their environment and which aren't. On the basis of such

intimate data, they design filing, bookshelves, desks, and select the rest of the furniture. "All you have to do to move in is put an ashtray on the desk and hang something on the wall."

Gwathmey believes that circulation space is a major element in office or residential design. "It's the most intensively designed space because it's perceived and used by everyone," he says. "It's not a throwaway and not an accommodation space." He doesn't simply mean the corridors but the actual sequence of movement throughout the space. This includes the reception area, secre-

tarial pool, and other pool spaces he feels establish the environment. Gwathmey calls them the "core," explaining, "we exploit the design possibilities of these areas, to make them the most 'intense'". The extensive use of glass blocks, reflecting surfaces, and a dramatic 15-foot-(5-m)- square photomural gives them a vivid personality of their own.

The effect is rich, and the style is widely copied—but not repeated elsewhere by Gwathmey/Siegel. "We're moving on to other ideas now," says Charles Gwathmey. "We have some new things going with glass blocks that you wouldn't believe."

Gwathmey/Siegel is currently designing a new desk system for Knoll International. Suitable for both modern and traditional interiors, it is made of mahogany, and there is no metal hardware, so it can't be dated. The system has many options. It combines a series of base pedestals, drawers, and file drawers. There are different shaped tops, some with curves, some with the executive L, to suit each need.

The system represents a venture into mass production of some of the furniture ideas that they've used successfully for many years.

⑥

⑤

❶ The conference room in the foreground and the office beyond are the few spaces with perimeter windows in the Evans Partnership offices. Through the masterful use of transparent surfaces, skylights, clerestories, and mirror-and-glass block, natural light penetrates the interior.

❷ Through the entrance door, the names of Evans clients can be seen behind the reception desk. The raised white letters cast shadows on the skylit wall.

❸ Gwathmey Siegel and Associates designed both the spectacular office building and the office within for their builder/developer client. Together they make an effective sales tool for Evans' construction services. The grand height of the building is evident at night, looking across the reflective pool.

❹ and ❺ An interior office seems spacious and light, its full-height glass-block wall lit with borrowed light. The marble-topped desk is custom designed. Oak cabinetwork and trim brings them together. This vertical layering is expressed throughout.

❻ The giant photomural of construction workers acts as a wall and defines the main gallery. The reflective ceiling makes the space seem even higher. The middle management space, service functions, and bathroom core are organized in single-height spaces to the right. These areas repeat the character of the executive spaces.

John Saladino Associates

John Saladino is a Yale graduate in fine arts and approaches his interiors with a painter's eye.

Interiors Magazine made him Designer of the Year for his "daring use of color and materials in contract design" and for "giving client and public exhilarating environments." They commend him for his cheerful use of color in a doctor's offices.

He is equally unrestrained in his own offices, selecting wooden trellises and a lowered ceiling for the entrance. Saladino has an unfailing sense of his own talent: "after all, my clients come to me, they don't come from real estate brokers." He spoke about his work for the cosmetics firm Almay Inc. as typifying his approach to design.

The art of designing for Almay was to create an illusion of space and glamor within a tight budget and to utilize that space as an appropriate marketing setting for visiting buyers. Space for him is the last status symbol in New York City. "We tried to combine image-making with the practicality of the office traffic flow and function," he explained. For example, the conference rooms double as exhibition space for the products where "the white tables become altars upon which those allure-making products are celebrated." Tall sliding doors open to demonstrate drug-store and display vignettes. Audiovisual equipment, folding modular tables, white cork walls, and two levels of lighting make this space totally functional.

There are office standards for desks and file cabinets, but the president's office combines antique with modern furniture and has an early-19th-century library table as a desk.

The result is a strong corporate feeling, and yet, in Saladino's words, "the offices have something of the privacy of the boudoir ...a sense of female luxury."

He conceptualizes space in terms of color and texture. The color scheme is appropriately based on tints taken from the Almay makeup palette. Peach, taupe, and off-white delineate the architecture and graphically describe the nature of the client. But expressing the products through the design wasn't simply a matter of color. He felt that glamor could be conveyed through materials and proportion. He has been bold enough to combine things not normally seen in offices, such as bath-tile floors with walls painted in high-gloss flesh tones that shimmer. The lighting, a combination of fluorescent and incandescent, and the coloring are designed to flatter employees and visitors, make them feel good.

Apart from blending the romantic with the technical, Saladino stresses the importance of creating an immaculate and rarified atmosphere with white desks, peach fabrics, and chairs with putty-colored frames. The chairs look like powder puffs, as soft as they can be for a posture chair, and are upholstered in a mixture of cotton and linen. All the other seating is covered in mohair plush to be both practical and luxurious.

The general wall colors are peach, the columns taupe, and the core walls white.

"In the cosmetics business, merchandising a product image is what sells cosmetics," says Saladino. Almay is also in the process of wooing good people to work for them. "If you want to work in the cosmetics field," he observes, "you don't want to work on a dark wool chair. That's what the old offices were like. It's important that *these* offices be magnetic."

①

②

❶ *In the Manhattan offices of Almay, manufacturers of cosmetics, two conference rooms, divisible by sliding doors, have white walls and table tops for accurate color readings. Concealed shelves in the smaller area are internally lit for display and photography. The Harter chairs were chosen because they look like powder puffs.*

❷ *The president's office is simultaneously richly textured and practical. Standard fluorescent fixtures are recessed in the acoustic-tile ceiling above the desk and seating area. The desk is an early 19th-century library table.*

❸ *The reception area sets the theme for glamour: oversized spaces, colors that flatter, and textures that glow. Saladino uses colors and materials not usually found in offices—bathlike ceramic tile, flesh tones, and shimmering surfaces. Linda White designed the banner; the petal chair is Saladino's design.*

❹ *In the secretarial areas, Saladino aimed for an "immaculate, rarefied atmosphere." To make them seem more expansive, he separated the desks with unframed glass partitions, rounded out the columns to make them softer and less obtrusive, and simplified the ceiling with one luminous plane.*

③

④

Pentagram

"In the consumer revolt against current architecture which has gathered strength over the past 20 years, the most damning criticisms have been

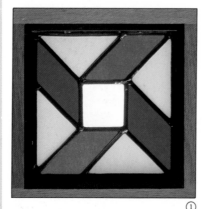

boredom and monotony, simplification and crudity of form and expression. We have impoverished our complex urban inheritance. We have lost our natural poetry and feeling for place, and we have made no place in building for our peers of other callings."

In the renovation of the London headquarters for Unilever House, architect Theo Crosby has tried to rectify that situation. He is a partner in Pentagram, the design firm with offices in London and New York. Pentagram is known for the corporate identity programs of such clients as Reuters, British Petroleum, and Cunard. Crosby's remarks appeared in "Pentagram Papers," which reflect the firm's professional interests in graphic design, architecture, and industrial design.

Unilever House, on the Embankment by Blackfriars Bridge, was one of London's last imperial baroque buildings. The interiors were "unemphatic Art Deco." Built in an "enormous hurry" in 1930, it was never quite finished. The exterior, with sculptures by Sir Reid Dick, has always been a splendid riverside asset and also an object of modernist derision for 40 years. Crosby has written, "It represented everything the Modern Movement was against—pomp, weight, wasteful and inefficient planning, and, above all, far too much on the site."

Pentagram was commissioned to renovate the building and to provide a new entrance linking it with a new office wing designed by Fitzroy Robinson and Partners.

The support facilities served a staff of 1,400 and included new conference rooms and a restaurant. The top floors were gutted and rebuilt for executive offices, and the existing offices were refurbished.

The problem was to redesign the existing building without destroying its character. Unsightly mechanical equipment was covered by a new roof. Pentagram added new windows on the executive floor, formerly a windowless attic. New sculptures on the cornice retain and modify the architectural expression. Fourteen sculptures, twice life-size, are being made by Nicholas Munro. Designed to complement the originals, the new sculptures will be in a new material of glass-reinforced plastic, which is colored to match the stone facade. A large arch, adorned by the same splendid decorative gates that were present at the old entrance, has been cut to mark the new entrance. (The old entrance will become the place for the new visitors dining room.)

Crosby has written: "Unilever has become, in 50 years, a truly enormous organization, spread across the world, employing every race and nationality. Something of this diversity is incorporated, in materials, artworks and gifts from member companies into the fabric." This was the basis of the

interior design theme, which also capitalizes on the original art deco interior.

The entrance hall, residential space hacked out of the old rear offices and lavatories, is intended to be an exercise in "integrated decoration to explore new territory." According to Crosby, "Basic themes, inherent in the original decoration, are elaborated in colored marbles, in light fittings and in the new capitals." Pentagram considers these interiors an "ambitious contemporary variation of Art Deco which also subsumes some of the romance and richness of Unilever itself." Sculptures by the Benin sculptor Chief Emokae, given by United Africa Company International, and a bronze of "Krishna Dancing," given by Unilever Hindustan, are the focal points of the new entrance hall. The German subsidiary has contributed stained-glass windows. A new chandelier from the Austrian subsidiary will grace the new visitors dining room.

The conference rooms and the executive offices are rich in detail, such as stained-glass office doors and custom wood-cabinetwork. They give credence to Crosby's notion that "building and interior furnishings provide a variety of convivial activities, where skill is evident, and instantly recognizable."

❹ A detail of one of the capitals in blue and gold plaster with bronze uplighters. The complex light box Pentagram designed at its center contains ordinary fluorescent fittings to illuminate art deco motifs used throughout the Unilever interior.

❺ The new north entrance to Unilever House has been cut into the existing facade and matches the detailing of a nearby opening. Within, a new stone arch and bronze gates from the old south entrance have been installed behind a glass canopy above which is a gilt sculpture by Bernard Sindall.

⑤

❶ A detail of a stained-glass door panel on the executive floor. The clear glass fulfills fire-code requirements.

❷ The new conference room incorporates a brilliant new art deco-inspired light box on the ceiling. Oak louvers diffuse window light and direct the view.

❸ In the main entrance hall with stairs leading down to the Watergate entrance, floors are patterned in travertine and colored marbles. The wall panelling in decorated mirror glass is by Diane Radford.

❻ and **❼** The chairman's office, with its' fine view of St. Paul's, has oak dado panelling and a new desk in oak and dark-green leather. The walls, covered with grass cloth and topped with decorative cornices, integrate the air conditioning in the room without losing the excellent high ceilings of the 1930 building.

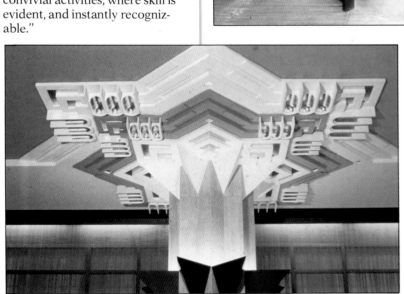

④

David Hicks

David Hicks' elegant country estate has been the testing ground for his creative ideas since he began redecorating it in 1960. "My major contribution as an interior designer," wrote Hicks in his book, *Living With Design*, "has been to show people how to use bold color mixtures, how to light rooms, how to use patterned carpets, and how to mix old with new." David Hicks has designed residences, hotels, shops, restaurants, and offices throughout the world, but he chose his library in a converted farmhouse to illustrate the design principles that have made him internationally famous.

The library: A very simple, symmetrical room with elegant proportions, the library has painted wood floors and a plain, painted plaster ceiling. Its four walls are lined with bronzed bookcases interrupted only by a large window and, directly opposite, a fireplace with a simple marble surround. The entrance door is centered in a third wall and integrated with the bookcase design. The door zones the room: to the right, in front of the window, is the desk; to the left, in front of the fireplace, is the seating area for reading or talking to visitors. The simplicity of the layout creates a feeling not of stimulation but of repose.

His library reflects the basic hall marks of David Hicks' style, especially in the way priceless antiques and luxurious materials mix with family mementos—portraits and heirlooms—and simple touches of comfort—throw pillows on the unmatched easy chairs. The beautiful and very old Turkish carpet that dominates the library belonged to Hicks' grandfather, and its brilliant red hues keynote the color scheme. The various reds, in fact, provide the library with a sense of warmth even as they are tempered by the luxurious textures: smooth leather bindings with gold titles; lustrous carpet; soft velvet. There are red draperies at the window, a red cushion on the satinwood chair at the desk. The red silk velvet that covers the wall behind the fireplace came from his grandmother's evening dress.

"Nostalgia to me is one of the great pleasures in life," says Hicks; and in his role as an interior designer he interprets his client's taste, style, and way of life, even if that client is himself. The library lighting is simplicity itself—three lamps with similar shades and variations of the same base. The lamps are placed precisely where they are most needed—one on the desk and the two others on tables at the side of each chair flanking

①

the fireplace. A picture light, over the portrait above the fireplace, is the only gratuitous accent.

Hicks upholstered the traditional wing chair and a club chair in two of the color-coordinated, geometrically patterned fabrics for which he is famous. In each case, piping of a contrasting color brings out their pleasing contours "I have been fascinated by furniture since I was ten years old," he says. In fact, embellishing traditional forms with his own bold-patterned fabrics is a David Hicks trademark—another aspect of mixing old and new that shapes his library's whole design.

③

②

❶ *Upholstered armchairs of compatible but dissimilar shape break the symmetry of the library's design. Upholstered in geometric fabrics designed by Hicks himself, they bring warmth, comfort, and a major note of informality to an otherwise formal layout. Above the fireplace hangs another family heirloom, the portrait of a 17th-century ancestor.*

❷ *The library is on the ground floor of this renovated wood farm building. Hicks added the porch on the left and the round attic.*

❸ *Aside from the telephone, Hicks' desk top features family photographs and other personal memorabilia, reflecting unabashed nostalgia and his penchant for collecting.*

❹ *The desk, made for Edwardian financier Sir Ernest Cassell, is a practical family heirloom with copious drawer space for storing papers. Placed in front of the wide, curtainless window, it gives Hicks a restful view of his gardens.*

❺ *A detail of contrasting shapes and textures that mix old and new—cool, crisply carved, polished white marble; sleek, bronzed bookshelves; warm, scarlet bindings. The lamp glow brings out the gleam of the gold titles. All the books in Hicks' collection will eventually be bound in shades of red.*

④

⑤

Terence Conran is something of a byword in modern design. He's the man who took the myth and mystique out of good design and made it accessible via his Habitat stores in Britain, Europe, and America.

Terence Conran

His own offices, studios, and workshops are housed in a converted warehouse space in London's Covent Garden, home of the Royal Opera and once the traditional fruit and vegetable market.

Conran Associates acquired an old banana warehouse on 28 Neal Street in the early 1970s, and when the company grew from 30 to 80 people in four years, they were fortunate enough to be able to buy an old 7,500 square foot piano warehouse directly behind them. The two buildings were grafted together by a stylish glass bridge (initially disputed by city conservationists who wanted something more Victorian).

The new warehouse space provided long, wide rectangular rooms on the ground floor and two other floors that were converted into studios for graphics and products and a large workshop with smaller offices around the perimeter. The large graphic-art studio enables designers and art workers to operate side by side, ensuring a close liaison and follow-through on corporate, retail, packaging, and in-store projects for clients such as Yardley, Lyons, and Akzo. The product-design studio is especially fitted to handle various materials and processes for clients such as Sony, Renault, and Marks and Spencer. A large workshop for building prototypes is designed so that cars, caravans, and boats can be driven into the building.

Every attempt was made to preserve the charm of the buildings in their historic settings, while adapting them to the modern needs of a comprehensive international design group. In spite of the many disciplines housed under the warehouse roofs, there is a remarkable consistency throughout the open-plan offices and design studios in the use of bold primary colors against a neutral background, broken up by colorful felt tack boards often cut on the diagonal.

Terence Conran's own office is stark: dark blinds offer privacy from the street. His chrome-and-black-topped desk is softened by a vase of fresh flowers, a feature that is seen throughout his group. The effect of his office isn't markedly different from that of the conference room or his directors' offices: there is a certain consistency in style for everyone who works for the Associates, which helps create an egalitarian atmosphere.

Carpeting is used throughout for its acoustic qualities and to balance the hard edge of the painted brick work. The furniture is largely Habitat, designed by the Associates. This is economical and a sound advertisement for the group. Corporate clients can see Habitat's furnishings *in situ*. Similarly, in planning interiors for others, the group rarely designs special furniture but draws on the Associates' existing ranges and finishes, except where specialized design is needed for conference tables and projection facilities.

Group needs have prompted creative growth. The Associates are becoming increasingly involved in the design of computers and the use of computers in design because of what they have learned via the needs of their own computerized administration and payroll.

The advertising and catalog needs for Habitat established in-house services that now have the experience—and space—to service outside clients. The group has additional features not always associated with even the most sophisticated design companies in big cities, such as a restaurant and a gallery displaying company work and that of individual artists and photographers.

①

②

③

④

(6)

(5)

(7)

❶ A detail of the seating area in one of the private offices in Conran Associates, London offices. Tack boards on a diagonal are both a graphic device and a functional hanging space.

❷ In the catalogue department, the entire wall is used to prepare schedules.

❸ All the walls in the office are painted white, and splashes of bright colors are used as a unifying element. This private office is outside one of the design studios and, like the rest of the office, it is furnished with the furniture available in Conran's retail stores.

❹ The desk in Terence Conran's own office exemplifies the attention to detail that is a hallmark of all Conran's designs.

❺ One of several drafting rooms in Conran's offices that are organized according to function.

❻ Conran's own office is on the ground floor of the building. Venetian blinds redirect the light from the full-height windows and provide privacy from the street. The door in the background leads to the model shop.

❼ The basement-level conference room is used for presentations and public exhibitions.

Elements of Design

Chapter 3

Ceilings

Ceilings used to be major decorative elements in architectural interiors. They were meant to be seen and admired. Elaborately coffered in wood and plaster, with painted panels and fancy plaster work, they demanded attention. Lighted indirectly, they became an illuminated plane, like the walls and floors.

Most ceilings today are conceived as simple, unornamented surfaces. They are designed to be inconspicuous. Yet ceilings are important in establishing the character and atmosphere of interior space. The ceiling height relative to the size of a space, the materials it's made of, its color, its texture, and how it's lighted all influence our perceptions. And the ceilings in modern office buildings must fulfill functional requirements as well as aesthetic ones. A simple, unobtrusive ceiling requires good design.

Office-building ceilings must grapple with the technological realities of high-rise buildings—structural and mechanical systems, electric and telecommunications distribution, and fire safety and lighting. A suspended ceiling can discreetly hide most of this clutter. In the offices below, the only evidence of such clutter are well-placed light fixtures, an occasional air diffuser, and a sprinkler head or two. Sometimes the building's structural module is expressed as well, with tracks built into the ceiling for moveable partitions. By careful attention to details, all the components can be organized into an integrated whole. They're all drawn on a *reflected ceiling plan*.
In addition to its utilitarian func-

tions, the ceiling, like any surface, reflects light and sound. As the biggest uninterrupted surface in the office (it's as large as the floor, of course, but the floor is covered with people and furniture), ceilings contribute significantly to the acoustics and the lighting qualities of a space.
Finished ceilings: There are two types of finished ceilings. The first, commonly used in residential construction rather than office buildings, is fastened directly to the underside of a roof structure. It allows no room for hiding utilities. Obviously, any ductwork and plumbing not accommodated within the ceiling will have to be below it. Suspended ceilings, the second type of finished ceiling, allow a space called a *plenum*, between the ceiling and the bottom of the structure above it for building necessities. Usually, suspended ceilings provide easy access to the plenum for maintenance, repairs, and changes in the maze of mechanical systems hidden above them, And they can, when installed according to recognized standards, provide a building with required fire resistance ratings.

Suspended ceilings are available in several different materials. *Acoustic tiles or panels* are an office building standard. Made of noncombustible materials—usually mineral fibers, fiberglass, or asbestos—they're best known for their sound-control capabilities. Their porous composition effectively prevents sound waves from being reflected back into a room. The degree to which they absorb airborne noise can be rated by a noise-reduction coefficient—NRC. In addition, acoustic

tiles and panels can offer fire protection, accessibility to the mechanical systems above them, and the capability of air circulation. They come in a variety of colors and textures, including fabric-wrapped panels and panels covered with a mirrorlike reflective film. Check carefully with manufacturer's specifications.

In most office buildings, the hung ceiling is continuous throughout, and partitions are either built to its underside or stop just above it. This saves time, money, and materials. In addition, the undivided space above the hung ceiling can be utilized as one giant air duct—usually for return air that is sucked back into the central air-conditioning system for recycling. However, sound waves, reflected from the underside of the structural slab, also travel through the plenum, from

one office to another. Even the most efficient sound absorbers allow some airborne noise to pass through it. So, for the best possible sound insulation in private offices, even with a sound-control ceiling, make sure that the office partition continues above the hung ceiling to the underside of the structural slab, caulked at the joint for an airtight seal. If the plenum is used for return air sound-insulated holes will have to be cut in the partition so that airflow won't be impeded. This costly procedure should be used in every space where absolute acoustic privacy is desired.

Acoustic ceiling tiles and panels have standardized sizes: a tile is 12 inches (.305 m) square; a panel is either 24 inches square or 24 by 48 inches (.610 m square or .610 by 1.219 m)—which coordinates with the standard sizes of recessed

①

fluorescent lighting fixtures. Either ⅝ of an inch or ¾ of an inch (15.88 mm or 19.05 mm) thick, they are available with different edge details: a shadow line or bevelled edge, which emphasizes individual tiles and panels; or a square-cut edge, which minimizes the joint between abutting tiles and creates a continuous-looking surface. The best-quality tiles have flush edges and nondirectional fissures.

You can glue tiles to the underside of flat, existing ceilings yourself, but suspended sound-control ceilings require professional installations to receive proper fire-resistance and noise ratings.

The cost and appearance of ceiling tiles vary according to the suspension system that you choose. The least expensive system employs a grid of visible metal *splines*, which are inverted Z or T shapes. They hold 2-by-2-foot or 2-by-4-foot (.610-by-.610-m or .610-by-1.219-m) panels on four sides. The panels are tilted into place and rest on the flanges of the splines; they're easily tilted out for access to the space above it. Standard lighting fixtures fit this grid, and air-conditioning grilles are cut into it when necessary. The splines vary in materials from painted steel to extruded aluminum, and their cost varies accordingly. The most elaborate exposed splines do triple duty as tile receptors, as air-distribution grilles, and as overhead tracks for moveable partitions. These are deluxe systems. In general, the rigid geometry of a standard exposed-spline ceiling contributes to the monotony of office spaces. If this standard system is offered by the building you're planning to lease space in, it might be worthwhile to negotiate with your prospective landlord for a higher-quality system: the concealed spline.

Concealed-spline systems show no visible means of supporting the tile. They have to be carefully aligned, and consequently, they're more expensive to install. Used in conjunction with square-edged tiles, they look almost monolithic.

Any ceiling reflects light to the space below it. In recent years, the ceiling as a light-reflecting surface has been reevaluated in office design. There has been a trend away from uniformly spaced ceiling fixtures to those that aim high-intensity light from below onto the ceiling surface. The ceiling bounces light into the office as indirect light. It's supplemented by work-top lamps. A simple, unbroken ceiling, with as few cutouts as possible, is required for uniform reflection. The concealed-spline system is ideal. Although the task/ambient lighting system has more impact in general office spaces, the idea of simple ceilings for private offices has great credence. Any reduction in the number of cutouts in the ceiling—for lighting, air-conditioning diffusers, and public-address speakers—makes the ceiling feel lighter and less oppressive.

One way to eliminate cutouts is to use the tile itself as a diffuser. The plenum area above the hung ceiling is designed to carry conditioned air to the room through unobtrusive, small adjustable openings in the tile. A foil backing prevents air seepage through the tile and insulates the plenum air space. Another way to eliminate ceiling diffusers is to use recessed lighting fixtures that also handle air. And trim, linear diffusers, well placed, are elegant alternatives to the common utilitarian diffusers that are much more prevalent. A note of caution: air-conditioning systems should be properly designed by mechanical engineers. The irregular surfaces of acoustic tiles and panels collect airborne dust particles, especially near diffusers where air movement is greatest. In time, even the whitest tiles become greyed. Plastic-covered tiles slow down the process. Periodic vacuum-cleaning will remove loose dust; gum erasers are useful for removing

②

small marks and smudges. Soiled acoustic tile can be washed with mild soapsuds that are applied with a wash rag wrung dry. Ceiling units can be repainted without loss of their acoustic properties. (Use a thin, vinyl-acrylic, flat wall-paint, but check first with the manufacturer's specifications.)

Aluminum panels make a completely different-looking acoustic ceiling. Once relegated to utility spaces, they are now being used in prestigious areas of the office, such as reception and board rooms. Aluminum-panel ceilings are common in Scandinavia, where colored rather than reflective surfaces are popular. They can be perforated with tiny holes, evenly spaced throughout the panels (available in sizes up to 24 inches [.610 m] square), which permit sound waves to reach sound-absorbent pads behind them. They need no maintenance, and holes can be cut in them for recessed lights. Aluminum panels are available in a shiny mirror-like

❶ *Ceilings can be an important source of acoustic control. Both of the ceilings shown here are interesting examples of suspended acoustic ceilings. This one is the Soft Look from Armstrong. The fabric-surfaced panels are fire-retardant and come in twelve different colors. Panels are fashioned with tegular edges to provide design interest and easy installation and removal.*

❷ *There are tiny perforations in the aluminum panels on this suspended ceiling. The panels cover a thick layer of acoustical padding that absorbs noise. The reflective panels make the ceiling disappear visually expanding the space at Garey Shirtmakers. Architect: Gwathmey Siegel and Associates.*

finish; crisp edges minimize the joints between panels. This sleek system reflects the floor below it and gives the illusion of a space twice as high as it really is.

Plaster or gypsum board are less often used office ceilings. Their residential allusions make an office seem gracious and unbusinesslike. They "fit" every room size, and there is no need to worry about grids or joints in an irregularly shaped room. Their relatively hard, dense surface reflects more sound waves than it absorbs. In private offices this is generally not a problem because the little noise generated by a single occupant can be absorbed by a carpeted floor.

Plaster ceilings—the wet system—is rarely used in office-building construction. Wet plaster is troweled in layers over metal lath or gypsum lath in separate applications—a scratch coat, a brown coat, and a finish coat over metal lath; and two coats over rock lath. Acoustical materials—usually vermiculite—are substituted for sand in the plaster mix for better sound absorption. Unlike regular plaster, acoustic plaster is extremely fragile and difficult to maintain. If it's painted, it will lose some acoustic properties. If you need sound control, use acoustic plaster only in the event that commonplace acoustic tiles are unsuitable.

Gypsum wallboard is a dry system. Panels 4 by 8 feet (1.219 by 2.438 m) are screwed onto metal furring channels (or wood in a nonfireproof building). The screwheads and the joints between the panels are filled with a special compound—*spackle*—and covered with tape to make a smooth surface. This smoothing is a critical operation: irregularities in wallboard ceilings are much more apparent than in wallboard walls because ceilings reflect more light. High-gloss paint emphasizes any surface blemishes. Use it with care.

Plaster and wallboard ceilings

offer design flexibility, and the opportunity for embellishment. They can be formed into interesting shapes—vaulted upwards or propped down in special areas, for example. The ceilings can meet the walls in a simple 90° angle, be softened with a curve (a cove), or be trimmed with a molding. They offer a modicum of flexibility for access to the space above because they can be cut and patched if it's absolutely necessary to get to the plenum space. As this is a dusty procedure, it's best to plan ahead. Provide unobtrusive access panels if possible or, better still, locate valves above a more accessible ceiling type. Plaster and gypsum-board ceilings can be finished in a variety of ways: in a smooth or

textured finish, covered with paper, or painted. In general, a smooth, light-colored ceiling is best.

Coffered ceilings exist in some old buildings that have been converted to office use. They can be built today, at great cost, to give a feeling of Old World charm to private offices. Modern realities, lighting and air-conditioning ducts, must be carefully integrated; and new construction in a fireproof building requires fireproofed wood.

Simpler wood ceilings can be made of oak or maple strips or planks usually used for flooring. Panels of wood veneer, scored to resemble individual pieces, can reduce installation costs. Veneers offer the opportunity to incorporate more exotic woods. But try to be consistent. If your desk is

wood, make sure that the ceiling is compatible.

Any finished ceiling can be designed with a **drapery pocket** at the windows—a recess for drapes, curtains, or blinds that conceals the hardware for hanging them. Then, for an uninterrupted window view, blinds can be pulled up when they're not needed for sun-control. A **lighting recess**, a continuous slot that can vary from 6 to 12 inches (152.4 to 304 mm), runs parallel to a wall. It conceals lighting fixtures that wash the wall with light. The slot, or **reveal**, can also be used to conceal air diffusers. A continuous recess along all four edges of a ceiling creates the effect of a floating ceiling. Scaled down to ¾ of an inch (19 mm), a reveal is still a crisp and elegant way to articulate the difference between the ceiling and the wall.

Exposed Ceilings:
Exposed structural ceilings are common in older office buildings and in lofts and factories that have been converted to office use. You can either work with them or suspend a new, finished ceiling. Exposed ceilings—a keynote of the high-technology style—have become increasingly popular as a stylistic alternative to typical office interiors. One reason for leaving a ceiling exposed is to retain the relatively high floor-to-floor

heights. Another is cost savings. On the other hand, the clutter of overhead pipes, conduits, and ducts can be unsightly. And sometimes when a high-ceilinged space is compartmentalized into small offices, the resulting rooms have awkward proportions.

There are several strategies for minimizing the disadvantages of exposed ceilings. One is to paint all the overhead clutter with white or light-colored paint matching the walls and forget about it. Paint can also camouflage awkward proportions of a too-tall private office. Establish a line 9 feet (2.74 m) or so above the floor. Paint everything above it a dark color—grey, black, or brown—and everything below it a contrasting light color. This reduces the apparent ceiling height, yet retains a feeling of "loft" in a high space. Another way to accomplish this is to "celebrate" a mechanical feature by painting air-conditioning ducts a bright color or emphasizing suspended lighting fixtures. Or you can hang a transparent plane of wood slats, or even an opaque plane of plaster, which creates a more intimate space below it yet allows you to "read" the dimensions of the larger volume.

A modified open-office layout that eliminates the slab-high partitions of private offices also eliminates awkwardly proportioned rooms. Freestanding partitions, 8 or 9 feet (2.43 or 2.74 m) high, can be built to enclose individual offices. Since the ceiling runs continuously above them, they're perceived as part of the larger whole and not as a vertical shaft of space.

Skylights are architectural assets worth preserving. They provide the cheeriness of natural light and the drama of an unexpected light source. Skylights have a practical, energy-saving use as well: since daylight is far brighter than any artificial light, there's no need to turn on the lights on bright days. If the skylights are operable, they can ventilate the office efficiently, getting rid of warm air trapped at the ceiling level. But make sure to use insulating glass to prevent winter heat-loss, and if your skylights don't face north, make sure they have reflective glass panes to prevent excessive heat-gains.

If skylight openings conflict with your office layout, you can redirect the light from the ceiling opening (as Barry Brukoff Interiors did in an office for The Coca Cola Company in San Francisco, made from their former warehouse as shown in the section called Clerical and Operational Areas.). Horizontal blinds—including opaque ones for a virtually complete light-seal—are available for sun-control. Most lighting designs incorporate artificial light fixtures in the skylight so that the light distribution is similar whether or not the sun's shining.

Not all exposed ceilings present interior design problems. Some, in fact, are designed to be seen. Their straightforward structure incorporates lighting and mechanical systems. Coffered concrete ceilings, sometimes called **waffles**, are best known; they provide a handsome, dignified office interior.

❶ *Original pressed-metal ceilings, like the one in this bank, were produced in large sheets and nailed into ceiling joists. Currently enjoying a revival, pressed-metal ceilings now come in panels that are easily installed on conventional suspension systems.*

❷ *The massive ceilings in the Boston City Hall are also part of the structure of the building. Their design is part of the building's style. Architect: Kallmann, McKinnell & Knowles. Interior design: I.S.D., Inc.*

❸ *A very unique and expensive ceiling of lacquered-and-incised wood at General Felt Industries, Knoll International in New York City. Access panels to recessed fixtures are camouflaged by the grid in the wood. Window-wall soffits, fascia, and induction units are enclosed in a plastic laminate. Narrow-slat metal blinds on the windows control light. Interiors designed by Charles Pfister of Skidmore, Owings and Merrill.*

❹ *Skylights functioning as horizontal windows are another design element in ceilings. This skylight in the office of Alan Felsenthal is the only source of daylight for this windowless space. Designed by Stanley Felderman, Ltd.*

❺ *In the New York offices of Pentagram, the ceilings were left exposed. The paraphernalia of lights, sprinklers, and air ducts were organized by layout and color into elements of design. Architect: Katrin Adam.*

Lighting

②

Lighting is a major concern for all office designers. Common sense tells us good lighting is crucial to effective work. Moreover, lighting accounts for a large percentage of the total energy consumption of a building.

The two basic elements which the office designer must consider are the cost of lighting and its efficiency. Speaking to the latter issue, efficient lighting is that which lights the work area thoroughly but does not create eyestrain for the office worker.

There are some basic strategies and simple rules for reducing eyestrain and fatigue. The first is to avoid high contrasts. The work that you're doing should be the most brightly lit surface in the room. Hot spots of glare elsewhere in the room, from overhead ceiling fixtures or from glossy surfaces, reflect light back into your eyes. These hot spots compete with the task at hand for your attention, causing fatigue. Non-reflective desk tops of leather or wood reduce potential glare sources. Careful positioning of lights will avoid hot spots on other office surfaces.

An often overlooked source of hot spots is the surface of the work itself resting on your desk top. The glossy surface of print or pencil lines, CRT screens and keyboards, sometimes reflects light into your eyes, distorting an image and making it difficult to read. This phenomenon is called veiling reflection and it is easy to test for: put a mirror on the surface where you'll be working; if you see a "hot spot," your lighting source will cause veiling reflections. Veiling reflections can be avoided by moving your desk.

①

Alternatively, you can switch to low-brightness lighting fixtures—fixtures with parabolic reflectors or prismatic lenses that change the angle of the light.

Another strategy for reducing eyestrain is to avoid a high contrast between your work (which is probably white) and your desk top. Dark walls and dark desk tops can be a problem. You should work in a space with some background illumination.

During the day, natural light may provide all the necessary background illumination, but at night it's best to use lights throughout a room. Some suspended or pendant lighting fixtures serve a dual function in this regard. They simultaneously light the work surface and the ceiling, providing both direct light and indirect ambient light.

Fluorescent light is most often associated with the office. It was invented in 1939 and works on a principal of energy-activated phosphors which coat the inside of a sealed glass tube. The phosphors are activated by invisible violet light which is produced when an electric current is passed through the tube containing the vaporized gases of mercury and argon.

A fluorescent lamp generates very little heat. It is efficient, delivering a relatively large amount of light per watt of power consumed (or 65 lumens per watt). The fluorescent light has a long life span which makes it economical. Moreover, it's doubly efficient because it does not heat the air thereby demanding that an air-conditioning system work harder to cool it down again.

There are a few factors to consider when using fluorescent lights in office design. Fluorescent is a linear light source. It does not produce sharp shadows and contrasts. There's no denying that it's an ideal source for lighting the

❶ Incandescent lights spotlight directional signs and help visitors find their way to the conference room at Thomson Travel Agency in London. Architect: Trickett Associates.

❷ Three different kinds of light are available in this office at Techner Apex. Large windows provide abundant daylight. A fluorescent light is surface-mounted above the desk and along the wall, incandescent wall washers give a feeling of warmth to the space. Designed by Warren Platner Associates Architects.

❸ In the corporate chairman's office of the Philadelphia National Bank, custom-designed pendant fixtures light the desk. Also, a line of recessed incandescent fixtures highlight a collection of duck decoys and other art objects. Designed by The Space Design Group.

❹ The round, recessed fluorescent light fixture echoes the shape of the table underneath it at Garey Shirtmakers. Color readings tend to be on the blue side under fluorescent lights, so shirt samples are best viewed close to the windows. Architect: Gwathmey Siegel and Associates.

❺ This custom-designed fluorescent fixture is doubly efficient because it's close to the work surface. Also, it projects light both upward and downward at the same time. This well-organized ceiling at International Paper is designed so that there's a sprinkler system and an air diffuser at every fixture location. Designed by the Space Design Group.

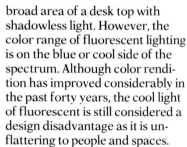

①

②

broad area of a desk top with shadowless light. However, the color range of fluorescent lighting is on the blue or cool side of the spectrum. Although color rendition has improved considerably in the past forty years, the cool light of fluorescent is still considered a design disadvantage as it is unflattering to people and spaces.

The other major light source is, of course, incandescent light. Incandescent bulbs have a tungsten filament which glows when heated. These bulbs are relatively inexpensive but they emit heat and are not particularly energy efficient (delivering only about 20 lumens per watt). The main virtue of the incandescent bulb is that its light is to the warm end of the color spectrum. It's the standard against which other light sources are compared. In addition to its flattering light, another advantage of incandescent light is that it's a point source which can be easily controlled.

In order to achieve the efficiency of fluorescents and the warmth of incandescents, many designers use a combination of the two in the office. Fluorescent light is often used at the desk with incandescent lights used for special purposes elsewhere. One effective use of incandescents is as a wall wash. If the walls of the office are bathed in incandescent light, the whole space seems incandescent and the office is warm and inviting. Wall washers, which can be either recessed or surface mounted, are designed to give an even spread of light along a wall.

In addition, or as an alternative to washing the walls with incandescent light, incandescent downlights can be used to complement fluorescent lighting. Downlights can light specific objects and areas such as tables or plants. Downlights are designed to spread light horizontally. Their directionality produces strong shadows. Downlights above a desk can function as

both ambient and task lighting but since intensity varies greatly with the distance between the source and the surface to be illuminated, it's much more efficient to use a light source closer to the work surface. Hanging pendant fixtures or desk lamps serve this purpose. The advantage of suspended fixtures is that they don't take up valuable desk space. On the other hand, desk lamps can usually be adjusted for the best light and to reduce glare. Of course the use of either a pendant fixture or a desk lamp offers an opportunity for displaying a beautiful object which complements the total office design.

Light tracks mounted with individual incandescent luminaires are a flexible lighting design solution. The luminaires can be adjusted to accent, downlight or wash a wall surface. Pendant fixtures can be hung from the track where needed. Exposed track lights and light fixtures contribute to the character of the office interior as opposed to recessed fixtures which are seen as part of the architecture.

Whether you combine incandescent and fluorescent, use pendants or downlights or desk lamps, selective switching can add flexibility and efficiency to your lighting plan. Selective switching allows task lighting and general lighting to be operated independently. This controls light levels and adds variety to office lighting combinations. Incandescent light can also be used in conjunction with rheostatic, or dimmer switches for even more control of the interior environment. Selective switching is initially more expensive but should reduce operating costs over a period of time as lights are used only as they are needed.

High intensity discharge lamps, a third source, are the most efficient (approximately 100 lumens per watt). First developed for lighting large outdoor spaces, they are now used in large office areas. Freestanding or mounted to office furniture, they provide indirect light bounced from the ceiling.

Of course, daylight is the most important, efficient, and pleasant light source available. In some offices, depending on windows and exposure, it might be possible to take advantage of natural light for several hours each day.

While the cost and efficiency of lighting are major concerns, there are important aesthetic considerations that should not be overlooked in the choice of office lighting. Lighting makes design come alive. Good lighting can make or break a design. Lighting can lend an air of elegance to common materials or conversely, it can make the most exquisite materials appear mundane. One lighting scheme can create the illusion of a warm, inviting, and dramatic office while another can make the same space appear cold, lackluster and monotonous.

③

④

❶ *A continuous track on the ceiling brings power to the open-plan work stations below it at the Farrell Grimshaw Partnership offices. Exposed fixtures, easily replaced, are part of the track. Above, a skylight parallels the path of the unit. Architect: Farrell Grimshaw Partnership.*

❷ *The office of Edward J. Safdie, formerly a private club from the Edwardian era, is lit indirectly with a high-intensity discharge lamp. The light bounces off the ceiling, highlighting the intricate plaster details. High-intensity lamps are being used more and more in open-office systems. Designed by Charles Swerz and Associates.*

❸ *A single exposed light would create glare but a series of them prevents it. Here, in the offices of Lea-Ronal, a row of such lights are used for general illumination. Suspended fixtures above the desk are good task lights. Designed by John Saladino, Inc.*

❹ *Circulation areas can be lit with lower-light levels than in office areas. Beautiful light fixtures can also serve as sculptures, as they do in this corridor at Alusuisse of America. The wall-mounted fixture shoots light upward and is the main focal point for the area. Architect: Samuel J. DeSanto*

Walls

①

Walls provide a sense of enclosure. They define space, and territory and afford privacy. They are barriers—for sound, light, vision, traffic, and fire. Exterior walls (in conjunction with the roof, of course) are barriers to the weather as well. The psychological implications of shelter cannot be ignored. Walls are the three-dimensional realization of the office layout; the firm plan. Within their thickness, walls conceal wiring and piping. Most walls make effective sound barriers, preventing the transmission of sound from room to room. And within a room, the finish of the wall surface contributes to its acoustic qualities. Hard surfaces, such as glass, brick, plastic laminate, wood, and plaster reflect sounds; soft materials, such as fabric, cork, and carpet absorb them.

The aesthetic importance of walls is well known; they're always in view. Of all the architectural elements, walls do the most to determine the appearance of space—its color and its character. Recently, the psychological and functional importance of walls in offices has been the focus of attention. This is a by-product of the debate about open-office planning. The purest open-office planning eliminates interior walls because they act as communication barriers. They also limit organizational flexibility because

most fixed walls inhibit layout change: relocating walls is expensive and time-consuming.

Any wall that helps support a building is called a **bearing wall**. Bearing walls were used in older office buildings—they were usually made of brick and covered with plaster. The last tall, brick-bearing-wall building, The Manadnock Building, designed by Burnham & Root, was built in Chicago in 1891. Sixteen stories high, it required 6-foot-thick walls for the first story—a loss of a considerable amount of rentable area. The brick bearing walls of older buildings can be stripped of plaster and left exposed for a handsome interior finish. Exterior bearing walls were replaced by a more efficient system—columns and **curtain walls,** which support no structural loads. This system is now typical of high-rise construction. Usually, interior walls, bearing or not, are called **partitions**.

Nonload bearing partitions can be demolished without disturbing the building. In older fireproof buildings, partitions were made of hollow clay tiles, gypsum block, solid gypsum boards, or metal lath and were finished with plaster. This produced a solid, dense wall with excellent sound-attenuating characteristics. Plaster is rarely used today. Drywall construction, faster and less expensive, is now typical.

In **drywall** construction, gypsum wallboard sheets are screwed to metal channels. The joints between the sheets and the holes made by the screwheads are concealed with tape and spackle and sanded—a job requiring skill. Properly installed drywall gives the smooth, seamless appearance of plaster. However, drywall construction just doesn't have the sound isolation properties of plastered solid walls. If you share a wall in common with other tenants or need complete acoustic privacy, such as in an attorney's office, this is a matter of some concern. Sound isolation can be

achieved with special hardware and installation techniques. Two layers of wallboard on either side of the metal studs are fastened by special resilient clips. The space between the studs is filled with batt insulation. The partition must continue from the floor to the bottom of the slab above, not just to the underside of a suspended ceiling. It should be caulked at the joint for an airtight seal. Otherwise, sound can be reflected to adjoining spaces from the underside of the slab.

Prefinished gypsum-board panels, covered with vinyl, eliminate the need for any further interior finishes. They fasten directly to the metal studs, and they are utilitarian in appearance.

Gypsum-board walls and plaster walls can be painted, finished with wallcoverings, or panelled with wood. When you choose wall finishes from samples, don't forget to hold the sample vertically because that's the way the finish will reflect the light when it's on the walls. If you don't, the colors will seem darker on the walls than the sample. (For the same reason, carpet will appear lighter than the sample if you don't hold the sample horizontally.) Remember, also, to look at all samples in lighting conditions that approximate those of the actual space. The light source, whether daylight, fluorescent, incandescent, or H.I.D. lamps, affects color. It is always best to test design elements under actual lighting.

Paint is the most common, most flexible, and least expensive way to finish plaster and wallboard partitions. Paint is versatile. Used monochromatically, it unifies all the vertical surfaces, including windows, walls, and doors—as well as the ceiling if it's made of plaster. Using more than one color, for example a continuous stripe around a room or painting one wall with a contrasting color, can change the apparent proportions of a room. You can emphasize handsome architectural de-

❶ *This 1903 San Francisco warehouse was converted into office space and the brick bearing wall was left exposed in the office of one of the partners. The brick is the structural exterior wall of the building. Steel reinforcements were added to the ceiling in case of an earthquake. Architects: Hellmuth, Obata and Kassabaum.*

❷ *An unusual, noninstitutional treatment for gypsum wallboard at the company headquarters of International Paper in New York City. Wall panels are wrapped in silk, adding texture and color to this office. Fine craftsmanship went into the careful alignment of the material. Designed by The Space Design Group.*

❸ *Another treatment for wallboard is displayed in the Boston offices of Tnemec. The site of this regional office is a high-rise apartment building. Two apartments were joined and renovated as an office. The architectural character was largely determined by using Tnemec paints throughout. The paint is usually applied to the exterior of airplanes, boats, and bridges; this was the first time it was applied to drywall and plaster. Extensive surface preparation was required but the effect was well worth the effort. The walls showcase the company's product and serve as a symbol of corporate identity. Architect: Rubin and Smith-Miller.*

tails such as doors, windows, bases, and picture railings by painting them a different color from the walls.

Using two or more colors is usually more expensive than using only one. New walls require a sizing coat and two coats of paint. U. S. landlords supply off-white. Anything darker sometimes requires more than two coats to cover properly. Again, increased labor and material costs will increase the price.

A paint job is only as good as the surface beneath it. The wall needs careful preparation. The responsibility for preparation of the wall should be clearly specified. The preparation of newly constructed walls can be either the painter's or the plasterer's responsibility.

Paint comes in three finishes:

high-gloss, semi-gloss, and matte, or flat, finish. Because they're reflective, high-gloss and semi-gloss paints show any surface irregularities in the surface beneath, so make sure they're well prepared. High- and semi-gloss finishes are easily washed clean. They're recommended for places where fingerprints are apt to appear—doors, windows, and their frames. (But even flat paints can be washed.)

Water-based paints are easy to apply. Paint spots can be wiped up before they dry. Solvent-base paints are more durable. They require more elaborate application and clean-up.

Wallcoverings give a more finished look to interior walls. Like paint, solid-color, smooth-textured wallcoverings unify wall surfaces.

Textured wallcoverings offer a more active surface. Patterned wallcoverings, either floral or geometric, are very ornamental. They have a powerful effect on an interior.

The most practical wallcovering is sheet *vinyl*. It is durable and easily maintained with soap and water. Dimensionally stable, vinyl is easily installed. It usually comes in 54-inch (1.37-m) widths. Some wallcoverings are available in matching upholstery-weight fabric, for designs that warrant integrating the walls and the furniture. A wide range of textured effects are imitated, some more successfully than others, in vinyl. The imitations include fabrics (linens and burlaps), leathers (suedes and pigskin), plaster, cork, patent leather, and wood.

Wallpaper is fragile. It's difficult to install because it wrinkles, tears, sags, and bubbles. It is also difficult to clean. Unless it's treated with a plastic coating, wallpaper is rarely used in offices and is usually restricted to low-use areas.

Tough paper-backings can be laminated to fabrics and applied to walls by any competent wallpaper installer. Just about any fabric can be custom-laminated to a paper back. Linen, jute, burlap, and silks are available as standard catalogue items. Grass cloth, woven bamboo, is available in many colors and textures. An acid-free lining paper is recommended under all light-color, paper-backed fabrics or for any fine-texture paper that is expected to remain on the wall for an extended period of time. Some paper-backed fabrics, including the fine-textured silks and linens as well as wallpapers, should be applied to a smooth, seamless surface. Rougher-textured paper-backed fabrics, such as grass cloth, and vinyl wallcoverings can be installed over less than perfect surfaces.

Stretched fabric is an elegant but expensive wallcovering that completely upholsters an interior.

The fabric is seamed vertically. It's installed from floor to ceiling over wooden frames fastened to the wall below. Patterns must be made in complicated rooms, to allow for cutouts for windows and doors. Softer looking and more luxurious than the same fabric glued to the walls, stretched fabric has two advantages: it hides any wall defects underneath; and with a layer of sound-absorbing material glued between the wooden frames, it provides acoustic control.

Other sound-absorbing materials can be glued into place like wallcoverings. Cork, available in different shades of brown, is an effective sound absorber. So are carpetlike fabrics (paper-backed polypropylene) which are specially designed for wall application. They are rated for their absorption characteristics. Because cork

and carpeting conceal pinpricks, they make excellent floor-to-ceiling tackboards.

Wood—warm, handsome, and durable—is always appropriate in office spaces. Indeed, for some people it's a mandatory symbol of success. Most wood walls are fabricated in cabinet workshops and installed on the job-site after the fixed partitions are installed. Often, storage cabinets and desk units are designed as part of the wall. Forests throughout the world supply exotic hardwoods for wood-panelled walls. East Indian laurel, Madagascar ebony, English sycamore, and French walnut are very, very expensive veneers; Brazilian rosewood is the most expensive of all. Mahogany, zebra, olive ash, and English oak are in a midexpensive range. Teak, American cherry, American white oak, and American walnut cost

less, but they are still expensive compared to other alternatives.

Custom woodworking usually entails using hardwood veneers— thin layers of finer woods glued to a less expensive backing. The backing is plywood or particle board, usually ¾ of an inch (19 mm) thick. The sawn edge must be finished with solid hardwood pieces or a "self-edge" of veneer. Traditional panelling uses larger panels surrounded by matching solid hardwood pieces for *moldings*, *trim*, and *rails*. Nontraditional panelling is more apt to be floor-to-ceiling planes of veneer.

Wood grain is a decorative feature. When a series of veneers from the same log (a *flitch*) are used together, their similar grain produces a strong pattern, especially when it's applied over a large area. Some possible veneer patterns are book-matching, slip matching, chevrons, and herringbones.

There are two ways to treat the joints in an expanse of panels. They can be emphasized with a groove or recess, or covered with a molding. The other alternative is to leave a smooth, flush appearance, which minimizes the joints.

Solid-wood panelling is also a possibility, using common and less-expensive species—birch, redwood, cedar, or pine. Usually, these panels are assembled on the job and are blind-nailed or glued onto furring strips. This type of panelling is already visually active. It shows every strip and every grain, so you should select clear grades without knots.

Wood flooring continued up a wall is sometimes an effective visual accent. In this case, it would be installed and finished by the flooring contractor.

After wood walls are in place, they have to be finished. At this stage, the wood color can be altered by staining or bleaching. Sometimes an inexpensive species can be stained to resemble a more expensive one. The next step is to use a wood sealer, which protects the wood from dirt and stains. The finish depends on the appearance you desire. Boiled linseed oil brings out the natural luster of the wood. Wax, which requires maintenance, produces a gleaming surface after it's polished. Clear lacquer is the most glossy finish. Remember to ask for samples of the finish you choose. They should be submitted for approval before work begins.

Demountable partitions save construction time and avoid construction mess because they are moveable and reusable. They're worth considering if you anticipate frequent changes in office layout. Demountable partitions slip over special floor tracks that can be installed over carpeting. They are fixed with ceiling tracks. In some systems, this track is fastened to the spline of exposed acoustic-tile ceilings; in others, drilled through the tile. Obviously, they're coordinated with finished ceiling heights and the ceiling layout.

Ordered as complete assemblies, demountable partitions are equipped with framing members, doors and frames, and wall-finish materials, such as vinyls, acoustic fabrics, or large glass areas. Some assemblies have integral electric fixtures and conduits for electric and telephone service lines.

Demountable partitions approach furniture in concept because they're separate and apart from the building structure. As such, they have tax advantages that offset their high initial costs. In the USA, they are eligible for tax investment credit. Also, they can be depreciated over a shorter time period than built-in walls, using a full accelerated depreciation method. To learn more about this, check with your accountant.

Some manufacturers have coordinated their moveable partitions with the design of their open-plan office systems. In effect, the partitions are ceiling-high panels that have the same details and appearance. Their components—

work surfaces, storage units, and lighting fixtures—are interchangeable with the open-office system.

Mirrors can be used architecturally in large, unframed sheets applied to a wall. They give the illusion that the wall they're covering doesn't exist—it seems to disappear. Since objects in front of mirrors appear an equal distance behind the mirrored plane, a single mirrored wall magically doubles the size of a space. Of course, they double the clutter as well. So, before you install a mirrored wall, make sure you'll like seeing twice as much as what's in front of it.

Mirror can be a dramatic finish material—suited to fashion-and-glamour-related offices. They should be placed so that they're not disconcerting. For example, don't put a mirrored wall opposite visitor's seating. Avoid aiming

bright lights at mirrors; they will create hot spots that might be reflected back into your eyes.

Good mirror work is expensive. Its cost is comparable to a teak-panelled wall. The best-quality mirrors are ¼ of an inch (6 mm) thick copper-backed plate glass. Be sure the back has been sealed to protect the silvering from scratches. Use as few seams as possible. Most installers recommend not cutting holes in mirror (for light switches, wall fixtures, and the like), so plan the wall carefully. All the edges should be ground smooth before the mirror is fastened to the wall. Professional installers use mastic to fasten mirrors to the wall—or to furring strips if they're needed to even out the wall in back. Mirror itself comes in many tints—grey, bronze, and pink shades. A base will protect the mirror from a zealous floor cleaner.

❶ *Book-matched acacia wood walls finish this private office in the Philadelphia National Bank. The flush wood panels are full height. The desk and seating area in this large office are delineated by the fascia suspended from the ceiling. Designed by The Space Design Group.*

❷ *Demountable partitions can be easily moved and rearranged as organizational needs change. These partitions can also be outfitted with raceways for electricity. Such partitions are becoming more and more integrated with furniture systems. Designed by DEGW.*

❸ *The use of a mirrored wall in the Los Angeles office of Vidal Sassoon effectively doubles the space. This kind of mirrored wall works architecturally to expand the space because it extends from floor to ceiling and from wall to wall. Joints that might destroy the illusion have been minimized so that the wall appears to be virtually seamless. Designed by Gwathmey Siegel and Associates.*

Walls With Glass

Early office bulidings used glass in interior partitions because daylight was needed for illumination. High **clerestory windows** allowed some light from exterior offices to penetrate interior spaces, even public corridors. The clerestory windows were operable for ventilation. Even when glass areas were at eye level, the glass was usually **translucent,** not transparent; it let in light, but obscured a view. Clear glass was used for control.

Since the 1950s, the transparency of glass, and its solidity, have been exploited. Many private offices are enclosed with at least one wall of glass—clear glass. There are several reasons for this change. First, office spaces are smaller. Space has become a luxury. Lighting and ventilating, now done mechanically, require lower ceiling heights, and higher rental costs require smaller office spaces. In tight quarters, there is a need to extend the visual limit of interior space. Glass can fulfill this need. Clear glass partitions are acceptable because privacy requirements in offices have decreased since the 1950s. Visual privacy is now deemed much less important than acoustic privacy. Being seen is less critical than being heard. In the U.S., most people close the door to their office only for important telephone calls or meetings. Moreover, the office environment has become more humane. The psychological benefits of exterior

views for people working in interior spaces can no longer be denied nor ignored. Glass partitions make it possible to have enclosed offices and views. Some organizations have even reversed the usual spatial priorities: they locate private offices along the interior core wall and support personnel along the perimeter. A glass wall separates them.

Walls with glass have other advantages: improved communications between staff members. It's easy to see if someone's at a meeting or on a phone call, saving time and footsteps. Supervision and control are easier as well. Should visual privacy be necessary, walls with glass can be fitted with screening devices such as blinds or draperies.

Clear glass can be colorless or tinted green, bronze, or grey. For visual interest—a tailored look—consider **wire glass**. It's available in handsome geometric patterns, pinstripes, and squares and is much more elegant than the chicken wire of long ago. Most building codes require some type of safety glass in partitions where the sill is less than 18 inches (.45 m) from the floor. Wire glass fulfills this function. Otherwise, most designers choose **tempered glass**. It's engineered to break in relatively harmless crystalline shapes if someone should walk into it. A decorative decal, glued to full-height glass walls at eye level, helps prevent this from happening.

If your organization needs complete visual privacy but you'd like to bring light to interior spaces, consider adopting the original solutions: clerestory windows or translucent glass. Etched, rippled, and hammered effects are available.

The frame that holds the glass in place is very important for visual appearance and aesthetic effect. A concealed frame, flush on the four sides where glass abuts adjoining materials, fosters the illusion of continuity of space on either side of the glass. An unframed door of tempered glass completes the effect. A heavier frame in wood or metal emphasizes the wall plane and makes a more obvious separation. Wiring can run concealed in a heavy sill.

Walls of **glass block**, popular when they were introduced in the

①

②

1930s, are enjoying a revival. Installed like masonry with mortared joints, they can be thought of as a solid wall that lets in light. Depending on the amount of privacy you desire, you can choose a pattern for visibility or for light transmission. Some patterns distort light more than others. Glass block is luminous in both natural and artificial light sources. For interior applications, a thin-line series, 3⅛ inches (79.3 mm) thick, is recommended. This series weighs 20 percent less than the standard series, 3⅞ inches (98.4 mm) thick, used for exterior applications. The thin-line series is available in 6- or 8-inch (152.4- or 203.2-mm) squares and 4-by-8-inch (101.6-by-203.2-mm) and 6-by-8-inch (152.4-by-203.2-mm) rectangles.

③

④

❶ *Glass walls on either side of this interior corridor create a sunlit secretarial area with a view. Architect: Hellmuth, Obata and Kassabaum.*

❷ *The enclosed offices on the right line the perimeter wall of this office building and face an open-office area on the left. To create a view for the people who work in the open office, as much glass as possible was used for the enclosed offices. Here, tinted glass defines form and creates spatial variety. (Mock-ups of the floor were made in clear glass but that didn't seem to show the form, so a tinted glass was used instead.) The enclosed offices were staggered for variety of form and to make a more interesting circulation route around the perimeter. Designed by The Space Design Group.*

❸ *Glass blocks can be laid like masonry and shaped into curved planes. Here, in the offices of The Space Design Group, a glass-block wall encloses a conference room and allows light into the lobby area. The conference room is kept private because the thick glass blocks are not transparent. Designed by The Space Design Group.*

❹ *The view from the corridor into a corner office at the Tandy Corporation in Fort Worth, Texas, is highlighted because of the interior glass wall. The door to the office is set into a floor-to-ceiling glass panel to make the wall as transparent as possible. Hardware and framing are minimal; window muntins throughout are black with round, natural oak rails at chair height. Architect: Martin Growald. Designed by Benjamin Baldwin.*

Free-Standing Walls

Freestanding walls reconcile the desire for spaciousness with the need for a sense of enclosure. They are built above eye level, yet never completely enclose a space, stopping short of the ceiling or adjacent walls. Free-standing walls define space and territory. They seem permanent, yet they allow for complete openness. They can be constructed and finished in many ways, including painted drywall, wood panels, fabric stretched over an exposed frame, or panels of tinted glass.

Whatever the construction, freestanding walls must be designed not to topple. They can be

fastened, with rods, to the ceiling or braced on at least one edge with a wall that intersects it.

Freestanding walls afford minimal acoustic privacy. Since you must rely on the floor and ceiling surfaces for sound absorption, carpet and acoustic tile are almost mandatory.

1 Free-standing, acoustical, silk-fabric walls are smooth on one side and structured on the other. Although they don't reach the ceiling and don't abut the walls, the enclosures shelter the managers' offices in privacy and seclusion. Architect: Tod Williams and Associates.

2 Lighting and air-handling systems are encased within the ceiling structure of this free-standing room. The entire room can be easily moved. Although the system offers complete acoustic isolation, the glass walls prohibit any visual privacy. Architect: Trickett Associates.

3 Painted high-gloss wall board at Robert Panero Associates gives privacy to clerical workers who sit near to the reception area. The enclosure gives them privacy but allows the floor space a sense of expansiveness. Architect: Susanna Torre.

4 In the same organization, panels are attached to a free-standing wall that separates the conference room from the desk area. The panels open for display purposes. Designed by Susanna Torre.

5 Free-standing walls, used as space dividers, are attached to columns in such a way as to emphasize a sleek industrial look in the offices of Juan Montoya. Exposed hardware enhances this look.

6 Architect Francis Duffy says that these free-standing fin walls are ''flexible but quasi-architectural.'' Used in a series on a large open-office floor, they define space for groups to work in. The fin walls provide services for storage, electricity, and other functions. Architect: DEGW.

Floors

Floors take a beating. They are subjected to more wear than any other surface of a room. Flooring materials vary greatly with respect to durability, appearance, cost, and the amount of maintenance each requires.

The "feel" of flooring is one of its most important characteristics. Its resiliency affects how comfortable it is to walk on and how it sounds when we walk on it. Hard flooring materials, including wood, masonry, ceramic tile, and most composition floors, are noisy; every footstep can be heard. Soft materials, such as carpet, cork, and rubber, create a relatively quiet atmosphere. They absorb the impact noise of footsteps.

The visual aspects of flooring are equally expressive. The floor is always in view, a background for furniture and people. Flooring can be designed to define circulation paths and seating areas. It can give a space the illusion of expansiveness (by using a continuous material and pattern throughout an installation). Or it can emphasize a division into smaller units (by using disparate materials or different colors of the same materials).

The relative initial cost of flooring materials can be outlined in general terms. Stone floors are the most expensive; tile and brick floors less so, but still costly. Vinyl, wood cork, and rubber flooring are moderately expensive; reinforced vinyl is inexpensive. Carpet ranges from inexpensive to expensive. But initial costs are only part of the story. Maintenance and any

replacement costs must also be considered and averaged over the life of an installation.

Carpet in the office is a status symbol. That's why the advertising slogan, "A title on the door…rates a Bigelow on the floor" was effective. In the 1950s, when the slogan was introduced, carpet was an expensive and not very durable flooring material. It was restricted to low-use areas and deemed a perfect reward for successful executives. Technological innovations in the last 30 years have improved carpet performance and lowered its price. It's now feasible in just about every office area.

The advantages of carpet are well known. Carpeted spaces are quiet. Carpet absorbs impact noise from footsteps and furniture. It provides acoustic control by absorbing airborne noises. In fact, carpeting made open-plan offices practicable; they'd have been too noisy without it. Carpet is versatile. It's available in a tremendous range of colors, textures, and surface designs. It provides visual softness and gives a finished look to interior spaces. It's a safe, nonslip surface. With preventive maintenance, carpet will retain its appearance for several years.

But carpet is not a permanent flooring material. When selecting carpet, you must ask, "How long will this carpet look good?"

The factors to consider, in order of importance, are traffic, fiber, appearance, including color and texture, and cost.

Traffic is measured in "walk-ons" per day, which refers to the number of people walking across the carpet. Moderate use refers to an area that receives less than 500 walk-ons a day, or 2,500 a week.

Private offices, executive floors, and conference rooms are in this category. Virtually any commercial-grade carpet will be suitable in these areas. Heavy-traffic use is 1,000 walk-ons per day. It usually means a moderate trackage of outside soil and moderate beverage-spillage, and a few areas where traffic funnels through. Carpet construction is more critical in these areas, which normally include clerical and secretarial areas and office-space corridors. Lower-pile heights and denser, tighter construction are necessary in these areas. Heavy-traffic areas are spaces that receive more than 1,000 walk-ons per day and 10,000 people per week. High-density open-plan areas, lobbies, and some public corridors in office buildings, particularly leased spaces where there are many offices off the corridors, are classified as heavy-traffic areas. In fact, carpet might not be the best solution for these areas. Consideration should be given to more durable flooring materials in such areas. Should you select carpet,

①

those with nylon fibers, either exclusively nylon or blended with acrylic or wool, are the only ones to consider.

Fibers: The most important factor in carpet performance is the fiber it's made of. Each fiber has distinct advantages and disadvantages that should be considered in carpet selection.

Wool represents the standard against which all other fibers are measured. It is one of the oldest natural fibers. It has high aesthetic appeal because it is soft and lustrous. Wool is easy to dye, easy to clean, naturally crush-resistant, resists burns, and resists soils. High static, and its possible allergenic properties are its minor disadvantages. The major disadvantage is its high initial cost, which has limited its use to only

1 percent of the contract carpet market. In the relatively small area of a single private office, wool carpet is affordable. Used throughout an installation, however, it can be prohibitively expensive.

Nylon is a generic name for the synthetic fiber used in 80–85 percent of contract carpet. Invented in 1939, it was first used in carpet in 1947. Nylon is the strongest fiber known. From the first, it offered carpets with superior abrasion-resistance and crush-resistance. Carpets made of nylon were easy to dye, but they had an undesirable sheen and high static. After going through several stages of improvement, fourth-generation nylon fiber now has superior soil- and stain-resistance and antistatic control. Changes in the fiber cross-section have improved both luster, and soil-hiding capabilities. Carpets of nylon can be used anywhere in the office. Nylon is often used in combination with other fibers to increase their sturdiness.

Acrylic (and modacrylic, a chemical variation) is the fiber that most approximates wool. It has a high color life and is easily adapted to styling possibilities. However, acrylic fiber has a low abrasion-resistance and it should be used only in light-traffic areas.

Polypropylene (also known as olefin) is most frequently used as a carpet backing and most famous as the fiber that artificial turf is made of. It's useful as an outdoor carpet because it's highly moisture- and stain-resistant, and when properly dyed, it resists fading from sunlight. Although polypropylene-and-nylon blends are used in Europe, it was never widely used as a face fiber because its very soft and only available in a limited selection of colors. Recently, however, polypropylene has been making a comeback. Low cost (it's one third as expensive as nylon), excellent stain-resistance (inherently better than any fiber), and its generic

③

resistance to ultraviolet light have made this fiber increasingly attractive in low-use, high-sun areas.

Blends combine the characteristics of two fibers. Blends, which constitute 10 percent of the contract market, perform in the ratio of the fibers involved. They're used for the following reasons: to reduce cost (a blend of 45 percent wool and 55 percent acrylic gives the qualities of wool at a lower price); to increase performance (a blend of 20 percent nylon and 80 percent wool and polypropylene and nylon carpets are more durable than wool or polypropylene alone); or aesthetics (a blend of 70 percent acrylic and 30 percent nylon tone down the shininess of an all-nylon carpet).

The most recent technical innovation in carpet fibers is the development of antimicrobial agents. Added to the dye, these antifungal and antibacterial agents reduce odors and virtually inhibit the growth of microorganisms in carpeting. They are useful in office areas where food is served, such as executive dining rooms, cafeterias, and vending areas.

Appearance: The carpet color is the starting point for a color scheme because it covers an inherently large area. Yet color has an important bearing on how soils and stains can be masked. If you select a color to suit the traffic

②

❶ *Not usually used in corporate offices, this 100-percent wool carpet is from Bloomsburg Carpet Industry. The cut-pile style was used in the executive offices, and in the outside clerical areas a carpet of different texture (cut/uncut) but the same color and fiber was used. The muted color creates a neutral background that sets off the sculptural form of the furniture. Architect: Daroff Design, Inc.*

❷ *Wear and tear from desk chairs constantly being moved back and forth is one of the biggest problems when office floors are carpeted. One solution is to use an area rug. The desk chair rolls on the wood floor, and the rug defines the seating area in the office. Designed by Jack Lowery.*

❸ *Another solution is to set the carpet into a floor recess. The perimeter of this floor is oak parquet, sculpted around the desk chair. The carpet was recessed into the floor so that it would be on the same level as the wood. This librarian's office at Providence Athenaeum was designed by Warren Platner Associates Architects.*

that an area will be subjected to, you can create a soil-hiding advantage. Soiling and stains show up more readily in lighter shades, so avoid them in heavy-traffic areas. Choose carpet the same color as the soil outside: reds in clay areas, greys in city grime. In addition, multicolored carpets, such as tweeds, moresques, heather effects, or better still, patterned carpets, mask soil more than solid colors. Luster levels also play a part because the brighter or shinier a fiber's luster, the more quickly a carpet will show soil.

The surface texture of a carpet is also important. **Level loop pile** is comprised of uniform, uncut loops. **Multilevel loops** have two or more loop heights for a sculptured carpet face. **Cut pile plush** carpets, as the name implies, are sheared to produce a smooth surface, and **cut and loop pile** combine the two textures. Loop pile carpets are better for hiding dirt and footmarks. In general, the smoother the surface, the easier it is to see soils and stains. Cut pile carpets show the imprint of footprints. Some cut pile carpets show shading or color variations as a result of changing light reflection as the carpet pile is displaced when it is walked upon. For most people, this enriches the visual effect, enhancing the feeling of luxury. But those who would rather avoid shading can select a carpet whose face fibers have been engineered, through luster and twist, not to show it. As the traffic becomes greater and durability more critical, consider using tighter gauge carpets with high densities and loop constructions.

Density can be calculated with a simple formula. Density (expressed in ounces per cubic yard)=

$$\frac{36 \times \text{face weight (oz. per. sq. yd)}}{\text{pile height (ins.)}}$$

A density of 3,000 to 4,000 is suitable for moderate traffic, 4,000 to 5,000 for heavy traffic, and densities over 5,000 are suitable for heavy-traffic areas. Some

carpet lines are designed for different densities, but with similar pile heights and appearance allowing you to select a high-performing carpet in corridors and a matching, but less-expensive carpet in continuous offices. This saves money.

Installation: Seams are the most critical part of carpet installation. The carpet should be installed with as few seams as possible. Most carpet is 12 feet (3.65 m) wide. (**Velvet** type capets are usually the exception to the 12 feet [3.65 m] width. Velvets are extremely smooth carpets in which the individual tufts are only minimally visible and the overall effect is that of a single level of fiber ends. They're so smooth that any seam would show, so they're best used in one piece. A 15-foot [4.5 m] width increases the installation possibilities.)

You must choose one of the two different installation methods: over a mat or glued directly to the subfloor. Studies have shown that a good-grade commercialtype carpet cushion increases the appearance retention of a carpet between 30 to 50 percent. Installing carpet over padding is, however, more expensive than direct glue-down as more materials and labor are required. Generally speaking, padding is better. However, direct glue-down is recommended in offices in two circum-

①

②

stances: The first is large open office areas where the carpet has nothing to be anchored to except on either end. The second is where carpet is subject to rolling traffic such as automated mail carts and wheelchairs.

Wear and Tear: Desk chairs pose a dilemma. "There's a tremendous pressure concentrated on the four or five points of a chair's casters rolling back and forth in the same path day after day," says David Kassell of Consolidated Contract Interiors. "The surface of low and tight carpet glued to the floor will retain its look, but the backing might delaminate. Conventional tackless carpet installed over padding is going to creep. The only way to protect a carpet completely is to use a carpet mat."

If you decide that your aesthetic sensibilities are offended by a carpet mat—or that mats are unsafe because chairs can skid across them at great speed—choose the chair casters carefully. Select the widest possible wheels—a 2-inch (50.9 mm) diameter is preferable —of the hardest possible material, stainless steel. These wheels work best on a low-pile, tightly constructed dense level loop nylon carpet.

Another option is to use **carpet tiles** instead of broadloom carpet. Carpet tiles are 18- or 24-inch (.457- or .610-m) square tiles of carpet. Some are manufactured to "lay in" without glue; others need a small amount of adhesive to stay in place. Carpet tiles have a different backing from conventional carpet. They're engineered so that they don't unravel at the edge and for dimensional stability.

Carpet tiles are the wave of the future. Besides being easy to replace for wear, they allow quick, easy access to underfloor ducts. This makes them extremely useful in offices where the layout is frequently changing. If an area where a chair with casters once sat becomes fully visible or floor outlets have to be relocated new tiles do the job without leaving scars. Carpet tiles have aesthetic advantages. If each tile is laid with the nap in a similar direction, the seams are virtually invisible. You can also lay the tiles to make a pattern and combine colors to achieve a custom look. Borders and special areas can be installed at no extra cost. Moreover, you can take them with you if you move.

A third solution is to design an office with a durable material under the desk chair and carpet elsewhere in the office. The desk area can float on an island of wood, ceramic tile, or masonry within a sea of carpet. Or, conversely, the carpet can be designed to be inlaid within a border of hard surface flooring, with the low seating area set on it. Care should be taken that the carpeting and its durable counterpart are at the same level so that you don't trip when you walk from one area to another.

A fourth way to combat wear under desk chairs is to use hard flooring throughout and place area rugs upon it, for the desired look of softness and for acoustic control. Ordinary carpet, cut and bound at the edges, works very well. Handwoven carpets, especially Orientals, work even better.

Preventive Maintenance:
Preventive maintenance goes a long way toward prolonging the life of carpet. Carpet allowed to soil heavily is difficult to restore and seldom retains its original appearance. It will need replacement long before it wears out. The largest portion of common soiling

③

is in the form of hard particles. Left in the carpet, their sharp edges abrade the pile fiber as effectively as sandpaper. Thorough vacuuming is the most effective way to remove them. "Thorough" means at least eight passes by machine in key areas, such as places where traffic paths funnel and converge—halls, the entrance to doorways and stairs, water fountains, and vending machines. These areas need daily vacuuming. Pay particular attention to entries and to transitions from hard-surface floorings to carpet. Spot cleaning should be taken care of daily. The sooner a spot is removed, the less likely it is to cause a permanent stain.

Flammability: The flammability and ability of carpet to resist flame-spread is a subject of concern and also confusion. There is no way to predict the performance of a carpet system without testing it empirically. The purpose of interior-finish regulations is to avoid rapid fire-spread. The flammability of a specific carpet and the level of resistance necessary to prevent fires from spreading to other parts of the building along a corridor are the questions that testing is geared to answer.

The "pill test" measures flame-spread. It's concerned with what would happen if carpet were the first item to be ignited—for example, if a lighted cigarette were

① Carpet tiles help solve the durability problem because they are easily replaced. Also, when used in conjunction with flat wiring, it's easy to get services like telephones and electricity to work stations in open-office systems. Courtesy of Interface Flooring Systems.

④

dropped on the carpet, would it spread across the floor to ignite draperies and furniture? All carpet sold must pass the "pill test."

Three tests measure the flame-spread resistance of carpet—hence the confusion. They are the Tunnel Test, the Chamber Test, and the Flooring Radiant Panel Test. In their pamphlet "Flammability Testing for Carpet," the Center for Fire Research of the Institute for Applied Technology, which is a division of the National Bureau of Standards, advocates using the Flooring Radiant Panel Test. "[It] is different from most other fire test methods in that it measures an actual property of the carpet and is not based on an arbitrary scale." The result of the test is reported as the critical radiant flux, and expressed as watts per square centimeter. The

② Durable ceramic tile is used to define the main circulation area at Best Products. The patterned carpet is functional in the office area because it hides soilage. Carpet pattern by Jack Beal is from a silk screen. Architects: Hardy, Holzman, Pfeiffer and Assoc.

③ Carpet tiles can be positioned to create a pattern such as in this Parisian lunchroom. Architect: DEGW.

④ These carpet tiles were laid with a contrasting border. This custom-look is inexpensively obtained with Interface Carpet Tiles.

higher the number, the more resistant is the material to flame propagation. A 0.45-watts/cm² rating is the minimum criterion for corridors and exitways of hospitals and nursing homes; only 10 percent of carpet meets this standard (Class A). Class B rating for other occupancies, is 0.22 watt/cm². Of course, local fire marshalls and some federal agencies set their own standards and choose the governing test. They vary from jurisdiction to jurisdiction and might include smoke-density standards. Check your codes very carefully to be sure your carpet is acceptable.

Resilient Floors

Resilient floorings are smooth-surfaced tile-and-sheet floor coverings that have the ability to recover from impact and pressure. Resiliency ranges from the limited capability of asphalt tile to soft cork and rubber floor coverings.

Resilient tile floors were the office-building standard for years, from the World War II building boom until just recently when they were challenged by carpet. The advantages of resilient flooring, however, are difficult to ignore. They are durable, stain-resistant, dimensionally stable, color fast, and easily maintained. Their glossy surface reflects light, and they're relatively inexpensive.

Most resilient floors are made by the same process—a plastic material is combined with fillers and pigments to produce a mixture that is processed into sheets of varying thickness.

Reinforced vinyl tiles are, by far, the most widely used of all resilient floors. Made of vinyl resins, asbestos fibers, and fillers, this material was previously known as vinyl-asbestos. The industry changed its name to delete the reference to asbestos. Reinforced vinyl can be installed above, below, or on grade because it is moisture resistant. The familiar "marbelized" look—beloved by facilities managers because it hides dirt so well, and hated by designers for its dreariness—is still available. In recent years, however, the colors of marbelized tiles are lighter and clearer; they usually look more distinguished if they're laid with the pattern lines running parallel, instead of alternating. In addition, reinforced vinyl tiles (sometimes shortened to R.V.T.) are available in solid colors (which will, of course, show shoe marks and scuffing more readily). They're also available in textured finishes that imitate the classic flooring materials. Maintenance has been simplified. They need never be waxed, only buffed. These visual improvements do

①

① Harry Torczyner's office was designed in the early 1970s when low cost, good quality office carpeting wasn't available and the building's standard flooring was vinyl asbestos tile. To upgrade the flooring, architect Susanna Torre chose a studded rubber tile, and it was used throughout these Manhattan law offices. Torre was attracted to the nondirectional quality of this new flooring and its resiliency underfoot. Also, in this office, the flooring doesn't detract from Mr. Torczyner's magnificent art collection.

② Designer Juan Montoya selected a reinforced-vinyl tile, polished to a reflective sheen, for his own New York offices. The utilitarian material was an esthetic and practical choice. The precision finish emphasizes the plane of the floor, and the tiles are not easily damaged in this busy, working office where ink and other art supplies are likely to spill.

wonders for general office areas that use R.V.T. The strictly functional connotations of this material, however, limit its use in private offices.

Cork and **rubber**, cut into tiles, are more appropriate for private offices. Cork tiles—a relatively expensive material, and a natural one—have a look of warmth and luxury. They are quiet and soft underfoot and have some sound absorption capability. With vinyl added as a protective sealer, they gain some durability, but lose some resilience. Cork floors require waxing to look well. **Rubber**, the most resilient floor, has had a comeback in recent years. Solid-color embossed rubber tiles have become emblemmatic of an industrial, mechanical style, and its crisp look belies its comfort. That's probably why they are popular in private offices, as well as in the high-traffic areas—corridors and elevators—for which they were originally intended. There are now

several facsimiles of the original flooring, developed in Italy by the Pirelli Company and used extensively in its headquarters building in Milan. Rubber tiles need washing and buffing.

Vinyl, in sheets or tiles, is the best-wearing and most expensive composition floor. It is soft and has a built-in luster that is easy to maintain. Most types need no waxing. Vinyl is available in realistic finishes that imitate slate, brick, wood parquetry, and ceramic tile. For private offices, most people prefer the original material; for the general office, R.V.T. is more economical. **Asphalt tiles**, at the other end of the spectrum, are the least expensive, hardest composition floor, they, too, are rarely used in the office.

Linoleum, one of the earliest forms of resilient flooring (it was introduced commercially in England in 1864), is not generally used because it doesn't perform as well as other materials.

Leather, cut in tiles, is another resilient flooring material. It can withstand light traffic, but its indentation-, stain-, and abrasion-resistance are low. Leather floors are luxurious, expensive, and require careful maintenance.

All resilient floors must be installed on smooth and level subfloors—either plywood or concrete. Solid-color vinyl and rubber bases, which finish off the floor, are usually installed when the flooring is laid. Straight bases have a less institutional look than covered bases.

Wood, Tile and Masonry Floors

Wood flooring was common in office buildings until the late 1940s. Then, judged impractical to maintain and expensive to install, wood was replaced by resilient flooring as a building standard. This was a great loss. The beauty and warmth of wood, a natural material, plus its inherent durability have made it a favorite flooring material through the ages.

Solid pieces of wood are used in flooring; that's why wood floors have such durability and permanence. Color and grain are inherent throughout each piece. Traffic rarely wears them through; the sander is the biggest wear problem.

Only hardwoods are suitable for office floors. Strip flooring is widely used. The strips, constructed from uniform tongue-and-groove pieces, can be glued directly to a level subfloor with a latex adhesive. The strips—generally 1½ by 12 inches (38.1 mm by .305 m)—are assembled on the job into parallel, basketweave, herringbone, or end-matched patterns. Their relatively short lengths prevent them from popping up.

"Palace" patterns and borders combine a variety of wood shapes and species to create more intricate patterns. Regardless of species, they are the most expensive wood flooring because so much labor is required to install them.

Corporate designers favor teak. It is incredibly stable and never needs expansion joints, even in long corridors. Oak, favored in older office buildings, is not specified as often today; nor are cherry, ash, and pecan because they are considered too soft. Their color, however, is often emulated through staining more durable hardwoods. They're used in the palace patterns.

The first step in floor finishing is sanding. At this time, their color can be modified—stained darker or bleached lighter. Then, a sealer coat is applied to bring out the grain of the wood and to make its surface impervious to stains. The traditional way to finish wood floors is to seal them with oil then apply wax to protect the sealer. Floors treated with sealer can be refinished without resanding. Waxed floors need daily maintenance to sweep up the dirt that might get embedded in the wax. Waxing one to four times a year and dry buffing as needed keeps the surface in top condition.

Polyurethane provides a hard-surface finish; it is useful in areas subjected to high-volume traffic. If this type of finish gets damaged, it can be sanded off and reapplied. Quality wood-floor contractors recommend the wax finish. If portions of it are damaged, it can be repaired without refinishing the entire floor. Wood impregnated with an acrylic solution is another possibility. This gives a permanent, abrasion-resistant finish that will never require waxing or other protective coatings. They are best suited to high-traffic areas.

Hardwood floors should never be wet-mopped. Water could raise the wood grain and cause the wood to swell and warp. If you use a liquid paste wax, make sure that it is solvent rather than water-based.

Tiles: Ceramic tiles are made of clay baked at high temperatures to form a durable, impervious flooring material. Tile floors are permanent, easily maintained, and less expensive than masonry. Tile floors offer versatility: they range from formal, slick monochromes to warm terra cottas, and they are manufactured in myriad shapes that can be laid in almost any configuration.

Ceramic tile may either be glazed or unglazed. Unglazed tiles don't present a wear problem unless they're very soft, although they can be prone to spot-staining from grease and oils. *Quarry tiles* are unglazed. Their color range, from yellow-reds through ambers, are the earth-colors of the clays from which they are made. Although quarry tiles can be waxed, it's unnecessary and usually, they're left in their matte finish. *Paver tiles* are generally thicker and larger tiles that are particularly suited to high-traffic or impact areas.

Glazed tiles have a surface finish fired integrally with the tile. This poses two questions about wear: will friction and grit wear down the surface? Will the glaze withstand traffic and impact? When choosing a tile for areas of concentrated foot traffic, those tiles that have an abrasive grain to provide additional slip- and wear-resistance are recommended.

You can choose tile for its sleekness, brilliant colors, and smooth surface or for its handcrafted, irregular look. Matching bases and trim pieces are available for special conditions—turning corners

or edging steps, for example. The choice of installation technique—setting and grouting—depends on the construction of the subfloor and the capacity of service the floor must meet. Thin-set adhesives or conventional mortar are the setting mediums.

Maintenance involves two factors: the face of the tile and the grout seams. As with most materials, preventive maintenance—frequent washing with mild cleaning compounds—is highly recommended.

Masonry: The important spaces in public buildings have traditionally had stone floors, and with

good reason. Stone floors last forever; they are easy to maintain, and they have great tactile appeal. If you use a masonry floor in your office, you can tap its allusions of ceremony, permanence, and elegance. Like most natural materials, stone has great visual interest. Marble, especially, comes in a variety of rich colors and veinings. Travertine, calcite, dolomite, serpentine, and onyx are the different varieties. Onyx is the most expensive type of masonry.

Granite, more monochromatic, has a range as well, from pink to grey. Slate, a sedimentary stone, has limited applications. It wears unusually well under heavy foot traffic, but it has a very low abrasion-resistance. Shoe nails and grit easily scratch it.

Stone floors are finished by polishing, honing, or sanding. Polishing produces a smooth, highly reflective surface. Honing produces a velvety-smooth nongloss surface. Sanding or abrasive treatment results in a flat, nonreflective surface, which is recommended for high-traffic areas.

All stone can be cut into tiles. The tiles can be laid in uniform rows for a relatively neutral background, or they can be arranged in patterns and combined with contrasting colors to further elaborate their instrinsically rich appearance.

Tile sizes vary from 6-inch to 24-inch (152-mm to 610-m) squares. Tile thickness varies from ⅜ of an inch to 1¼ inches (9-mm to 32-mm). Thin tiles can be reinforced with a fiberglass backing for greater durability.

There are two methods for installing them thin set and mud set. **Thin set**, which refers to a thin layer of mastic, requires an absolutely level subfloor of concrete or plywood. Most installers prefer concrete subfloors: they transmit less vibrations, thereby reducing the possibility of cracking or loosening the stone, and they expand and contract at a rate similar to stone, reducing stress. **Mud set**, a ¾-of-an-inch (19-mm) setting bed that acts as both an adhesive and levelling factor, is the traditional installation

method. Don't forget to compensate for this thickness when the stone abuts another material. The difference is usually made up within the threshold of a door.

Masonry floors need periodic washing with a mild household detergent. Oil should be immediately wiped up before it causes a permanent stain.

④

Window Coverings

Large windows, and many of them, have always been the goal for office-building design. At the end of the 19th century, the architects of the first skyscrapers developed a prototype in Chicago. With two operable windows flanking a fixed pane in the center, the Chicago–style window completely filled the space between the structural elements of the facade. It was the maximum possible size. This window type became a classic and was eventually used in every building type. It was transmogrified into the suburban picture window.

Technical and structural innovation in office windows followed. Glass sizes increased; installation improved; double glazing, various coatings, and integral filtering additives in the glass made possible entire window walls. But, as Richard G. Stein points out in his book *Architecture and Energy*, tall buildings with large, sealed windows have severe drawbacks. They depend upon "massive" use of mechanical heating and cooling to compensate for heat exchange through them. Most window walls have low insulating values; they allow heat-loss in winter and heat-gain from direct solar radiation any time of the year. This consumes energy.

Building design can address some of these problems. One technique is orientation. If the building is laid out along an east-west axis, most of the windows will be on the north and south sides. There is no direct sunlight on the north facade. The south facade is subject to direct light. Exterior adjustable sunshades can divert these rays if the building has no overhangs or permanent sunscreens. It's more difficult to screen the relatively low-angled rays of morning and afternoon sunlight on the east and west facades. On the east and west, tinted or reflected glass can be effective. Such glass also reduces glare—irritating excessive brightness—as it diffuses the sun's rays.

Window Coverings: To solve problems of glare and direct solar radiation, offices in older buildings and those in curtain-wall buildings designed in pre-energy-conscious days must depend on window coverings. Often, window "treatments" have cosmetic value, hiding ugly radiators, pipes, and unit air conditioners.

Window coverings perform other functions. They provide visual privacy. They block unsightly views because although just about any window is desirable, not all views are ideal. Even if shades, draperies, or blinds are never opened, the office retains a feeling of space expanding beyond its confines. Windows are powerful—they're usually the first thing you notice when you enter a room. Because of this high visibility, window coverings make a large contribution to the charac-

①

②

③

① *Before the current widespread use of air conditioning, operable windows were the main source of climate control in office buildings. Some advocate their return because people derive satisfaction from having control of their work environment. This copper-clad window, circa 1910, is in Pentagram's New York office.*

② *At Mortgage Guaranty Investment Company, afternoon sunlight is modulated by sliding, adjustable louvered panels of natural wood. Interiors designed by Warren Platner Associates Architects. Architect: SOM.*

③ *Large windows are desirable in offices. A heating convector spans this broad window at Standard Brands Research Center. The laboratories have tall, narrow windows between the round service towers. Architect: Warren Platner Associates.*

④ *In the Citicorp building, all windows are fixed and the climate is controlled by a computer, although tenants have switches on their floors to override it. Architect: Hugh Stubbins and Associates, Inc.*

⑤ *Code requirements necessitate a safety bar across the floor-to-ceiling window in the offices of fashion designer Halston. Plexiglas rods were used so that the view is not obstructed. Architect: The Gruzen Partnership.*

⑥ *There was no view from the windows in this office of Margo Berk, director of Temporarily Yours, so window blinds were designed as part of the wall decoration. Flexalum Decor Blinds by Hunter Douglas, Inc. Designer: Dexter Design.*

ter and appearance of an office. Even if they're not needed for sun-control, many people want them to finish or soften a room.

Most blinds, shades, draperies, and shutters can be adjusted for mood and circumstance. For example, sun-control might be necessary only certain hours of the day or seasons of the year. Privacy

needs are not constant. Draperies are desirable to shut out the darkness only when you're working late. Window coverings can be used in tandem. If your building requires a standard window covering to give a uniform appearance on the exterior, you can mount the covering of your choice in front of it in your office.

Venetian blinds, in existence since the days of ancient Egypt, are probably the most widely used office window covering. Their principal advantage is that they allow light and air to penetrate, yet they provide privacy. Venetian blinds are designed so that their stiff, horizontal vanes can be adjusted 180°, to any angle between completely open to completely closed. Left open, or completely horizontal, they diffuse light and thus reduce glare. In this position, blinds with thin vanes seem to disappear. Vanes (or slats) are available in wood and metal in widths varying from ⅝ of an inch to 2 inches (15.88 mm to 50.8 mm). Once commonly used, the widest vanes have a vintage look today. Blinds are available in hundreds of colors and many finishes. Two or more colors can be combined for a decorative striped effect. Each surface of one vane can be coated with a different color for decorative effect and to conserve energy. A bright, reflective color on the surface toward the window deflects solar radiation and reduces heat-gain and air-conditioning loads. Although the interior surface might be a dark color, it won't absorb heat.

Horizontal blinds are usually mounted within the frame of the window opening. They give a neat, architectural look. Venetian blinds can be pulled up completely. If they're mounted in a ceiling recess, they disappear until they're needed. One drawback of Venetian blinds is that their horizontal surfaces do catch dust and grime that seeps in at window openings. Preventative maintenance is best: make sure the blinds are dusted often.

Venetian blinds are often used in problem windows. Individual vanes can be cut to fit irregularly shaped openings. They might lose some adjustability: usually they have the tilt function but cannot be drawn. If you desire the flexibility of Venetian blinds but find the geometry too spare, you can easily combine them with softer-looking draperies.

Vertical blinds, like Venetian blinds, are based on the principle of adjustable vanes. They, too, can be regulated to control light and privacy and can be surfaced in two colors. The vanes of vertical blinds, which are made of strips of fabric or plastic, are mounted from a top track and rotate top to bottom. The vanes are from 3½ to 6 inches wide (88.9 mm to 152.4 mm) and overlap when the blind is closed. They can be pulled aside and stacked like drapery when you need to clean them or open the window. If there's enough room (at least 2¾ inches [69.85 mm] clear for 3¼-inch [82.55-mm] vanes), vertical blinds can be mounted within the frame of individual windows. Be sure to check for protruding window hardware first. Sometimes there s an advantage to mounting the blind from floor to ceiling in front of the window. The long line of vertical elements emphasizes a room's height and can also conceal radiators and air conditioners below the window. Similarly, wall-to-wall installations make a small window seem larger and can compensate for poor window placement by disguising the window's location. If the vanes are properly adjusted, you will only see diffused light, not the source. If the vanes are not likely to be blown about by air currents, they can hang free. If you anticipate their swinging, you can purchase blinds with a second bottom track or a bottom chain (which might interfere less with air convectors). Vertical blinds collect less dust than horizontal ones because gravity works for them.

Shades range from the most utilitarian to some of the most decorative ways to cover a window. Fabric roller shades are the least expensive. They're best used in individual windows that are not too wide. Shades are useful in rooms requiring total light control. Blackout shades are made of opaque fabric and are installed with a special side trim to prevent light leaks. Roller shades are often installed in conjunction with other window coverings. Roman shades are an exotic variation on the

traditional shade. As they are pulled up, fabric gathers in the folds, and the shades hang with varying degrees of softness. They're usually designed to be partially drawn.

Shades have less flexibility than blinds. They can be designed to let in light or be totally opaque. Their translucence depends on the face fabric and the backing. Sometimes it is helpful to mount the shade from the bottom of the window and have it close toward the top. In this way, you can achieve both light and privacy.

Draperies introduce a soft, residential feeling to office surroundings. They control light and privacy and offer some acoustic absorption depending on their thickness and size. They might also afford some protection from drafts, which was one of their original functions. Two types of draperies are often used in tandem: sheer, translucent casement cloths at the windows and heavier, lined draperies flanking them.

Available in a large variety of open-weave and sheer fabrics, **casement cloths** function to soften and diffuse light. They're usually a neutral color because light filtering through them, will take on their color and tint the whole room. All fabrics used for window coverings must withstand the ravaging ultraviolet rays of the sun. Casement cloth, which is rarely drawn, takes a particularly cruel beating. Synthetics, especially polyester, last longer than natural fibers in ultraviolet light.

Casements usually hang inside the window frame, close to the frame and the glass, and extending close to the sill. They hide the dirt on windows. Fabric from 200 to 300 percent of the width of the window is necessary for graceful and ample fullness. Casement cloth (and more opaque fabric) can also be hung from a track in smooth, flat panels. Special hardware enables the panels to be easily drawn across the entire width of the window or to stack one behind the other. Panels can never be completely retracted because at least one panel is always visible.

Draperies can camouflage and conceal architectural irregularities such as off-center windows. Although draperies can be drawn

across windows to shut out light, they usually hang to the side as decorative elements. As a rule, plain fabrics, similar to the wall color, make the transition from solid wall to clear glass. They encourage visitors to look through windows. Moderate color contrasts direct attention toward windows. And draperies of bold colors and unusual patterns call attention to themselves rather than to the windows. Drapery fabric should be colorfast and dimensionally stable so that it doesn't shrink or stretch. It should also be strong to withstand the wear and tear of opening and closing. Linings increase draperies' durability and opacity. The drapery pocket at the ceiling of some office-building windows hides the

②

①

③

track for a neat, finished look.

Draperies are expensive. The required yardage for face fabric and linings is substantial. Draperies usually hang floor to ceiling and two to three times the width is required for a full, luxurious look. Custom fabrication and installation are expensive and so is the regular cleaning they require. In addition, their life expectancy is limited. You can expect them to look good for only three to five years. The longevity of both casements and draperies depends on the fabric and its lining, the color (blue dyes fade especially quickly), and the microclimate of their location. Exposure to the sun, abrupt changes in temperature, and exposure to warm and cool air currents from convectors and air conditioners all affect the durability of drapes. Casement and drapery fabric must meet the flammability requirements of governing codes.

Shutters are a more permanent and more architectural window covering. Shutter panels can be fitted with moveable slats, which regulate light as blinds do. There are two types of shutters. Single, floor-to-ceiling panels (hinged or on tracks for access to the window) are designed to stay in front of the window, with only occasional access. The second type are designed for frequent opening and closing. They're usually built as a series of panels, hinged in pairs or sliding on a track. Shutters can be built of metal or wood to match any office decor.

④

❶ *Vertical blinds conceal an unsightly view at the 77th Street Sports Medicine Clinic. An ash-wood unit was built into the far wall to provide storage and to conceal the radiator. Although the windows don't actually cover the width of the rear wall, the wall-to-wall blinds give the appearance that they do. Architect: Marvin Mitchell.*

❷ *Sheer fabric diffuses the light from these greenhouse style windows. Courtesy: Flötotto.*

❸ *Levelor blinds are used to create a wall in this interior conference room. The adjustable vanes permit the occupant of the office to control the degree of privacy.*

❹ *A wall of shutters is an attractive solution to the problem of window coverings. Shutters provide a flexible means for controlling light. This Boston office of Prudential was designed by Daroff Design, Inc.*

⑤

❺ *Roman shades are usually designed to be at half-mast. Opaque shades can be strong visual elements, but they have the disadvantage of blocking both light and the view. Designed by Ellen L. McCluskey Assoc.*

❻ *Formal draperies are a traditional style of window treatment. At this executive office, the full-height draperies emphasize the grand proportions of the room. Designed by Jack Lowery.*

⑥

Rooms With A View

②

The saying goes, "Commands a view." There's no question that an office with a spectacular view signifies a place of power and importance. A corner office with two vistas conveys this even more. The higher you go, the more desirable the office, as the horizon is rendered ever more distant.

On a more fundamental level, a beautiful view gives pleasure. We're linked with the natural order. We know the weather, the time of day, and the season at a glance. What up close would seem chaotic blends with the advantage of height into a larger pattern. From a distance, we perceive order in the natural landscape and the urban one.

An intermittant glance at a distant horizon gives your eyes a chance to refocus after close work. This visual rest relaxes eye muscles and reduces fatigue.

Framed by the office window like a painting, a view should be treated as a work of art. It is a major element of decoration in the office interior. Locate your desk to make the most of it. Your visitors will appreciate a glimpse as well.

With any window, there are problems to be solved. **Direct sunlight,** which can be uncomfortable to be in and *glare,* bright light that can be uncomfortable to look at, must be controlled. If your office is in a building with tinted

①

glass or large overhangs or on the north side of the building, the problems are already solved. If not, choose curtains of open-weave casement cloth. They don't obscure the view when they're drawn. Nor do thin-slatted Venetian blinds and operable vertical blinds if they're properly adjusted. That's why they're so popular. If you desire the privacy and feeling of warmth that drawn draperies provide at night, make sure they stack beyond the window frame during the day.

If your office requires a unit air conditioner, place it on top of the window, where it will least obscure the view. Or, better still, try to build it through the exterior wall.

A good view is potent. If a window is large enough and at eye level people sitting 60 to 70 feet (18 to 21 m) away can enjoy it. Some strategies enable you to share the advantages of a spectacular view. One is glass partitions that impose no visual barriers between your office and interior office spaces. They can be screened off with curtains or blinds when privacy is needed. Or you can make a point of keeping your door open.

1 *Twenty-four-foot-high ceilings were walled with glass windows at Weyerhauser Technology Center, located in a heavily wooded area of Tacoma, Washington. The open-office system was positioned on a diagonal so that the magnificent view is apparent from all work stations and circulation aisles. Architect: Skidmore, Owings and Merrill. Interior design associate: Charles Pfister.*

2 *Every interior space gets a view of the Manhattan skyline because of these carefully placed openings in the fabric panelled walls at BEA, Citicorp. Architect: Tod Williams and Associates.*

3 *This executive office at Johns Manville world headquarters outside Denver overlooks the panoramic vista of the Colorado Rockies. In the foreground is an interior glass wall. Draperies were provided for privacy but they are rarely used. Architect: The Architect's Collaborative. Interiors designed by The Space Design Group.*

4 *In Lea Ronal's windowless office, attached to a factory, John Saladino created an interior, skylit courtyard almost like a Japanese garden. Vertical blinds on the interior wall further enhance the illusion of a window overlooking a garden.*

5 *Author Jeffrey Archer positioned his desk close to the window in order to take full advantage of the view. His London office overlooks Big Ben.*

④

⑤

③

Doors

Because a door is both a barrier and a means of access to the space beyond it, every door has a ceremonial aspect. The design of entrance doors usually acknowledges their symbolic importance. But doors to offices are so commonplace that their design is usually taken for granted. Unless these doors are hopelessly flimsy or badly in need of refinishing they probably won't make a negative impression. On the other hand, doors are an ideal place to make a positive impression; they are where the private office begins.

Most office buildings supply flush (unpanelled), 36-inch- (1-m) wide doors, with metal frames and butt hinges. The height, which varies from building to building, is usually 7 feet (2 m). Should you choose to deviate from building standard, there are several factors you can vary to make a door a significant design element. The first is to increase the width or height. Extrawide doors seem gracious. Just make sure there's ample room for the swing, which will extend further into the room. In tight quarters where wide doors are warranted, conference rooms, for example, consider sliding doors. They have no swing. Office doors should never be narrower than 32 inches (1 m), to allow wheelchair access into any room. Full-height doors make space seem expansive because the ceiling continues, relatively unimpeded, on either side of the door.

Since doors are strong elements in the composition of both sides of the wall they're part of, so they should carry out the design theme of the office. Through the use of special finishes, such as wood veneers, lacquer and plastic laminates, or applications of leather or fabric, a variety of effects can be achieved. Other techniques such as employing panelled or ornamented doors or doors with glass vision panels also emphasize the door itself. When using special door types, the hardware also deserves attention. Unusual hardware such as high-quality pivot hinges (attached to the door at the floor and ceiling) or olive knuckle butt hinges (exposed hinges of almost sculptural design and special finishes, such as brass, bronze, or stainless steel—all of which can be polished or satin-finished— provide functional and aesthetic accents. Upgrading the hardware in an existing door or switching from building-standard locksets and knobs to lever handles, for example, can make an appreciable difference.

A note of caution: Doors and their frames in office buildings must conform to local fire codes because they might be needed to deter flame-spread. All stock doors are classified according to construction and labelled by type, conforming to recognized standards. (In the USA, the National Board of Fire Underwriters classifies five types of fire doors, A-E; each is suitable for a different application.) Any custom-made door must be independently tested and certified before it's installed. Check with the local codes.

The door placement affects office furniture layouts. As a general rule, locating a door near one wall, rather than in the middle of the office, offers more flexibil-

①

②

③

④

⑤

⑥

ity. Of course, other factors, particularly the window location, also have to be considered.

Door location affects layout and lighting and circulation on the other side of the office wall. This is most obvious in long corridors outside offices of equal width. Here, office doors can be equally spaced or the doors to adjacent offices can be paired. The resultant rhythm is a strong design element.

For the most part, Americans usually keep their office doors open while they work alone inside. A closed door is a signal to others that the occupant is with a visitor or otherwise temporarily inaccessible. This signal has a different meaning in other cultures. Anthropologist Edward Hall, in his book *The Hidden Dimension*, has compared Germany and the United States: "The meanings of the open door and the closed door are quite different in the two countries. In offices, Americans keep doors

open; Germans keep doors closed. In Germany, the closed door does not mean that the man behind it wants to be alone or undisturbed,

or that he is doing something he doesn't want someone else to see. It's simply that Germans think that open doors are sloppy and disorderly."

❶ An all-white, full-height door at the end of a corridor in the offices of *Printsiples* was designed by Judith Stockman and Lee Manners. Lever hardware was used as a visual accent, and the curved wall adds visual interest.

❷ The deep-red African marble lobby in the Chrysler Building is accented by art deco elevator doors. Each door has a different wood inlay pattern. Architect: William Van Alen.

❸ Antique doors were installed in the law offices of Richard Golub. Most of the day, the doors are left open; they're closed only during private conferences with clients.

❹ In London, code requirements necessitate the use of a glass panel on doors. Therefore, glass inserts are a graphic feature of British office-door design. An oval window is part of this door at the Booker McConnell offices. Designed by Zeev Aram and Assoc.

❺ Chinese red columns (of lacquered cardboard), an expanded wood threshold, and large round grips for opening the sliding etched-glass door emphasize the ceremonial aspect of entering the corner conference room at BEA Associates. Architect: Tod Williams and Associates.

❻ Hinges, handles, locks, and stops are important details of door design. At the offices of GFI/Knoll International, the clear-glass door between the reception area and the partners' office can open parallel with the wall because of the recess for the stainless steel pull. Architect: Skidmore, Owings and Merrill.

Table Desks

"An executive who is really a directing, thinking, planning head of business, doesn't need a desk with drawers, unless for storing cigars and golf balls for his periods of relaxation and recreation. As a matter of fact, many large executives have abandoned the desk altogether, replacing it with a large table." W. H. Leffingwell, one of the first management consultants in the United States, wrote this in 1925.

Tables are still a logical alternative to pedestal desks if you spend most of your office day meeting with others. Even small offices can be laid out with free-standing tables that accommodate three or four visitors. This has practical planning advantages. If an office doubles as a conference room, perhaps separate conference rooms for small meetings are unnecessary. If small conference rooms were eliminated, the total square feet required could be reduced. This saves money.

Back units or credenzas handle other desk functions, including storing documents, supporting machines and telephones, and acting as a holding area for work in progress. This frees the table top from clutter. It eliminates the bother of straightening up for visitors. It also eliminates the temptation for visitors to read your mail upside down.

Forty years after Leffingwell, another expert in office planning theory, Robert Propst, restated the advantages of a table in the office, used in conjunction with other work surfaces. His important work *The Office: A Facility Based on Change* was an explanation of the Action Office open-plan system that he developed, but what he wrote is applicable to private offices as well. Propst showed how a table offers options. A table offers the "ability to have uncompromised conversations over a neutral surface," wrote Propst. "A personal work surface covered with papers is a highly compromised and distracting condition to conversation."

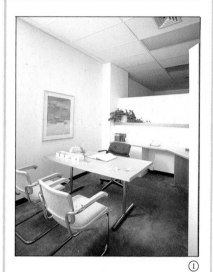

①

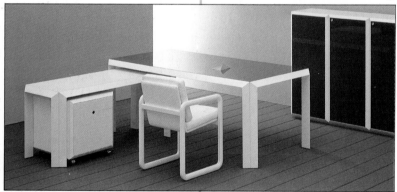

②

③

④

Propst favored "roundish" tops because they offer users the "ability to adjust laterally" around it. People can sit face-to-face, the most formal situation, or for a more relaxed conversation, they can sit catty-corner. If they need to look at documents together, they can sit side by side.

Legs at the edges of the table top might restrict these seating possibilities. Recessed legs or a central base with a cantilevered top are more flexible. Make sure that a cantilevered top is engineered to prevent tipping and strong enough to support the weight of someone sitting on it. To provide stability, some slender bases need a concealed plate bolted to the floor slab. The plate is ultimately covered by the finished flooring. Obviously the table has to be installed before the flooring. This requires coordinating the flooring and furniture schedules.

Just about any material is suitable for table tops—glass, wood, stone, plastic laminate, or leather. Tops are available in many shapes. The choice depends upon the room size, the number of visitors, and your personal style. If it's important for you to sit at a recognizable place of authority, then a round or square table isn't suitable because it offers no single visual "head"; every position is equal. Rectangular and oval tops have a place of authority along a long side. One shape that clearly expresses authority is a truncated circle. The straight edge is the power side; visitors sit along the curve.

To take advantage of the inherent flexibility of a table desk, make sure the chairs have mobility. They should be on casters or glides or light enough to be picked up and rearranged.

Of course, when there are no meetings, the table desk is available as a large work surface, which is another advantage. Some incorporate pencil drawers just for this purpose.

(5)

1 Neville Lewis, chairman of his interior design firm, located the drafting room in the sunny corner on the premises and relegated to himself a shipshape, small office with the classic Omega desk-table as its centerpiece. The Omega is in the Museum of Modern Art Design Collection.

2 Talete, a German system of office furniture, is residence-scaled geometric shapes with protruding angles deliberately kept in check. Miter-joined corners of the white writing desk recess inward as do the edges of the cabinet fitted with shelves and wire-reinforced dark-glass doors. Designed by Pierluigi Ghianda and Gabriele Regondi for Rosenthal.

3 Race office systems set storage nearby along walls, freeing up a round-table work surface stage center. Drawer units cantilever out from a baseboard-level Race "beam," which can also house telephone, CRT, and word-processor wiring. Designed by Douglas Ball for Sunar.

4 The writing surface of this Linea Direzionale desk is Italian walnut veneer inset with leather and grooved to hold pencils and pens. The desk bases are covered in rifled stainless steel. Matching bookcases stacked on storage units have tempered-glass doors. Designed by H. Von Klier for Olivetti.

5 The sleek, lacquered Saratoga desk is leather-panelled and wide enough to pull several chairs up to. Storage is out of sight—a slim pencil drawer on the sitter's side. Designed by Vignelli Associates for Poltronova.

6 To make the O'Neill and Borges law office feel airy and larger, architect Marlys Hann kept colors light and furniture shapes spare—Herman Miller Ergon chairs and a file unit on casters. The custom-designed table-desk top is wrapped in leather, its simple column base anchored under the carpet with a flange. The red step ladder to reach law books is a sculptural shape itself.

(6)

Pedestal Desks

Freestanding pedestal desks have been and are the most widely used style of desk. Their origins are the freestanding tables in the libraries of great 18th century European—especially English—residences. Though a few examples survive from the late 17th century, the pedestal style did not become common until the Queen Anne and Georgian periods. Usually made of walnut or mahogany, the desks were designed to support heavy volumes and serve as writing desks as well. They were grand pieces in every way, scaled for large, important public rooms. Their tops were often inlaid with leather, an added enrichment providing an unusually comfortable writing surface and a minimum of glare. The pedestals themselves were cabinets containing storage space for books, papers and writing implements.

Modern styles: For today's office functions, the pedestals have been modified to facilitate information storage. Pedestal desks are available in every style, material, and price range. In its simplest form it is a hollow-core door, surmounting two approximately 28-inch high file cabinets, each of which may contain two file drawers, four storage drawers, or a combination of one file drawer (on the bottom, to prevent tipping) with two storage drawers.

If the pedestals do not provide enough storage there are two possibilities: you can buy units with matching pedestals, called credenzas, which are freestanding; or you can choose a desk with an "executive L", in which a storage cabinet is attached at right angles to the desk proper. The executive L gives you more work space at your desk; it is great if you like to spread out. The separate credenza, on the other hand, makes it easier to compartmentalize work tasks—and work machines. Other features to look for are built-in openings in desk tops for wires and telephone cords. A 10-year study by architect Michael Brill shows that most people prefer wood desks—even imitation wood—to any other material. Oak, a light wood, is becoming increasingly popular for moderately priced desks, supplanting walnut and rosewood. Exotic, burled wood veneers, whose interesting patterns come from twisted trees, are sought after for expensive desks. Leather desk tops—and leatherlike vinyl—are being used again today for the same reasons they were originally used: they feel luxurious, provide a good writing surface, and the dull texture of their surface reduces the glare from overhead lighting.

①

②

③

❶ This Gwathmey Siegel design for Knoll International features modular pedestals that can be combined with cantilevered work surfaces of various shapes and sizes. Tops can be adapted to specific uses: larger sizes for executives, curved tops for receptionists. The elements are available in four mahogany finishes and dark plastic laminates; materials can be mixed.

❷ Ward Bennett's love of simple, geometric forms "without gimmicks" is evident in this Capsule desk he designed for Brickel Associates. Shown here in ash with its matching credenza, it is also available in walnut and Carpathian elm burl. Its sophisticated details include a full circumference stainless steel base—whose reflective qualities make it appear to float—and side finger pulls.

❸ A single pedestal desk with a machine extension is one of the many combinations possible in the flexible system designed by Bruce Hannah for Knoll International. Three basic components—a modular pedestal, a leg, and a variety of top sizes—make this a highly versatile system. The pedestals and leg are made of steel and covered in black, red, or brown plastic panels. The top is available in wood veneer or plastic laminate.

❹ This handsome, straightforward desk, shown here with a management return, was designed by Douglas Ball for Sunar. Its rectangular forms are moderated by the bullnosed work-top edge, curved on both the executive's and the visitor's side. Finished in three shades of oak—the lightest is illustrated—and in mahogany, it has optional built-in wire management, and various pedestals. Matching credenzas and floating pedestal models are also available.

❺ The exposed surfaces of this Georgian-style desk are of European walnut burl and cherry. Each pedestal contains a file drawer and two box drawers. The work top is available in all wood or with leather inserts. An overhanging conference top can also be used with the pedestals shown here. By John Widdicomb, Inc.

❻ A sleek aluminum structure supports its diverse components and serves as wire raceway for this innovative desk. Designed by Bruce Burdick for Herman Miller, its individually articulated elements accommodate both office papers and electronic equipment. Each component can be ordered separately; top surfaces are available in dark and light oak veneers, black laminate, glass, or marble. The drawer cases are made of polyurethane structural foam.

Partner's Desks

The original partner's desks were used in English banking houses in the late 18th century. They were designed so that two partners sat opposite each other, knee to knee. Each could check on the other as they counted money. The desk pedestals contained drawers to hold money. They opened in both directions for mutual supervision. Richly carved mahogany, with gleaming brass fittings, partner's desks acquired an aura of wealth and prestige. Soon they were popular, often for personal use, outside the financial world. Because they symbolize success, some executives today continue to use them, either antiques or reproductions.

Today, the partner's desk concept appears in offices in different forms and for different reasons. One reason for two people to share the same workspace is lack of space. Sometimes it's impossible to subdivide one office into two separate and equal smaller ones. Sometimes the resulting split would produce two tiny offices. Sharing the space, and the desk, is an obvious solution. Sharing an office also saves resources and money. Both partners get general illumination from the same source, although individual desk lamps are a good idea. Both partners have the same access to files and documents or electronic information if they share a computer terminal.

One set of visitors' chairs is sufficient; they can use common lounge seating. Both partners can enjoy the same view and the same art objects. They each need, however, separate telephones.

Another reason for two partners to share one space is personal and symbolic. Some partners want to work together in the same room. They need and enjoy the interaction; they like the efficiency.

Partners can work side by side or facing each other. They can use a common work surface or have separate ones. The size and shape of the room dictates this as much as the working relationship between the partners. One thing to consider is visitor seating. Try to arrange it so that a visitor can keep both partners in view. If the partners are spread out too far, a meeting might seem like a tennis match.

Some desks are designed for more than two people to share. At such close range, however, it's difficult to achieve any privacy for telephone conversation. The space under a large common surface can be used for storage cabinets and file drawers.

②

①

③

④

❶ Partners sit side by side at this 5-by 12-foot (15- by 36-m) worktable designed by Charles Pfister. On the left, a solar bronze glass door with polished stainless steel frame provides direct access to the conference area. A painting by Morris Louis hangs on the far wall. Architect: Skidmore, Owings and Merrill.

❷ A genuine, antique partner's desk where two partners sat opposite each other. Originally, these desks were used in banking establishments and the money drawers opened from both sides so that the partners could keep a constant check on each other. Because the desk was associated with banking, it became a status symbol in offices. Modern adaptations of the partner's desk changed the money drawers to file drawers for storage. Desk from the Desk Shop, Oxford, England.

❸ At their own offices, designers Lynn Jacobsen and Richard Orbach of Creative Perspectives purposely sit at separate desks that face each other to facilitate a two-way collaboration.

❹ Barbara Schwartz and Barbara Ross of Dexter Design Inc. work in tandem on all jobs, and they decided it would be more information- and time-efficient if they shared one joint office-conference space. Their desk is a formica-surfaced contemporary partner's desk in the shape of a solid D—the Dexter firm logo. Above the desk is a painting by Larry Zox. The rattan coffee table in the foreground is above standard height—20 inches—so it doubles as a writing surface where clients can take notes.

Credenzas and Other Storage

The credenza, which gained widespread usage during the Italian Renaissance, was a carved wooden sideboard that stored dishes, linen, and silverware. Its name, from the Latin *credere*, to trust, hints at an earlier use: before becoming an elaborate piece of furniture, the credenza was a table where food was tasted, to guard against poison, before it was served.

Today the only poison likely to be on an office credenza is a cup of coffee from the vending machine. Credenzas supplement desk functions. They provide storage and additional work surface. They're usually located directly behind the desk for quick access from a swiveling desk chair (allow at least 42 inches [1.06 m] for the chair to clear). Credenzas can work just as well if they're placed to one side, perpendicular to the desk.

Most desks have a matching credenza of the same height (29 inches [.737 m]) but a shallower depth (18–20 inches [457–508 mm]). Like the original sideboard, credenzas are designed to sit against a wall or in front of a window. The width varies with the components you choose. Like pedestal desks, credenzas are designed to be used as a system. You can choose the elements to suit your work style and your storage needs.

Credenzas are equipped with the same drawer options that desks have: box drawers and file drawers. In addition, they're fitted with doors to store high or bulky items. Some credenzas come with bar units; some have sliding shelves for machines, such as recorders that can be stored below desk height but have controls that require access. And some credenzas can be ordered with a knee space instead of a storage cabinet (32 inches [.813 m] is about the standard). This transforms the credenza into a second desk.

Credenzas free the primary work surface. They're an ideal place for telephones, calculators, or computer terminals. Most credenzas are fitted with grommets and have internal raceways to handle wires and cables. Placed against a wall, the space above them is ideal for display.

In recent years, some manufacturers have introduced high-back units that perform the same function as credenzas but expand storage capabilities by providing shelves above the work surface. Like the office systems to which they're related, they usually incorporate task lighting below

①

②

the shelves. Since they're too high to use in front of a window, they're not suitable for every office layout.

If the uniform look of coordinated desks and credenzas doesn't appeal to you and yet you need more storage and work space than a desk alone can supply, consider other possibilities: you can adapt some other furniture, for example a rolltop desk, or an armoire, to serve as a back unit. Or you can design a desk with sufficient storage and a large enough work surface to satisfy your needs.

③

④

⑤

❶ *A wall unit in the chairman's office of MGIC makes maximum use of the space behind the desk. The custom-designed unit includes a closet and overhead cabinets for storage. Designed by Warren Platner. Architect: Skidmore, Owings and Merrill.*

❷ *Lawyer Richard Golub makes unconventional use of an antique rolltop desk positioned behind his French provincial table. The desk's drawers hold his files, the writing extension serves as a telephone stand, and the other surfaces display his plants and art objects.*

❸ *An expanded credenza incorporates both a work surface and storage space. File cabinets form the base of the work area and includes a kneehole space. This area frees the table for conferences. Overhead storage includes both task and up lighting above the shelves. Designed by Neville Lewis Associates and Kaneko/Laff Associates.*

❹ *Because the president of the Norlin Corporation likes to work standing up, his office was designed with a wraparound credenza. The shelves provide plenty of storage space and a waist-high work surface. There's a desk and a conference table in an adjoining room. Designed by James Stewart Polshek.*

❺ *One of the standard components of the offices at the Ford Foundation is a system of brackets positioned behind the desk. The brackets support either shelves or cabinets.*

Desk Chairs

Sitting in chairs is an acquired, cultural trait. We could forego chairs completely, squatting or kneeling instead. "A chair is really the first thing you need when you don't really need anything," said communications design consultant, Ralph Caplan, "and is therefore a peculiarly compelling symbol of civilization. There probably are few more powerful symbols in contemporary life."

One reason chairs make good symbols is that they can assume almost any form. The functional requirements of a chair are basically rather simple. A chair need only keep the user's buttocks above the floor to qualify as such. Because they are immediate and minimal human environments, chairs are proving grounds for aesthetic and technological ideas. Few architects and designers can resist the urge to attempt a new design. A chair can be the most expressive piece of furniture in the office. Some have such a distinct identity that we even know them by name: Mies van der Rohe's Barcelona chair; Marcel Breuer's Chesca chair; and a leather chair named Joe, shaped like a baseball glove, are some examples.

But whatever its form, through the ages and across most cultures, a sitting position has meant authority. By extension, the chair is the seat of power. Our language expresses this: "an endowed chair in a university," "to chair a meeting," and "Chairperson of the Board." The most concrete example of the chair as a symbol of power is the throne.

Far too often, desk chairs are chosen for their throne-like, ceremonial qualities. Looming large behind a desk, these high-backed chairs frame the user with expensive upholstery fabric or, more commonly, leather. Upholstery details, including buttons, tacking, and stitching emphasize luxury. Such chairs far overpower all the other furniture in the room.

Even without going to extremes, desk chairs are usually larger than other chairs in the room and certainly never smaller. The device of identifying chair models by job category—secretarial, managerial, and executive—reinforces the office hierarchy and the chair as status symbol. As standard practice, manufacturers offer a product line that is comprised of variations on a basic design: secretarial chairs are small and armless; managerial chairs are larger-scaled and have open arms; and executive chairs, approaching throne-like dimensions, have closed arms, the widest seats and the tallest backrests.

Unfortunately, choosing a chair solely for status ignores the "fit" between the user and the chair. Large secretaries assigned small chairs and small executives who get big ones, can have problems. Women executives, particularly, have difficulty finding a chair to fit their status and their bodies.

Yet the basic consideration when choosing a desk chair should be proper body support. Poorly designed chairs can be a cause of backaches—the occupational hazard of office workers. They can contribute, as well, to varicose veins and a variety of heart and other circulatory ailments. Sitting in a chair is an unnatural position for the human body; it puts a strain on the thighs, buttocks, neck, shoulders, and especially the back. Sitting for prolonged periods can cause discomfort. Desk–bound office workers have more back problems than any other group except bus and truck drivers.

Seating for office workers has been analyzed by those in the field of **ergonomics.** Ergonomists study the human body in relation to the physical environment, especially the workplace. They've developed guidelines for office seating that have resulted in handsome, well-designed chairs that meet high standards of comfort and aesthetics. Ergonomically designed chairs are available in just about every style and material, compatible with any office interior, from space age to traditional, and in every price range. In fact, lowly secretarial chairs were, at one time, better designed than too soft, over-padded executive desk chairs. To discover if a chair is indeed comfortable after you've been in it for a while, try to spend as much time as possible in it before you buy. Here are some things to look for when buying chairs:

The *seat* should be properly adjusted so that your feet rest on the floor without dangling. Legs are heavy—about 17 percent of your body weight—and there should be no pressure on the underside of your thighs. If you find you're crossing your legs frequently, it might be to relieve some under-leg pressure. In addition, make sure that the seat's not too deep. There should be clearance between the front of the seat and the back of your knees; the front edges should be padded. If there's pressure behind your knees, your feet might fall asleep. The density of the seat cushion should be firm enough to prevent you from sinking too far into the cushion. Usually 1½ inches (241 mm) is maximum. And if the seat has a slight hollow and contour, it's usually more comfortable.

Make sure the **backrest** supports the lumbar region—the five lower segments of the spine—so that it can maintain a natural, concave curvature. The cardinal rule is to keep the small of your back in contact with the chair back. Some chairs—for example the Diffrient Chair designed by Niels Diffrient, or the Wilkhahn FS line office chair designed by Klaus Franck and Werner Sauer—follow you through the basic office positions: relaxing on the telephone, sitting up straight with a

① ② ③ ④

visitor, or leaning forward over the desk. Avoid too–soft back-cushions in all seating, not just desk chairs. If the lumbar region is not properly supported, the spine curves conversely, and this can induce backaches. Good support increases comfort by distributing back pressure over a large area. The top edge of the backrest should be high enough to provide good support when the chair is tilted backwards. And if a thronelike high back appeals to you, make sure your neck is properly supported in a comfortable position.

Armrests should be adjustable so that, when you're using them, your shoulders will not hunch up. They should be long enough to support your forearm and base of your hand, yet short enough so that your fingers won't get jammed under the top of your desk. Armrests shouldn't restrict movement; if they do, perhaps you shouldn't have them. Secretarial chairs have no armrests because they get in the way of typing. If you like to sit close to your desk, make sure the armrest doesn't get in the way. And use your armrest often, to help you get out of your chair. Too much sitting is unhealthy. Try walking around your office occasionally to get some exercise.

Actually, desk chairs are designed for mobility. They have a swivel mechanism, which makes it easy to rotate around to reach every desk surface. Tilt mechanisms allow a variety of body positions. They enable the chair to work like a rocker. Casters allow movement across the floor. Caster selection depends on the flooring material. The largest diameter casters of the hardest possible material, usually stainless steel, are recommended for carpets. Hard rubber casters are recommended for hard floors. Chair glides, small metal buttons, are generally used for pull-up chairs, which don't need mobility, yet should be easy to move.

❶ The Mobius caned executive armchair, designed by Ward Bennett for Brickel Associates.

❷ Ergon chair components include cushioned lumbar surfaces. Designed by Bill Stumpf for Herman Miller, Inc.

❸ The durable "skin" of the Leonardo Operational chair is heat-fused and puncture-resistant. Designed by Paul Tuttle for Atelier International.

❹ Harter's 8700 series desk swivelchair looks soft but its leather seat cushions are reinforced with sinuous steel springs. Designed by Earl Koepke and the Harter Design Staff.

❺ The Verde 700 desk chair from Finland. Designed by Yrjo Wiherheimo for Vivero.

❻ The thronelike Xanadu high-back armchair is upholstered in glovelike leather. Stendig, Inc.

❼ Padded backs and seat heights of desk chairs in the Pelly collection adjust via a three-way lever under the seat. Designed for Pledge.

❽ The leather-contoured Diffrient Executive Chair pivots at two crucial points to support the small of the back. Designed by Niels Diffrient for Knoll.

❾ Vertebra® Integral Arm Executive Seating is designed by Emilio Ambasz and Giancarlo Piretti and produced under exclusive license from Openark® B.V. by Krueger.

❿ All six chairs in the Paradigm line are developed around the same size seating shell. Designed by Richard Schultz for Stow/Davis.

⓫ German Wilkhahn FS High Back chair. Designed by Klaus Franck and Werner Sauer. Exclusive U.S. production rights licensed to Vecta Contract by Wilkhahn GmbH. U.S. and Canadian patents applied for.

⓬ Swivel-tilt armchair designed for Steelcase by Warren Platner.

Visitor's Chairs

A famous fast-food chain deliberately designs its seating to look comfortable—the backs are padded—but the seats, hidden by the table, are uncomfortable, uncushioned molded plastic. In this way, customers are made to feel welcome, yet simultaneously encouraged not to linger. You, too, can choose chairs that suit your purposes for office visitors. As opposed to the fast-food chain, however, you'll probably want to make your visitors comfortable.

You can choose visitors' chairs that look similar to your desk chair. Since visitors' chairs don't require mobility, specify floor glides or a sled bottom instead of casters. Tilt mechanisms are unnecessary; it's unlikely that visitors will lean back and put their feet up on your desk. Having all the chairs alike, however, expresses the notion of equality of status. If you want to express that you, as its occupant, are the most important person in your office, choose a variation of your chair design instead. Select a visitor chair with a lower back, or choose an armless version of your desk chair, or upholster a similar visitor's chair in a different, less-expensive fabric. The overall effect of using a unified chair design is usually one of dignity and restraint.

If you desire more variety and expressiveness, choose a chair for its sculptural qualities. Obviously, visitors' chairs should be compatible with the other furniture in the office. But you can choose a traditional Queen Anne chair because you love its lines and not worry that its straight back was not ergonomically designed. Visitors spend relatively little time in them, so for visitors' chairs, comfort is not the major issue. Telling your visitors how you feel about them—their importance relative to you—is, perhaps, a greater consideration.

In general, look for light, moveable chairs. They give a feeling of spaciousness—especially in a small office. Select a chair that looks good from every angle. Don't forget, visitors will probably see its back first (if your desk faces the door); you'll always be looking at its front. Make sure the seat isn't too low—unless you want to intimidate visitors by being seated high above them. Remember, high, firm seats are easier to get in and out of than low, soft ones. Chairs with armrests seem more gracious and are more comfortable than those without.

Chairs made of wood are appropriate in both modern and traditional interiors, while metal and plastic chairs definitely have a modern connotation. Generally speaking, it's much easier to coordinate a straight-lined modern desk with an antique chair, than the other way around. The former expresses an eclectic style; the latter is harder to pull off—probably because a desk is the dominant piece of furniture in an office.

Seating arrangements influence interactions. The most formal way to arrange visitors' chairs is to place them directly across the desk from you. Face-to-face situations is the preferred arrangement for competitive situations; it's difficult to avoid direct eye contact, and you can closely monitor every expression. In this case, the desk protects you and acts as a barrier, discouraging long interactions. If you prefer more informal communications at your desk, place the visitor's chair to one side of it. Corner-to-corner arrangements still allow eye contact, yet are more relaxed.

Be realistic about the number of visitors' chairs you need. Pare the number to avoid cluttering your office. If you find that you can't accommodate enough visitors at your desk, perhaps you can use a table desk, or hold meetings in a nearby conference room.

①

②

❶ *The chairman of the board of Allied Chemical installed near his desk Smith & Watson's reproduction Bank of England chairs. Based on a 1760 Chippendale design, the back height and leather padding of this seating is proportioned to be comfortable yet austere. Interior design by Ellen L. McCluskey Associates.*

❷ *In the adjacent offices David Hicks designed for his managing director and his financial director in London, visitor seats are variations of American classics—Charles Eames' swivel-based chairs in his aluminum series.*

❸ *The chair designed by Mies van der Rohe was chosen for its classical lines in this executive office at Prudential (NEHO) in Boston. The chair can be drawn to the desk or turned to face the couch; it looks good from any angle. Interior design by Daroff Design, Inc.*

❹ *The former offices of Harold Evans at The Sunday Times in London also used chairs designed by Mies van der Rohe. As visitors' chairs in a small office, they are substantive without being bulky. Designed by Terence Conran.*

③

④

Lounge Chairs and Sofas

Lounge chairs and sofas, used for informal conference areas in offices, are the ultimate office luxuries. Lounge seating—fixed arrangements of upholstered chairs and couches—require large floor areas. The private office big enough to accommodate a lounge seating area has the luxury of space to begin with; the semireclining position, suggesting relaxation rather than business as usual, expresses the luxury of time as well.

Almost any padded chair or sofa is suitable for lounge seating groups in an office. Just be sure they're not too soft or too low. Lounge chairs should be easy to get into and out of. They should provide proper back support, maintaining the concave curve of the lower back, and they should not throw your body into uncomfortable, awkward positions. You'd be surprised how many do.

The size of the office determines lounge furniture layouts. The most efficient arrangement incorporates the pull-up chairs at the desk as one side of the vis-a-vis. The most lavish arrangement is comprised of full-size sofas facing each other across a low table, remote from the desk in a separate area of the office.

Lounge seating arrangements are usually anchored by a low table. Make sure that the one you choose is large enough to hold the inevitable papers and reports that will find their way there. People prefer to sit opposite each other and, at some slight angle, near the arms of sofas rather than squarely in the middle. Right-angled arrangements, therefore, are most conducive to good conversation. But be sure to provide enough room at the inside corners so that everyone has enough leg room. Avoid a crowded feeling that would detract from the sense of expansiveness, which is, after all, the primary purpose of lounge seating. A corner table, used as a spacer, is also useful for holding a telephone.

Most sofas are available in two- and three-seating positions, with a one-seat version that's basically an armchair. Seating arrangements in an L-shape or a U-shape provide the necessary conversation corners. Uniformly upholstered elements of matching design, they create a serene, dignified look— popular and appropriate in modern-style offices. If you prefer the more gracious, almost residential quality of a traditional style, choose disparate elements— sofas and lounge chairs that complement each other's shape but are of different designs. Use the lounge chairs as sculptural accents against the more horizontal lines of the sofa. Consider wing chairs, for example. Just make sure that any lounge seating you choose is in scale with the other furniture in your office and does not make the room look overcrowded. Again, the feeling of spaciousness is the key to the success of lounge seating areas.

Because it's used in large areas, the fabric used to upholster lounge seating has a great effect in determining the office image. In general, smooth-textured fabrics suggest elegance, sophistication, and sleekness. Leathers, suedes, shiny vinyls, velours, silks, and wool flannels are some examples. On the other hand, ruggedness, naturalness, and warmth are the general impressions conveyed by woven, more textured fabrics such as tweeds, corduroys, linens, textured vinyls, and woven cottons. It's best to stick with solid, neutral colors and soft textures; they tend to reduce the apparent bulk of large furniture pieces. And they're easy to live with, day after day. Avoid big patterns—they're distracting, and they get tiresome. Leather, because of its splendid feel, its durability, and easy maintenance, is a wonderful, albeit very expensive, choice in any office. Durable wool weaves are another good choice. As a general rule, it's best to choose neutral colors and let the textile fabrics provide interest and contrast.

The trim used in some lounge seating adds a pleasant contrast to upholstered forms. It has a practical purpose as well, protecting vulnerable outside corners such as chair arms and the top of backrests from wear and tear. Wood is most often used for this purpose because it's so pleasant to touch and adaptable to both traditional and modern designs. Metal and plastic serve the same function, while projecting a cooler and more modern feeling.

The best-quality upholstered furniture has cushions of goose down and feathers; synthetic materials such as dacron and polyurethene have more problems—they tend to flatten— but are acceptable substitutes. Under no circumstances should you select lounge seating using polyvinylchloride for stuffing; during a fire it emits a toxic gas.

③

④

❶ A red L-shaped sofa is used in the reception area of this San Francisco office. The red is used both for the boldness of the color and to emphasize its form in this otherwise neutral space. Designed by Hellmuth, Obata and Kassabaum, Architects.

❷ Laura Ashley's desk is turned toward the window so that it takes up a minimal amount of space. The major portion of this office is a relaxing seating area.

❸ A custom-designed seating area from the same office as in photograph number 1. As in the reception area, the sofa in this office is L-shaped. The same fabric is used on all seating. The sofa is a place for conversations, the table for more formal meetings, and the work surface is for paper work and telephones. The Ergon chairs are from Herman Miller. Designed by Hellmuth, Obata and Kassabaum.

❹ The furniture defines different activities in this fashion designer's office. At left is the reception area, next to it a worktable, then a seating area, and at right, a conference table and another worktable.

Telephones

It's difficult to imagine an office without a telephone. In fact, for many people, a telephone is the only thing they must have in order to conduct business. In today's business world, the telephone is the key communications instrument. Other than face-to-face meetings, it's the most personal way to exchange information. Moreover, it satisfies

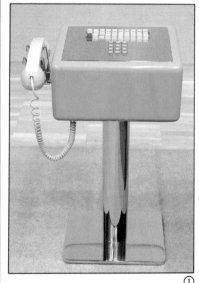

the need for efficient, dependable high-speed communications.

Computerization, with its resultant miniaturization, has dramatically affected telephone technology. Today, individual instruments can protect the users' privacy and handle complex connections within the office as well as conference calls that include many parties. The most modern phone systems virtually eliminate switchboards, except in huge installations that handle hundreds of daily incoming calls. In smaller offices, the speed and ease with which calls are distributed reduces the work of

receptionists and makes the private office more self-sufficient. Secretaries and support staff can be more productive because the phone system now handles some of the routine duties.

The state-of-the-art of telephones changes so rapidly that an office can very quickly be dated by the instruments. The crank, the dial, the hold button, and push buttons are features that made previous developments obsolete. Obviously, the office planner must work closely with a phone company representative to arrive at a phone system that will provide the essential features for an efficient office as well as allow for modification and expansion.

There is enough hardware and equipment available to meet just about every office phone requirement, and thanks to miniaturization, the space needed for central wiring is much less than it used to be. But you will have to plan your phone system carefully in advance to allow for such things as the size and color of phone units, the switch-room space and power requirements, the wiring size and methods and the interrelationship of employees by telephone.

Recent developments have combined the communications capability of a telephone with those of a computer. The phone components offer automatic dialing, hands-free talking, and last-number redialing. The computer component stores frequently used phone numbers —up to 81 of them—that can be called up from memory and automatically redialed. A screen can be programmed to list the calls that must be made that day.

The touch-tone dial enables electronic data, as well as the voice, to be transmitted over regular phone lines. A *modem* (for modulator-demodulator) can convert the digital data from a computer memory to a form that can be transmitted over a phone line. As the phone system is already a worldwide system, this hookup potential makes it possible to link computers all over the world. On the other hand, any compute hookup with a modem

connection requires two phones: one for voice communication and one for data transmission. This signifies a return to the multi-phone installations of the Dark Ages of telephone technology— before the hold button was invented.

When you plan your office phone-systems, remember to allow for telephones in places like conference rooms, lounge seating areas, and outside conference rooms—any place where

employees gather is a logical location for a telephone. If you are arranging for a phone in a gathering place like a conference room, try to make some arrangement for privacy for the phone user.

In the private office, the phone is frequently moved about. Keep this in mind, and allow for wires coming out of desk tops and auxiliary surfaces. You must also allow for access to cables for repair work.

Today's telephones are a far cry from the black boxes of the past. Your telephone company representative can show you a wide range of phones, some of which emphasize streamlined design; some gadgetry. One appealing option is replacing the ringing bell with blinking lights or buzzers. This eliminates some of the distracting noise in an open-plan office. The important thing, once you have the system worked out, is to be certain that the phone is handy in every location where it will be needed.

④

⑤

❶ A free-standing phone set in a lacquer box on a mirror-polished stainless steel pedestal. A phone like this that doesn't take up desk space is worth considering, but advance planning is necessary for locating under-floor phone lines. Designed by Warren Platner for Knoll.

❷ Built into a drawer, this phone slides out of sight when it's not in use. The control board next to the phone also operates the lights and the door to an adjoining conference room. Designed by Christopher Owen.

❸ A small table keeps the telephone off the desk of Charles Agee Atkins, managing partner at The Securities Group. The focal point of the room is the antique Regency desk. Interior design by Zim-Lerner, Inc.

❹ The telephone on the desk of the secretary to the chairman of the board of Interconnect Planning Corporation, a private telephone company, looks like a standard handset and functions as the last terminal in a very sophisticated computerized telephone system. This equipment has memory privacy and conference call features. The floor outlet was carefully coordinated by architects Rubin and Smith-Miller, who also designed the custom desk.

❺ One of the many components of the Herman Miller Action Office System is this phone stand that keeps the phone off the desk, freeing more work space.

❻ A phone integrated into custom-designed furniture, the receiver is on the side and a steel disc for interoffice and outside lines is set in the stainless steel apron of a credenza in the Manhattan conference room of GFI/Knoll. Designed by Charles Pfister of Skidmore, Owings and Merrill.

Electronics

Electronics have entered the executive office in the form of calculators and stock market indicators. In the next few years, in efforts to increase productivity, the executive office will become automated. As executive and management salaries account for 75 percent of the payroll, the value of automation to executive functions is obvious.

Most of todays' executives don't know how to type. Nor do they want to learn. This means that until voice-activated computers, which eliminate the use of a keyboard, become a reality (perhaps in 5 to 10 years), executives will use keyboards and terminals to get information quickly but not to enter data. This means that the desk-height extension or credenza is now adequate for executive use. However, when terminals are used for long stretches of time, they must be ergonomically designed. They must, like typewriters, be at the right height to work with comfortably.

The increasing use of electronics in the office will ultimately change office design considerably. The introduction of telephones, typewriters, and copy devices did little to change the basic desk design, but with the use of computers, work surfaces of the future will be simpler, more basic supports. As Swiss architect and furniture designer, Fritz Haller says, "Computer technology is growing faster than furniture design." It's been predicted that in 5 years, the shape of the terminal will be flatter and smaller. No doubt by that time the terminal will be an integrated part of the executive office. The executive of the future will use the desk-top computer to view information either in a data base or in the form of electronic mail created by the secretary at his or her work station. The executive's own work will be transmitted to other executives' work stations or to managerial personnel.

In addition to changing the traditional desk, automation should change other office furniture because it eliminates the need for bulky files. Offices will rely on computers, rather than paper, for everything from stock quotations and library documents to airline schedules and daily correspondence.

At the moment, CRT units are heavy and bulky items. The trend, of course, is to smaller and smaller equipment and components so that the terminal does not take up valuable desk space. For now, the terminal is best located in a back unit that allows easy access. In any event, some designers have grouped all the electronics in one console and not allow them to dominate the office space.

In designing for the office computer, wiring is a vital consideration. A wiring system that allows for connections to other computers is important. If there is a company "mainframe," the individual computers must be connected to it. Moreover, if the computer is used in conjunction with a telephone, extra phone lines and phones must be installed.

It's very important to have the proper lighting for computer work, especially if the computer is being used for long stretches of time. The computer screen should not be against a bright surface like a brightly lit window. This can cause eyestrain and fatigue.

①

②

❸

❶ For two partners at GFI/Knoll in New York, Skidmore, Owings and Merrill designed a swiveling custom case of mirror-polished stainless steel to house the Quotron screen set on a credenza in the office that the men share. To the left, the Quotron keyboard that activates transmittal of information on the screen.

❷ Trading rooms rely on electronics for communication and processing orders. This traders' room features a special custom-designed worktable that the architects developed in collaboration with the dealers. Electronic monitoring boards were located so that they could be seen by everybody, and a conveyor belt system was included to transport tickets. Special lighting was developed so that the monitors would be lit without glare. Designed by Interior Concepts.

❸ Some executives want machines that work for them out of sight. A Lanier dictaphone slides inside a Sigma Executive Credenza, and this custom unit, veneered in oak, walnut, teak, or Carpathian elm burl, can store a great deal else. Behind touch-latched hinged doors, box and file drawers, dictation machine slides, and adjustable shelves are offered in seven different compartment configurations. Stendig, Inc.

❹ This custom-built console in a real estate office includes a telephone, calculator, audio system, and other controls. A CRT unit is installed on the left. All these systems are conveniently located behind the desk. Designed by dePolo/Dunbar.

❹

Accessories

Design solutions to office space must be viewed as total concepts. Every element of the design must be respected and must add to the total effect. Office accessories are the finishing touches. They complete the design statement and carry the style and character of the rest of the design elements to their logical conclusions.

Desk accessories can be special objects that give pleasure to the user as long as they carry out the design of the total office. Accessories are sometimes the only way that office users can control their own environments. They might be the only personal objects allowed in an organization where conformity is a goal. If your accessories are unique, they are a way to provide office visitors with information about you. Interesting accessories can also trigger informal conversation.

In addition to their design function, desk-top accessories perform specific tasks. Primarily, they can organize office clutter. You don't have to fumble for pens and pencils if they're at hand in a permanent location. Some pen sets are even equipped with secret microphones, adding to their usefulness in an unexpected way. Blotters, no longer necessary for drying up ink, are useful for reducing desk-top glare. Diaries, clocks, mail openers, scissors, paper-clip containers, and ashtrays organize office paraphernalia. In- and out-trays direct traffic flow as they organize.

①

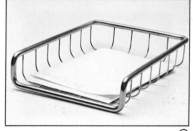

②

Choose accessories that are pleasant to touch and pleasant to look at. Well-designed accessories need not be expensive, and their effect can be crucial in the total office design. Repetitive elements,

③

especially in open offices, act as unifiers and tend to tie an interior together. Rather than many discrete elements, they can be seen as a design theme woven throughout the interior. Pentagram, a

design firm with London and New York offices, has carried out a design theme with the help of its office accessories while at the same time adopting a sort of business signature. They've managed this through the use of the color red. All of their office accessories, including wastepaper baskets, phones, and in- and out-trays are the same bright color red. In addition, exposed pipes in the offices are painted the same color. This device integrates the office space while giving it and the business a unique personality.

❶ *The custom-designed desk can double as a conference table, and accessories are kept to a minimum. Designed by Doris La Porte Associates.*

❷ *Prototype of a stainless steel outbasket by dePolo/Dunbar.*

❸ *A stainless steel pen holder for the desk by dePolo/Dunbar.*

❹ *The sculptural forms of these desk accessories echo the interior architecture in this office at Jones, New York. Designed by Juan Montoya.*

❺ *Scissors and ruler set designed by Vignelli Associates, Inc.*

❻ *An eclectic combination of furnishings and accessories that could easily be adapted for home use. The office of Patricia McMillan, vice president of a public relations firm, reflects the personal style of its occupant. The wall behind the desk is a bulletin board on which schedules, stories, and bits of design inspiration are hung. The Flexalum Decor Blinds are by Hunter Douglas, Inc.*

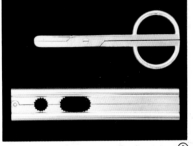

⑤

④

⑥

Lamps

A desk lamp is a sculptural accessory with a practical purpose: it carries out a design theme as well as lighting the desk top. In addition to its practical and design functions, a desk lamp has subtle psychological ramifications in the modern office. Simple as it may sound, being able to turn a lamp on or off humanizes the office environment. In pre-energy-conscious days, a master switch controlled whole floors of overhead lighting fixtures. A desk lamp saves on energy as well as allowing office occupants to control their own light.

Desk lamps can play a major role in creating atmosphere in an office. Because the desk lamp is at eye level, it gives a more intimate feeling to the room. Moreover, an eye-level light source is more flattering to the face than over-head lighting, which can create harsh contours.

Also, desk lamps must comple-ment the design of your office. Architect's drafting lamps have a classic beauty, although they may be considered too utilitarian by some people. A change in lamp shade can dramatically alter the appearance of the lamp. Remem-ber that a lamp can take up precious space on the desk top, and pay special attention to the size of the lamp base. When choosing a desk lamp, you should also bear in mind the electrical outlets in your office. If your desk is free standing in the center of the room, for example, managing the electrical wires can be a bit of a problem unless you've specified a floor outlet at the desk location.

Of course, the most important function of a desk lamp is to illuminate the work surface. Most desk lamps are adjustable and are light enough to be moved around until the optimum illumination with minimum shadow and glare is achieved. Since the light source of a desk lamp is at eye level, a shade is required to eliminate glare. Some lamps are designed with lenses that prevent veiling reflections: they direct light so that it does not bounce back into your eyes from the lighted surface.

Some offices have overhead fluorescent lighting that can be harsh. You may remove the tubes in these overhead luminaires and rely solely on your desk lamp for illumination. You'll have to use a lamp that provides some indirect light for background illumination so as to reduce light contrast ratios, a source of eye fatigue. You can provide this indirect light by using a translucent shade or by using a lamp that casts some light at the ceiling as well as the work surface.

Desk lamps can be equipped with incandescent or fluorescent lights. Incandescent light gives a warm quality and is preferred by most people.

①

②

④

③

❶ Tizio lamps, designed for Artemide by Richard Sapper, have a counterweight system and a swiveling base to make them adjustable to nearly any angle within a 37-inch (1-m) arm-reach. A high-low switch controls light intensity.

❷ Both desks in this office at Creative Perspectives have a local source of light from traditionally styled architectural lamps. The light directed by the flared shades covers a wide area. The lamps supplement the dramatic lighting provided by the track lights on the ceiling.

❸ Tiffany lamps are as much a source of light as they are art objects. The handsome lamp in Richard Golub's office matches the Tiffany accessories on his desk.

❹ At Associated Metals and Minerals, the lighting was designed to meet the client's demand for an energy-efficient lighting scheme. Local control of lighting was provided for all work areas and individual offices to keep energy consumption at the level required for work. Architect: Jack L. Gordon.

Plants

Plants are living sculptures. They bring color, texture, and a variety of form into the office. They enliven interior spaces by softening the regular geometry of buildings and furniture. In addition to their visual charms, plants bring some of the intangible delights of the outdoors into the office. They foster interest and provide the satisfaction of nurturing something and watching it grow and flourish. They are a welcome natural element in an artificial environment.

Color, texture, pattern, and shape are the design criteria for matching a plant to an office. A plant supplier (who usually also handles maintenance) can provide detailed information, including photographs, on a wide variety of plants that will grow well in your office environment. Fortunately, most plants thrive in the environment of an office where temperature, humidity, and lighting levels are well controlled.

If you feel you need specialized help in selecting your office plants, you can avail yourself of the services of an interior plantscaper.

①

Placement is the key to keeping office plants thriving. A dying plant will spoil any interior. But proper placement will go a long way in ensuring good results.

Proper lighting is crucial. The position of the plant in relation to windows as well as the amount of direct and indirect sunlight from those windows will affect the office plant. Some plants must have natural light while others can survive very well on artificial lighting. With the latter, artificial lights attached to timers can regulate light on weekends.

Because plants can be damaged by toxic fumes from paints or other chemicals, be sure to schedule the installation of interior finishings so that plants are the last items to arrive.

The availability of water is an important consideration in the selection of office plants. The best way to maintain plants is to make it easy to water them. Plants placed on a high shelf or suspended overhead might prove difficult to water. Moreover, plants hung high off the floor tend to dry out more quickly and therefore need more frequent watering.

Plants in the office have definite design functions. In fact, when the first open-plan office was introduced in Germany it was called **Burolandschaft**, or office landscape. Plants were used profusely, and several species were combined for maximum density. They were used to screen areas, to define circulation routes, and to separate work stations. They were also used to identify status by setting apart an executive area. Plants still perform all these functions in today's office.

Make sure that your plants are in proportion to the size of their surroundings—a plant that is too large will dominate a space while a too-small specimen will be inconsequential. And, of course, plants grow, so maintenance should include clipping and pruning to keep the size constant. Plants can be used alone or grouped for different effects. When you group plants, you can repeat the same shapes or use different ones in combinations.

Plant placement is very important. In large groupings, plants, along with color and graphics, give identity to large areas or whole floors. Like works of art or other display items, plant locations should be thought out in the design stage so that considerations can be made for lighting and water availability. Remember that in addition to lighting for growing purposes, lighting can be used to bring out the sculptural qualities of plants. For example, up-lights on the floor can give a plant a dramatic presence.

The planter is also a design element—it should be an appropriate size and shape for the plant and must complement the interior design. Also, the planter should be large enough to hold the original nursery container. This prevents the shock of transplant, and it facilitates removal if the plants must be replaced. Some designs require built-in planters complete with their own water supply. Self-watering planters, which cut down on maintenance, are available. Make sure that planters are watertight to prevent leaks and ruined floors. The planters should be on glides or casters so that the plants can be easily relocated.

Placement of Plants for Plant Maintenance

Low Intensity Areas— plants can be placed just about anywhere with a task/ambient lit space, some discretion required.

Chamaedorea:
    Neanthe Bella Palm

Dracaena:
    Janet Craig Dracaena
    Warneckei Dracaena
    Corn Plant
    Madagascar Dragon Tree

Howeia:
    Kentia Palm
    Paradise Palm

Philodendron:
    Cordatum
    Heartleaf Philodendron

Scindapsus:
    Devil's Ivy
    Pothos

Spathiphyllum:
    Golden Pothos
    White Flag
    Peace Lily

②

When considering plants for the office, don't forget cut flowers. While generally more expensive than potted plants, cut flowers are an unfailing source of delight. Cut flowers are also very potent: you don't need a large formal arrangement to make an impact. One or two brightly colored flowers can enliven any office. Be sure to change cut flowers frequently so as not to let them wilt.

③

① *Many people make the mistake of using small plants when a bigger one would be more appropriate. Here, a ficus tree sets off a secretarial area at Genatt Associates. The tree is large enough to be in scale with the space around it. Designer: Robert K. Lewis Associates.*

② *Planters can also define a space, and their shape, size, and material can be strong decorative elements. These handsome ceramic planters add character to this office space. Ron Collier and Associates.*

③ *These formal palm trees act as columns, announcing the corridor at Thomson Travel in London. The exotic palm also has a symbolic association for a travel agency. Designed by Trickett Associates.*

④ *Plants are an important part of the architectural environment at Central Beheer. Cared for by employees, plants can humanize the working environment in any office. Architect: Hermann Hertzberger.*

Medium Intensity Areas— plants must be placed within four feet, or closer, of any fixture with a down-light component.

Fuchsia:
  Fuchsia
  Lady's Eardrops

Primula:
  Primrose
  Polyanthus Primrose

Sinningia:
  Gloxinia

Senecio:
  Cineraria

Begonia:
  Painted Leaf Begonia

Brassaia:
  Schefflera
  Umbrella Tree

Cacti:

Chamaedorea:
  Bamboo Palm
  Reed Palm

Chrysalidocarpus:
  Areca Palm

Cissus:
  Kangaroo Palm
  Grape Ivy

Dieffenbachia:
  Giant Dumb Cane
  Tropic Snow
  Exotic Dieffenbachia
  Gold Dieffenbachia

Ficus:
  Weeping Fig
  Fiddleleaf Fig
  Indian Laurel
  Abidjan

Wideleaf Rubber Plant
Variegated Rubber Plant

Hedera:
  Needlepoint Ivy
  Glacier Ivy

Nephrolepis:
  Boston Fern
  Tall Feather Fern
  Lace Fern

Philodendron:
  Emerald Queen Philodendron
  Laciniatum
  Split-Leaf Philodendron
  Red Princess Philodendron

Plectranthus:
  Swedish Ivy
  Candle Plant
  Prostrate Swedish Ivy

④

High Intensity Areas— Plants must be within one foot of the fluorescent down-light component, or must receive direct light from an H.I.D. or Fluorescent fixture (as in a hanging planter).

Begonia:
  Wax Begonia

Chrysanthemum

Cyclamen

Asparagus:
  Sprenger Fern
  Plumosa Fern

Chlorophytum:
  Spider Plant

Crassula:
  Jade Plant

Dizygotheca:
  False Aralia
  Spider Aralia

Fatsia:
  Japanese Aralia

Phoenix:
  Dwarf Date Palm

Polyscias:
  Balfour Aralia
  Ming Aralia

All Succulents

Art in the Office

Today, corporations are playing a role that was filled by the church in Medieval times. Corporations are becoming major patrons of the arts. Their patronage is expressed in offices filled with pictures and objects that add a sophisticated touch to the environment. "I see this as a tremendous amenity," says Mar-

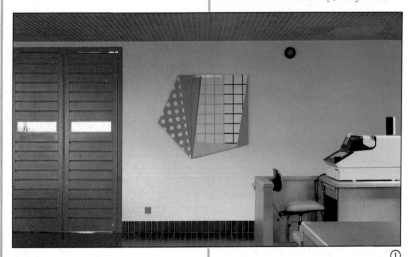

vin Affrime of the Space Design Group. "So few people get to live with art. It's wonderful to bring art into the mainstream. People can see it as they walk down the corridors, as they enter the building, as they're having lunch. It tells them that a corporation cares for their cultural pleasure."

An art program for an office must be determined in the early planning stages so that budget allowances can be made, and the finishes and lighting can be designed with artwork in mind. A new breed of office expert—the art consultant—will advise an organization about its collection.

The most often heard advice is to buy for the pleasure and enjoyment of the organization and the people in it.

The art budget is an organizational decision. But even where museum-quality pieces are beyond the budget, you should buy the best quality possible in any given price range. Organizations with smaller budgets are often tempted by posters even though they have no intrinsic value and cost the same to frame as more valuable works. Concerning an office art budget, designer Doris La Porte said, "I'd rather buy less expensive furniture and spend more on art and accessories, if I had the choice. Nobody's going to get excited about a sofa, but a painting is a learning experience."

Remember that office art need not be limited to any particular medium. Folk art, photography, and any type of graphic piece can form the basis of a collection. Even the company logo or a display of products can be conceived and provided for as art objects if they are visually attractive. And don't forget that furniture, including desks, tables, and armoires, can be considered art and have a functional as well as a decorative place in the office.

The most important consideration for art in the office is that it be well displayed. The size should be appropriate to the wall it's on; the colors should harmonize with those of the interior spaces; and it should be well lit so that it can be properly seen. Artificial light should not distort the color. This means that locations for art are usually determined in advance. Good potential locations include the end of an axis, along a corridor, and above a credenza.

Scale of the art object must relate to the space that it's in. A painting on a wall that several people face in a large open area has to be strong enough to "read" for those far away, yet at the same time interesting for those who walk up to it.

Decisions must be made about installation heights so that there is a consistency throughout the office. Will the paintings or prints be rotated or will they remain in one place? If they are to be moved, you will want to avoid nail holes. A picture molding can provide flexibility for art that is to be regularly rearranged.

In addition to installation height and placement, you must consider how the art is to be framed. Do you want to use a single frame finish consistently or would you prefer a variety of frame styles? If you decide on a variety of styles, you must be sure they complement one another.

Environmental sculpture can serve as office art in addition to graphics. Sculpture includes

large-scale three-dimensional objects that modify a space as well as small precious objects that have personal meaning for the owner. Sculptures are more unusual in office interiors because they ordinarily take up valuable floor space.

Careful attention must be given to the display of sculpture in the office. Sculpture bases are important. They shouldn't overpower the piece. Proper lighting will bring out the contours and textures of a sculpture. Incandescent lights, a point source, are better than fluorescent lights, which don't have any punch.

④

⑤

③

❶ For IBM Basingstoke, artist Sue Ridge was commissioned to create a series of artworks she refers to as her enamels. The works feature a grid pattern that echoes something the artist saw in the design of the building. Subtle colors were used so that the enamels wouldn't conflict with the primary colors Michael Aukett chose for the interiors.

❷ To preserve the 16th-century frescoes in his Rome office, Architect Evaristo Nicolau made a graphic design of the exposed electrical wires.

❸ Mario Bellini's office is on the top floor of a converted convent in Milan. A photomural of the cloister below covers his office wall. Real sculpture contrasts with the photographic illusion. Architect Bellini designed all the furniture.

❹ The executive floor corridor at International Paper showcases some of the artwork that has been acquired through the corporation's active art program. The Space Design Group, who designed the headquarters, selects the art, a unique collection of works of wood or paper—gentle reminders that forest products and paper are the business of IP. Many corporations sponsor similar art programs organized around different themes: regional artists, folk art, textiles, and so on. Shown here is a Japanese mulberry paper collage by Maud Morgan and a wood sculpture by Pino Pedano.

❺ This private office in Arlington Virginia was designed as a neutral background for a fine collection of 20th-century art. The Calder mobile is silhouetted against the window on a raised platform. Designed by dePolo/Dunbar.

Designing Office Spaces

Chapter 4

Entrance Doors

You enter an office long before you get to the front door: You bring a bundle of impressions to that door as you walk through the neighborhood to reach the building; as you pass through the lobby; and as you wait for the elevator. So that front door either confirms those impressions or dispels them.

You expect the image of the entrance door to be carried through in the design scheme beyond. That announcement could be billboard bold, a large environmental graphic, or it could be super discreet. Perhaps double doors have been used, expressing exclusivity. Or perhaps the door is made of glass and frames interior views that entice visitors.

Next, you reach for the door handle, shaking hands with the firm. Finally, you enter.

Apart from symbolism, the door has other functions. First, it must conform to fire regulations. Secondly, the door, as well as its frame, should be secure, providing protection against break-ins and thefts. Thirdly, if your office has no mail room, a mail slot could be incorporated in the door's design, for mail delivered out of hours. A heavy door may be impressive, and level changes architecturally intriguing, but both should be avoided because they will inconvenience handicapped visitors. For the sake of the handicapped, too, lever handles should be easily manipulable. Finally, the entrance door could be equipped with a buzzer so that the receptionist, without having to leave the desk, can open the door from within.

①

The materials an entrance door is made of is important. Doors should be durable and cleanable. Metal pushes, pulls, and lever handles are easily cleaned and give a solid feeling to that metaphorical handshake with the firm. Hinges, pulls, and stops can also add to the effectiveness of the entrance.

②

③

④

❶ The "D" on the entrance door to Dexter Design is both the company's logo and the push that swings the door open. This small office is so well designed and space-efficient that it gives the appearance of a much larger work area.

❷ A standard-size door is converted into a billboard graphic for Garey Shirtmakers by affixing the company's logo to the side of the entrance door. The space is further increased by the door swing on the floor. Designed by Gwathmey Siegel and Associates.

❸ Special pivot hardware was installed to operate this super-large entrance door. The image created by this entranceway, both posh and impressive, is another example of the front door functioning as an introduction to the company. Designed by Christopher Owen.

❹ Fire regulations in England specify that entrance doors be made, at least partially, of glass and that they swing out into the corridor. Built to conform with these laws, the entrance to Lindustries also incorporates lighting into the door design. Designed by Planning Unit.

❺ Instead of a graphic logo, this massive glass door serves as an introduction to BEA, Citicorp's offices. Continuous lighting and flooring also opens the expanse of offices seen from the elevator. Fire doors are concealed on either side of the reception desk. In the event of fire, the hidden door would slide out of the core recesses and barricade the offices, providing a regulation area of refuge for employees. Architect: Tod Williams.

❻ This oversized wooden door and its symmetrical accessories set the stage for the traditional decor within the offices of Allied Chemical. Designed by Ellen L. McCluskey Associates.

⑤

⑥

Reception Areas

Desk Area: The receptionist's desk affirms the entrance door's message: You have arrived, and this is what we are like. The desk the receptionist sits behind to greet visitors establishes the company's style immediately. As such, the desk's position must be prominent, but also one from which the receptionist has direct visual contact with the front door, to see who is coming in. The desk shouldn't sit above floor level, obliging visitors to look up into the receptionist's face. The receptionist is there to greet, not to judge.

Imagine the Statue of Liberty as an office building. This may give some idea of the double function the receptionist's desk serves. An emblem of welcome, it is also a place where work is done. It must be functional and at the same time convey the company's image. Packages, messages, mail, and incoming calls—all are received here, not to mention visitors. In smaller offices, the desk should be equipped with a buzzer controlling the entrance door as well as a small pass-through for parcels. The telephone is essential. Cubby holes, each labelled with an employee's name, are useful and convenient repositories for messages. If the receptionist types, the typewriter should be placed so that the receptionist has enough privacy to concentrate and enough light to see the task at hand. Finally, television monitors may be provided for security purposes or for calling up information, such as addresses or frequently called phone numbers, from a computer's memory bank.

①

②

③

Despite all this, the receptionist's desk must stand as an island of calm, far removed from the chaos outdoors. A short raised screen between the visitor and the cluttered desk behind it will provide the receptionist with a place to fix reminders, messages, often-called telephone numbers, and so on. The desk should not be overly inviting. As opposed to other desks in the office, the receptionist's is no mere convenient horizontal surface. Visitors (and employees, too, for that matter) should not be tempted to dump things there. A raised surround will clearly discourage this.

Seating Area: In his play *Waiting for Godot*, Samuel Beckett presents the human condition as one of perpetual anticipation of someone or something that fails to materialize. While this might strike you as less than congenial, the truth is that some part of our lives is spent, to a certain degree, waiting, often enough in the reception area of an office.

Here, though, the situation need not be so bleak as that of Beckett's lost souls. Special lighting, somewhat moody rather than task-oriented, can at once indicate the actual seating area and create visual pleasure for visitors. Flooring that is different from that used throughout the office, and perhaps different from the flooring around the receptionist's desk could further define this space.

Of course, seating is absolutely necessary here. Comfortable seating enhances the welcome already established at the entrance. Seating might be built-in or provided for by a quartet of Mies van der Rohe's Barcelona chairs, two on either side of a steel-and-glass coffee table (the ultimate cliche of waiting-room luxury). As most visitors will be strangers; they will feel least awkward in individualized seats—separate chairs or, at least, separate cushions. At ease, the visitor must nevertheless be kept alert because there is business to get through. Seating that is neither too low nor too soft will get this point across. Indeed, some companies go so far as to furnish their reception areas with backless benches in which visitors won't care to linger for long. Fabrics must be durable because in any busy day, seating is in for

④

considerable wear and tear.

Walls give a company the chance to show off a little. A handsome logo cries corporate identity, while display cases or shelves featuring the company's products will further serve to impress. Fine art—paintings, drawings, or prints attractively framed and judiciously hung—could proclaim a company's wealth and taste. These embellishments will also offer visitors something to look at while they wait. As for magazines, these are most appropriate in the offices of doctors and dentists, where anxious patients need as much distraction as they can get.

In smaller offices with lighter traffic, the reception area can serve as a conference area as well, equipped with table and chairs. While this may not be the most formal of arrangements, it is certainly a practical one, and it saves space.

⑤

❶ The color scheme in this British Graduate Appointments Office is bright, cheerful, and friendly. The specially built reception desk effectively hides clutter from view. Designed by Pierre Bötschi.

❷ An industrial worktable is custom-converted into a reception desk at the offices of The Kooper Group. Industrial light fixtures hang from cables purchased at a marine suppy house and plastic stick-on letters spell out the name of the firm. Behind the free-standing wall is a Xerox machine. Designed by Eisenman and Enock, Inc.

❸ Barcelona chairs are a classic symbol of corporate luxury. But at the offices of General Felt Industries, Knoll International (producers and distributors of the chairs) the furniture also serves as corporate identity. Reception area designed by Charles Pfister of SOM.

❹ Utilitarian functions can be built into beautiful furniture. This oak message unit is part of a reception desk designed by Judith Stockman and Lee Manners.

❺ Reception areas are sometimes enclosed for either security or privacy. The receptionist at the offices of FMI controls the visitor's access to the inner offices. This particular area works well because it is part of the business office but the receptionist is not entirely isolated from coworkers. Mural designed by Sue Ridge. Architect: DEGW.

❻ Visitors to Creative Perspectives, a design firm, are by appointment only, so this reception area doubles as a conference room. Designed by Richard Orbach and Lynn Jacobson.

⑥

Executive Suites

Like the reception area, an office's executive suite—comprised of the board room, the chief executive's offices, and private conference rooms—serves two purposes: It is where a company's key people meet and work and the symbol of success, status, and power. When located on a high floor (or at least on the point) more expensive-looking variety—might be employed in its executive suite. Oak remains constant throughout the office, but its significance changes. High ceilings, a spaciousness the rest of the office lacks, and generously proportioned furniture could further advertise corporate self-confidence.

The executive suite is not for visitors' eyes only. It reminds the executives themselves of their positions within the company. They see themselves surrounded by visual (and symbolic) confirmation of their own importance.

A secondary reception area at the threshold of the executive suite—a smaller-scaled, and possibly posher version of the main one—can add to the aura of grandeur.

①

uppermost floor of the several a company might occupy), the executive suite is literally something to be aspired to—the proverbial room at the top.

An approach to this part of the office could easily be ceremonious. Showmanship and luxury could be in order to let visitors know they are entering a special place where momentous events occur with breathtaking frequency. Costly materials signify power. For example, if an office is panelled in red oak, English oak—a more expensive and (more to the

②

③

④

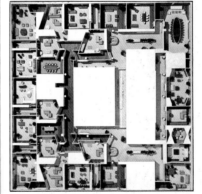

⑤

❶ Walnut-burl desks are both impressive and functional in this executive secretary area at Smith Kline. The wide open expanse of space creates a pleasant working environment. Designed by Daroff Design, Inc.

❷ This waiting area in the Smith Kline lobby matches the executive floor. The Barcelona-like chairs and the lavish tapestry by Helena Hernmark create a comfortable and inviting seating area for visitors. Designed by Daroff Design, Inc.

❸ Part of the same project detailed in illustration number 5, these enclosed telephone booths are located outside the board room and are a pleasant amenity for visitors. The booths provide privacy for visitors who need to communicate with their home offices during sessions of the corporate board meetings. Designed by The Space Design Group.

❹ Some executive floors use corridor space for executive secretarial areas. The art, wood ceilings, wallpaper, and generous use of space create an extraordinarily pleasant environment. Even the files are concealed behind custom woodwork. Designed by Ellen L. McCluskey Associates.

❺ International Paper's executive floor is shown in this model. The white spaces denote service areas such as elevators and kitchen space. The model shows all board and conference rooms, private offices, and secretarial areas. Placement of desks and chairs is meticulously planned. Space for the telephone booths as shown in photograph number 3 appears in the upper-right-hand corner of the model. Designed by The Space Design Group.

The executive secretary's desk, aside from its practical functions, should be an impressive one. The person who sits behind it is a denizen (if no deity) of a company's Mount Olympus, and someone most executives would be lost without.

Status symbol or not, executive secretaries have a job to do—or, rather, several of them. The desk they occupy no matter how sumptuous, must be one equipped for the full range of secretarial activities, and the chair must be a

Executive Secretary Areas

secretarial chair. If bookkeeping is one of the secretarial duties, the desk should have ample ledger space. If the executive's office itself has no files, the secretary's desk should be placed near them, to provide easy access.

As executive secretaries often go about their jobs in the corridors just outside executive offices, good desk lighting and proper ventilation is essential for them.

In addition to paperwork, executive secretaries must deal with people, too. So, the desk and chair should be placed for direct eye contact with the executive. The desk should be positioned for executive secretaries to protect the entrance to the boss' office and screen visitors, as well as calls. Despite this guardian-of-the-gate role, executive secretaries should never sit at a desk in the direct path of office traffic, where messengers might mistake them for the receptionists and drop parcels

there. Comedies of errors involving executive secretaries mistaken for receptionists can be further avoided by locating the former's desk in an enclosed area.

It should be noted that executive secretaries' function and status are changing, a state of affairs bound to affect design considerations pertaining to this company employee.

❶ This custom-designed work station creates a private office within an open space. The free-standing wall of this executive secretary's office at Barber Oil is made up of files that provide protection from distraction by people passing by in the corridor. Although the enclosure provides adequate privacy, it is also highly visible to both her employer and visitors. Designed by Gwathmey Siegel and Associates.

❷ A former California warehouse was converted to office space for Coca-Cola. The high-tech design includes an exposed ceiling, skylights, and colorful graphics. The desks were staggered on a diagonal to ensure privacy. Designed by Barry Brukoff Interiors, Inc.

❸ At the law offices of Brobeck, Phlager and Harrison, custom enclosures provide privacy and hide desk clutter. The free-standing walls create two circulation lanes. On the left, a wide lane for heavy traffic, and on the right, a smaller lane provides access to both the files and the executive offices. Designed by M. Arthur Gensler Jr. and Associates.

❹ Video monitors are becoming increasingly common in offices. At Smith Kline, a guard station in the building's lobby contains security monitory devices for the headquarters. The cameras monitor people entering the building.

❺ A bronze glass wall behind the reception desk on the executive floor hides a monitor that informs visitors of the conference meeting schedules and carries an inhouse program. The unit is not visible when it's not in use. Designed by Daroff Design, Inc.

Board Rooms

①

②

③

More than any other room in an office, the board room is the embodiment of a company's inner workings, the tangible manifestation of a corporate entity. Unlike other office interiors, the board room, on general policy rarely is used for anything else but meetings. Like other office interiors, it can declare a company's status. But, more importantly, design here expresses a corporate activity as much as it conveys status. The board room's layout—its unifying table surrounded by a family of chairs—is the expression, in design, of how a company is run.

The board room could be off a smaller reception room, for conversation and informal business, as well as a place in which to wait. Direct access to the board room from the main entrance is advisable, and adjacency to toilet rooms is a necessity.

The board room itself should be in its design, an impressive environment that will encourage board members to rise to the occasion. Frivolous decor should be avoided—it is as uncalled for in this serious space as is frivolous behavior.

The room is dominated by the conference table and the chairs around it, which together constitute the arena of corporate decision-making. The table should be 29 inches (74 cm) high, though 26 inches (66 cm) is now coming into fashion. Various table shapes lend themselves to board meetings. A round table is most suitable for up to 12 people, while a rectangular table is best for up to 20. For more than 20 people, various table shapes are recommended: boat-shape, U-shape, circle, oval, or triangle. The design and shape of the board-room table can express company hierarchy by emphasizing different seating positions.

As for the chairs, these should be comfortable, fairly soft seats for hard thinkers. Less commodious observers' chairs may be lined up against the walls.

In addition to the obvious table and chairs, a considerable battery of audiovisual equipment might be necessary in board rooms if presentations are to be made. Screens, if there are any, should be visible from every seat in the room. Some may require small projection rooms just off the board room; for others, rear-screen projection suffices. Taping facilities are useful if not a word

① Portraits of the founders of the Philadelphia National Bank adorn the walls outside the board room. The space serves as a waiting area for visitors who make presentations to the board.

② Inside the same board room, a circular table unites 25 board members by eliminating the hierarchy imposed by a square table. Lighting fixtures are custom designed, and the tapestry is by Sonia Delauney. Designed by The Space Design Group.

③ Muted colors, curved chairs, and sleek design create a comfortable environment for long meetings. The Rotunda chairs are used as a design theme throughout the offices of Xoil Energy Resources, Inc. Designed by Vignelli Associates.

④ Individual microphones are raised by a separate platform to ensure that all speakers will be heard in the board room of Shell International's London offices. The grill conceals a projection room. Designed by Buzas and Irvine.

⑤

⑥ The Hotel van Eetvelde in Brussels was designed by Victor Horta. One of its grand rooms is now used as the board room by the Gas Board.

⑥ The conference table in the board room at ATT Long Lines is made of a synthetic that looks like lacquer yet is stain-proof and durable. The table is made in sections so that it can easily be rearranged. Adjacent to the board room is an executive waiting room. Architect: Kohn Pederson Fox. Interior design: dePolo/Dunbar.

⑦ In the same board room, an English oak lectern matches the finish of the walls. Controls for audiovisual presentations and room lighting are built into the lectern, and the top bar conceals a small reading light. Designed by dePolo/Dunbar.

⑦

④

of the meeting is to be lost, while microphones are useful in large board rooms where every word spoken must be heard by all present. Telephones should be placed in a separate area.

Air conditioning in the board room itself must keep the air fresh, smoke- and body-odor free, especially since such rooms often have far less window space than more frequently used areas.

Executive Dining Rooms

With rich materials and striking design, the executive dining room can convey a sense of exclusivity, telling those who dine here that they have earned their right to do so—and that the company can afford to take good care of its personnel.

Aside from its symbolic value, though, the executive dining room saves time. If the room is attractive, execs won't want to go out to lunch, which means that they will have to spend less time out of the office. Cost-effective dining rooms like these (some of which even include bars) also provide pleasant surroundings, a welcome change of pace.

There are times, though, when work-related matters make eating here a not entirely social occasion. In such cases, the executive dining room can double as an executive conference room.

The executive dining room should be near the kitchen and should be provided with ample space for storage. No matter how lavish the design, it must not be a difficult room to clean. Proper ventilation is essential, as are durable fabrics on the chairs. The dining room should be situated so that most noise does not filter in from outside.

①

②

❶ The simple style of traditional Early American furniture creates a friendly, homelike atmosphere in this executive dining room, reflecting the personal preference of Joseph E. Brooks, chairman of the board of Lord & Taylor.

❷ To visually enlarge a small interior executive dining room, one wall was panelled with mirrors. The table is actually two units; it can expand to seat 14, or it can be separated to accommodate two smaller groups of diners. The cast-paper relief is by Louise Nevelson. Designed by Daroff Design, Inc. for NEHO Prudential.

❸ Elegant goblets from a line of glassware designed by Vignelli Associates for CIGAHOTELS.

❹ In most offices, valuable corner space is reserved for the private office of the highest executive. However, at Chase Manhattan Bank the corner space is used for an executive dining room. Consequently, diners are treated to a spectacular view of the city. Designed by Skidmore, Owings and Merrill.

❺ The Space Design Group wanted a dining room that would put their clients at ease; a social rather than a corporate space. An intimately scaled dining room was created with the use of low seating and a square table. The space also doubles as a conference room. Designed by The Space Design Group.

Employee Cafeterias

As more and more people come to work in offices, companies are paying closer attention to the quality of office life on all levels. A well-designed and pleasant-looking employee cafeteria presents an opportunity for the firm to show the people working for them how much they matter. The very look of this large room will communicate a good deal about how a firm views its employees.

Like the executive dining room, the employee cafeteria offers a change of pace within the office environment. However, while the decor might be seductive, it should not be overly so. Rather, the tone set could be lively so that dining becomes a kind of pick-me-up. Aside from sensible layout and attractive decor (not to mention good food), a view from a large window is desirable here as well, especially if people spend most of their day at work in windowless interior spaces.

Although a company need not go overboard with its employee cafeteria, certain requirements must be met for this room to succeed. First, there should be a variety of seating. Some prefer to eat lunch in groups, others prefer a more confidential tete-a-tete, while still others wish to maintain their privacy and eat alone. Office life may be regimented, but dining in the office need not be. Secondly, acoustics should keep noise levels down. Many conversations will occur here. They should not merge into an uproar. Thirdly, the cafeteria should be well-ventilated, to prevent food odors from lingering. Fourthly, floors here, if not tiled, should be covered in antimicrobial carpet, that will further reduce odors and prevent mildew. As for kitchen layout and machinery, a food consultant will be able to offer the employer or designer the most salient advice.

Smaller firms may find big, elaborate spaces beyond their means if not altogether unnecessary. Still, they might provide lunch rooms for their employees. Attractively designed, these can prove to be pleasant amenities, as well as time-savers.

①

❶ The staff restaurant at BP Limited's Britannic House is visually expanded with a mural by Edward Bawden. Designed by DRU.

❷ Partitions and wide corridors divide a very large space for 300 diners into smaller areas. The deliberate use of natural woods is a design theme used throughout the headquarters of International Paper, which produces paper products. Designed by The Space Design Group.

❸ The employee cafeteria at the West Office Building of Deere and Company was designed to glitter. Glass tables catch reflections from centerpiece light fixtures/flower containers, glassware, flatware, and the overhead silk swags. Designed by Kevin Roche John Dinkeloo and Assoc.

❹ An interior space can be expanded with a wall mural. At Smith Kline, photomurals by Elliott Kaufman serve this purpose. Each floor at Smith Kline contains its own lunch room for employees, so a different photo was commissioned for each space. Designed by Daroff Design, Inc.

❺ The stand-up lounge at IBM World Trade Americas/Far East Corporation headquarters is for brown-bag lunches or snacks from nearby vending machines. The collage of flags, assembled by Charmayeff and Geismar Associates, becomes an abstract mural. Designed by Edward Larabee Barnes, FAIA.

Executive Bars and Baths

Executive baths, replete with sauna, steam room, and exercise apparatus, are the last word in luxury. Here, lavish materials such as marble, chrome, and expensive tiles are in order, as are towels with the company logo on them. Some might argue that busy executives actually need such baths when they are on the go and must relax for three-quarters of an hour before the next nerve-wracking, high-pressure appointment. The truth is that these rooms are status symbols, pure and simple, and should be treated as such. Installing a special bathroom in an office building is expensive enough because it entails the addition of new plumbing and a hot water heater (in most buildings, wet columns carry only cold water); venting fixtures; and having to raise the floor for toilet and shower waste lines. If a firm decides to go through with all that, it might as well go all the way with the decor, but its existence shouldn't be too obvious.

The executive bar—a room in itself, concealed behind cabinet-work or only a large closet—is a luxury proclaiming status and wealth (particularly in offices of the entertainment industry). The bar might be located in the waiting area outside the board room, in the conference room, or in an executive lounge. In any case, if the bar is a wet bar (that is, one including a sink), it must be situated near a wet column. A dry bar (one with no running water) is somewhat less opulent and might be thought of as a glorified liquor cabinet. Small refrigerators are useful in both wet and dry bars.

①

②

③

④

⑤

⑥

⑦

❶ At Jones New York, an executive bar is connected to the conference room. The bar is built into a semicircular, free-standing divider that offers privacy in the office space behind it. Designed by Juan Montoya.

❷ A bar is built into a wall recess in the executive lounge at International Paper. Designed by The Space Design Group.

❸ A prefabricated, compact bathroom designed by the Farrell/Grimshaw Partnership consists of a stainless steel lavatory, a warm-air dryer, and a water heater.

❹ This executive bath is replete with symbols of corporate status, including towels monogrammed with the company logo and lots of marble. A handy phone extension is also provided. Designed by Christopher Owen.

❺ The most provocative design element of the bathroom in Pentagram's Manhattan office is the spectacular view of the Flatiron Building. An historic New York landmark, the Flatiron Building is perfectly framed by the large window. Architect: Katrin Adam.

❻ General Felt Industries/Knoll International commissioned the last word in luxury with this executive bath. Recessed lights frame a wall of mirrors, and polished black granite is used throughout. Designed by Charles Pfister of Skidmore, Owings and Merrill.

❼ The high-gloss finish of this custom-designed bathroom unit is made of synthetic material, but it resembles a lacquered surface. It is both rich looking and very durable. The upper cabinet conceals a mirror and shelves for bathroom utensils such as electric razors. A handy electric towel-dryer is positioned to the right of the unit. Designed by dePolo/Dunbar.

Clerical and Operational Areas

Clerical and operational areas offer an opportunity for truly human design. More than any other part of the office, they are most in need of improvement. Although, perhaps, the duties clerks perform are often regimented and repetitive, this is no reason to assign them to spaces that only reinforce the regimentation and monotony. Many ideas as to how to make clerks at once happier and more productive workers through design are currently afloat, but there exist no hard and fast rules.

The main point in any design concerned with the clerical area is to give each individual a sense of personal control over the environment and personal involvement with it. If only within the limited space they occupy, office workers should be allowed the chance to express themselves—perhaps in the form of extra desk surface for framed photos or knickknacks and the like or a vertical surface for taping up reminders or other more lighthearted printed matter.

Intent on their typewriters, word processors, or video screens, operators may not only feel depersonalized, just another face in the typing pool, but isolated from their co-workers as well. This unnecessary condition can be remedied by positioning desks so that employees have eye contact with others around them (indeed, strong white-collar unions in Germany and Sweden have inisted upon it.) Operators must also have unobstructed peripheral vision, so as not to be taken by surprise when people come up to them. So that workers don't have their backs to oncoming office traffic,

unforeseen approaches can be avoided by placing desks to the side of circulation paths.

Breaking down a massive typing pool into small clusters will avoid the sensation of being swallowed up by a bureaucratic machine. Such small, more comprehensible units could instill their members with a team spirit. Files, which are good dividers, can be used to break up areas, and at the same time they can be designed to absorb sound. Their backs provide display surface for anything from office memoranda to more personal decorations. In any event, overcrowding a clerical area to the point of inducing claustrophobia is counterproductive whether it saves space or not.

The individual work station is a private domain. Lighting for it must be sufficient. The chair must be a good one, offering constant back support. The desk or work station should be selected for the activity or equipment. There are many different possibilites.

Proper height for equipment is essential so that office workers don't have to reach up or bend down (tables with adjustable heights should in theory eliminate whatever height problems present themselves). Also, desks should not be placed so close together that office workers cannot move without colliding into one another.

In general, clerical and operational areas must be wired for electric typewriters, telephones, computer terminals, and word processors. The latter should be placed in distraction-free, glare-free spaces surrounded by sound-absorbing material. Finally, proper ventilation should be provided.

①

②

❶ This multifunctional Lucas furniture system provides interlocking desks and incorporates the automation of clerical work. The system uses natural oak and steel to provide work surfaces, screens, and storage space. Designed by John Sager.

❷ Functional file cabinets are easily converted into desks in the New York offices of Pentagram. Additional storage is provided by overhead cabinets. The straightforward design of this small office affords enough space for two people to work comfortably. Interior work directed by Katrin Adam.

❸ Low storage cabinets define small groups within a vast word-processing department. Low-level lighting won't cause glare on the screens. Chairs are provided not for visitors but for inhouse staff to consult with the operators. Designed by Daroff Design, Inc. for Prudential.

❹ A detail from the same office, this name plate is an example of how almost any work space can be personalized, giving employees a sense of control over their environments. Designed by Daroff Design, Inc.

❺ Routine clerical tasks are prime candidates for automation. In changing the nature of office work, electronic data and word processing profoundly affects office design. Lighting levels, miles of cables, noisy printers, and an influx of programmers must be accommodated. This equipment, by Wang Laboratories, is in a showroom designed by SRC Design Organization, Inc.

❻ These work stations are part of an extension that was built onto the Deere and Company headquarters building. The aluminum ceiling reflects light directed upward from desk fixtures. The low-partition work stations in this totally open office floor overlook a skylit garden. Architects: Kevin Roche John Dinkeloo and Associates.

③

④

⑤

⑥

Corridors and Coat Closets

A corridor is a means to an end; it is also full of design opportunities where visual points can be scored with merely a shift in lighting levels or spatial proportions. As the most-used spaces in an office, corridors might also be the most intensively designed ones.

Aside from their function as transition spaces, corridors also provide convenient places for informal meetings.

One totally unsurprising element in a corridor is its coat closet. In the days of lockable private offices, these were not so necessary, but today the mass of workers with no offices of their own need secure places to stash their belongings before settling down to the morning's chores. To perk up a corridor, coat-closet doors might be wrapped in fabric for the sake of visual variety or made to stand out in some other way. Otherwise, freestanding wardrobe units that match other storage units can be employed, especially in open-plan offices. In full view, they provide security for personal belongings.

①

②

③

❶ Long, platform steps are accented by a deep reveal above the base of this corridor. The base details emphasize the change in levels and draw attention to the bar in the lobby beyond. Designed by The Space Design Group.

❷ A remarkable assortment of materials, textures, colors, and surfaces were used in the design of the Italian Trade Center in New York. One unifying theme, however, is a series of horizontal white bands that begin wide and far apart on the bottom floor and get narrower as they travel through the offices. Designed by Design Collaborative.

④

⑤

❸ Two side-by-side corridors on the executive floor at Smith Kline. The tinted-glass wall on the left conceals the fire stairs and service core. The right side is left free to be an art gallery. Designed by Daroff Design, Inc.

❹ A U-shaped corridor is visually straightened out by installing a mirror at a 45-degree angle. (The mirror also reflects a Duane Hansen sculpture.) The glass blocks allow daylight into an interior space. Designed by Susanna Torre.

❺ As part of the office landscape system at SuCrest Corporation, custom-made free-standing closets were built to line the corridors. Bold graph-

ics were used throughout the floor. Designed by Wayne Marcus.

❻ The right wall on this open-office floor at International Paper is the core wall for the building. By positioning closets at right angles and installing mirrors, the core wall virtually disappears. Designed by The Space Design Group.

❼ In the open-office floor at Pentagram, full-height gym lockers are used by employees for coats, umbrellas, and other paraphernalia. In addition, the lockers serve as floor partitions. Design directed by Katrin Adam.

⑥

⑦

Libraries

Office memoranda may come and go, but books remain. They should be treated with due consideration in the design of any office space. While some firms may prefer to keep their books on shelves arranged along a corridor's walls, others will want to set aside a room for them and make this their library.

The office library can figure as a design feature, in which case particular attention should be paid to the material used for shelves (metal is more economical, wood more luxurious—and more expensive). Indeed, shelves themselves can have an architectonic presence of their own, the books a multihued arrangement that will stand out. In law offices especially, it seems appropriate for weighty tomes to be displayed because they are a symbol of what the firm actually does.

Whether the library is shown off or kept from public view, a number of guidelines should be followed in its design. Ascertain, first, what the floor loads are. Once you know for sure that the floor will not cave in under the weight of the volumes with which you plan to stock your library, you can begin thinking in more specific terms. Adjustable shelves are the most efficient. Once the library starts burgeoning (as it inevitably does), more shelves can be squeezed in. To determine just how much actual shelf space you will need, reckon that approximately ten books take up about a foot of shelf. Also take into consideration varying book sizes because library shelves should be designed for books of all sizes (unless a firm has use only for textbooks, say, and knows perfectly well its library will never include the latest paperbacks). Special shelving will display books prominently to highlight works of particular interest.

Before deciding on an approach to the library space, determine exactly how the room is to be used. Will frequently consulted books be stored here or little-used records? Will people come in to sit down and research or purposefully browse? Once a library's function is set, a number of points should be borne in mind. If the library is to have both stack space and reading areas, each should have its own lighting. Reading areas—those where the most concentrated library work goes on—should provide people with enough room to spread out books and papers and with surfaces where out-sized reference works can be conveniently consulted. Here, tables and chairs are essential, but you might provide lounge chairs as well for those times when the weary reader wants to abandon books and take a break. Views, down corridors or out

①

windows, will offer further relief from the printed page.

Marshall McLuhan, the late communication specialist, suggested that books are becoming obsolete. Perhaps libraries devoted solely to books may be outmoded. So besides books, a firm may wish to store films, tapes, slides, or microfiche in its library, in which case special temperature and humidity controls should be included.

No matter what a library holds, some sort of cataloging and information retrieval systems are necessary. Such elements should also be incorporated into the design, whether they be assigned to card catalogues or computers. If computers are used to call up information (as they often are in sophisticated law offices, where the most obscure case can appear at the press of a button), the glare from their terminal screens should be deflected from the reading area.

Along with printed matter, office libraries should help researchers along their way. Pens, paper, and copying machines should be available and, perhaps, typewriters (these last two placed so that their distracting sounds can be muffled).

③

④

❶ *When the architectural firm of Hellmuth, Obata and Kassabaum designed their office in San Francisco, they placed their library in an open space underneath a bridge that connects to another level of the office. The library is easily accessible to everyone. Displayed on steel shelves, the books also serve to decorate the walls.*

❷ *An unusual feature of the Italian Trade Center in New York is the librarylike display of wine, Italy's biggest export. The use of contrasting colors and textures creates the illusion that this large area is broken up into two rooms. Behind the wine library is an elaborate bar area. Designed by Design Collaborative.*

❸ *In a small office like Dexter Design's, every inch of space is important. In order to get the most of their valuable space, a wall is converted into a functional place to house reference volumes. The wall library continues along the length of the corridor. Designed by Dexter Design.*

❹ *Of all the library spaces featured on this page, the research library at Standard Brands Research Center is the most traditionally designed. Here the library is a separate space that houses technical and reference volumes and current scientific reading. A glass-window wall divides the library from the second floor hall and provides a spot of light and color to an otherwise white environment. A touch of corporate identity is introduced by displaying a collection of artifacts from the early days of the company. Designed by Warren Platner Associates Architects.*

②

Conference Rooms

In a sense, conference rooms are like board rooms without the ceremonious atmosphere. Many of the same factors should be taken into consideration when designing them, such as special air-conditioning requirements (conference rooms, too, are often interior spaces); ancillary rooms for audiovisual equipment; telephone access; and the inclusion of a wet or dry bar.

But while board meetings may have an air of solemnity about them, conferences tend to be less formal affairs. It is at conferences that presentations are often made for the first time, issues are raised, discussed, and resolved.

The design of the conference room should provide a calm, neutral backdrop for visual presentations, with lighting that emphasizes the materials presented. If products are to be presented, they must be illuminated clearly and without color distortion. In addition to projection screens, the conference room could include a magnetic board and display walls on which to tack up material—these for the more nuts-and-bolts aspects of a presentation. In case of presentations that cannot be made over a table, there should be space to line chairs up auditorium-fashion—which means moveable chairs (and flooring across which chairs can be pushed with minimal effort).

It has been said that conferences of more than eight to ten people frequently go awry, partly due to its participants' being cramped together around a table whose vast expanse only encourages them to raise their voices higher and higher or encourages them not speak up at all. Smaller conferences, of five to ten people, work best when held around an oval table whose chairs—spaced neither too close nor too far apart from one another—pivot in all directions, enabling the other participants to politely face whomever is speaking. In addition, the conference room's walls should not encroach on the table.

③

①

②

⑤

⑥

④

tentious partly because it is exposed, but the friendly atmosphere is enhanced by the skylight, plants, and ceiling fan that decorate the area.

❹ The floor of the conference room at Nabisco Brands was raised so that the convector at the window would not obstruct the view for those seated at the leather-wrapped table. Silk wall panels conceal a rear projection screen. This space is also used for board meetings. Swanke Hayden Connell, Architects.

❺ Two wall mirrors face each other in the conference room at Richardson-Vicks headquarters. The mirrors serve a dual function: they visually expand the space and they reflect the Connecticut countryside. The conveniently placed bench provides alternative seating for long meetings. Designed by Kevin Roche John Dinkeloo and Associates.

❶ Detail of a conference-room plaque is part of an integrated signage system at Prudential Insurance Company. The device announces when the room is being used and prevents disturbing interruptions. Designed by Daroff Design, Inc.

❷ As a piece of furniture, the conference table can be designed in many different shapes and sizes. The multifaceted perimeter of this custom-designed table gives every person a special place. Designed by John Franklin.

❸ At the English firm of Farrell Grimshaw Partnership, a corner of their open office is used as a conference area. The space is relaxed and unpre-

❻ The high ceilings and huge windows at Weyerhauser Technology Center provide a truly spectacular view to almost everyone who works on this open-office floor. The conference area is set far enough away from the general work stations to prevent distraction from other employees and ensure privacy to those seated around the table. Architects: Skidmore, Owings and Merrill.

Files and Storage

Although pundits predict paper's eventual disappearance from offices throughout the world, the fact remains that today, it is still very much with us, if not overwhelming us altogether. American offices alone turn out 600 million pages of computer printout, 234 million photocopies, and 76 million letters in a single day, each office worker contributing his or her daily share of 45 sheets of paper to this veritable deluge. These millions and millions of pieces of paper constitute the heart of information that makes offices function. They cannot be done away with—at least not just yet. Despite much talk of paperless offices in the not-too-distant future, "hard copy" seems inescapable.

The question, then, is what to do with all this paper. It would be nice if you could just throw it all out when the day ended and start fresh the next morning, but of course, offices do not operate that way. The most common means of storing paper is the file cabinet. Built into wall space, as they are in many handsome integrated systems, file cabinets will match the rest of the decor and stand out as architectural elements. Color-coded, the files within can provide a certain visual interest. File cabinets should not have more than five drawers in them, unless your employees happen to be giants who can see into any top drawer, no matter how high.

One alternative to the file cabinet is the sort of storage system favored in Europe, where files are exposed on shelves and kept not in file folders but in binders. Another is a series of files on tracks, a space-saving solution in which one file can be slid aside so that a person can get to the file in back of it. Or perhaps you might opt for mobile files, in which dead files are whisked away while active ones are kept close at hand. Finally, you might consider transferring all files onto microfiche, which takes up less space than paper, while stowing the originals away in some remote location.

Hard copy may be unavoidable but computer tapes offer a very compact means of storing records. The information filling 10,000-filing-inches' worth of paper (which take up approximately 728 square feet) can be transferred to computer tapes that take up only 20 square feet. The contents of an entire filing cabinet will fit onto a mere two discs of tape. Computerized files also require retrieval systems that call up files, at the press of a button or the wave of a wand over a coded label, from computerized storage bins. Aside from its convenience, this method makes files relatively inaccessible, thereby precluding the misfiling that can wreak havoc on systematically stored records. As with all computers, those storing records also require humidity and temperature controls (especially during hot weekends when the office building's air conditioning is turned off).

①

②

③

④

⑤

⑥

⑦

⑧

❶ It has been said that in the future, paper will all but disappear from offices, replaced by electronic devices. In the meantime, vertical files are recommended for personal use in smaller work spaces. Courtesy: Steelcase, Inc.

❷ File cabinets seem to disappear when built directly into a storage wall as they are in this office at Transammonia; a functional design solution that saves space. Designed by Gwathmey Siegel and Associates.

❸ Files can be used to support work tops and function as partitions in large office spaces. At the Sainsbury Centre for the Visual Arts in Norwich, England, files are arranged to create a work area. Designed by Foster Associates.

❹ Tucked away in a remote corner, this small space stores samples in a designer's office. A closeable door hides the storage system from view. Designed by Juan Montoya.

❺ This Minitrieve System by the Supreme Equipment and Storage Systems Corporation is a computerized file retrieval. Information security is assured because access to the files is limited to the operator of the computer. The system saves space and the wand prevents misfiling by reading out coded labels on all filed material.

❻ Lateral files from Steelcase provide easy access to material and create an organized environment for storage.

❼ Moving banks of storage trays save aisle space in this file system at Pentagram, New York. Banks can be fitted to store anything from paper to computer tapes to disc packs.

❽ In Europe, files are often kept in binders as opposed to closed drawers. This Haller system provides components for storing these and other kinds of records.

Coffee-Breaks and Kitchen Areas

Work may be the one thing in life that sustains us, but neither man nor woman can live by work alone. We need variety in the day's routine. A firm ought to provide a space for that mini-siesta, otherwise known as the coffee break. The visual impression should be at once soothing and distinct from that of the rest of the office, signalling a change in tempo for employees. Furthermore, the coffee-break room shows employees that their employers care about them.

There should be places for people to sit and relax. Employees can stash their snacks in a small refrigerator or pantry cupboards, while the employer supplies coffee and a coffee maker. Stove and sink might be provided, as well as counter space. Vending machines might be included, too, and a water fountain, which should be designed so that handicapped people may drink from it as well. Finally, garbage disposal should be seen to, to circumvent the inevitable mess of cups, saucers, and spoons.

①

Fire Extinguisher

②

③

1 Well-organized elements built into the wall at the end of the corridor include a drinking fountain, a coffee machine, storage, and a fire exit. The recessed fountain saves valuable space in the busy hallway.

2 Fire extinguishers should be prominently displayed in all cooking areas. This simple label (in the employee lunch rooms at Smith Kline) could be a lifesaver during an emergency. Designed by Daroff Design, Inc.

3 The space between two elevator banks was converted to an employee lounge at Johns Mansville's temporary headquarters. A fresh pot of coffee is always available. Designed by The Space Design Group.

4 Lounge areas are places where employees can meet informally and exchange information. The lounge at IBM in Bristol is a cheerful environment for such activities. Designed by Rock Townsend.

5 The lounge area at IBM in Amsterdam provides an additional amenity for employees: vending machines that dispense all kinds of snacks. Designed by DEGW.

6 This kitchen area at Thomson Travel in London was designed for maximum efficiency. Storage for cups and saucers is built into the counter, and bins for silverware are attached to the wall at left. The cash register on the far side of the counter indicates that this is not a place to get a free cup of coffee. It also looks as if this counter provides employees with food as well as drink. Designed by Trickett Associates.

7 A coffee brewer sits on a counter in the lunch room at Midwood Industries. Soft, indirect light above the counter is a change from high light levels on the open-office floor. Designed by John F. Saladino, Inc.

Mail Rooms

The mail room is the office stepchild, that forgotten place somewhere down in the basement where employees sort out thousands upon thousands of envelopes, the import of whose contents they may never guess. In many offices today the process of sorting mail is exactly what it was a hundred years ago, the rooms in which it occurs little changed from their *fin-de-siècle* forebears. Some companies make an effort to integrate the mail room with the rest of the office by using the same furniture system there as is used throughout. But it goes without saying that in most instances these spaces are ripe for change in terms of design.

For the time being, though, certain aspects of the mail room will remain the same. In any mail room, ample work surfaces and cubby holes are essential, as well as special areas for scales, stamps, postage meters, and electronic weighing machines. Designate as the mail room a space near the back door so that messengers can have direct access to it without having to traipse through the entire office, where enough traffic flows back and forth as it is. In corporate office buildings, the mail room should be located near truck access, to facilitate loading of outgoing mail as well as deliveries. In small offices with limited space, set aside a special area for mail-room activities and equipment.

Thanks to automation, the nature of office mail is now beginning to alter. Moving mail-machines laden with the day's

post roll out the mail-room door of their own accord, following an invisible, chemically treated low-pile carpet path and making preprogrammed stops. Half R2-D2 and half pony express, this robot-like device saves both time and personnel. Even more advanced are the computer networks that transmit messages from office to office. These circumvent the U.S. Mail altogether and do away with the need for letters, stamps, envelopes, and, for that matter, mail rooms, too.

① If robots are the wave of the future, then the Mailmobile from Bell and Howell may be showing us that the future has arrived. This automatic, self-propelled vehicle follows a chemical path, stopping at preprogrammed intervals. The Mailmobile can deliver and pick up letters, interoffice memos, packages, and anything else that would otherwise be delivered by company employees. Obviously, the Mailmobile could be very cost efficient for large companies. Designed by Bell and Howell.

② Most mail rooms are located in the basement or an interior space. More often than not, they are crowded, cramped, and poorly designed. This mail room in a major energy company is the rare exception to the rule. Here the standards of design are the same as in the rest of the company. The well-organized space provides many compartments for storing mail and horizontal space for sorting, weighing, stamping, and wrapping

②

packages. Mobile hampers move the mail. Large windows flood the area with sunlight. Designed by Neville Lewis Associates and Kaneko/Laff.

3 At IBM World Trade Americas/ Far East corporate headquarters, a conveyor belt carries mail and memos to six different places within a three-story building. The system runs on trolley lines through the ceiling. The system saves time and money for IBM, since a lot of paper work must be distributed efficiently in this major corporation. Designed by Edward Larabee Barnes, FAIA.

4 Many components of an office system are combined in this Action Office Mailroom. Shelves and cubbyholes for storage accommodate themselves to all the general paraphernalia of a mail room. Work surfaces and storage for machines are also provided. The functional assembly saves space in cramped quarters. Designed by Herman Miller.

5 This work area at Album Graphics clusters functions to save space and employee time. In this small space, the reception area, mail room, and copying facilities are effectively combined. Located by the front door, the receptionist can monitor visitors' access to the second floor. A storage and wrapping area for outgoing mail is tucked away under one counter. Architect: David Hirsch.

Spaces for Machines

As offices become more and more automated, firms will come to devote more attention and space to the machines that will do their work for them. Back in the days when computers and copying machines were thought of as ultramodern, ultrasophisticated luxuries, these were proudly displayed for all to see and marvel at. Now that they are more commonly used, however, they are best kept in rooms of their own—rooms where they cannot be tampered with, and in regard to which certain design considerations must be borne in mind.

Computer rooms must include special humidity and temperature controls. When it comes to climate, these machines can be fussier than human beings, especially when the building's air conditioning is shut off and they are left to fend for themselves. Unlike human beings, however, computers carry on contentedly in rooms with no view whatsoever. Indeed, they should never be located near windows, so a constant temperature can be maintained around them. The usual fire protection—water- or foam-filled extinguishers—should not be used in computer rooms because they would only ruin costly equipment. Instead, a device that extracts oxygen from the air should be employed (such a device, though, is effective only in an airtight space). In rooms containing whole networks of computers, be sure to provide adequate space for connections, unless you want a veritable botanical garden of visible, tendrillike wires creeping across the room's walls and floor.

Copy rooms and photostat rooms need proper ventilation and sufficient light. Provide ample storage space in these rooms for paper, ink, chemicals, staples, tape, scissors, and so on. Conveniently placed waste bins are essential for those sheets of paper one can throw away without upsetting the workings of the entire firm. Table space is necessary here, too, particularly if the copying machine is not equipped with a collator. Include storage racks, as well, for work to be picked up.

A resilient-tile flooring is recommended, specifically a multicolored one on which stains from ink or chemical spillages won't show. Insofar as positioning the machines themselves goes, comply with manufacturers' special requirements (often enough, the contract between you and them gives you no choice in the matter). This way, when a machine breaks down and the manufacturer sends a repairperson to fix it, he or she cannot refuse to do so simply because you've placed the machine just where you were told to place it—in a location where all the heat the machine generates is dissipated and where there is enough space for its inner workings to be completely accessible. The manufacturer may also suggest certain conditions in which the machine will operate best and most efficiently. These, too, should be heeded so as to avoid water damage and the like.

Equipment rooms can be located either centrally or in a more remote zone of the office, depending upon how much a part of the service core they are and how many people are expected to use them.

The question of how much actual space to devote to machines has no hard-and-fast answer. Equipment design is in a state of flux. Today's behemoth of a copier may shrink to more reasonable proportions tomorrow.

③

①

②

❶ A Quotron machine, set into its own beautifully lacquered cabinet, looks like a working piece of sculpture. Positioned outside the president's office at BEA, an investment management company, the machine overlooks the library and open-office space, acting as a message center for everyone. Architect: Tod Williams and Associates.

❷ The Gilman Paper Company in New York uses a custom-colored yellow copying machine to match its files and storage. At the time of purchase, this was the biggest copying machine made, but the model has since been superseded by even larger machines. The free-standing copying machine is used by everyone on the floor. Designed by Environetics, Int.

❸ This computer room at Associated Metals and Minerals has its own supplementary air-conditioning system that operates independently of the building's system. The room is continuously air-conditioned to maintain temperature control for the delicate equipment. The programming area is in the foreground, and the computer room is behind a glass window in the rear. Architect: Jack L. Gordon.

❹ Careful consideration should be given to where noisy machines are placed. At this international corporation, all the equipment is grouped together in an acoustically isolated area. This well-organized environment includes telex, facsimile, and copying machines. At left, clocks above telexes show different time zones from around the world. Facsimile machines (at right) electronically read out and transmit printed information. The office supervisor sits at bottom left. Designed by Neville Lewis Associates and Kaneko/Laff.

❺ Equipment room on The Daria, a yacht that often functions as a moving office. All equipment was grouped together for easy and efficient serviceability. The communication and navigational equipment includes telex, TWIX, and satellite hook-up machines. Design: Douglas Barnard, Inc.

Stairs

One problem many offices share is their spatial monotony. The eye may be pleased—with color, with light, with form—but the level remains constant throughout, and the space stirs no sensations in the body. This is especially true when an office is located on a single floor or communication between its floors is effected only via the elevator.

Stairs between floors of an office will relieve this sense of predictable, unrelieved flatness. Going up or down a staircase built of any material offers an experience radically different—spatially, temporally, and psychologically—from that of walking across a floor. Just as a stroll outdoors can clear your mind, walking upstairs or downstairs within an office can create a sense of moving on. Also, the rhythm of walking upstairs or downstairs differs from that of walking across a floor. It produces

a change, not only in level, but in tempo from an office routine that can prove stultifying. In view of this, when designing a staircase, pay particular attention to the dimensions of risers and treads. The less steep a staircase, the more soothing the rhythm of descent and ascent.

Of course, stairs can be constructed only at great expense within a standard office building. The structure of some buildings prohibits it, while in others if a staircase is to be built at all, it can

only run in strict accordance with the structure. Some building codes limit the number of floors that can be linked internally this way, while others limit the materials that can be used. Check your local codes on this.

Aside from their visual, physical, and psychological effects, stairs can be practical features as well. They are more appealing than elevators, and less cramped. What's more, people don't have to wait for them. Indeed, communication between an office's floors will be improved when people know they need not bother with packed, snail-paced elevators to get from one floor to another but can enjoy a physically pleasing walk up or down a flight of stairs.

❶ Valuable window space is rarely used in corridors; that's why this stairway at Milbank, Tweed, Hadby and McClary is so luxurious. The design of the open balustrade lets in the light and expands the space. Architect: Swanke, Hayden, Connell.

❷ The half-landings of these "dog leg" stairs are used to house reference books for this law firm. This means that everyone has ready access to the most commonly used law books without having to travel to the library. Designed by M. Arthur Gensler Jr. and Associates.

❸ Open-riser stairs connect the mezzanine area to the first floor at Album Graphics. The risers are opened to allow light to filtrate to the first floor, and they give the staircase a feeling of playfulness. Architect: David Hirsch.

❹ Spectacular circular stairs connect the executive floors at Coca-Cola's world headquarters in Atlanta, Geor-

gia. The period Neo-Georgian style is all the more striking since it is set in a modern office building. A skylight above the executive floors floods the stairway with natural sunlight. Interiors designed by John Chaloner. Architect: FABRAP, Inc.

❺ This E.F. Hutton staircase connects the executive floor with the reception area. The stairs are embellished with a three-dimensional silk sculpture by Karl Rosenberg. Interior designer: Ronald Bricke and Associates.

❻ An internal stairway connects two floors at International Paper. These stairs were provided so that employees wouldn't have to wait for the elevators. An informal seating area was added to the base of the staircase. This area serves as both a waiting area for visitors and an informal conversational space for employees. Design: The Space Design Group.

Open Office:

AVAILABLE SYSTEMS

Open-office systems are designed to facilitate most details of office life. You can get coat hooks, blackboards, telephone stands, planting pots (with a grow-light above them), and signs emblazoned with your name. But when all is said and done, open-office systems come in two basic varieties, each with its own particular aesthetic.

One type emphasizes the hardware and connectors that hold the system together, thus creating a businesslike, efficient-looking atmosphere: a vivid image of office process. The second approach strives for simplicity and sedateness.

Most systems are available in a vast variety of materials, including wood and fabric and plastic-laminate, and offer numerous color options. It's safer to choose a neutral color for the system, though, and save accent colors for painted surfaces and discrete pieces of furniture. Systems are expensive and expandable. They are an investment you will be living with for a long time.

Theoretically speaking, all open-plan systems can accommodate an office's every function—mail room, conference room, and so on—while at the same time integrating them within a single, unified design. The simplest open-plan systems are composed of screens, panels, and desks. Screens afford some visual privacy. They absorb sound and divide the office into smaller spaces. New screens can disguise existing furniture. If they are above eye level, the mismatched desks won't show. Freestanding screens are also useful for defining conference areas and providing some acoustical privacy.

Panels are available in three height ranges: low panels (up to 48 inches [122 cm]) create a feeling of privacy when you're seated, yet allow you to see or reach over the top when you're standing. Panels about 60 inches [152 cm] high offer more visual privacy, though if you're tall enough, you can still see beyond them. The tallest freestanding panels are about 80 inches [203 cm] high. They provide the maximum privacy but can be oppressive if employed throughout an installation. Tall panels are useful for defining departmental areas. They should be combined with shorter panels, particularly in areas where eye contact is necessary. Ceiling-height panels are available in some systems as well. Sometimes, the panel heights are used sym-

①

bolically, too—to express rank, in which case the more senior employees have the highest panels, and so on down the line.

Another system is comprised of panels and panel-hung components. Here it's difficult to tell where the screens end and the desks begin. In these systems, the panels support the other elements, either along one edge—a cantilever—or along three sides, which envelop them in a C-shaped configuration. Either way, the stations can be slid back-to-back, sharing a panel between them. This saves panel costs but presents a problem should a work station have to be moved, in which case one set of components will be left without a panel. Of course, another panel can be added, but

②

unless there are extras on hand, this can take time. If you anticipate frequent layout changes, try to avoid delays by designing truly independent work stations or choosing a more flexible layout.

Another type of open-office system is more furniture-oriented. Each work station has an individual identity and can stand alone. These systems are generally more massive than panel-hung systems and generally preferred by executives. The Marcatre system (de-

③

❶ Designed in the Bauhaus tradition, the Bayerische Ruck building in Munich, Germany, is completely furnished with the open-plan system by Haller. Each floor is composed of three circular spaces housing about 20 to 30 people. All work stations are clustered around a central core to maximize teamwork. Building architect: Uure Keissler.

❷ A section through the Race system shows the padded acoustical panels and the central raceway that brings power and cables through the structure and electricity for up lights. Desk tops and storage are cantilevered from the raceway. Designed by Douglas Ball for Sunar.

❸ Free-standing work stations complement the geometric forms of the Weyerhaeuser Technology Center, designed by SOM. The system, designed by William Stephens for Knoll International, minimizes hardware and connectors.

❹ Mobile System by Flötotto, a West German company, features moveable storage walls.

④

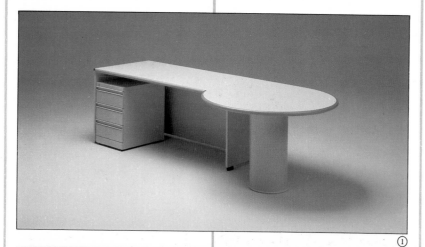

①

②

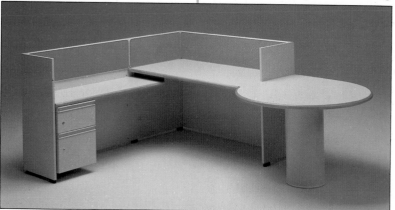

③

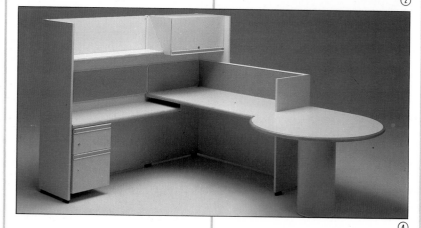

④

signed by Mario Bellini), Knoll International's Stephens system, or Herman Miller's C-forms can all be used in private offices. L-shaped configurations in particular are appreciated for the optimum work surface and storage they provide.

Open-office furniture systems can provide a sense of enclosure—a function once the exclusive province of architecture. Now, some systems are usurping another building function: that of distributing power. Such systems arrive prewired. All electronic equipment can be plugged into its components, while the system in turn plugs into the building's components, acting as a kind of gigantic extension cord. One work station can also plug into the next, so theoretically the number of taps into the building's distribution system can be reduced. This can save money, though in prac-

tice local codes and labor unions limit such a setup. In any case, make sure the distribution points are carefully located so that each work station will be serviced by electricity, phone lines, and if they are necessary, computer cables. The advantage of a system with wire-handling capabilities is that all its furniture conceals all wires thoroughly.

Open-office systems have taken over the function of lighting, too. Most systems offer built-in lighting fixtures as optional components. Light fixtures are located close to work surfaces, usually attached to the underside of storage cabinets, but plug-in lamps are available as well. These provide *task lighting*—that is, direct light at the work surface. Not only is such light practical, but psychologically, it gives individual workers a greater sense of personal control over their immediate

surroundings because it can be adjusted to suit their needs at any given moment. ***Ambient lighting*** —that is, enough light for general illumination that need not be as intense—also can be supplied by fixtures designed in conjunction with furniture systems. Sources of ambient light are mounted above eye level and provide low-level indirect light bounced off the ceiling. Another source of indirect lighting, independent from the work station, is the tall, free-standing fixture called a kiosk (so named because of its shape). Of course, overhead ceiling lights can be used in open-office planning. In recent years, however, some task/ambient lighting solutions have created attractive office interiors. They are softer and less monotonous than most schemes that use uniform overhead fluorescent fixtures. Well-designed task/ambient lighting is energy-conserving and

also delivers better quality light—to where it's needed—at less watts per square foot than the conventional overhead fluorescent lighting.

Another component that's available with some systems is a "sound conditioner." This is an electric device that emits ***white noise***—random sounds of all frequencies—or ***pink noise***, which emphasizes higher frequencies. The sound conditioner's purpose is to block intrusive office noise generated by people and machines on the office floor. The intention is to provide a constant sound level that will create acoustic privacy. The analogy most often used is that of individual conversations getting lost in the larger noise of a busy restaurant. It should be added, however, that no one knows just what the long-term effects of exposure to white or pink noise are.

⑤

⑥

❶ through ❺ This series of photographs shows how the Marcatré System can be changed by adding additional components. The system was specially designed to incorporate a circular surface for conferences, eliminating the need for a separate table and saving floor space. As the need arises, this system can double as a work space, expanding left, right, forward, and backward. Designed by Mario Bellini in Roman oak veneer combined with gray, white, or beige laminates.

❻ The Herman Miller Action Office, designed by Robert Propst, is the granddaddy of all panel-hung systems. It can accommodate virtually any size or height; it can service every office function; and it is available in almost any finish. Everything from phone stands to coat hooks is included in this system. In fact, the options are so varied that prospective customers are supplied with a computer service to help specify their orders.

Open Office:

DESIGN CONSIDERATIONS

The best open-offices plan give the staff a modicum of privacy while promoting interaction and improving traffic flow. The worst ones are like stepping in a hornet's nest. When considering an open-office plan, think first whether your organization can use it. Law firms, for example, where the privacy of attorney-client meetings is a prime concern, do not lend themselves to open plans. Design or publishing companies, on the other hand, adapt admirably to open plans, because their business requires group interaction and because new projects may call for frequent revision of staff groupings.

Whatever the firm, executives will probably dislike losing their private offices, at first. A study conducted by Lou Harris for the office-furniture manufacturer Steelcase showed that 88 percent of its executives thought the biggest drawback to the open plan would be their own loss of status. The best solution for many organizations may be a hybrid design, combining the best features of both conventional and open-office plans.

If an open-office plan fits your organizational needs, you must consider whether you can find the right space. You will need a large, open-floor area, with enough clear distance between columns and other obstructions to accommodate the office system you intend to install. The open plan, moreover, works best in spaces with high ceilings. Too low a ceiling traps the staff in a "pancake" of space and reflects too much noise.

High ceilings also leave room to install a raised floor so that distribution grids for electric, computer, and telecommunications equipment can be installed out of sight.

Design considerations:

Open-plan systems can give the user a voice in office planning. Employees may work at stations tailored to their needs—left- or right-handed, for example—and convenient to the appropriate equipment and files. At the same time, individual work stations may be located according to an office's operating procedures and paper flow. In recent years, environmental and organizational psychologists have developed sophisticated methods for interpreting office-user needs. Based on information gathered from interviews, questionnaires, time logs, travel logs, and group meetings, these experts provide a program of the physical and functional requirements that are the prerequisites for a design.

If you are contemplating an open-office system for your organization, ascertaining user needs is the first and probably most exciting part of the process. At best, the programming phase of open-office design is an effective way to involve employees in new facilities and educate them about projected changes in office location and routine. It is important, however, to give the workers real choices. If you simply dole out the most desirable locations and equipment based on job category, the staff will feel cheated. Beware of system advocates who claim that

floor-space requirements can be reduced. Panel-hung components, they say, take up less floor space than freestanding desks, so you can rent less square feet for the same number of people or increase the number of people in a given space. This claim is spurious for all diagonally oriented layouts and even for most right-angle layouts. Where such cramming is possible, gains in real estate will usually be offset by lower employee morale and decreased operating efficiency.

Drawbacks to open plan:

Lack of privacy—especially acoustic privacy—is the most serious disadvantage of any open-office plan. Lou Harris's Steelcase poll revealed that the company's office workers felt the single most important factor in getting the job done is the ability to concentrate

without distractions. Privacy for telephone calls and meetings was especially important to managers and professionals. If you're considering an open-office plan, you should solicit the advice of another office expert, the acoustics consultant. Each space will have different acoustic characteristics, depending upon its dimensions and materials, but there are some general rules to follow. Any open-office system needs carpeting to absorb sound and mask footsteps. Also, choose an office wall-system with good sound-absorption capabilities; each manufacturer provides ratings. And make sure the system doesn't leak sound between panels: A card should fit tightly through any joint. Remember, too, that the higher the panel or vertical divider, the more effective it will be at blocking sound. Of course, the easiest way

②

to stop noise is at its source: replace telephone bells with blinking lights; group noisy equipment in one area; and distribute work stations as far from each other as possible. Nonetheless, you don't want a room that is silent. Aim for a constant level of background noise which masks individual speech and increases the sense of privacy.

Advantages to the open plan: A well-designed open-office plan gives employees a sense of space and freedom. Ideally, no work area will be more than a few steps from a window view. It will be clear to anyone who steps from one type into the other that an open plan creates a greater sense of autonomy than either a closed cubicle or in-line desk arrangement.

Aesthetic considerations aside, the open plan lends itself particularly well to small- or medium-size offices where the emphasis is on interaction. Advertising companies, architectural firms, publishers, and designers are all good candidates for the open-office plan. Open arrangements make it easier for different professionals to work as a group, each lending expertise at the moment it is called for. Two private walls give enough space for both personal decorations and work display. Also, such companies are often most liable to staff expansion, reduction, and realignment. The open plan means that walls, desks, and equipment can easily be moved to accommodate changing conditions.

❶ *The large spaces of this former bakery now house a major store planning company. The original structure—steel ceiling joists and brick walls—were left exposed, but its industrial look is softened by the rounded forms of the office furniture system and its neutral-color fabric. Designed by The Design Collective, Inc., using the Haworth system.*

❷ *Lack of acoustic privacy—especially for conversations—is the major complaint in open offices. Sound-absorbing panels, acoustical-tile ceilings, and carpeting help reduce distracting noises. Noisy telephone bells should be replaced by blinking lights; phones should be located near acoustic panels. Courtesy: Sunar.*

❸ *Designer Barry Brukoff provided office space for Stanford University by converting its former gymnasium. He added a balcony along one wall, which now accommodates the reception area, conference rooms, and private offices. Noisy office equipment is grouped under acoustic canopies. Special solutions were devised for lighting this enormous space. General illumination is provided by custom tubular lighting fixtures and suspended metal fixtures; each work station has its own task lighting.*

③

Johnson's Wax:

FRANK LLOYD WRIGHT

T his building is designed to be as inspiring a place to work as any cathedral ever was in which to worship," wrote that great visionary of 20th-century architecture Frank Lloyd Wright of his administration building for S. C. Johnson & Son in Racine, Wisconsin. In office design, as in nearly every other aspect of architecture, Wright was ahead of his time. Here he created a vast open-office plan area, forerunner to today's open offices. Aside from additional file cabinets, brought in to contain today's paper explosion, the space re-

mains basically unchanged since it was built in 1939—and still works.

The main area, known as the Great Workroom, is 128 by 208 feet (39 by 63 m) and scored by dendriform columns, 21 feet 7 ½ inches (6.5 m) high and spread on a 20-foot (6-m) grid that employees dub golf tees. Most of the clerical workers occupy the main hall, while supervisors sit along the perimeter and a low mezzanine connected to the ground level by metal spiral stairways placed at convenient points. Generous proportions offer enough room to rearrange the departments without altering the building's structure. Wright himself designed desks and chairs for nearly 100 employees. The desks feature swing-out bins instead of drawers and above the work surface, provide a second level of storage. Chairs, upholstered in red, match the hard Cherokee red-brick and red-kasota sandstone of the walls. The curved forms of both desk and chair echo those on the building's architecture.

What is perhaps most extraordinary about the Great Workroom is its quality of spaciousness and light. The building is essentially viewless (windows would only have looked out on a dull industrial landscape) and centered around the central hall. Diffuse light filters in through an exterior

glazing of Pyrex tubes laid like bricks as well as through a glass roof, creating an almost dreamlike ambience.

And yet, as Wright observed, the building stands as an "architectural interpretation of modern business at its best." The floor, at one time covered in linoleum, had a hard, brilliant gleam to it, as would befit the headquarters of the manufacturers of Johnson's Wax. Today, red carpet covers the floors, but the spirit of American free enterprise, at once down-to-earth and soaring, remains. "When you go into the Johnson Building, interior space comes free," wrote the architect. "You're not aware of any boxing in at all. Restricted space simply isn't there. Right there, where you've always experienced this interior constriction, you take a look at the sky!"

Indeed, offices have the reputation for being constricting spaces. But Wright understood that office work keeps big business humming and that big business, especially in America, beckoned to many as an open field of unlimited opportunities for growth and gain. An ode to the American work ethic, his building is extraordinary, in part because it manages to capture so successfully that sense of openness and limitlessness in what others have seen as a mere bureaucratic machine: the office.

1 Frank Lloyd Wright on the mezzanine of his 1939 S.C. Johnson and Son administration building. Wright pioneered open work spaces, long before anyone dreamed up the phrase "office landscaping."

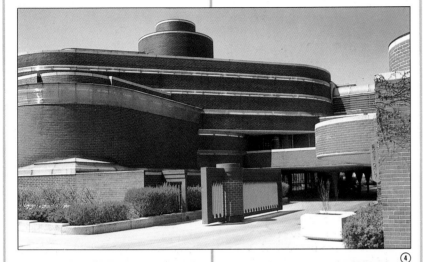

2 Wright custom-designed almost every component of the building, including these bird-cagelike elevator enclosures.

3 Wright explored the decorative possibilities of light-diffusing glass tubing for both walls and ceilings.

4 The same materials—brick and glass tubing—are used on both the exterior and the interior.

5 In 1938, Wright wrote of this Great Workroom: "This building is designed to be as inspiring a place to work as any cathedral was ever in which to worship." The two-story-high dendriform columns and the quality of the light help make it so. The original furniture is still in use. More file cabinets have been added through the years.

6 The entrance lobby is ringed by a mezzanine. Here, as elsewhere, the lighting, a combination of natural and artificial light sources filtering through two layers of glass tubing, gives warm and shadowless illumination at all times.

7 A covered bridge leads to the Johnson Research and Development Tower Wright designed in 1950.

8 and **9** Wright's shaping of the total work space extended to designing all the furniture. The padded back of the chair tilts, and the armrests are high enough to be functional. Companion desks, their curvatures echoing the shapes in the building, have swing-out bins instead of drawers.

Ford Foundation:

ROCHE, DINKELOO & ASSOCIATES

The office as an urban Eden: the concept seems a contradictory one. What could be less of a paradise than an office? But Kevin Roche, John Dinkeloo & Associates, in the 1968 Ford Foundation Building in New York City, managed to unite these two opposing ideas. Here offices for 350 people—executives, for the most part—look out from two sides onto a skylighted, lush, enormous interior garden, designed by Dan Kiley, and enclosed by a glass wall 12 stories high. The garden's climate, a mean level between New York outdoors and the offices within, allows for temperate-zone planting. This marks the first time plants were used in an interior in this way and as such constitutes a veritable tour de force. Each office features sliding glass doors that look out onto the court (and across to other offices within the building as well), which is open to the public. The building's rectangular forms and the garden's wilder ones present a dramatic juxtaposition of the artificial and the natural, an expression of urban and work environments and a relief from them.

①

The offices themselves feature luxurious, rich materials throughout, forcefully expressing the personality of a powerful organization. Warren Platner designed new office furniture, including a desk with the sort of retractable slatted rolling top that covered rolltop desks of old (here it functions as a cover for files located in secretarial desks) and a pedestal that integrates a telephone as well. Desks are of mahogany and bronze, with dark-brown leather insets. Typewriter stands are made of bronze as well. Telephones—trimline handsets with push-button dials, used here for the first time—rest on free-standing pedestal units. Directly over each desk hangs a pendant fixture shedding both direct and indirect light; defining space and efficient for working.

The building itself mirrors the organization's hierarchy. Executive suites and the dining room occupy the uppermost floor, along with the chairman's office. The auditorium and board room are located on a lower level.

The office as Eden? Perhaps not. But certainly, the Ford Foundation Building acknowledges the fact that if much of life today revolves around planned work, there exists another part of it that is effortless, unpredictable, and free.

❶ *The Ford Foundation's vast interior garden space extends beyond its glass facades and ties visually with open spaces in a prestigious New York neighborhood. The lush garden is in spectacular contrast with its urban setting.*

❷ *Office spaces are open to the garden via sliding glass panels. Architect Kevin Roche calls it a living room for the whole Foundation, the spatial expression of their common organizational aim.*

❸ *The ceilings, the walls, and all the furniture were custom-designed by Warren Platner as one unit. These standard components can be switched and rearranged, and although the offices vary in size, they have one quality standard—luxe.*

❹ *A detail of the custom-designed mahogany desk shown at right. Trimline handsets with push buttons were used here for the first time.*

❺ *The double, facing secretarial desks incorporate two phones in a brass plate. Typewriters sit on their own polished bronze pedestals. Sliding mahogany tambours cover files in the style of old roll-top desks.*

❻ *Pedestrians experience the garden as soon as they pass through the revolving doors. The eucalyptus trees will eventually grow 150 feet up into the great court. Lush seasonal plantings include tulips, begonias, chrysanthemums, and poinsettias.*

②

③

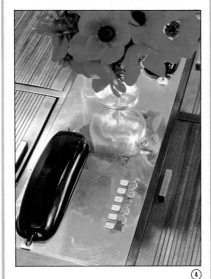
⑤

④

⑥

Best Products:

HARDY HOLZMAN PFEIFFER ASSOCIATES

An adventurous client and an architectural firm known for its innovativeness and ready wit here team up to offer a corporate headquarters in Richmond, Virginia, that features an open-plan office with remarkable interest. Hardy Holzman Pfeiffer Associates achieve, in this 68,000-square foot (6,324-sq m) office space, ever-changing vistas by playing off the rectangular orientation of its work stations against the building's curved glass-block wall. Because of this, the entire office space is never perceived at once in all its intimidating vastness but rather only in sections at a time, thereby humanizing it in terms of scale. Space here is further broken up into smaller units by architect-designed dividers, painted colonial blue and detailed like a 19th-century wardrobe. Delightful as these appear, they also serve such serious functions as housing all wiring for telephones, lighting, and computer terminals.

Other factors conveying a sense of warmth and intimacy include circulation paths marked by soil-age-hiding, cozy-looking floral carpet or durable, old-timey ceramic tile (the former marks

subsidiary paths, the latter marks the main one); residential-looking task lights, that look more like the kind of lamps one finds in living rooms across the land than anything else; the very daylight itself, soft and diffuse (and bright

②

③

enough for there to be little need for artificial lighting during the day), which pours through the enclosing 2-story glass-block wall; and the absence of traffic noise from the highway outside, accounted for by the building's curved entrance facade.

The witty juxtaposition of incongruous styles here marks this as an office space where pleasure was as much on its architects' minds as practical considerations. The water-lily carpet (adapted from a Jack Beal silkscreen of 1977) and the tiled floors, out of some turn-of-the-century café; outdoor fountains harkening back to the Italian Renaissance and a moat, surrounding the building, conjured up from the Middle Ages; wardrobelike dividers redolent of the 19th century; and the corporation's superb collection of contemporary art (which this section of the still-incomplete headquarters was intended to display) —all these bespeak a light-heartedness and equally light hand found in office interiors all too rarely. Work may never be all fun, but that's no reason—or so the architects seem to say—for the work environment to take itself as seriously as all that.

❶ Recycled Moderne eagle sculptures set by architects Hardy Holzman Pfeiffer and Associates gives a clue to the architectural allusions inside Best Products' headquarters building. The curved facade is translucent, and transparent glass blocks are set in a diamond pattern reminiscent of 16th-century Venetian masonry.

❷ The main circulation path inside the building follows the curve of the façade. It's tiled in a pattern you might see in 19th-century office buildings. Lily-patterned carpeting, inspired by a Jack Beal silkscreen, is used in open-office areas.

⑤

④

3 The two-story glass block wall admits a soft, even light. The curve conforms to the shape of a superhighway that borders the site. At night, from the highway when the interior light shines through, the building appears weightless.

4 An extensive, well-placed art collection helps maintain a human scale throughout the headquarters. Here, Andy Warhol silkscreen portraits of Marilyn Monroe are visible from the lobby and the second level of open offices, which are on a mezzanine.

5 Floral carpeting, residential-style task lights, and small-scale Colonial houses for files, storage, and services give work stations a feeling of warmth and intimacy.

6 The office of Frances Lewis, executive vice president, is an intense compression of art history and cross-century furnishing taste. Private offices are in the back of the building, facing planted gardens and a meadow.

⑥

Central Beheer:

HERMAN HERTZBERGER

With Dutch architect Herman Hertzberger's 1973 office building, Central Beheer, an insurance company in Apeldoorn, the Netherlands, the humane working environment becomes a reality. "The question was to make an office building," writes the architect, "which would be a working place where everyone would feel at home: a house for 1,000 people." In doing so, Hertzberger abolished the sort of floors, stacked one atop the other like so many pancakes, that characterize so many office towers throughout the world. In their place, he provided 9½-by-9½-foot (3-by-3-m) modules, a series of spaces which, though articulated, are not defined by any walls. The modules are linked both horizontally and vertically and can accommodate anywhere from one person to four people. To-

gether they form a corridorless, open working space, ambiguous enough to seem at once continuous and divided up into smaller areas that individuals can appropriate for themselves. In such a space, the worker feels at once private and involved in the building's larger life.

Not only does Central Beheer's modular structure encourage individuality and self-expression; its interior design does so as well. Furniture can be arranged within the modules in any number of ways, while the grey, fundamentally unfinished backgrounds—of exposed concrete and concrete block—virtually cry out for completion via personal touches. Time here is as pliable as space and decor because employees at Central Beheer are free to work flexible hours and need not adhere to rigid schedules.

(1)

(2)

(3)

(4)

(5)

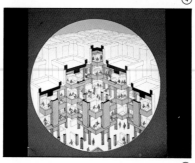

(6)

As Hertzberger movingly writes of his office building, "free choice possibilities stimulate the occupants to add their own color, so that everyone's choice and point of view are brought to the surface … It is not a question of everyone being alike, but … of everyone having the same opportunity for being different. By investing care and love in the things which no one else can do for them, which a person can only do for himself, the occupants appropriate the building and from being its users become its inhabitants."

❶ Central Beheer has many entrances. These access paths have the scale and sociable connotations of a Mediterranean village street.

❷ The staff exploit the possibilities of individual expression in their work spaces. Clutter is certainly not an issue here.

❸ A work space personalized by modifying air diffusers into an owllike mask.

❹ The exposed block walls cry for embellishment—here a portrait of the architect, Herman Hertzberger.

❺ The regularity of the facade belies the spatial richness within. Large windows let in lots of light.

❻ The cutaway section of part of the building shows its great spatial variety.

❼ An employee and his family can lunch together at the restaurant. Visits are encouraged to break down the barriers between work and home.

❽ and ❾ In this unique office building, both the space and the management style is designed for maximum flexibility. The offices are readily adaptable to expressions of individuality, and the working hours of employees vary according to individual needs.

Willis Faber & Dumas:

FOSTER ASSOCIATES

"Most office buildings raise standards for the visitor and gradually dilute them towards the user—traditionally expressed by the entrance lobby areas with finishes and fittings that gobble up the top slice of funds and reflect a total disparity with the working floors. The reverse is true," says architect Norman Foster, "at Willis Faber & Dumas, an office for 1,300 employees, in Ipswich, England, designed by Foster's firm. Here, Foster notes, "movement is open, literally in the sun, and social contact is natural and relaxed across the spectrum of the company. Orientation is immediate; you always know where you are. The barriers are few and seldom visual."

Indeed, the entire space is visible from the building's entrance lobby. Doors are virtually nonexistent. Two large escalators slice through and connect two upper-office floors, terminating at the roof, where they are covered with a large skylight, through which natural light filters down into the interior offices.

But it is the building's curving facade that first announces the theme of maximum visibility. It is composed of glass panels suspended from above, with no metal frames but rather metal clips

①

holding the panels together. While offering workers contact with the outside world, it reflects, as architecture critic Reyner Banham writes, "every detail of East Anglian urban architecture from Low Gothic to High Brutalist." At twilight, on the other hand, the whole building glows from within. Faceted into panes of bronze-tinted glass, the facade was specially designed from a prototype that the architects developed for their own office. Its components are now commercially available.

Spectacular though it is, the glass facade also answers the needs of the employees working inside the building. As Foster has written, "The suspended glass wall was a response to the notion that most people are happier being able to see the outside, provided they do not suffer some discomfort as a consequence." Because the amount of glass used here is generous, it is not only those workers sitting by the windows who get a view—everyone else does, too.

The building's interior meets workers' needs as successfully as its exterior. "We placed an emphasis on raising standards and providing amenities to attract the most talented, competent people," Foster notes, "and to keep them happy enough with their working conditions so that they would be highly productive in their jobs." In

light of this consideration, along with two office floors, a number of amenity facilities were provided: swimming pool, coffee bar, gymnasium, and restaurant. The roof, covered with sod, serves as a picturesque landscaped garden. "The proportion of amenity area to work area is high," Foster points out, "especially if the near acre of roof garden is included in the equation." Such amenities, incidentally, have become increasingly common in offices, because they draw both the best and brightest and make for healthier employees, physically fit enough to cope with job-related stress and fatigue.

②

③

(4)

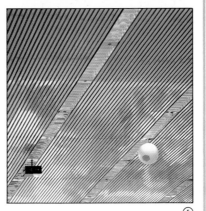

(5)

(6)

❶ *Willis Faber and Dumas, international insurance brokers, have insured some famous forms of transport—the Titanic, the NASA moon buggy. By day, the continuous glass façade of the headquarters reflects downtown Ipswich. At night, the wall disappears and the town gets a view inside. The building is energy-efficient, despite having "the largest continuous glass wall assembly in the world." A sodded-roof terrace for the company restaurant provides good insulation. Also, the building covers its entire site—hence the irregular shape.*

❷ *Work stations set back from the perimeter leave a circulation zone. The reflective, bronze glass panels are suspended from the structure. They have minimal hardware to obstruct the view. Floor troughs carry wires and cables to the work stations in the completely open plan.*

❸ *Amenities are stressed. The 75-foot pool is flush with the lobby floor and directly visible from the lobby.*

❹ *An atrium, filled with palm trees, escalator banks, and sun, begins at the rooftop pavilion and slices through two working floors to the lobby below. It gives the building, packed with 1,300 people, a modicum of spaciousness.*

❺ *In the sleek, all-services ceiling system, aluminum strips house fluorescent lights set with parabolic reflectors to maximize down lighting. Holes in the aluminum plates accommodate sprinklers, smoke detectors, and night lights. Air flows through spaces between the aluminum sections. The reflective surface helps conserve energy.*

❻ *The escalator ends in a rooftop pavilion housing a restaurant.*

This double-ended ferryboat, built in 1924, used to ply the bay between San Francisco and Sausalito. Some 30 years later, it was retired and then bought and gutted by a firm that wanted to convert it into a restaurant. This, however, was not to be the boat's ultimate fate. In 1964, the industrial design firm of Walter Landor and Associates bought the vessel and went about converting it into their floating international headquarters (other offices are located in 13 other

upper and lower decks—with 10 to 15 designers in each. In addition to these, there are private offices for designers, while Landor himself has his office in what was once the Captain's Cabin, which still has its original wood stove. The original general passengers' lounge on the top deck now serves as the firm's conference room, panelled in redwood and natural fir and lit by nautical fixtures of the 1920s. One wheelhouse is lived in by a full-time caretaker while the other is given over to Landor's

Museum of Packaging Antiquities, a display of thousands of packages. The museum is open to the public by appointment.

①

Ferryboat:

WALTER LANDOR & ASSOCIATES

②

cities, including New York, Mexico City, and Tokyo).

Package design, corporate design, exhibit design, environmental design—all go on in this floating office, which accommodates anywhere from 90 to 100 employees—designers, marketing consultants, photographers, researchers, and technical specialists. Additional facilities for 25 other employees occupy an adjacent pier building. A flexible cable between ship and shore feeds the ferry, carrying telephone cables, electricity, gas, water, and sewerage.

The boat itself is divided up into four studios—port and starboard,

③

❶ *In its day, the Klamath, built in 1924, carried 1,000 commuters past the Golden Gate Bridge on each trip across the bay from San Francisco to Sausalito. Now, moored along the San Francisco waterfront, the ferryboat houses a floating population of 90 to 100 designers, photographers, and marketing specialists, who staff the industrial design firm Walter Landor and Associates.*

❷ *A deckhouse above the main- and the saloon-deck levels of offices displays the Landor Museum of Packing Antiquities—tobacco and nail boxes, Victorian gramophones—memorable shapes and graphics tracing a century of package design and technology.*

❸ *Four studios set along port and starboard on both decks have sensational views of the bay or the San Francisco skyline. Work surfaces and walls in the drafting areas are pervasively white, but the original fine wood-beamed ceilings are left exposed.*

❹ *Redwood and Douglas fir panel the private offices on board, including Walter Landor's own work space, the original captain's cabin, which still has its vintage wood stove.*

❺ *The conference room on the saloon-deck level has its share of electronics for audiovisual presentations, but the architectural grace of this space is its old, subtly curved, tongue-and-groove-patterned raftered ceiling.*

❻ *The tree-planted decks are splendid spaces to stay on board for lunch. A flexible cable connecting the boat to the shore carries telephone, electricity, gas, sewerage, and water lines. Electronic equipment installed along the ferry's hull minimizes corrosion.*

④

⑤

⑥

Victorian Residence:

LAW OFFICE

①

P erhaps it is thanks to Charles Dickens that in our minds, lawyers and Victorian interiors are inextricably linked. Of course, in Dickens the lawyers are always overworked and underpaid, if not wholly unscrupulous, and the Victorian interiors always filled with gloom. But at the San Francisco law firm of Kutsko, Moran and Mullin this is hardly the case. The firm's 3 attorneys, 5 secretaries, and one receptionist (along with a dozen other attorneys who rent space here) occupy a converted Victorian mansion in Pacific Heights, built in 1899 for a gold-mine owner, that is a prime example of adaptive reuse. It is, as well, a wise alternative to the anonymity and high costs of large office buildings. In a large building, Kutsko, Moran and Mullin would have been just one of a hundred firms. At their present home (which provides 6,000 square feet [2,358 sq m] of office space), their corporate identity boldly stands out, while the Victorian ambience strongly evokes the tradition of the law.

The mansion is eminently suited to the practice of law. Attorneys and their clients need private offices to meet in—offices the rooms provide—large enough so that conferences can be held in any of them. The basement is given over to copying machines, an employees' lounge, and space

for tenants' secretaries.

Residential amenities have been preserved wherever possible. Showers, such luxuries in office buildings, already existed here, enabling fitness-minded lawyers to take noontime jogs. Fireplaces, framed mirrors, stained glass, carved wooden balustrades, parquet floors, wainscots, wallpaper, rugs, loveseats, and a turrett right out of the Gingerbread Age—all add character to this atmospheric office space. Original features that had been lost or destroyed were duplicated, with the help of photographs, when the firm took the mansion over, in a successful attempt to achieve an authentic Victorian look. Only the kitchen was gutted and reborn as the law library. Of course, certain practical changes were called for as well. The mansion had to be replastered and rewired, and new plumbing had to be installed.

Today, although word processors tend to blow the mansion's fuses and the only parking available is on the street, the many advantages this former residence offers over the typical office space are readily apparent. Here the office presents itself not as a harsh alternative to the home but as a milder, warmer place, at once serious and lighthearted, and in the end, it's far more welcoming than many more conventional offices.

②

1 Fourteen grandly proportioned rooms attracted Michael Kutsko, Richard Moran, and Ronald Mullin to a turreted 1895 Victorian mansion in San Francisco. The attorneys converted the parlor floor into offices for their firm and rented the other rooms to other lawyers to amortize the cost of extensive restoration. That cost, well over $100,000, included searching out craftsmen to replace gingerbread trim and replaster cornices. The roof, wiring, and plumbing system had to be replaced, too.

2 In Ronald Mullin's office, originally the informal parlor, the mirrored fireplace is mahogany and the double-layered wood doors are mahogany on the inside and oak on the exterior to match panelling in the adjoining room.

3 Michael Kutsko's office was once the family dining room.

4 Richard Moran set his antique desk in the family parlor. The mansion was built by Edward Coleman, a gold-mine owner, and partway through the restoration, Coleman's niece presented Kutsko, Moran, and Mullin with old sepia family photographs showing the mansion's rooms at the turn of the century. So the partners were able to search out antique chairs and Oriental rugs capturing the shapes and textures of those Victorian interiors. A lighting designer replicated the chandeliers.

5 Stained-glass windows that had been stolen from the house before the lawyers took title in 1974 were spotted at a flea market by a sharp-eyed real estate agent. Rescued, the flower-themed glass panels were reinstalled behind the restored oak staircase.

6 The kitchen was the one major space totally gutted and changed, transformed into a law library for the firm.

③

④

⑤

⑥

Industrial Loft:

PENTAGRAM (LONDON)

Lofts transformed with varying degrees of success into living spaces are common enough these days. But when a respected and adventurous design firm such as Pentagram establishes its London headquarters for 50 employees in a loft space, something special happens. With close attention paid to the most seemingly insignificant details, the result is an interior at once handsome and unpretentious, filled with creative clutter yet not at all messy. Corporate identities, information, environment, and product design were all conceived under high ceilings and exposed pipes that form an industrial backdrop to the sophisticated processes of design. Windows, too, look out on industrial vistas: the Grand Union Canal and Paddington Station on one side and on the other what Pentagram jokingly describes as "the best view of East Berlin you find in London."

Like most design studios, Pentagram's is an open-office space. The first floor is given over to reception and meeting and dining areas (in the latter, lunch is provided daily to the staff, an amenity at once social and time-saving) and the second floor to studio, workshop, and darkrooms. Here, the open plan makes for flexibility as projects and teams change. While shelving for supplies and equipment subdivide the interior, it is light and airy enough

to make participation in the studio's ongoing if somewhat noisy activity well near unavoidable. For privacy and presentations, staff members hie themselves to one of two conference rooms, the smaller of which is equipped with slide projectors.

Perhaps the most noticeable unifying element here is the color red, a theme that recurs in Pentagram's New York offices as well. Even the exposed pipes have been painted red and accent the space as strikingly as the red accessories, red telephones, and red typewriters do.

Visually satisfying, the space is practical, too. One particularly noteworthy feature is the carpet tiles used throughout. Rather than being glued down, these grip the floor and are therefore easily ripped up and replaced when paints or inks are spilled, as inevitably happens in design studios.

①

②

③

④

⑤

❶ Pentagram's 50 graphic and product designers, its model makers, its secretaries, and its Cordon Bleu chef flow through two floors of a renovated industrial loft space in London. Everyone contributed pounds and pence to plant a young London plane tree at the front door. Address numerals introduce the clear red that inside defines typewriters, sprinkler pipes, and desk accessories.

❷ Pentagram's storage philosophy is "anti-cupboard," so files and saws and braces and bits are in the open in the product design workshop.

❸ Signs and tiles are kept simple in Pentagram bathrooms and show the company's penchant for organization and their use of graphics.

❹ One dining-room wall is a cheerful profusion of antique signs all relating to food. The tables are similar to the white work tops in the design studios.

❺ and **❻** Architects on the mezzanine and designers below have spectacular views of 19th-century transport—London's Grand Union Canal and Paddington Station. The windows provide plenty of light. The open plan is easily divided into spaces for working groups, who share facilities and equipment.

❼ Storing projects in sight in slatted bins controls clutter and is access-efficient. Open-top containers, not drawers, hold personal belongings.

⑥

⑦

Townhouses:

IBM EDINBURGH

IBM, a patron of fine, modern architecture, undertook its first restoration of a historic building in Edinburgh. Buchan House faces prestigious St. Andrews Square in Edinburgh's New Town, designed by Craig in 1767. Once the address of laird's mansions, it is now the heart of the business district.

To provide office space for 120 people in a multinational corporation and preserve the character of a historic urban site was a complex planning project. Four buildings were involved: two of the earliest buildings facing the square, and two less distinguished buildings around the corner on North St. Davids Street, built later in the 18th century. The result was part restoration, part conversion, and part new construction—a collaboration between Covell Matthews Partnership of Edinburgh, who were responsible for the exterior work and new construction, and London architects Rock Townsend, who designed the interior. Their sensitive solution respected the needs of both interior and urban design.

They restored the exteriors of the two St. Andrews street buildings and the fine Georgian interiors as well. They preserved the facade of the two North St. Davids Street buildings and then tore down the rest. Behind the restored facade they built a new building.

Private offices face the street and preserve the original scale. What really makes the planning work is the lighting. From the street, pedestrians can't see obtrusive overhead fluorescent fixtures. Instead, "uplighters," free-standing indirect fixtures, provide general illumination and maintain the historic character. The building seems to glow.

In renovating Nos. 21 and 22 St. Andrews Street, the architects retained the original rooms and their neoclassic details as much as possible. Painted pastel green throughout, the townhouses provide general purpose and teaching spaces and some private offices. Mechanical services—air conditioning, electricity, and communications—are concealed within the existing structure, or run in the corridors, hidden by a suspended ceiling.

(4)

(5)

(6)

❶ *IBM chose an important historical part of Edinburgh in which to slip offices for 120 people in their data processing division. They restored two 1767 houses on St. Andrews Square, kept the facades of the adjoining buildings around the corner, and constructed a new building behind them, screened from view.*

❷ *The stone facades, porticoes, and grand chimneys of all four Georgian houses were patched and cleaned up. The compartmentalization of the original rooms was kept so that looking in from the square, the offices are compatible with the domestic rhythms of the street facades.*

❸ *The Georgian rooms are used for private offices, teaching, and exhibition spaces. Typical lighting in these areas is free-standing fixtures that bounce light off the walls and ceiling and emphasize the finely sculpted cornices and capitals in high relief.*

❹ *A new reception desk sits between Neoclassic columns. The interiors are painted pale green, a color widely used in interiors in the 18th century; it is light-reflective without being chilly.*

❺ *Suspended ceilings in the corridors conceal air-conditioning ducts and major mechanical feeds so that the original details could remain intact. The L-shaped configuration of the four original buildings screens large open-office floors, where most of the employees work. Furniture throughout is deliberately modern.*

❻ *A section through an office in the restored buildings shows how mechanical services were discreetly concealed in the floors and ceilings. Desks lamps and telephones plug into floor outlets, so there are no wires underfoot.*

Architect's Conversions

To the untrained eye, a broken-down iron foundry, an abandoned monastery or a defunct butterscotch factory might seem ready for demolition. But to the architect and designer such structures present an immediate challenge for creative conversion.

Old buildings, even those on the verge of decay, can provide unusual space and good light; a gift for the architect or designer seeking uncramped and imaginative working environments for their studios and offices. It is often easier and more challenging to convert raw space than it is to adapt impersonal office buildings to the needs of a creative team. It is also more fun.

Many old building contain unusual features like original structure, carved arches, and woodwork. These details can add old world charm and grace to any working environment.

People seem to enjoy working in former factories or convents, and the environment certainly has added client appeal. The unique qualities of converted offices provide the client with proof of the architect's creative ability to effectively adapt existing structures.

①

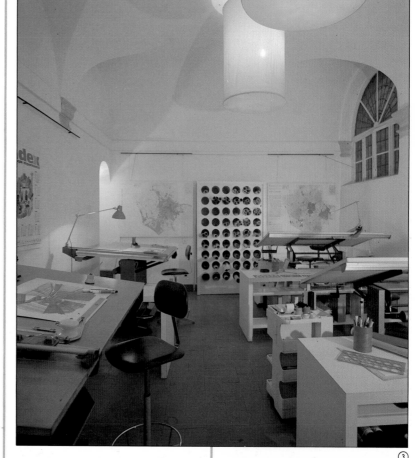

③

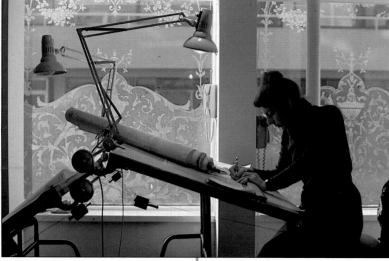

②

④

⑥

⑦

⑧

⑤

❶ Hulme Chadwick, in London, converted a historic pub into offices. The exterior of the building was left intact.

❷ The etched-glass windows are part of the original building, and they provide privacy from pedestrians while allowing plenty of light to filter into the drafting room. Not shown in this picture is the sophisticated computer system, which is in great contrast with this antique setting.

❸ On the via Giulia, in a historic section of Rome, a former residence was converted into the design studio of Evaristo Nicolau. In the 15th century, the building was the home of a wealthy family. Once part of the stables, this street-level room was converted into a workroom/office. The high windows provide privacy from pedestrians. Architect: Evaristo Nicolau.

❹ Since the 15th century, many different rooms were added, and there are several level changes throughout the building. In the reception area, and throughout the building, the electrical wiring on the ceiling was made into a graphic design.

❺ The Taller de Arquitectura, led by Ricardo Bofill, is an interesting group of economists, architects, and poets who bring the concept of urban theater to architecture. This former cement factory on the outskirts of

Barcelona is the focus for Walden 7, a "city in space" of some 5,000 dwelling units designed by the Taller. Given its agglomeration of silos, mechanical plants, and underground passages, the Taller assessed the potential of each for work and leisure.

❻ A design studio in one of the silos of the converted cement factory shown below.

❼ Mario Bellini converted a former convent into his offices in a historic section of Milan. The design studio shows the original oval windows. There are also model shops for industrial design in this building. Architect: Mario Bellini.

❽ One end of Bellini's office was made into a greenhouse. A photomural of the cloister below covers the other wall. The Il Colonnato table and the Break chairs were all designed by Bellini for Cassina.

Adapting Spaces

Chapter 5

Advertising Agencies

Advertising agencies know the value of advertising. Most agencies want their offices to have a unique, memorable look. They also try to appeal to their clients. An agency that wants to do ads for financial institutions, for example, generally aims for a look of substance.

The reception room is the first chance to establish the image of the agency, and as it's often used as a waiting room, it's a good opportunity for the agency to sell themselves. Therefore, reception rooms usually display the names of the agency's clients.

The heart of the advertising agency office is the screening room, which is, in effect, a sales room that brings together clients and the agency's work. Naturally, since the client is making decisions about an agency in the screening room, everything possible is done to ensure the client's comfort. The same attention, or perhaps even more, is given to the audiovisual facilities that will present the agency's ideas. Most screening rooms have projection facilities and a screen for viewing commercials. Both 35-mm and 16-mm formats are used. The screen is often flanked by two video screens—one for black and white and one for color—so that the client can see the work on the same scale as the viewer will eventually see it. From the client's point of view, the seating at the conference table must be comfortable and there must be clear, direct viewing from every seat. The audio facilities and the acoustics in the room need to be good,

not only for the presentation but also for the very difficult format of the discussion that inevitably follows.

In addition to the main screening room, many larger agencies have other screening facilities. These are set up as viewing rooms and are used to see rough cuts and commercials before they're finished. Though these rooms can be large, they're generally more workmanlike in character. Chairs with writing tables attached are often used, and there is less emphasis on comfort than in the main screening room.

Individual offices in an advertising agency allow for a wide latitude of style. At the former

offices of the J. Walter Thompson agency, executives were encouraged to decorate their offices with furniture and fixtures they found comfortable and pleasing, and to help them the agency collected fine period pieces. Going from one Thompson office to another was like moving through a series of drawing rooms. Another of Thompson's rules was no closed doors. When they moved into the 11th floor of the Graybar Building in New York City, they removed office doors and installed 26 wrought iron gates and grilles behind which the top people worked in clear view of anyone passing by: a distinctive interpretation of the open office.

①

②

③

One unusual aspect of advertising agency offices is that executives frequently do some of their own typing or at least their creative typing. This means that many people besides secretaries need appropriate surfaces for typewriters as well as correct lighting and electrical facilities.

An advertising agency has a tremendous amount of intermix among departments. They very often have a special department called Traffic where people keep tabs on the status of various projects, but people have to move from department to department as well. This requires a thorough study of adjacencies to make the most efficient use of time.

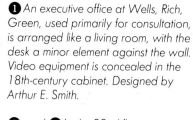

④

⑥

❶ An executive office at Wells, Rich, Green, used primarily for consultation, is arranged like a living room, with the desk a minor element against the wall. Video equipment is concealed in the 18th-century cabinet. Designed by Arthur E. Smith.

❷ and ❸ In the 32nd-floor screening/conference room at Benton and Bowles, the screen wall is a permanent black-and-white composition. The inner rectangle serves as a border for the projected image. Cabinets below are for storage and contain speakers. Designed by The Space Design Group.

❹ The names of their clients are etched in the smaller glass panels in the reception area at Manoff Geers Gross. Two clocks give New York and London time. Finishes of oak and linen are used throughout the office, matching the decor of the London office. Designed by Pentagram.

❺ At French Gold Abbott Kenyon and Eckhardt, the carrels occupied by account executives are formed of simple varnished screens against the balustrade of the raised creative area. The floors are raised to give better scale to the small individual offices. Designed by Pentagram.

❻ The conference room at BBDO in London was designed by Duffy, Eley, Giffone, Worthington.

⑤

Architects and Designers

①

Architects and designers inherit the image of an archetypical work place: the skylit *atelier*, or studio, patterned on those of the Ecole des Beaux Artes, where students receive instruction in design. Whether it is a school or a work place, the core is the drafting room, a timeless open space that even today is the heart of the architect's or designer's office.

Drafting demands good lighting. Hence, whenever possible, the skylighted location for deep spaces and further illumination by adjustable lamps known as architects' lamps in the United States. Drafting tables—the architects' equivalent desks—require a large surface area to hold large drawings. They also need a nearby reference area almost as large again as the drafting table for materials constantly referred to in the course of work. Architects must have ready access to plan file-drawers, catalogues, and other support areas of the office, including libraries for samples of materials and products.

Computers have begun to invade the drafting room—at least in the firms that can afford them. Computers are useful in all sorts of calculations, including structural and mechanical computations as well as cost estimating and facilities planning. (Computer-

aided design—CAD—can perform repetitive drafting chores much faster than its human counterparts.)

The working drawings of the 4.4 million square feet of office interiors for the Sears Tower in Chicago, Illinois were produced entirely on the computer-plotting system of Environetics International, Inc. Lawrence Lerner, its president, advocates placing the computer in the drafting room. Lerner thinks that the computer should be operated by designers not operators so that eventually the designers will come to use the computer as a tool just as they do felt-tip pens and yellow tracing paper. The computer is also useful in the designers' office because of its word-processing and text-editing capabilities for specifications and contracts.

One of the most spectacular features of many architects' offices is the lack of single–office rooms. In addition to the drafting room, the architects' and designers' office must include conference rooms to present work to clients. The conference room should have facilities to display lots of different kinds of presentation boards, models, slides, video tapes, overhead projections, and films. Lighting should be adjustable in order to show models, drawings, and material samples at

their best. The lighting should also be as flexible as possible in an effort to simulate actual conditions. In addition to formal conference and presentation rooms, space is also necessary for informal conference areas for meeting vendors and sales representatives outside the drafting room. Additionally, there may have to be some provision for the printing of drawings in the house or, alternatively, provisions for messengers who will handle this chore.

Open-office-plan drafting rooms have traditionally been very successful for architects and designers because design projects require the coordination of thou-

sands of small details. The drafting room, where easy communication is essential, allows for openness and effortless interaction. An open plan allows flexibility for staffing various simultaneous projects.

Architects and designers often see the potential for adapting existing buildings to offices. They've converted abandoned train stations, water mills, and factories. But like any business, they choose a location and an image depending on the clients they wish to attract, and their office locations range from prestigious high-rise buildings to water towers.

1 The drafting room in the shared Manhattan design offices of Bray-Schaible Design, Inc. and D'Urso Design, Inc., is a former artist's studio overlooking Bryant Park. The walls separating the main room from the windowless space on two levels to the rear were removed, and an existing curved stairway was exposed.

2 Architects Rubin and Smith-Miller's drafting room is in a New York City loft. The shelving in the rear defines separate areas for each of the partners. A remnant from this former factory is the stamped-metal ceiling.

3 The upper drafting room of Hellmuth, Obata and Kassabaum's San Francisco office is under the roof of a former warehouse. Inconspicuous high-intensity discharge lamps shed even light. The work stations for project architects along the windows are used elsewhere for office staff.

4 Hulme Chadwick and Partners stripped, gutted, and completely renovated a dilapidated pub called the Bromley Arms for their new offices. The company was the first U.K. architectural firm to purchase and install a computer for drafting and design. All the work stations at Hulme Chadwick plug into the CPUs (central processing units).

5 The drafting room of The Space Design Group is in an office building in New York City. To get the maximum ceiling height, acoustical tiles were glued directly to the ceiling slab, leaving the beams exposed. Many large windows and custom-designed suspended lights make individual drafting lamps unnecessary.

Consulates

Embassies are government ministries located in foreign capitals. Consulates are subordinate posts in provincial cities in the host country. Embassies and consulates have several functions. Their consular sections look after the interests of their own citizens who are living or travelling in the host country. They issue travel visas to citizens of other countries. Their less public function is to monitor and report political, economic, commercial, and military events in the host country. Trade commissions are less complicated. Located in major commercial centers, their official function is to foster trade.

Like their professional and business counterparts, the offices for government vary in scope and scale. In general, they are designed as administrative outposts, with good lines of communication to their home offices. They are interesting because they embody both an official and a national identity in a foreign land.

Plaques, flags, or portraits of the powerful swiftly convey the official nature of government offices. The presence of military personnel who act as security guards reinforces it. Unfortunately, in recent years security has become an extremely important design consideration. Obviously, security and hospitality to the public are at cross-purposes. Embassies and consulates throughout the world have had to face this vital issue.

National identification helps visitors from the host country form an impression about the country they might travel to or trade with. And for nationals who visit or work in them, it gives a feeling of a home away from home.

National identification can be expressed in several ways. Display is perhaps the simplest—using posters, photographs, and objects that highlight a country's geography and culture. Another way is to recreate the environment of the home country using indigenous interior finishes and furniture. Trade commissions display national products; exhibition spaces for trade shows and screening rooms for films and slides are important adjunct spaces. And usually, architects and designers from the home country are commissioned to design the project, with the assumption that their work will be an example of their national cultural sensibilities.

Because instantaneous long-distance communication is critical, these foreign outposts house sophisticated equipment in relatively large areas. Secure areas for confidential files and shredding machines are also necessities in embassies and consulates. Space outside the building for motor pools, a prerequisite of power, is another design consideration.

①

②

④

⑥

❶ *From the street, the blue column can be seen through the gateway. It indicates to the passing pedestrian the presence of the Ivory Coast Consulate behind a New York City townhouse facade. The male and female figures that guard doorways in traditional tribal architecture are abstracted here as columns. Architect: Susanna Torre.*

❷ *The small offices of the Malaysia House in London are located in a building on Trafalgar Square designed in 1922 by Sir Aston Webb. The building was completely renovated to accommodate a conference room, a library, a showroom, and offices for the staff and the commissioner. In the entrance hall, Malaysian woods and pewter were used. The ceiling was made with timber slats and randomly arranged multicolored balls. The same detail, with darker timber, is used in the basement auditorium (photograph number 4).*

❸ *The commissioner's suite of offices was located on the top floor of the building, where the large glass walls provide a staggering view of the square and the Strand. The interiors were lined with Malaysian materials as a symbol of national pride. The carpet was specially woven in a rattan pattern that is used throughout the building.*

❹ *A small screening and lecture room is located in the basement. The screen is concealed behind panels of pin boards, and the speakers are housed below. The air-conditioning outlets are invisible in the elaborate ceiling ornamentation. The Malaysia House was designed by Pentagram.*

❺ *The ambassador's office in the Ivory Coast Consulate is used on his frequent trips to New York. The wood carving of a bird deity was done by an artisan of the native Senufo tribe.*

⑤

Dentists

①

Dentists' offices should, of course, show concern for the patient. Is the waiting room, for example, designed to alleviate a patient's anxiety and stress? Comfortable seating, pleasant fabrics and textures, and soothing artwork help to accomplish this as do carefully chosen colors. Studies have shown that warm colors—red, orange, and yellow—tend to be arousing and can cause an increase in blood pressure, palmar sweating, and restlessness. Cool colors—especially blues and greens—produce a calming effect on the central nervous system. Isolating the reception room accoustically so that the sound of drilling can't be heard, also reduces stress.

The treatment room, or operatory, can be designed for patient comfort, as well. Windows, for example, give both the patient and the dentist a feeling of release in a relatively small space.

A wide range of equipment and practice methods provide many options for designing dentists' offices. The operatory is the core of the general dental practice. As interior designer Jain Malkin points out in her book *The Design of Medical and Dental Facilities*, dental journals have published numerous time-and-motion studies over the years illustrating the quest for efficiency. Most dentists now use assistants and prefer maximum flexibility. While a patient lies in an adjustable contour chair, the dentist has the option to work either from a seated position or a standing one.

Dentists can choose from among several delivery systems— the way they will actually treat patients—and set up the operatory

accordingly. Most treatment rooms are set up specifically to be right-or left-handed, although if more than one dentist will be using it, an ambidextrous layout is possible.

Cabinets, utilities, equipment, and even door placement vary according to the personal preference of the dentist. According to Malkin, 8 feet 6 inches by 11 feet 6 inches (2.6m by 3.5m) is an optimal size, although in reality, many dentists have to settle for smaller treatment rooms.

Operatories need shadow-free illumination. The operating light, usually designed to deliver 2,500 foot-candles, should be ten times brighter than the work tops and the room surfaces. Usually, two or three four-lamp fluorescent fixtures will supply the necessary 200–250 foot-candles. The colors in the operatory should be subdued. Intense hues, or high-contrast patterns may make it difficult to match the colors of crowns.

Operatories are utility-intensive with complex requirements for

plumbing, compressed air, suction systems, natural gas, and electric power. If medical gases, oxygen, and nitrous oxide are used for analgesia, strict fire and building codes govern their storage and arrangement. The walls that support X-ray machines have to be structurally reinforced. The timer button that activates the X-ray equipment should be a minimum of 6 feet (2m) from the machine.

The requirements for all these services vary with the equipment and the manufacturer. Malkin recommends working with a reputable dental equipment dealer during the design and working-drawing phase. She recommends individual shut-off valves for air and water at each

operatory so that the entire suite doesn't have to be shut down if the equipment in one operatory needs repair. Malkin also advises specifying carpet with synthetic backing rather than jute. In the event of flooding, the synthetic backing will remain dimensionally stable and will not rot.

The other requirments for a general dental practice are a laboratory, sterilization and storage spaces, and a business office where charts and records are stored. Many dentists have a patient education area as well. A private office is for the dentist's convenience and comfort; patients rarely visit there, so it doesn't have to be a large office.

Pedodontists are dentists who

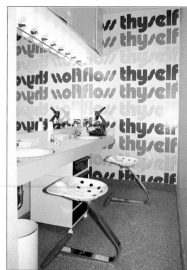

②

③

④

work exclusively with children and their offices should be designed for youthful patients. Although orthodontics, the branch of dentistry that deals with straightening teeth and correcting malocclusions, deals with some adult patients, most are young.

The waiting rooms in these specialists offices should be child-proof and easily maintained. The furniture should be small scale and covered in washable and durable fabrics. Special activity areas, a blackboard, paper, and pencils and a place to use them, provide necessary diversion for younger children. Some orthodontists and pedodontists find that if they arrange their dental chairs in groups called bays, peer pressure keeps crying to a minimum. As a precaution, at least one private-treatment room might be provided to isolate recalcitrant patients. The group arrangement is economical because there is less initial partition work. Adjacent chairs can share supply cabinets.

Orthodontists and pedodontists need private offices large enough for initial consultation.

The other dental specialties that treat adults—oral surgeons, periodontists, and endodontists—have requirements similar to a general dentistry practice. In addition, they require recovery rooms for their patients.

⑦

⑤

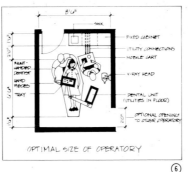

OPTIMAL SIZE OF OPERATORY

⑥

❶ *A cheerful reception area puts patients at ease in this California office. The receptionist should be able to see the waiting area and control the access and circulation to the inner office. Designed by Jain Malkin, Inc.*

❷ *In this patient-education room, a dental hygienist teaches proper dental care to patients, promoting preventive dentistry.*

❸ *Patients bring their own tapes and earphones to this relaxed, unusual open dental office. Architect William Weber Kirsch designed the space, the ground floor of a former spice factory, for Dr. Bruce Marcucci.*

❹ *A play area in the waiting room is important for dentists who specialize in working with children. Designed by Jain Malkin, Inc.*

❺ *The operatories in this converted spice factory combine modern equipment with antique dental furnishings.*

❻ *Illustration of the optimal size of an operatory. Many dentists settle for a smaller size than this, and the layout of the operatory really depends on the dentist's individual style. Designed by Jain Malkin, Inc.*

❼ *Six chairs are placed side by side in this orthodontist's office. Peer pressure keeps the young patients in line. Designed by Jain Malkin, Inc.*

Doctors

Alleviating a patient's anxiety is a critical issue in the design of medical offices. So is improving the efficiency of doctors and their staff. Well-designed medical offices emphasize the human factor as well as circulation and office layout.

Functionally, the typical medical suite is divided into administration, patient care, and support services. The administrative spaces include the waiting room, reception area, business office, and storage space for medical and insurance records. Patient care includes examination, treatment, and consultation rooms. Support services include nurse stations, laboratory, X-ray, darkroom, storage, and possibly a staff lounge.

In general, medical offices are usually comprised of many small rooms connected by a corridor. Patients move from the front office (the waiting room and reception area) to the back office (the examination and consultation rooms). The doctors and staff usually enter the back office through a secondary entrance and rarely appear in the public areas. Each doctor travels between examination rooms and a private consultation room, although not all doctors see patients in consultation rooms. Obviously, if they do, the consultation room should be near the examination rooms. The consultation room also serves as a small reference library and a place to rest.

The location of the administrative office is strategic because patient circulation pivots around it. An arriving patient checks in here, and departing patients should travel past this space to reschedule appointments and, in the United States, to pay their bills.

A patient forms the first impression about a doctor from the waiting room. If the waiting room is comfortable and cheerful, it will put the patient at ease. A place for coats and umbrellas should be provided, wheelchair patients need an area to wait in, and patients in casts need a room to stretch out in.

A visit to a doctor or a dentist is traumatic for many people. According to interior designer Jain

③

④

②

Malkin, who specializes in medical facilities, patients fear the invasion of their personal space even more than they fear unknown medical procedures. In her book *The Design of Medical and Dental Facilities*, Malkin shows how these psychological needs can be met by good design.

Seating arrangements can help to allieviate stress if individual seats are spaced relatively far apart, and patients are not forced to sit together or stare at each other. The number of seats depends on the individual practice and the doctor's scheduling procedures. High-volume specialities, such as obstetrics, need larger waiting rooms than low-volume specialities, such as psychiatry. There should be enough seating to accommodate two seats per patient per doctor-hour because many people bring a friend or relative with them when they visit their doctor.

According to Malkin, lack of confidence in the doctor breeds anxiety in the patient. In the waiting room, she advises using soothing colors and textures. Live plants, not plastic, suggest health. Image is important, as it is in other

①

kinds of offices. For example, surgeons usually try to convey a conservative image in their furniture selection and office decoration. "People need to feel that the surgeon is a serious person not subject to frivolity," Malkin says.

The concern for the patient extends to the back office. Corridors need to be well lighted and wide enough for wheelchairs and gurneys (wheeled stretchers). The examination room's design should give the patient as much personal privacy as possible. If patients have to remove their clothes, a changing cubicle with a mirror and a place to hang clothes is necessary. An 8-by-12-foot (2.5-by-3.7-m) examination room is usually large enough. The examination-room door should swing into the room so that it can shield the patient from the gaze of people walking by.

If a patient has to walk from one room to another with bare feet, the floor should be carpeted. The furniture in the consultation room shouldn't act as a barrier between the patient and the doctor. Ponderous desks with flush fronts are not usually recommended.

There is some controversy about windows in medical suites. The demands of patient privacy conflict with a desire for natural light and views. As a result, many rooms in a medical office are interior and windowless. However, windows in medical offices are most useful if they begin at least 4 feet (1.2m) above the floor. Furniture can be placed beneath them, and they provide privacy. The size of rooms in medical offices seem to work best as multiples of 4 feet (1.2m)—8-foot-wide (2.4-m) examination rooms and 12-foot-wide (3.7-m) consultation rooms. Therefore, if medical-office buildings are designed with continuous window walls, the mullions should be 4 feet (1.2m) apart.

The examination room is the doctor's work station and should be set up for the individual doctor.

For maximum efficiency, all the examination rooms should be identical. Examination rooms should be well lit. Some specialists require adjustable lamps that provide high-intensity light. The examination table, equipment, and cabinets for instruments and supplies vary with each specialty. Likewise, the support areas—the nurse stations, laboratories, and X-ray rooms—vary with the type of practice and its size.

Medical offices, like all health-care facilities, are subject to the most stringent flammability requirements for interior finishes. The specifications for carpet, upholstery fabric and fillings, wall-coverings, draperies, and adhesives for wallcoverings must be checked for conformity to the governing fire codes. Likewise, code requirements for exits and for storing combustible gases and supplies must be considered. Among other relevant codes are those that provide for the handicapped. Toilet rooms, entrances, and elevators should be barrier-free.

⑤

⑥

❶ *The reception room for the 77th Street Sports Medicine Clinic can seat 29 patients for the 7 doctors who work in this clinic. The design of this area recognizes the fact that most people come to the doctor's office in pairs, and the layout provides lots of leg room for people in casts or wheelchairs. Architect: Marvin B. Mitchell.*

❷ *A consultation room in the same clinic uses warm wood and matching chairs for the doctor and the patient to create a relaxing atmosphere.*

❸ *This well-organized laboratory doubles as a storage room for medical files. Architect: Neski Associates.*

❹ *Signage and a chart rack outside the examination room adds to the patient's privacy and is very efficient for the physician. Architect: Neski Associates.*

❺ *The surgery room at the office of The Foot Care Group. The treatment rooms are linked by a corridor (gait testing) to the functional core of the office. Architect: Rubin and Smith-Miller.*

❻ *The most characteristic architectonic device employed in the Foot Care Group offices was the creation of a continuous zone of clerestories and cover lights above all the rooms. Both natural and fluorescent light is shared and borrowed between all the rooms in this runners clinic. Architect: Rubin and Smith-Miller.*

Fashion Designers

Fashion designers require offices that express a personal variation on the theme of glamour. They need a sense of showmanship in their office space as well as a strong personal statement. Creativity in the office design enhances the spirit of flair and excitement that will help them to sell themselves and their clothing designs. The high-visibility spaces in a fashion office are the reception area and the showroom. Both these areas need to emphasize the personal signature of the designer, but these areas must be flexible in their use of space. Showrooms must be large enough to seat clients comfortably during a presentation. The latest trend in fashion sales is the use of videotaped presentations rather than live models. This demands that attention be given to the placement of video equipment.

Privacy is an important factor to be considered in the fashion office. Because the element of surprise is a necessary ingredient to the fashion industry, the designer's workrooms should be high-security areas. They are best located away from the main office traffic routes. In addition to privacy, the designer needs good lighting for sketching, sewing, and selecting fabrics. A sample room of design resources should be in the vicinity of the private designer offices; often it is located in the office of the head designer.

The sales area of the fashion designer office is in the public section of the space. Salespeople need desk space for taking orders. A conference table can be used in place of a desk because it is friendlier and less forbidding. During the market season when buyers visit the offices frequently, tables should be arranged for privacy so that potential competitors don't see or hear what another store is buying. Sometimes included in the sales area or contiguous to it is a space for entertaining out-of-town buyers. This entertaining area usually includes a kitchen for the preparation of food and drink.

①

②

1 Designer's room outside of the president's office at Jones, New York is covered in taupe-colored linen. Display space was more important than storage, so the linen was scotch-guarded and sketches, swatches, and photographs can be pinned up anywhere. Steel shelving extends along the underside of the custom-built laminate cabinets. Designed by Juan Montoya.

2 Halston's New York offices occupy a two-story space in the prestigious Olympic Tower. Mirrored doors divide the space into a conference room, an office, and two salons. The 13-foot- (4-m-) high doors hinge open to create one large room used for fashion shows. Separate from this space is a large workroom, the administrative suite, designer's studio, and a resource room for sample fabrics and accessories. Architect: The Gruzen Partnership.

3 Yves St. Laurent Enterprises' New York executive offices are designed around a suite of 1931 art deco office furniture. Designed by Jed Johnson and Judith Hollander, Associates. Architect: Michael Hollander.

③

Lawyers

For most businesses, the automated office is something for the future. But two types of organizations—the extremely large and wealthy multinational corporation and, at the other extreme, the small, labor-intensive autonomous company—are rapidly moving into the future. Of the latter, the law firm is typical of a business that is taking advantage of the convenience and flexibility of automation.

The contemporary law office is in a period of transition. In the past ten years, law firms have been producing more and more of their contracts, briefs, and general paperwork on word processing

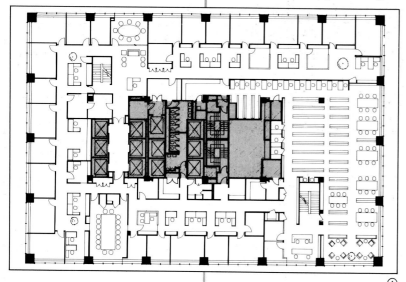

machines. Moreover, paralegals are joining the contemporary law firm and taking on routine legal duties. All this has forced a new approach to space planning in the design of law offices. The changes being made in law offices today portend the changes that many

small office industries will experience tomorrow.

Mary Ann Altman, a partner in the management consultant group Altman and Weil, Inc., specializes in legal economics, and is a member of the Pennyslvania bar, and an expert on law-office space planning. She writes, "The equipment and the training of personnel to operate word-processing machines represents a large investment. The ultimate return on investment depends on the output and the productivity of the equipment. Many firms realize that their investment will be returned only if the equipment is used for 6 to 8 hours a day. In this way, word processing is making changes in law offices' approach to space design and utilization."

Moreover, the use of this equipment changes the secretaries' job: because typing is done by a specialist, the secretary can do more administrative work and can work for more than one attorney. This shift in secretarial function affects space planning. For example, where does a secretary who works for more than one attorney sit?

One space-planning modification has already occurred in many offices. Word-processing centers have been established to group equipment and operators in one location. Within that center, the particular needs of word-processing specialists must be considered, including eye contact with other operators to relieve boredom; nonglare lighting, particularly on equipment keyboards and display screens; comfortable chairs; and good acoustic isolation, especially from the noisy printers.

Large law firms have come to depend on administrative/word-processing teams assigned to groups of lawyers. In a typical configuration of this sort, one might find, for example, litigation lawyers sharing a word-processing specialist who operates CRT and high-speed output equipment, a typist with a standard electric

typewriter, and an administrative secretary who directs the efforts of the entire team and acts as the liaison between the lawyer and the clerical support staff.

Another change in the modern law office is the appearance of the paralegal. The arrival of the paralegal again changes the law office layout. While paralegals don't need offices equal in size to those of the lawyers, they do need privacy and noise-control so they can concentrate on their work and handle telephone calls. Some law firms provide for their paralegals by means of standard full-height partitions that form discrete of-

3 The reception area, with another view of the conference room. Book-matched rosewood walls, used throughout, contribute to the image of solidarity and stature.

4 A detail of one seating area in the reception area. Law offices need separate seating areas—or at least individual chairs—so that adversaries in legal actions won't be forced to sit close to each other.

1 A venerable San Francisco law firm, Brobeck, Phlager and Harrison, occupy five floors in a high-rise building. They wanted their office to express tradition and continuity. The plan of the reception level shows that the library was given a prime corner location. Gensler and Associates were the interior architects.

2 The conference room at the end of the reception area (shown below) overlooks the Oakland Bay Bridge. The glass wall permits the interior space to share the spectacular view.

fices. Other firms use moveable, free-standing offices that allow for more flexibility.

The basic unit of the law office is the attorney's office, and the most crucial determining factor in the design of the attorney's office is the confidentiality of the client's case. This need for confidentiality between lawyers and clients will no doubt keep the cellular office concept intact despite changes in other aspects of the total law office. In fact, special construction procedures in modern office buildings may have to be utilized to isolate conversations within each office: the walls enclosing each office are continued through the space above the hung ceiling so that noise won't travel.

Very often the layout of the attorney's office requires a secretarial corridor outside the private office. The desire to bring natural light to this area often conflicts with the need for visual privacy. This problem is frequently solved with the use of clerestory windows utilizing clear glass above eye level or by using a full-height translucent glass wall between the secretary and the attorney. Both these methods allow light to penetrate into interior spaces while still ensuring privacy.

Within the attorney's office, where paperwork tends to get out of hand, a conference table for discussions with clients and a separate back unit for paperwork makes sense. Clients feel more comfortable about the confidentiality of their own case if they don't see materials pertaining to the cases of others. In any event, there must be ample storage space for paperwork as well as for reference materials.

In addition to staff and computer office space, another major element in law office planning is the law library. Mary Ann Altman has pinpointed five major changes that have taken place in library planning in the past ten decades. First, law firms have discovered that their library is an impressive

public-relations device. This implies that more care might be invested in the design and construction of libraries and that they may be visually prominent. Secondly, libraries should be planned to use computerized research equipment. Today, even small firms can avail themselves of data through telephone hookups with a remote data bank. Thirdly, the proliferation of microfilmed materials require library space for readers and printers. Fourthly, more and more medium and large law firms are considering adding trained law librarians to their staff. The librarian needs an acoustically controlled office with file cabinets for purchase records and book supplies. Lastly, the law library, like all libraries, should be planned with expansion in mind. As more and more opinions are printed and purchased, the growth rate of the average law library is likely to accelerate.

The law-office designer must consider the question of file storage and, particularly, centralized or decentralized files. The decision will vary with the type of law practice and the layout of the office. Mary Ann Altman explains that "the central files are more and more becoming a storage space for files in suspense status, either used infrequently or awaiting closing." When law firms are on two or three floors of a building, the use of centralized filing becomes cumbersome, and many firms have decentralized the files and created a file room on each floor.

In addition to their ordinary files, some firms require security file rooms for the paperwork on confidential cases. Sometimes, security file rooms are combined with workrooms and are remote from the flow of office visitors. These war rooms, as they are sometimes called, are considered a work space where papers and materials can be left in a state of disarray while they're being worked on by lawyers engaged in

①

antitrust, trade-secret, or other high-security cases.

All law offices provide some sort of reception area where clients announce themselves and wait to meet with their lawyers. Even in small reception areas, it is best to provide separate seats rather than large sofas because sometimes the clients waiting in the reception area may be adversaries in emotional legal battles. If space permits, two or more separate waiting areas can be planned adjacent to a reception area that serves only to receive clients.

Most law offices need conference rooms where meetings at-

tended by several people can take place. Many similar firms use the law library as a conference room as well. Other firms favor a series of small conference rooms that can be put to a variety of uses.

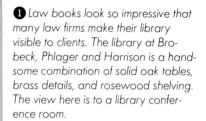

1 Law books look so impressive that many law firms make their library visible to clients. The library at Brobeck, Phlager and Harrison is a handsome combination of solid oak tables, brass details, and rosewood shelving. The view here is to a library conference room.

2 Full-height glass panel opposite the glass entrance provides a view of the board room with its parchment-finished table and leather-upholstered chairs. The walls are covered in wool fabric. Similar colors and textures are used throughout.

3 A detail of one of the 126 attorneys' offices.

4 Rosewood office doors, part of a storage wall in the secretary corridor, are hung on pivots so that the wall is uninterrupted. Brass nameplates are integrated with the doorknobs.

5 Custom secretarial stations in the foreground and paralegal stations in the background are positioned in the main corridors. The paralegal stations have clear glass to the ceiling above their enclosed padded walls for visual and acoustical privacy.

MR. PLATT

Producers

Film and television producers have relatively simple requirements for their offices. They need screening facilities and conference rooms and office space for their creative and administrative staff, with the usual requirements for files, storage, and copy machines. No less programmatic, but much more intangible, is the office image. In a field that prizes high visibility and strong personality, office spaces must not only support creativity but also express it. The office of Henson Associates, producers of the Muppets, is no exception.

Jim Henson, the Muppets' creator and producer, was attracted by the elegance of a turn-of-the-century New York townhouse. The problem was to convert it to office space for his dynamic organization without destroying the fine architecture that made it so appealing. Interior designer Warren Hansen and architects Maitland/Strauss/Behr, working as a team, came up with a solution that is part restoration, part renovation, and part new construction

They designed a puppet-assembly workshop as a new two-story extension to the rear of the existing building. Natural daylight floods the space through two large skylights. The workshop entrance is at street level, adjacent to the reception room and rehearsal spaces.

The building is zoned vertically, linked by an open central stairwell, a major element of the existing building. A screening room, the former library, is on the

second floor, along with the merchandising and art departments. The third level is the executive level of this small corporate headquarters. It contains Henson's office, a small conference room, and offices for other producers. The fourth floor houses the accounting and clerical departments. A new skylight on the roof and a new plant-filled lightwell bring natural light to the reception area and the open-office spaces adjacent to the stair. The openness throughout the building cuts through the departmental stratification. An interior stair continues to the roof, where Henson has a small retreat.

The image and attitude of Henson Associates is conveyed with whimsical elegance. This theme was the reference for design decisions, ensuring cohesiveness. "Everything was done with a slant to make it more 'Muppet-like'," recalls Warren Hansen. "For example, the screening room windows are covered with formal draperies. And the draperies are made of tie-dyed canvas."

Obviously, Jim Henson admires fine craftsmanship. He requested that the original detailing and materials be preserved. He preferred furniture and furnishings that were handcrafted rather than mass produced. As a result, antique carpets, handcarved tables and chairs, and handwoven fabrics fill spaces that have refinished wood floors and panelling. No fake details were added. The new additions are straight-

forward and cleanly detailed. Color was the other unifying element. Red, gold, and off-white were chosen for their warmth. A gold-tonality carpet covers the central stair and the small open-office areas that surround it.

Personalized work spaces are the rule. Henson's private office contains momentos that were made for him by friends—among them, a stained-glass panel depicting him and puppeteer Frank Oz with Bert and Ernie. Special work stations were designed for the puppet makers, who like to work on a brown-paper surface. Warren Hansen designed recessed, pressed fiberboard work tops wrapped with paper that could be removed and resurfaced.

①

②

1 Jim Henson's office is filled with unique, handcrafted objects and personal mementoes. The moose head—it lights up—and the stained-glass panels were made by friends. The sofa is hand-carved by Wendell Castle. The elegant room, painstakingly refinished and restored, serenely encompasses it all.

2 A former library, virtually intact, is now the screening/conference room. Moveable panels, covered in hand-woven silk, conceal video equipment. The chairs and the conference table are based on a Shaker design. The draperies exemplify whimsical elegance; they are tie-dyed canvas.

3 The gold, red, and off-white color scheme first appears in the entry foyer. The colors, chosen for their warmth, are used throughout the building to give the design cohesiveness. Wood doors open to the skylit reception area and open stair.

4 Three specialized work surfaces—a drafting table, a built-in light box, and a table-desk—show the complexity of the art director's work. No fake architectural details were added to this third-floor office. Personal and work-related display, warm colors, and natural materials enliven a straightforward interior.

5 The third-floor conference table is used for meetings, lunches, and small gatherings. The incandescent down lights are dimmer-controlled so that the light level can be adjusted for different activities.

6 A two-level extension was added to the building to house the puppet-assembly workshop in a large open area. Work stations were designed to puppet-makers' special requirements.

③

④

⑤

⑥

Built-in deadlines give publishing offices a sense of excitement and a lively atmosphere. The intensity level seems to correspond with the publication schedule. Daily newspapers are the most frenetic, book publishers relatively sober, and magazines in

Publishers

between. Their office layouts, however, reflect the different ways they gather, package, and distribute information.

The heart of a newspaper, the newsroom, is a classic open office. Reporters and editors sit in a large open space, arranged by departments. The newsroom is a work environment that demands and facilitates communication. The concept has remained valid for centuries; only the technology has changed. Every desk has a typewriter, or increasingly, a word processor. Reporters outside the office can hook up to the automatic electronic network via the telephone. The well-designed newsroom must be able to handle numerous cables and wires.

A newspaper's advertising and circulation departments can also be large open areas. They are also prime candidates for office automation. Other departments include production, which pastes up each edition, finance, planning, and legal. A library for collecting indexed articles, and occasional conference rooms are standard. So are the relatively large private offices for the publisher and the editor-in-chief who receive visitors.

Book publishers function best with cellular offices. The editors need enclosed offices with doors to keep from disturbing others when they meet with authors and

①

staff. They also need quiet when they read manuscripts. Copy editors, in particular, need distraction-free environments. Moving a book from manuscript into printed form requires constant coordination between several departments: production, editorial, design, and copy editing. It's helpful if the circulation between departments is easy. Other departments are publicity, subsidiary rights, and archives. A library makes an effective corporate symbol.

Magazines can go either way in terms of spatial layout; the choice is really a function of management style. It's not possible to say that the editors, proofreaders, and researchers who work for weekly magazines are installed in open offices and their counterparts in monthy publications work within enclosed rooms. The layout and art departments of magazines are usually large and in open studios because graphics and design are important components.

②

③

1 A cork wall at Workman Publishers becomes a giant planning schedule. Architect: Mayers and Schiff.

2 Sliding glass doors enclose the private offices at Workman Publishers. Moveable metal shelving divides the central open space into areas according to project needs. Architect: Mayers and Schiff.

3 The traditional style of the library at Oxford University Press reflects the fact that they are the oldest publishing company still in operation.

4 At the reception area on each of the ten floors at Harper and Row, a signpost identifies the particular publishing department. The signage system, designed by Chermayoff and Geisman, is used throughout the office, including a cylindrical signpost on the street in front of the building. Architect: Smotrich and Platt.

5 Lucas Programme desks, screens, and storage were used throughout the two floors occupied by the editorial and advertising departments at the Bristol United Press Building in England. The layout, based on copy flow, was determined by the Evening Post's work study department. Architect: The BGP Group.

6 The newsroom at the Providence Journal is divided only by glass partitions, so that the space is open for communication in the newsroom tradition. The editor's round desk is in the newsroom, his conference area behind glass. Architect: Warren Platner Associates.

④

⑤

⑥

Traders

Communication is crucial in the fluctuating markets in which traders deal. Whether they buy and sell securities, currencies, commodities, or financial futures, traders need up-to-the-moment information. In local marketplaces or exchanges, traders had instant communication face-to-face. Today, telephones and electronic monitors make it possible for them to hook up with other traders and other markets, often several at once. Some traders work from home.

This is a hectic and stressful business. Split seconds can make a difference of hundreds of thousands of dollars. Traders are often desk-bound for hours at a time. Those who deal in world markets that span several time zones work very long hours and rarely leave their offices during their working day.

Trading rooms should be planned to minimize fatigue. Work stations no longer have to be lined up in front of the Big Board; with computerization, a trader refers to an individual VDT screen for quotations and processes orders electronically. Work stations should be oriented so that traders see each other. Electronic monitoring boards and video display screens should be easy to read and glare-free. Telephones that are equipped with flashing lights rather than bells help to keep the noise level down. To minimize distracting others, the phones should also be equipped with built-in voice amplifiers. Air conditioning and ventilation should be finely tuned. The tangle of wires should be hidden, yet accessible, and the trader's chair

①

should be comfortable and provide support.

Areas for unwinding, remote from the stress-filled trading room, render comfort and provide relaxation. Lounges, shower rooms, and dining rooms are, in some cases, less perquisites of privilege than humane necessities. Not all traders are lucky enough to work in offices equipped with them.

The trading room, a specialized office environment, deserves a lot of attention. In a way, it's a prototypical automated office for professionals. Well-designed trading rooms recognize the nature of the work and acknowledge the importance of job performance. Yet, a checklist of design considerations is really no different for a trading room than for other office environments dependent upon electronics. The checklist items clearly illustrate how the human factor has to be considered in conjunction with technology.

Trading rooms need a clerical staff, the back office, to process the transactions that are made. Though some traders work as small, independent entities, most are part of large financial organization.

②

③

❶ The trading room in the London office of a Japanese corporation, Mitsubishi Trust, was designed in 1978 by Pentagram.

❷ The design aimed to capture some of the qualities of a Japanese interior. Pine panelling and sliding doors with shoji screens were used throughout. Le Corbusier chairs, a matching leather setee, and a specially made low table with tubular chrome and dark-red briotte marble are part of the formal dining room.

❸ The dealing or trading table is a series of working desks. The central black polished wood construction houses a double-decker filing system incorporating the standard Reuters equipment. The leather work surface rests on a heavy frame containing the cables and filing trolleys. The four dealers face one another, with two secretaries at each end of the table.

❹ The stockbroking firm of Rowe Rudd acquired a Victorian banking Hall in London for their headquarters. The design plan by Pentagram focused on the electromechanical dealing or trading boards.

❺ The kitchen displays the same precise design elements and color scheme of the offices.

❻ Well-organized communication equipment is a vital part of the trader's daily operations.

❼ A view of the director's dining room shows the application of the company logo on ashtrays, napkins, and menus. The decorative patterned woodwork allows for lighting and air conditioning.

④

⑤

⑥

⑦

Working at Home

Currently, 2 percent of the population in the United States work at home. While this might not seem like a large number, it is increasing every day as large businesses become more flexible and new businesses begin at home.

There are a number of advantages to working at home, advantages that seem hugely appealing to the office worker who is struggling with a long daily commute. It allows a worker to have a flexible schedule independent of corporate timetables and building schedules. Working at home also saves money by eliminating the cost of transportation, restaurant lunches, and the necessity of an elaborate working wardrobe. It also encourages the adaptive use of existing buildings, such as lofts and warehouses that can be converted to living/working spaces. A less specific but still important advantage of working at home is that it allows for an integration of life and work.

That being said, there are real disadvantages. When office functions and residential functions must be combined in limited space, there are often sacrifices to be made. And when a space is used for both living and working, potential infringements of noise and privacy must be carefully avoided. This sharing of space can sometimes lend a less-than-professional atmosphere to a business, which can be detrimential if clients have to visit the home/workplace.

Two of the major disadvantages of the home office are largely psychological. A home office allows no physical or mental relief from the pressing demands of work. One is never off the job, and some people find it difficult to leave their work behind under these circumstances. In addition to the constant pressure of work, the home worker is sometimes plagued by a feeling of isolation. There is little contact with others to provide a feeling of camaraderie, and there is less opportunity to share trade news and information with people in the same field.

One of the first considerations for the home worker is zoning laws. If space is rented in an office building there is no question that the use is a legal one. But in some communities, "commercial use" in a residential zone is illegal. By the same token, "residential use" in an industrial zone can also be illegal in some areas. The latter was a problem for New York City artists who needed large space for their work. They found space in manufacturing lofts but had trouble living there: there were no municipal services such as garbage collection, police protection, schools, and so on. Changing industrial zoning to residential is harder than the other way around. And suburban locations have similar restrictions where zoning laws are established because residents feel that commercial businesses would reduce property values, bring traffic to residential neighborhoods, and annoy neighbors.

It is important to check local zoning codes. Some of the regulations that apply to residential businesses include:

• Restrictions about the actual area of the residence that may be devoted to business.
• Restrictions about signs
• Restrictions about the type of business that may be conducted. For example, lawyers may not be allowed to practice while interior decorators may. Some communities prohibit stock brokers and veterinarians but allow dentists and counselors. In her book *Worksteads*, Jeremy Joan Hewes mentions that in California, actors' agents and talent scouts are prohibited from working at home. This law is intended to protect the unwary job seekers from the casting couch.

In some areas, zoning codes are becoming more flexible. In fact, mixing business and residential uses is being actively proposed to

②

③

❶ Photographer Les Carron converted an air-conditioning office in Manhattan into a combination studio and weekend pied-a-terre in town. First, the space was cleared of partitions and office paraphernalia. Brick walls were exposed, the floors were stripped, and the dropped ceiling was disassembled. Shown here is a free-standing wall that separates the studio from the office. A stained-glass panel takes advantage of the ample light in the loft. The butcher-block table serves eight, either for family dinners or business lunches. Lighting throughout the loft is controlled by a dimmer switch. Designed by Proposition Architecture.

❷ Carron's circular office in the center of his New York City loft serves as a reception area (door on right) for models and houses three desks. In the center is a lightbox for viewing and editing photo jobs.

❸ The vintage 1890s Brunswick billiards table provides recreation for both the home and office. The table is used for relaxation during breaks in shooting sessions. It has also been used as a prop in many of Carron's photographs.

revitalize central business districts that have virtually no life after dark when workers and shop keepers have fled.

The other kinds of laws affecting working at home—building and safety codes—are less flexible and with good reason. Building codes and fire laws are designed to protect inhabitants from potential hazards. They are concerned with fire safety, minimum standards for electrical wiring and plumbing, light, and ventilation. If a residence and an office are combined, then the standards for each must be met. A residence requires adequate kitchen and toilet facilities. A work space requires proper lighting and ventilation. Electric power requirements in an office tend to be greater than those in residences. Lighting, air conditioning, and office equipment can all contribute to making heavy demands on a home system.

There are other safety issues to be considered in the home work space. Valuable records need safe storage. They should be stored in a fireproof building, which is not typical of most frame houses. Some people rent vault space elsewhere for protection. One author reported storing her original manuscript pages in the refrigerator until she could put them in fireproof safekeeping.

Good design is a crucial element in the success of the home work space. It can make the difference between a space that works and one that becomes a hindrance to business. As Hewes pointed out in her book *Worksteads*, "The distinguishing feature of all worksteads —that they combine living and working places—can be an asset in the competition for capital. Particularly if his business has been operating for at least six months or a year, a worksteader can demonstrate efficient use of space and resources and clear savings in overhead, which are indicators of good management and a healthy enterprise."

①

②

③

❶ *Architect Michael Schwarting's studio above his loft space (shown in photographs numbers 5 and 6). By placing the studio above the rest of the space, Schwarting created a feeling of openness while hiding his office clutter from the living area.*

❷ *Painter George Negroponte did all the major construction work in his loft. Free-standing screens or planes were employed to divide the space into places to eat, to sleep, and to work. These subdivisions were more like territories than rooms because space was defined rather than contained. Architect: Rubin and Smith-Miller.*

❸ *Behind the wall shown in the above photograph (number 2) is this wide-open work area and dining area. Only the bathroom and an adjacent dressing area beyond the kitchen were completely enclosed.*

❹ *The bedroom in Negroponte's loft is part of the same screened-off area as the work counter shown in photograph number 2.*

❺ *Each area in Michael Schwarting's loft serves dual functions. The dining room is also a conference room; the living room is a reception area. Schwarting left the cast-iron columns intact and filled the living area with classic brentwood and modern furniture.*

❻ *The dining/conference room is spanned by a bridge in this two-story space. The walls are used for presentations and display.*

④

⑤

⑥

The Convertible Office at Home

①

Convertible offices are those where office activities and living activities take place in the same space. Convertible offices can be difficult to live with because they provide no physical separation between living and working. Often because there is no physical separation, it is difficult to achieve an adequate psychological separation. The person who functions in a convertible office space often finds it difficult to relax when surrounded with unfinished business, even when the weekend rolls around.

On a more positive note, there are real advantages to the convertible office. Today's trend in offices is to become more homelike. The idea of graciousness and expansiveness is becoming more appreciated because office space is at a premium. For example, private dining rooms and office kitchens are becoming an increasingly popular status symbol in an organization. With the convertible office, the normal homelike atmosphere has advantages to be exploited. Moreover, the trend toward more humanistic office furniture makes it easier to integrate working furniture into the living home without the jarring effect that was inevitable with uncompromising metal desks.

Essentially, there are three kinds of spaces needed for the convertible office: a place of retreat for undisturbed work, a place to meet with people for work and conversation, and a place to store records. Sometimes all these functions can be achieved in one place, but more often a selection of living spaces can be alternatively used for work functions. For example, the dining room can be used as a conference room while the living room can be used for informal conferences. A sofa used for meetings can convert to a guest bed. Chairs used in an office can also work well at the dining-room table.

Storage becomes very important when office and home functions share the same space. One solution, which really should be a goal in any office, is to limit paperwork as much as possible. But, of course, there will be essential paperwork in any business. Storage systems can be adapted so that they not only hold business files but also function as other furniture as well. Flat files, for example, can be covered with a plastic-laminate top and serve as a coffee table. It should be kept in mind that the repetition of uniform elements helps to organize a space visually. If a file cabinet can't be afforded, papers can be stored in similar-size boxes, baskets, or file folders.

One of the biggest challenges in the convertible office is to achieve an atmosphere of professionalism while allowing for a homelike atmosphere. A room has to be able to change character and function for the different roles that it will be playing at different times.

The most difficult things to establish are the amenities appropriate to both living and working. For example, if you use your living room as a conference room, it would be helpful to provide an office-phone extension in the same place. For strictly residential use, you wouldn't necessarily have a phone in the living room but you

⑵

should not have to send clients to the bedroom or kitchen to make a call. It is difficult to maintain an air of professionalism when business must be conducted from a bedroom phone. If the dining table is going to be used as a conference table, you will probably need more light than is required by the average dinner party. A rheostat, or dimmer, can achieve the desired effect without sacrificing the live-ablility of the room.

The smallest possible office, which makes no demands on other available floor space, can be contained in a closet. The depth of a standard closet is deep enough for a workable desk top. A flush-panel wood door or a plastic-laminate panel resting on top of a two-drawer file provides a built-in desk. Bookshelves can be mounted to the back wall of the closet to provide additional storage. A light mounted beneath the lowest shelf provides good light just where it's needed. Some

⑷

⑸

⑶

❶ *One way to conceal the home office is with a prefabricated system. When closed, Function Wall is an unobtrusive, made-to-measure wall panelled in fabric, mirrors, or veneered wood.*

❷ *The panels slide open and disappear into side pockets. The lights go on automatically, revealing a choice of functional environments.*

❸ *A complete home office with work surface, audiovisual center, and pull-out filing center is one environmental option. Other options include a bar with refrigerator, a library, a washroom, a fortified safe, a coat closet, or a hideaway bed.*

❹ *Every detail in Function Wall has been carefully considered. The black-stained ash, natural ash, or mahogany veneers are book-matched. The edges are hand-bevelled and the wooden handles hand-carved.*

❺ *Function Wall was designed by Herbert Hirche for International Contract Furnishings, Inc.*

①

②

fluorescent light fixtures are available with an electrical outlet so that an electric typewriter can be plugged right into the light. The wall space between the desk top and the first shelf can be used as a tack board for relevant display. The advantage of the closet office is that it allows you to close a door to hide work in progress. There is no need to take time to straighten up and give the area a semblance of neatness.

In addition to the work area itself, the entrance to the convertible office needs consideration. Check the route from the front door to the office space. This is a good place to dispel any impression of lack of professionalism. A cluttered entrance area can give a bad impression even if the actual work space is beautifully designed.

When considering the entrance area, give some thought to security. Is there a way to screen potential visitors before opening the door? If not, installing a peephole can be a good idea. Some people don't use their home addresses on their business letterhead even when the office is located right in the home. Instead, they rent post office boxes and use only that address for business correspondence. That way, they can use the telephone to screen visitors.

③

❶ Terence Conran's home office occupies one end of his living room in his Queen Anne house. He uses the office to work on weekends. The simple desk is characteristic of many of Conran's furniture designs.

❷ Interior designer Barbara Halpern's office at home is filled with Victorian antiques, fabrics, and wallpaper from that era and showcases her design approach. Her dining-room table serves as an all-purpose work surface. Samples and files are stored in built-in cabinets. Halpern keeps paper work to a minimum because storage space is limited.

❸ Michael Rubin's apartment is an example of a convertible office/bedroom. The bed is built into a sleeping loft and is out of sight when the architect is working at his desk. Designed by Rubin and Smith-Miller.

❹ and **❺** The top floor of this duplex apartment in Manhattan's Olympic Tower is often used for informal business meetings. (The lower floor encompasses the living areas.) The coffee tables in this office can be raised electronically to provide a full conference table. Other cleverly hidden electronic controls in this apartment are for windows and moveable walls, sound systems, and lighting.

❻ The author Jeffrey Archer has strong views on offices. He disapproves of the standard type of executive office and prefers smart, casual surroundings for work. Nearly all of Archer's writing is done at The Vicarage in Granchester or abroad, but he uses this London home office for meetings, interviews, and other work.

❼ The floor-to-ceiling windows throughout the penthouse flat provide a spectacular view of the Thames. Although the building is in the Thames flood zone, it hardly affects Archer's tenth-floor apartment.

❽ Archer's desk is in one corner of the L-shaped space. (There are four more rooms off this one.) The furnishings are light and sleek.

The Separate Office at Home

If you work at home, you are faced with a different set of goals, advantages, and problems in establishing your office space. There are two basic at-home office setups: an office that is a convertible part of the general living space and a totally separate and distinct office space. These setups are discussed in the previous two sections.

An office that is separate from other living quarters immediately resolves one aspect of a sensitive issue: privacy. Containing the office function also helps to put the office at a distance psychologically. The door or doorway becomes the filler between the office and the outside world. The office can be declared as off-limits to children. If you share your home with others, the totally discrete office allows for simultaneous but separate activity in another part of the house.

The most private of all separate offices has a totally separate entrance. This is more easily achieved in a suburban location and often involves a landscaping alteration to allow for a new path, door, and doorbell. A back door, from the residential space to the office space, is often desirable. Converted garages or bedrooms often readily allow for dual access and can be available as full- or part-time offices. This type of readily accessible office is particularly useful to professionals, such as physicians, lawyers, accountants, and therapists. (Remember that suburban attached-offices are subject to zoning laws that protect local communities from extra traffic, congestion, and the commercial invasion of a residential neighborhood.)

Totally separate working quarters have a tax advantage over a convertible office. Though the tax laws are always changing, the latest interpretation in the United States is that the portion of your property that's used *exclusively* for business can be treated, for tax purposes, as property separate from the personal portion of your home. A desk in the bedroom obviously does not meet the requirement of "a totally separate office." Similarly, a guest bed in the office can disqualify a space for a tax deduction. A legitimate attached office can be used by professionals on weekends or during the evening for additional income and tax deductions. Be

①

②

(3)

(4)

① and ② Designer Douglas Barnard created a study under the eaves in this London flat on Upper Brook Street. Barnard has a special affection for this study because it "seems to have a special impact on most people who see it. The study exudes quiet warmth almost like a cloister." The room is lit by the small circular window and strategically placed lamps. The walls are covered in suede cloth and the sleeper sofa is upholstered in a Duralee cotton corduroy. Previous to Barnard's renovation, the space had been a totally neglected storage area.

③ Architect Philip Johnson's one-room studio on his estate in New Canaan, Connecticut—a testing ground for his architectural ideas—was designed as a solitary work place. Light from the rectangular skylight and the large window is supplemented by artificial lights.

④ Exterior view of Johnson's study. The building has no historical precedent. Mr. Johnson says only that he "wanted to try a lonely tower on the hill."

⑤ This well-organized office is part of Peter Katz's living room. Katz, a graphic designer, covered cardboard file boxes with black paper to give the shelves an orderly appearance.

sure to check with a tax attorney or accountant on the tax-related status of your home office

A home office must provide for adequate sound insulation. Jeremy Joan Hewes, in her book *Worksteads*, recounts how a consultant engaged in international trade installed the telex machine that was essential to his business in his clothes closet. The machine was too noisy for the office portion of his loft and needed some sort of acoustical shielding. The closet provided the sound isolation that he needed and is so effective that it smothers even the clatter of printing messages that

(5)

arrive from Japan during the night. In addition to noise considerations, the separate office must take into account electrical use. Make sure that there is adequate power if a residence is "retro-fitted" for office use. The house lights shouldn't dim when the X-ray machine is in use. Office lights shouldn't flicker when the toaster is plugged in.

If a separate room, a spare bedroom for example, is converted into office space, the design considerations are similar to those of the private office anywhere. In this case, you have the large advantage of a residential scale. Moreover, you have amenities that have become goals in commercial space and whose lack is so often lamented. Your windows probably open, and unless you add them yourself, you have no fluorescent lighting and no acoustic tile. Finally and crucially, you have the freedom to design a space with human scale and dimension.

When designing an office as part of a residence, try to retain the best features of the existing building. This modification of existing areas can be particularly successful in an urban townhouse. For example, a dining room makes a fine conference room, a living room a good private office and various and assorted bedrooms can be converted to more offices.

If there are two entrances to the building, try to use them both to separate functions and circulation. In loft spaces, separate areas can be created that are screened from the larger area, by low partitions, for example, yet are open to them at the same time. These areas participate in all the aspects of open-office planning including the joys of openness and problems with privacy. In the case of the loft, there is no one answer that satisfies. The individual must determine a solution to suit both the demands of work and the limitations of space.

①

②

③

❶ *The working elements of this architect's home office in Sausalito, California, are displayed as part of the office design. By having a separate office, this architect's work in progress can be readily available, but he doesn't have to live with the clutter when he's not working.*

❷ *This studio is part of an extension that was built onto the home of Lillian and Zenas Block in Salisbury, Connecticut. Lillian Block is a painter, weaver, and textile designer, and the studio was built for all these functions. Not shown in this picture is her husband's office, which is off to the right of the counter in the right-hand corner. Because the counter was kept low, Zenas Block also has a view out of the windows on the left.*

❸ *Exterior view of the Block house extension shows the large windows beyond the screened porch that, together with the skylight, flood the studio with light. A separate entrance to the studio is near the chimney, part of the original house. Architect: William Ellis.*

❹ *and* **❺** *Reverend Patrick Tuft is the vicar of St. Nicholas, Old Chiswick, in London. His vicarage is a new building in the Georgian style that was designed by the Norman Haynes Partnership. The house was specially designed for a vicar and includes a meeting room and a private study on the ground floor. Rev. Tuft's study is an eclectic mixture of antique furniture, books, toys, and magazines.*

④

⑤

Office Electronics at Home

In his *The Third Wave*, a description of postindustrial society, Alvin Toffler predicts "a return to cottage industry on a new, higher, electronic basis, and with it a new emphasis on the home as the center of society." This dramatic change is a function of the shift from an industrial society where people produce goods to an "Information Society" where more people manipulate information rather than things.

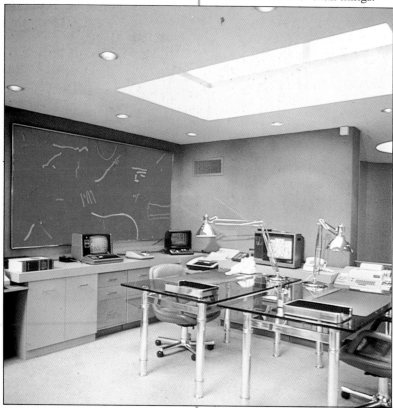

Toffler predicts that two levels of workers would first make the transition to the "electronic cottage." The first is the "low abstraction" office workers. For the most part, they require few direct face-to-face transactions in the course of their work. The tasks they perform—entering data, typing, retrieving, preparing invoices, and so on—are already carried out in the office on electronic machines. These workers need only electronic network connections from their homes to central electronic files. And the technology to connect them, the telephone, already exists. Through an electronic device called a modem, remote computer terminals can be connected to others in a computer network by telephone lines.

The second level of office workers for whom working at home is most feasible at the moment is what Toffler calls the "ultrahigh-abstraction" workers. He is referring to researchers, for example, or economists, policy formulators, or organizational designers who require both "high density" contact with peers and colleagues and time to work alone. There are times, after all, when even deal makers need to back off and do their homework.

We are already seeing a trend toward more flexible hours and work locations. The crucial demand is getting the job done and less and less emphasis is placed on how and where it's done. In fact, many office workers are working at home right now. Computer programmers, word-processing operators, and consultants who work for large organizations can work away from large corporate headquarters. They are geographically remote yet they can plug into their electronic data network where all the information necessary for their work is readily at hand. This setup is different in concept from traditional examples of working at home where the workers were independent professionals or entrepreneurs. How-

ever, Toffler suggests that "at a deeper level, if individuals came to own their electronic terminals and equipment—purchased perhaps on credit—they would become, in effect, independent entrepreneurs rather than classic employees—meaning, as it were, increased ownership of the 'means of production' of the workers." This would increase decentralization and decrease the need for large facilities.

Already there are many professionals who work at home, including consultants, human service workers, teachers, art dealers, investment counselors, insurance agents, and writers. These people only occasionally touch base in an office. They all can use small business computers to take care of their needs, and they have no need for computers.

The design criteria for the use of computers in the home is the same as for electronic devices in the office building. The furniture must be strong enought to support the equipment. Though computers, terminals, and VDTs will undoubtedly become lighter in years to come, today many of them are quite heavy. In addition to being sturdy, the furniture that supports the equipment must be at the correct height; desk height is too high. It's also important that light in the room not be reflected by the CRT screen. The best equipment has adjustable keyboards and tiltable screens, but this is available only when the keyboard and the screen are separate elements. As the printer can be quite noisy, it's best if it's located in a sound-isolating space with some acoustical dampening. Wire management will demand some attention. Each component has to be plugged into a power source, and there will be cables that run from machine to machine. The power supply must be adequate and the electric circuits must be properly wired. Finally, to connect with remote locations by telephone, a separate instrument has to be provided.

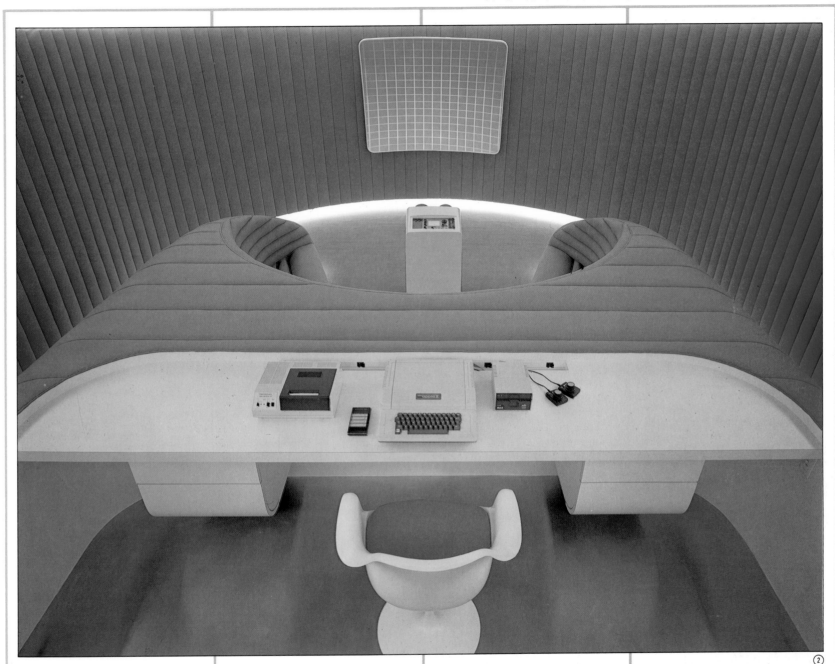

②

The design implications of the home office are unclear. Is a computer terminal dumped on a desk top in a bedroom a desirable way to work? How will the demands of privacy be met in a work situation where there is no separate office space? How can the disadvantages of isolation be overcome? Who will ensure that proper lighting levels and ergonomic factors will result in a work environment that is healthy and humane?

❶ *An international metal trader's office has been integrated with his living space. Traders have to be in constant communication with world prices, and so this work area includes a telex, Reuters Teletype, computer, television, and commodities-trading-service monitor, and an electronic typewriter. Designed by Creative Perspectives.*

❷ *Architects Doug Michaels and Richard Jost designed this media room in a Texas residence. The telephone links the terminal with an office computer and other computer networks. The video projection screen replaces a CRT screen. This room is also used for home entertainment with video games. The furniture and neon lighting were custom designed.*

The Moving Office:

CARS, BUSES AND VANS

Moving office combines travel and work. A moving office can bring people and services to remote locations: a train or an airplane modified by political campaigners, a van converted into a legal clinic, a coach turned into a library. More often, a moving office—in the form of an automobile, a helicopter, an airplane, a yacht—serves those who have neither the time nor perhaps the inclination to separate transportation and work when they travel from the office to an airport and from their office to their home.

Of course, motion affects work output in the moving office. Stability, quiet, and repose cannot be plugged into a moving vehicle. Some people are more adversely affected by motion than others. Studies have shown that passengers who face backward cope better with travel than those who sit looking in the direction of travel. Because they don't subject their bodies to unconscious alternating bracing and relaxing (in anticipation of traffic stops and starts) rear-facing passengers are far less distracted during the trip and more relaxed when they arrive at their destination. They can concentrate more fully on their task during their trip. Sitting backward is actually safer as well, because the body can better absorb impact in this position.

Communication is a crucial element in the moving office. In the field, it's relatively easy to link up with established networks. Film crews on location, for example, try to park near public telephone booths. In transit, however, ever more sophisticated solutions are required. Douglas Barnard, who has designed the interiors of corporate jets, helicopters, and a yacht, points out, "The moving office does not have the luxury of fixed communications lines, and yet, when one is away from a home office and support staff, communication becomes doubly important." Radio is usually the basis of communication to the home office, as well as the destination. Dictation machines and recording systems with elaborate controls can complete the onboard system.

But it's private transportation, free from fixed routings and timetables and designed for comfort and efficiency, that has become adjunct office space. Flexibility is a powerful selling point for corporate airplanes and company cars. The criteria for their design is comfortable seating, leg room, easy access, and a high standard for interior finishes and appointments—storage consoles, built-in telephones, and perhaps a bar.

Private transportation ensures that in traveling from one destination to another, little time is lost. For example, A. G. Nielsen, the pollster, was known for drafting memos in his blue Fleetwood Cadillac. *Everybody's Business* recounts that his "moving office" had a blue shag rug to match. Robert Moses, a public servant, used his car as a conference room on wheels. *The New York Times* wrote: "He maintained several offices, one of which was his limousine: so eager was he to use every minute that he often held meetings in his car, taking his guest along in whatever direction Mr. Moses happened to be going. When Mr. Moses had finished talking with his guest, a second limousine, which had been following, would pick up the guest and take him back to his office while Mr. Moses continued on to his destination in the first car." Both men are reported to have worked 60 to 70 hours a week.

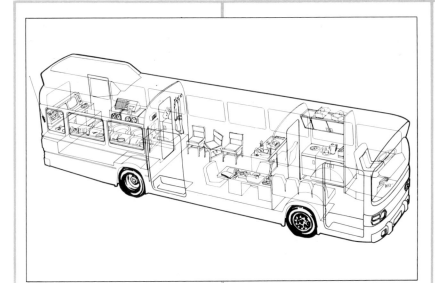

③

⑤

④

❶ A standard Leyland chassis and cab, with its own generator in tow, was painted gray so that it wouldn't attract attention to its interior electronic office. Inside is a mobile recording studio, complete with kitchen, sleeping quarters, and full air conditioning.

❷ The interior of the above van was designed for the English recording studio Island Studios by the Farell Grimshaw Partnership and Gray Coppack Designs. All floor, wall, and ceiling coverings are acoustically absorbent.

❸ Sketch showing the possible adaption of a British Leyland National bus as a film processing and cutting studio. The coach's relative freedom from space-restricting features presents designers with many different alternative uses for the vehicle.

❹ and ❺ In addition to 12 swirl chairs plus a 4-seat conference area, this bus is equipped with galley, bar, toilet, and videotape unit. The styling of this Willowbrook Spacecar was based on sketches by Willowbrook chairman George Hughes.

The Moving Office:

BOATS AND PLANES

Usually, moving offices are custom-designed interiors within prefabricated shells. It would be prohibitively expensive to design from scratch the perfect bus, van, truck, helicopter, airplane, or ship. A bus chassis, for example, has the potential to be an emergency room or a library. A large aircraft, such as a 747, can seat 300 passengers; the same fuselage as Air Force I, the U.S. President's moving office, accommodates far less. (However, the corporate jet, as we know it, is usually designed to carry about eight passengers and a crew of two.) Upfitters supply the interiors. They offer basic interior packages, and they also build to order.

Limitations exist. The moving office has to be safe and mobile as well as comfortable. Passenger needs must be reconciled with transportation design and regulations. Giles Aureli, Chairman of the Department of Industrial Design at Pratt Institute, emphasizes that structure, fuel, and safety considerations, dictated by international, national, and local regulations, influence interior design. For example, the seating arrangements in corporate jets are proscribed by exit requirements. Likewise, the size of the furniture in a rolling conference room has to be scaled to the legal maximum width of the van, truck, or bus that houses it. Fabric choices are limited by flammability standards,

①

②

③

a particularly acute problem in selecting materials to kill internal noises in helicopters and airplanes. Flammability as well as other safety requirements apply to ships, too. Aureli points out that those of the U.S. Coast Guard are particularly stringent.

Toilets and showers on board pose issues of portability, sanitation, and maintenance. Running water brings up the general question of weight. For any vehicle, additional weight means higher fuel consumption. Weight is absolutely critical in airplanes. It is inversely proportional to permissible passenger and baggage loads and/or distance. In an airplane that employs lightweight materials, the weight of stored

❶ The Daria is a 500-ton ocean-going office complex that was designed by Douglas Barnard, Inc. for a Dutch Antilles corporation. The ship can sleep 20 guests and 16 crew members. Its special features include a Long Ranger helicopter (seating seven), a 50-knot Donzi speedboat, and a 30-knot diesel sport fisherman. The ship was designed with a complete helipad, including firefighting and refueling facilities. The entertainment system includes a complete disco layout with full light and video shows, smoke machines, and advanced sound systems.

❷ One of the main public areas on the ship is the dining/conference room with facilities for 16 people. Upholstered wall treatments were used throughout the ship to help control engine noise. Other public areas include a lounge/library with facilities for smaller business meetings; a deck area, which can be closed or open to the sea air, that can seat 12 for conferences; and a sundeck with wetbar. To accommodate the guests, all the staterooms on the ship are equipped with built-in desks.

❸ The communications room aboard the Daria includes the most advanced navigation system available. The electronics are military standard. Included are high-frequency and satellite voice and telex communication, scrambler, and other electronic protection devices. The electronic, propulsion, and support facilities were designed by Nick Myers of London and DeVries Scheepsbouw of Holland. The naval architects were H.W. DeVoogt and Zoon.

water and plumbing lines makes running water—especially for showers, but also for galleys and lavatories—an expensive option.

Aureli points out that painting the exterior of corporate jets imposes a penalty in fuel consumption—about 10 percent more than if the stainless steel exterior were left unadorned. In addition, the average corporate jet is repainted twice a year to maintain its appearance.

Security, for property and passengers, is another reason for moving offices to have unobtrusive exteriors. A travelling recording studio, for example, might not like to call attention to its valuable contents. And as Douglas Barnard points out, travelling executives can be vulnerable to security problems depending upon the type of business they represent. The security system of the moving office must be highly flexible to meet the needs that accompany changes in locale and protect against industriual espionage as well as overt violence.

The aesthetics of the moving office pose a unique set of challenges. It must maximize the available space and fulfill its passenger's need for a safe-looking, hospitable, and spacious environment. Passengers in any vehicle, but particularly in airplanes, can be subject to feelings of claustrophobia. One way to overcome this is to make the windows seem as large as possible. Another is recessed cove lighting along the length of long vehicles, such as airplanes and buses. This tends to make the side walls recede and make the interiors appear more spacious.

①

②

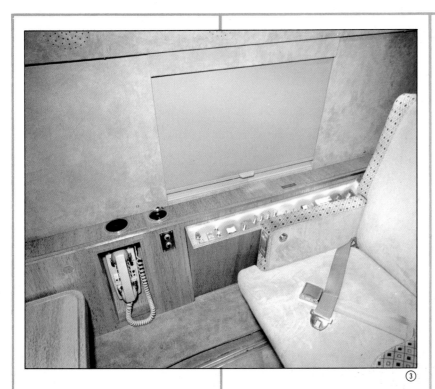

❶ A Grumman Gulfstream II was converted into a combination meeting center, hotel, and office in the sky for a Texas company whose executives are frequently sent to the Middle East. The interior incorporates space for two separate business meetings. The chairs and sofa convert into berths and all the tables double for both eating and conferences.

❷ The lines on the exterior of the Gulfstream II give the plane a sense of motion even when it's standing still.

❸ Communication controls are readily available. Wood veneers were laminated to foam sheets to reduce weight on the Gulfstream II. The plane interiors were designed by Douglas Barnard, Inc.

❹ The interior of this Augousta 109 helicopter was also designed by Douglas Barnard, Inc. For many businesses, the helicopter is the fastest, most efficient means of transporting executives for distances of up to about 300 miles. This particular helicopter is used by a corporation for short air commuting in western Europe. The chopper includes ample storage for paper work, briefcases, refreshments, and a small amount of luggage. Leather and suede were applied to the interior walls and ceiling to help control sound. Seats are upholstered in wool fabric for wear and comfort.

❺ Space is at a premium in the confined quarters of a jet. The lighting on this corporate plane emphasizes the height of the interior in order to relieve claustrophobia.

④

⑤

The Portable Office

①

For some people—consultants, journalists and sales personnel—the nearest telephone booth is the only office space they'll ever need. They keep track of incoming phone calls with live telephone answering services or message recording machines. If they have to be notified instantly, they use electronic paging devices, **beepers**, whose range is now equal to the distance between Frankfurt and Zurich. The telephone connects them with a network into which they can plug briefcase-sized computer terminals. There's room to spare in the briefcase for microfiche readers, dictation machines, and calculators.

Portable telephones will fit in the briefcase, as well. Their transmitter and power source have become so miniaturized that you don't need a limousine to transport them; you can carry them yourself. These battery-powered telephones will make travellers independent of the telephone booth.

Computerized switching using **cellular** technology will drastically increase the feasibility of portable telephones. Presently, their use is limited by the available channel space. In the New York City area, for example, there is a six-year waiting list to gain access to channel space. Of the approxi-

mately one thousand radio telephones now operating there, only twenty conversations can occur simultaneously. When U.S. government approval is granted for cellular telephone systems, tens of thousands of users will be accommodated.

Electronic pagers, limited because they can only receive signals but not transmit them, have become increasingly sophisticated. The range, once limited to 10 to 20 miles, is now 300 miles. Numerical LED readouts on the beeper inform its possessor of the

telephone number to call or a coded signal. Within two years, alphabetical readouts will be added that will display four messages of up to 20 characters each. Tiny magnetic tapes will be incorporated in the beeper to store the messages, which could range from "Buy" or "Sell" to "Take your medicine".

According to Kenneth Iscol, President of Telstar Communications, the most revolutionary development in personal communications is **voice mail**. "Any touch-tone phone can become a mailbox

for receiving voice messages. Also, you can send messages to one person or hundreds of people simultaneously, without typing, without owning any hardware. A push-button phone becomes your own computer terminal." Voice mail uses computer technology to digitalize, store, and reproduce human speech. Messages can be forwarded at given times, at given dates up to seven days in advance. "Another reason voice mail is revolutionary is there is no direct communication," says Iscol. "However, with business calls, it turns out talking directly to others is necessary only 20 percent of the time. For the other 80 percent, the telephone becomes a post office for sending or receiving messages anywhere, anytime with no delay. When you think that the average business call takes two and one half tries, seven minutes to complete, and the time and effort to send a letter or a memo, the advantages are obvious. It's convenient, it beats time zones, it leaves you more time to be productive. And all you have to do is pick up a push-button phone in your home, or a cellular telephone in your briefcase. You can go anywhere and be on top of things. You'll never need an office."

③

②

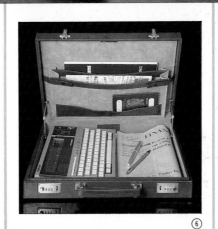

❶ *The DYNA T-A-C Portable is a hand-held radio telephone that provides all the capabilities of a business telephone. It is designed to work within cellular systems that utilize computerized switching. Cellular systems are presently being tested in two United States cities. Courtesy: Motorola, Inc.*

❷ *Electronic pagers, such as this BPR 2000, informs of incoming calls and reads out a number to call back on a display screen. Courtesy: Motorola, Inc.*

❸ *The OPTRX pager from Motorola has a tone alert and optional voice and read-out for messages.*

❹ *The Sony Typecorder is a completely portable typewriter that features many word-processor conveniences, such as instant editing, deleting, inserting, and steno capacities.*

❺ *Stylish accessories for the portable office include a brass card case, a tuck-away umbrella, a leather briefcase, a sterling silver pen, a date/address book, a calculator with its own pencil and writing pad, a fountain pen, and note pads.*

❻ *The Typecorder is small enough to fit into a briefcase.*

Office Planning

Chapter 6

Planning Office Spaces

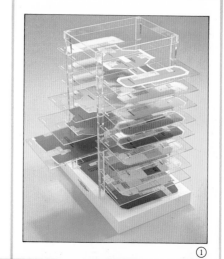

①

Before an organization can rent or build office space, it has to determine how much space it needs. Space requirements vary according to managerial style and budgets. They adapt to the module of existing buildings, to coordinate with column spacings, window mullions, and overhead-lighting patterns. New buildings have the luxury of being designed from the inside out.

The total number of square feet that an organization needs is the total space for all employees, the ancillary and support areas, and circulation. Minimum primary circulation requirements are fixed by fire laws, for access to fire stairs and building exits. Intradepartmental circulation factors establish spatial density. Obviously, circulation varies with the size of the building core (where elevators, stairs, toilet rooms, and mechanical spaces are usually located) and the configuaration of the building. John Worthington, a partner in the London firm Duffy Eley Giffone and Worthington (DEGW) Architects and Space Planners, cites a study of four German office buildings made by his firm. In the *Architect's Journal* he reports that the actual office areas account for 27 to 44 percent of the total area. Structure, vehicles, ducts, circulation, social areas, and special production areas—for building maintenance, informa-

tion exchange, and supply—account for the rest.

Worthington points out that office automation has had an effect on the way space is distributed. The increasing number of managers and professionals has called for an increase in support spaces for individuals and groups. He divides them into ancillary functions (localized meeting rooms and file and copy centers) and central support areas (computing, conference rooms, and cafeteria spaces). Between 30 and 40 percent of the useable area (the space left over after the building core and the primary circulation are subtracted from the gross area of the building) are now allocated to these functions.

Another change is that not only do professionals and managers require more space than the clerical operators they're replacing, but also more space than plans based on status standards would allow. A great deal of their time is spent meeting with others —sometimes as much as 50 percent. They need larger spaces for meetings, and they need privacy. In an open plan, their work stations should incorporate a place for meeting and be separated from other employees by greater distance than usual to prevent distraction. More enclosed conference rooms are being programmed as well. One conference room per 100 em-

②

ployees used to be the planning rule of the Quickborner Team (the German management consultant group); now, they plan for one for every 30 to 50 employees.

Changing office technology has modified other spatial requirements. For example, a word-processing work station with a printer and central processing unit takes up 50 percent more space (76 square feet [7 sq m]) than a secretarial work station with an electric typewriter on a desk extension (52 square feet [5 sq m]). Architect James Rappoport points out that some buildings designed

for the pre-electronic boss and secretary are obsolete because the automated setup can't be efficiently laid out in the space that used to house the boss and secretary between the building core and the exterior wall.

Some organizations will probably always link job and office size. Government agencies, for example, usually have strict guidelines for office size according to rank. The U.S. General Services Administration, for example, allows 500 square feet (46 sq m) for their highest rank—GS 18 and 100 square feet (9 sq m) for GS 12 and

13. By the same token, in organizations where office size reflects the job category, an executive vice-president might be assigned 230 square feet (21 sq m) and the

③

assistant vice-president, supervisors, and managers 100 square feet (9 sq m). Some organizations also link furniture standards to job titles.

Projection for space requirements should be made department by department and should extend for the length of the lease. Room for expansion can be accommodated by renting more space than present needs dictate and subletting it until it's needed. Or, the lease can include options to rent additional space at a later date.

Spatial requirements must be considered in conjunction with adjacency requirements. Which departments should be near one another, which can be on separate floors, and which in separate buildings? Some spaces might require room on more than one floor, stairs, for example; or rooms that require high ceilings, such as TV studios; or large meeting rooms, mechanical equipment rooms, and conveying systems.

The computer can be a useful tool for designers to keep track of the information collected during this phase of the planning operation. Once the data is collected and entered into a computer's memory, it serves as the basis for analysis of area requirements, work-station types, equipment, furniture inventories, department growth, and the budget.

❶ An acrylic planning model shows space allocations on floors in the Financial Times of London. One of the earliest steps in the planning process is to determine how the required adjacencies work in an actual building. Architect: Trickett Associates.

❷ Overhead view of a work station shows provisions for two separate work areas: a conference table for meetings and a desk for paper work. Spatial requirements for each office worker must be determined during the programming stages of office design. Courtesy: E.F. Hauserman Company.

❸ Wiring requirements must also be considered during the planning stages. Here a construction photograph of a stockbroker's office shows a raised platform that will house and conceal the wiring for computers, telephones, and the other electronic equipment in the future offices of Smith, Barney, Harris and Upham. Designed by Neville Lewis.

❹ Ancillary function areas need to be predetermined when allocating space. Often, these areas have special requirements for mechanical equipment or extra-height ceilings. The media room is an ancillary area that is used by many employees but is not assignable to any one person. Designed by PLM Designs.

❺ All planning options and possibilities can be visualized in three dimensions with Haller Systems planning aids that include the use of 1/20-scale models.

④

⑤

Planning the Total Image:

IDENTITY

Each organization has specific budgets, needs, goals, and plans. It has its own attitudes toward employees, visitors, clients, and vendors. The design of an organization's office reflects these attitudes from the initial planning stages. Taken together, they comprise what in design terms can be called the firm's *image.*

Image is not added in the form of finishing touches. It does not appear with the color of the paint. Image is a component of the programming process and pervades every design decision. Image is inherent in all aspects of the physical environment, long before the front door is opened.

Location is the first tangible clue to an organization's image—a clue people pay attention to. Indeed, when a prestigious New York law firm moved from Wall Street to mid-Manhattan, the mere shift in location became front-page news. Consider, then: is the office in a high-rent district? In an up-and-coming neighborhood or in a deteriorating one? Near other offices of its kind? Is it in a suburban office park? In your home? In a conventional office building? Not only the general neighborhood, but the street, the building, its lobby, and the number of floors above the street that must be traversed before reaching your office—all create an impression on visitors before they even reach the front door.

The physical environment provides information about the people and groups connected with them. It sends out messages that we're culturally conditioned to look for and interpret: "A title on the door rates a Bigelow on the floor" spells it out clearly. But most messages are read almost unconsciously—which is what enables them to operate so powerfully.

Image is important for two groups of people—the staff and outside visitors. Most designers and architects feel that the major concern of their clients is to be provided with pleasant work environments that will attract the best people. Marvin Affrime of the Space Design Group has said, "I tell my client that a well-designed office is the strongest comment a chairman can make to the office boy: 'We Care.' I think it's stronger than salary."

Sensitive to the environment, employees get employer-conveyed messages through the design of their offices. They get

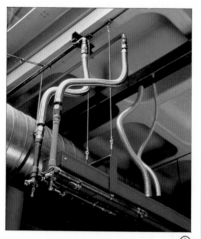

the point—all too well—when they walk through their firm's elaborate reception area and into poorly lit, crowded back rooms in which they labor eight hours a day. Knowing that one flight up executive offices present a striking contrast to their own domain only makes matters worse. While employees may not always be able to articulate their exact reasons for feeling mistreated in such a situation, they interpret the clues the environment provides easily

enough and respond to them.

As for potential employees, they are most sensitive to the personnel office. The personnel offices of large organizations are often the places where people form their first impressions of their future employers. Unfortunately, many firms neglect this department, at least in terms of the image it conveys through its design. Is there a pleasant place to wait? Is there a place to fill out an interview form in privacy? Does the interview room provide privacy and a sense of confidenti-

ality? Answers to these questions, positive or negative, tell potential employees something about the firm before they even so much as see the work space that might be provided for them.

Office visitors also receive messages from the office environment. Good design can inform visitors that a firm is different from others in the field. This can be suggested in ways more subtle than putting the firm's product up on a stand in the reception room.

For a long time, the United States government deliberately decided that their offices should appear utilitarian so that taxpayers would not think their money was being squandered on expensive furniture and lavish environments. This resulted in demeaning, drab environments for the people who worked there as well as for those who visited. Of course, government offices need not duplicate Versailles. But on the other hand, a low budget need not entail an ugly, depressing environment, either.

Some organizations feel that they should appear "utilitarian—no frills." Others feel that they should appear, "prosperous, traditional." Such messages can all be translated into concrete, visual terms. Some messages can all be translated into concrete, visual terms. Some materials, for instance, are inherently more luxurious than others and indeed are synonymous with luxury. Also, more space, properly deployed, usually seems more luxurious than less space. Still, a small amount of space need not look meager or mean. A small, well-lit, reception room can be designed to appear spacious and let people know as directly as a larger one can that their arrival is important.

While a successful image is an appropriate blend of the familiar and the unique, radical departures from expected norms could be poor business practice. Whatever the approach, it should be consistent. Layout, lighting, color, and furniture should be consistent with budget requirements and consistent with the firm's logo, paper forms, stationery, signage, and graphics. No detail is too small to be considered.

❶ Tnemec cleverly exploits their company's product by using a super-reflective paint on their interior walls. The wall surfaces display their product. The painted mannequin announces the entrance to the company headquarters in Boston. Architect: Rubin and Smith-Miller.

❷ Industriallike interiors are the antithesis of posh, expensive ones. Exposed lighting, wiring, air conditioning, and mechanical parts used as decorative elements suggest a no-frills atmosphere. The exposed ceiling at Middlesex Poly was designed by Rock Townsend.

❸ Another example of the industrial look, the little red office in the Kooper Group offices. Designed by Eisenman and Enoch.

❹ The stone elements used in the reception area of the executive floor of Prudential's NEHO Boston offices have rich symbolic meanings. They allude to the Rock of Gibraltar, the company symbol. The portal configuration of Walter Dusenberry's red travertine sculpture, Porta Lucia, also suits a place of arrival and departure. Designed by Daroff Design, Inc.

❺ Office locations also have symbolic associations. The townhouse setting for Hanover Acceptances suggests that this company is different from conventional offices. The antique accessories give further clues to the personal preferences of the occupants. Designed by David Hicks.

❻ The art deco lobby in New York City's landmark Chrysler Building is a prestigious introduction to any of the offices on the upper floors. Architect: William Van Alen.

Getting Advice from Design Professionals

The planning process begins with a need for new space. There are several reasons for this need. Michael Saphier in his book *Planning the New Office*, lists four reasons: the need for more space; the need for a better location; the need for more efficient space; and the need for better-looking space. The need for a different location and a new organization's need to establish itself are two more reasons.

Moving to new offices is a complicated process that takes time from the first idea to putting flowers in the vase in the reception room. If your lease is up in two years, now is the time to begin.

Organizations can choose to build new quarters, move to renovated quarters in existing buildings, or redecorate existing office spaces to make them more efficient and attractive.

Design professionals can be useful to a project from the start. In the planning stages, they can help with the project in the following ways:

- Compare available rented spaces to determine suitability and relative cost including construction or renovation.

- Analyze the existing operation, inventory furniture, and define space standards for new quarters.

- Prepare budget analyses, in cooperation with a real-estate consultant, of alternate strategies such as buying, building, or leasing space.

Obviously, a large corporation planning to relocate hundreds of miles from its present location has to consider taxes, zoning laws, relocation of personnel, transportation, community impact, amount of land or space to purchase, and so on. However, the goals are the same for both large and small organizations: to establish the broad parameters for choice and to consider the feasibility of alternatives.

Once the need for a change and the economic parameters of the move, the budget, are established, the programming phase follows. Most design professionals work with the client to develop the program—a statement of an organization's goals expressed in terms of area requirements and adjacencies. It describes how offices should function and what services they require. This can be useful in searching for suitable new locations. If a building needs a loading dock, if all the executives require private bathrooms, or if stairs connecting floors are desirable as a secondary means of circulation, these special needs have to be spelled out so that suitable buildings can be located and unsuitable ones eliminated without wasting time. If open-plan offices, are desired, some buildings are more suitable for this concept than others. Professional advice and experience are therefore useful at this phase. Design professionals can also review a building lease on behalf of their clients.

Interior designer William M. Leonard points out in *Administrative Management* (December, 1981) that the difference between a good lease and a badly negotiated one can mean tens or hundreds of thousands of dollars over the life of the lease. Having layout drawings prepared in advance is a major benefit during negotiations. The main parts of the lease that should be examined are the work letter, rent commencement, and continuing rights.

The ***work letter*** is the portion of the lease that spells out the improvements a landlord will make on his property before a tenant moves in. The work letter identifies the items the landlord will supply and in what quantity; this is usually referred to as "the building standard." The work let-

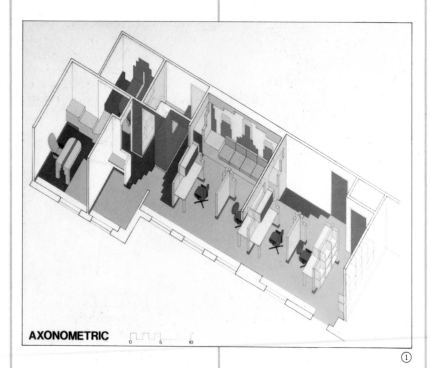

AXONOMETRIC

0   5   10

①

ter spells out formulas for arriving at "allowances" for building standard items and systems of credits or substitutions should you choose different ones. The items needed to create a basic space are air conditioning, floors, acoustic ceiling tile, a certain number of doors and frames, and square feet of wallboard partitions and light fixtures. Payments for items above building standard, including more of an item or one of

better quality, and substitutions and credits for less expensive items are agreed upon in the work letter. Custom items—internal stairwells, custom cabinetwork, additional air conditioning, and other specialties—are also spelled out in the work letter.

Rent commencement—the date on which rent begins—requires a knowledge of design and construction schedules.

The designer's advice can be

helpful in negotiating **continuing rights**—maintenance and security and utility services.

A move to new quarters provides the opportunity for reevaluating established practices and procedures; the programming phase is the time to consider new equipment, new filing methods, new telephone and communication lines, and new copiers and copier procedures. Even if all the changes are not implemented at

the time of the move, a master plan can be drawn up so that adequate power and capabilities can be provided for. These matters are easy enough to plan beforehand but are costly and time-consuming to add later.

Management consultants can give advice on communications, paper handling, office automation, and so on. However, many design professionals are qualified to make suggestions because of their familiarity with some, if not all, office equipment and procedures.

The program should be approved as the operational document on which all decisions are based. Once the program and preliminary cost estimates—bound to be very broad at this time—are approved, actual design can begin. At this point, however, many decisions have been made that will affect the final solution.

Design does not exist in a vacuum. It must be applied to a specific site, a specific location. Therefore, the **preliminary design** is based on a real location. It shows the allocation of space according to real needs in terms of a real site. Preliminary design is a source of excitement to designers and clients alike. It represents the first time the "problems" of an organization are solved by a spatial concept that translates the needs of the client into a three-

❶ *An axonometric drawing showing, in scale, the placement of walls and furniture. The drawing is a tool to help clients visualize the dimensions and shape of a design. The presentation drawing shown here, the New York office of an import/export firm, was prepared by Arsene/Lambros design.*

❷ *Architects Skidmore, Owings and Merrill's conference room is set up with accessories, furniture, and fabric swatches so that executives of Manufacturers Hanover Trust can make selections for their private offices.*

❸ *A study model of a new furniture system, the S/4 Series, designed by dePolo/Dunbar for Dunbar Furniture. The chairs are in production by the same company. The mannequins are used to show scale. Courtesy: dePolo/Dunbar.*

②

③

dimensional solution. At this phase, planning sizes and spatial densities should be reviewed.

The next phase is **design development**, where any problems that were present in the preliminary phase can be cleared up. At this point, **lighting** and **acoustic consultants** and **mechanical** and **structural engineers** might be required. Interior finish materials and office furniture and equipment are chosen. Perspective drawings or scale models are usually presented at this phase to give as complete a picture as possible of how the new office will look.

If the budget allows, a full-scale mock-up of a typical interior space—a private office, a work station—should be erected at this stage. Mock-ups offer an opportunity to refine details and make improvements. Mock-ups also encourage participation and feedback when comments and suggestions are entertained and implemented. Short of a full-scale mock-up, employees should be encouraged to visit showrooms and try out the furniture—especially office chairs because as far as comfort in the office is concerned, they are most critical.

The next phase is preparation of the construction documents—the drawings and specifications that make it possible for contractors to build the space. The construction documents are, of course, based on approved plans. They show whatever is necessary to fully explain the project and to determine its cost. A complete set includes floor plans that show construction, furniture layout, and lighting layout and telephone and electric plans that show outlet locations. Drawings of custom-designed cabinets and any special items—door frames, doors, convector enclosures, stairs, handrails—are included. They are usually organized by building trade—all the interior finishes, for example, are put in schedules on the same sheet to make it easier for the

painter to estimate the cost and to find the information to do the job when the time comes. A separate list of specifications—in note form—accompanies these working drawings. The specifications clearly describe procedures, standards, and responsibilities in more detail than the drawings do.

Construction documents are used by the contractor to establish a price for construction. Contracts with suppliers for furniture, furnishings, communications, and moving are prepared as well. The carpet specifications are particularly important because of their large expense. The design professionals advise in the bid-negotiation process.

The next phase is periodic job visits to make sure the work proceeds in accordance with the contract documents. Design professionals can coordinate the move and oversee installation of the furniture and interior fittings, as well.

Architects and designers can set up procedures for making sure that once it's occupied, the office space they've designed will be flexible enough for an organization's needs yet maintain design standards. At the time of the move, the designer can provide equipment manuals, signage guides, and maintenance programs for fabrics and finishes. They'll allow in-house staff to

make decisions about operational details. (IBM requires them.) Some design professionals suggest **post-occupancy evaluations** as an alternative to educating and training in-house staff—especially when complicated systems furniture is involved. They inspect their clients' offices every six to twelve months, to take care of the inevitable changes and modifications most dynamic organizations expect.

You should choose design professionals on the basis of their previous work. Look at offices they've designed. Ask for a reference. Design is a problem-solving profession. Designers provide service—their job is to offer advice

③

within the constraints of your budget and your organizational goals. You should ask for and expect a design solution that suits your organization. In general, the more clearly your goals are defined, the easier it is to formulate a design solution.

On the other hand, as a client you should set up an apparatus for decision making that has authority and speed. Design professionals, who are in effect advising you how to spend your money, will not proceed to the next stage until they have approval to do so. Slow approvals or countermanded decisions can be costly and time-consuming.

Each professional organization has developed contracts that spell out the responsibilities and obligations of design professionals. Their professional associations will send them upon request.

Design professionals charge for their services in a variety of ways, and four systems are given below as examples. Each firm has usually worked out the systems best for them. (1) A fee is charged on the basis of time expended on the project by establishing a rate for principal's and employee's time. (2) A fee is charged as a percentage of the total client's cost, usually billed periodically. The total service is broken down into phases. Payment is usually due at the completion of each phase. (3)

A fixed fee is negotiated after the scope of the work is determined. (4) A fee is charged based on a multiple of square feet. The services for engineers, acoustic consultants, interior plantscapers, and other professionals, depend upon specific situations. Reimbursable expenses, such as long-distance phone calls, travel expenses, and printing bills, are usually billed directly.

Warren Platner

To illustrate his approach to office design, Warren Platner, one of America's most respected architects and designers, chose the office he created for the director of research at Standard Brands, manufacturers of packaged food and liquor products, located in Wilton, Connecticut, and employing 230 people. "Here," says Platner, "there is nothing special for status, but everything special for function, because the Director has a special job."

The materials used are consistent with those of the rest of the building: exposed structural steel, brick walls painted white, exposed lighting fixtures, carpeted floors, and natural-oak furniture (designed by Platner himself). Special features are for function, not appearance: linen-covered panels in the vaulted ceiling and mounted behind the credenza wall absorb sound, while the director's desk and conference table have a leather top "so papers don't slide around," as the designer explains.

Still, this office is nevertheless a special place—"a place for thinking, sharing, and meeting with other people"—and has a definite presence of its own. A round conference table, rather than a desk, is the main piece of furniture. No one sits at its head, which makes it eminently suited as a place for discussion. The chairs grouped around the table are on castors so that they can be moved. Desk functions are taken care of by a separate credenza. Aside from the conference table, Platner

①

②

also included, for less formal meetings, a window seat in a very large bay window that commands a sweeping view. "A more relaxed, contemplative discussion of ideas can take place sitting around in comfortable seating," the designer comments. "It looks relaxed, it's a symbol, it says 'come over here and sit down, I'll spend a little more time with you.' This, I feel, is another example of a conventional and real need solved in an unusual way."

The director's chair faces a wall—"the largest unbroken surface in the room," Platner remarks —which happens to be a chalk-

board for people in the conference area to draw on. "It's usually covered with complicated formulas and equations because it's desirable to leave the information there," he continues, and adds that a roller shade was provided that "pulls down to cover and conceal it for confidentiality." The face of the roller shade is a world map, appropriate for a corporation with concerns as far-reaching as Standard Brands'.

If any element marks the director's office as a prominent one, it is the lighting. The office itself projects beyond the face of the building. With glass skylights

③

④

❶ Architect Warren Platner delights in solving "ubiquitous prototypical needs" in unique ways. The low window seating in the research director's office.

❷ The help of the public in evaluating new products is vital to the work at Standard Brands Research Center. This stair connects the main entrance with public spaces—tasting rooms and test kitchens—and the executive offices on a lower level. The rich lighting, integrated with the architecture and sculptural elements, enhances the experience of climbing the stairs.

❸ and ❻ The director's office was conceived as a conference room.

❹ The interior finishes are consistent throughout the building—exposed structural steel, painted brick, and exposed light fixtures. The furniture is of natural oak, here used in the open laboratory work places with metal files.

❺ In the director's office, the bar, toilet, and coat-hanging space are concealed behind louvered oak doors.

❼ The main conference room has two light sources for seeing new packaging the way a customer would: fluorescent, used in supermarkets, and incandescent, common in homes. When the blackboard rolls back, it exposes oneway glass to monitor food-tasting in the adjacent room.

⑤

⑥

around the room's perimeter, "the sky," as Platner notes, "is on the ceiling." Natural daylight falls through the skylights onto chalkboard and credenza, filtering through electrically operated Venetian blinds. The center of the ceiling, rising up above the conference area as a vault, features a very large fluorescent fixture that incorporates incandescent lighting (to "punch it up," Platner says), which sheds general light. Incandescent fixtures are also provided in the skylights so that at night the room is lit with a combination of fluorescent and incandescent light.

While the office is primarily functional, status symbols do crop up here, nevertheless. The office has its own lavatory as well as coat-hanging space and a bar. Platner, however, views the bar not only as a social amenity but also as functional as well. After all, he points out, "A beverage department is an important subsidiary of Standard Brands."

The director's office is one space in the Research Center. Platner took similar care in designing the building, its site, and its interior spaces: offices, laboratories, conference rooms, research library, and cafeteria.

⑦

Kevin Roche John Dinkeloo & Associates

When Union Carbide decided to move its headquarters from Park Avenue in New York City to Danbury, Connecticut, everyone knew that some major changes were in order, especially the architects, the distinguished firm of Kevin Roche John Dinkeloo & Associates.

"I spent months in the old Union Carbide building observing," Kevin Roche recalled, "after which I argued to get rid of different sized offices. Everyone needed the same amount of space and equipment to get their jobs done. In the existing headquarters, office size was a symbol of prestige, not function. The standards of existing offices were a problem for managers because furniture and finishes and office sizes changed depending on status. They were playing games with people who were doing a job. I felt it was important to get rid of the perquisites, get rid of the management costs, get rid of the costs of stocking, moving and upgrading furniture, and to get rid of the highly structured reward system tied into the physical layout."

Executives, too, had their qualms. Their offices were too large, they said, too pompous and ceremonial. They didn't like the sense of isolation and felt uncomfortable with the extreme disparity between their offices and those of the other employees. They

realized, too, that their office planner had not been able to keep up with organizational changes that required layout alterations.

The architects' solution was

①

unique. In Union Carbide's new headquarters in Danbury, 2,358 employees will eventually work in private offices. The entire corporation has the space standard throughout: a standard module, 13 feet 6 inches by 13 feet 6 inches (4 m by 4 m), the optimum size, the architects believed, for working alone or with small groups. For larger groups of up to 10 people, a conference room of the same dimensions is provided. Each office has a window. "This improved the lot of the lower-level employees," Roche noted, "and it treated everyone in a more egalitarian way." As for secretaries (there is one secretary here for every three professionals), they occupy core areas that include support spaces—copy rooms, file rooms, meeting rooms, and so on.

The problem was what to do with all those offices. If 2,358 offices were laid out side by side

on both sides of a corridor in a building one story high, that building would have to be 2.6 miles (4 km) long. Rather than opt for this unlikely edifice, the architects designed a four-story building with an undulating perimeter that allows the maximum number of offices in a relatively short expanse. The construction is extremely simple—reinforced concrete slabs. Office heating and air conditioning is provided by perimeter window units, as in apartment houses. The walls are drywall. Each individual office has excellent acoustic insulation as well as operable windows that reinforce the residential quality and scale. Four-level parking is provided in the center of this building so that

②

the lake-studded 674-acre site the building occupies goes unmarred and no one looks out their office windows onto a parking lot.

Before the building was constructed, each employee was given a choice of interior decor. The architect's office devised 15 different office interiors each costing the same. These interiors represented different styles—traditional, transitional, contemporary, and modern—along with different layouts and accessories. Each office was designed with a wood floor-border into which a standard size 8-by-12-foot (2.4-by-3.6-m) rug could be set. Domestic-style light fixtures were selected to further deinstitutionalize the office. As for furniture, some components were designed by the architects, while others were standard pieces.

Fifteen full-size mock-ups of the furniture and accessories were

built and installed in the old Union Carbide building, along with 15 scale models that were twice dollhouse size. From among these, employees could choose their own office interiors, taking as much time as they wanted to make up their minds. Only one rule held once a choice was made, the employee had to stick with it. The selection process was computerized, which formed the basis for ordering and inventory and provided a good system for maintenance and replacement.

"Some people were concerned that the whole thing might look visually disorganized, but actually it works quite well in practice," Roche noted. "It was interesting to see what people chose. For one

③

thing, they didn't choose what architects might choose—high-design chairs and desks. That was the least appealing choice. Employees tended to a middle ground of selection. Also, even with a mock-up, many people were unable to visualize the finished office. For example, a glass table-desk was not a popular choice, yet when they saw it in the actual building; many people wished they had chosen it. It was also very interesting that the traditional-style office was not popular at all. We are repeating this process in our design for another client, and we have eliminated that style completely.

"At the beginning of this project," Roche recalled, "if you had asked me before I designed this what the building would have looked like, I never could have imagined it." Now, though, it seems as if Roche hit upon a solution more ideal than he'd at first thought. "I'd like to encourage every person to design his or her own office," he mused. "Some people don't care if their offices are red or green, but a lot of people do. The architect can provide a service and help people make a selection. Designers have to remember that they are dealing with real people. The only way I know to do that is to constantly talk to and interview them. That's the touchstone of designing anything."

④

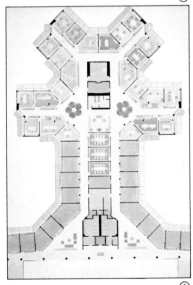

⑤

⑦

⑥

⑧

❶ through ❸ Kevin Roche John Dinkeloo and Associates' design for the Union Carbide Corporation's new headquarters is unique. It provides for 2,358 private offices, all with windows, all the same size. Moreover, employees were given the opportunity to choose their office design. Shown are mock-ups of three of the 15 possible choices. Each interior solution cost the same. The variables were layout, color, accessories, and furniture style. Full-scale mock-ups and scale models were set up in the New York office before the corporation moved. Employees could try out the arrangements and furniture before they made a decision. There was only one rule: no second choices.

❹ The building, shown during construction, is designed to be highly energy-efficient. All the windows have double-insulated glass and reflective awnings to control solar gain.

❺ This plan shows a portion of the building—a pod. The undulating perimeter of the four-story building affords each office a view of the Connecticut landscape. Service spaces are centrally located.

❻ A mock-up of a conference room, used for meetings of eight to ten people. It is the same size as the offices and furnished, like them, in an uninstitutional manner.

❼ The building, surrounded by trees, occupies less than 2 percent of the site. This model shows how the offices encircle the central parking garages, so cars are out of view. Dining rooms, medical services, mail rooms, and lounges are located in the middle of this large building.

❽ This office mock-up features a modern roll-top desk by Dunbar.

Karen Daroff

SmithKline is the fastest growing manufacturer of prescription drugs—ethical pharmaceuticals—and over-the-counter products. As their market is worldwide, the space to which they were relocating (in Philadelphia) had to be appealing to domestic and foreign visitors. Furthermore, the space had to be flexible, secure for people and information, durable, and maintainable.

With this in mind, Daroff Design Inc. set to work. "We try to research the company we design for very, very carefully," Karen Daroff comments. "Each has its own unique ideas about how they want to accommodate their employees, and how they want to be perceived by the public. And you have to learn to read between the lines. SmithKline is a closely knit, community-oriented company, which had achieved remarkable growth in a short amount of time. They wanted to retain the close-knit quality between employees and executives, many of whom had known each other all their working lives. They used words like 'substantial,' 'high quality,' 'not garish,' 'comfortable but not luxurious' to describe the working environment they wanted. To the public, they want to project the image of being exactly what they were—no artifice."

Karen Daroff worked closely with the client to develop a design program. SmithKline had already chosen a building for their corporate staff and excutives. Here the client wanted as many offices as possible along the perimeter of the building and presented the designers with the sort of extensive filing requirements Daroff calls a "challenge."

"We worked with their in-house staff to develop space standards that were based on the building which had been chosen before we were hired," Daroff explains. "We developed a flexible system of exterior office: an A office, 20 by 13 feet [6 by 4 m]—to be assigned to a vice-president or used as a conference room—that could easily be divided into two B offices, 10 by 13 feet [3 by 4m] each. The lighting and mechanical systems required no changes. A metal storefront system, that ran parallel to the window wall, could easily accommodate partition changes, and worked well within the building module." The storefront system allows light to penetrate the interior of the operations floors where the support staff is located. Its metal is brown anodized aluminum, its full-height tempered glass tinted bronze. The doors and fixed panels beside them (allowing for a wardrobe on the office side) are wood, which in addition to having what Daroff calls "a crisp, sculptural quality," provide a warm backdrop for the secretarial areas.

In addition to the architectural core that contains the elevators and washroom, Daroff provided two offset tenant cores on each floor. These accommodate office services as they are required—lunch rooms, for instance, or mail rooms. On the legal-department

floor, a law library was housed in the tenant core.

The tenant core serves as an organizing element of the design. Painted a distinct color on each floor, it serves as a visual landmark. The tenant cores' outside walls were designed to accommodate the extensive file cabinets the corporation required as well as closets and storage space.

Indeed, colors and textures were systematized throughout the office. These became more highly textured as one moved upwards through the ranks of management.

The firm wanted its employees to participate in design decisions from the start. All enclosed offices were designed to accommodate individual choice within a pre-selected range of fabrics and furniture that ensured the continuity of the design concept. Employees who were to work in the office's open-plan areas were invited to see a mock-up of that area and asked to make suggestions. It was an opportunity for

employees to participate and preview their new environment. Some suggestions were incorporated—a file drawer of a certain type was added, for instance, as well as a large work surface for unusual equipment.

In certain instances, Daroff Design employed some of technology's latest advances in the SmithKline offcies. Of particular interest is the wall behind the reception area that elegantly houses a TV monitor informing visitors of the conference-center meeting schedule and carries a daily in-house news program. Here, too, is a TV camera aimed at the elevator bank for security purposes. Audiovisual television, which combines video, slides, and film, has also been used in the large meeting room. Equipped with theatrical lighting, this room requires only minimal adjustments in order for live broadcasts to originate from there: a first step toward teleconferencing capabilities, which Karen Daroff cites as one very definite future trend.

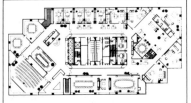

❶ *Smith Kline's World Wide headquarters occupies eight floors of a 24 story building in Philadelphia. Their separate lobby, entered from the building lobby, serves as the corporation's initial reception area and visitor control point.*

❷ *The executive reception area repeats the bronze and travertine finishes and subtle colorations of the lobby, chosen to project an image of warmth and substance. The sculpture by Clement Meadmore is part of an executive art program.*

❸ *Executive secretaries at Smith Kline have their own sculpture—solid bronze nameplates with engraved lettering.*

❹ *A different accent color gives identity to each of the seven operational floors. Lateral files are recessed in the walls of tenant cores, which also house lunch rooms and other support facilities.*

❺ *Plants define a waiting area outside a vice president's office on an operational floor. The perimeter offices are enclosed by a modified glass storefront system.*

❻ *and* ❽ *The largest meeting room at Smith Kline gets a dramatic, wide-angle view of Philadelphia's center city skyline. The batik silk tapestry by Shar Bickel serves as a backdrop for presentations.*

❼ *An antique Japanese screen is the focal point of the office of the president and chief executive officer of Smith Kline. The table desk and telephone credenza are oak burl.*

George Nelson

It would be nice if office environments would get more humane," says world-renowned architect George Nelson. "But if you look at the published stuff, they really aren't. It's bland, pretty, comfortable, with a sprinkling of abstract art, with some grape ivy that's easy to bully—but that's not humane." But Nelson feels that as more and

more professionals join the corporate ranks, they will want working environments with more appeal. They are high paid specialists who can be vocal about what they like and want.

"It's a cliche that a humane environment is a place where people like to go," he declares. "What are the ingredients? I think it's a place where people perceive that they have control over their

mini-environments. Because all the boss has is control. The boss can get up and sit at the other end of the room. The boss has a door to shut. The boss has someone there who cuts off unwanted visitors and phone calls."

Nelson is quick to recognize that all employees want, to some extent, to feel like bosses. "Everyone wants to be able to do the same thing," he observes. "They also want to do something to their own territory to mark it as theirs. They want to personalize it with the eternal Polaroid of their loved ones. They like their names on the door—or at least on the doorway, and labelled with a name instead of a number."

Nelson made some discoveries of his own about what a humane environment was when his firm was commissioned to design the interiors for the Aid Association to Lutherans (AAL) building in Appleton, Wisconsin. Finding none of the existing furniture systems suitable for the project, the firm set about designing their own. As Nelson recounted in *Ideas* Magazine, "AAL gave us a test area, an existing department in their old building. We got Luxo lamps and clamped them to the desks. You wouldn't believe the excitement this caused. So I checked and found that nobody in Appleton, Wisconsin, had ever seen a Luxo lamp. So I went back and talked to these people, and what I gradually discovered was that all these people felt quite helpless. They don't make decisions, they just stamp here and sign there. You

②

③

④

give them a Luxo and they can adjust it to light whatever they want. This gradually developed into the notion that people's happiness in a workspace related directly to the degree of control they have over their environment."

The furniture system Nelson designed incorporated as many built-in user options as possible, conceived as both functional assists and sources of pleasure. He designed an adjustable lamp, a plug-in sign, a book holder, a personal planter, a built-in waste receptacle, and an adjustable blind. "People laughed when they

saw the blind," he recalls. "But they all decided that they wanted one when they realized that it gave them control over the degree of privacy they had."

The system is designed to appeal to the sense of touch, which in Nelson's opinion, is all too often overlooked. He wanted the work station to "look good to feel." The inside of the work station—"like a jewel box"—is made of soft fabrics, pleasing to touch, that have an acoustic value as well. The exterior, on the other hand, is shiny and hard. "It's similar to being in a car," Nelson says. "When you're inside, you're only

in contact with soft things." The corners of the desk and accessories are round so that they will neither snag clothing nor cause bodily harm.

The problem with juxtaposing shiny steel and those soothing, softer materials is that this cannot possibly be done without a joint—a problem Nelson turned to his own advantage. Here he used the joint as a connector strip into which all accessories and panels plug. The panels, in turn, join together with a one-inch gap between them. This provides visual and psychological relief and allays the claustrophobic feeling of being completely enclosed.

The elements of the system fit together as a series of components resting on bases. Detachable, the bases permit the furniture layout to be organized and checked before the desk is actually assembled. If later changes should prove necessary, they can be achieved without altering the basic structure. Components are all additive while the desk is a freestanding piece of furniture.

The conference room, as conceived by Nelson, is particularly interesting. It is made up of free-standing panels forming a circle. Inside the circle stands a round table topped with a cafe umbrella and lit by adjustable lights. The umbrella serves as an inexpensive

"ceiling," creating so convincing a sense of enclosure that some employees went so far as to congratulate Nelson on designing a truly soundproof conference room.

Design styles may come and go but for Nelson, design's real mission is the creation of more humane environments. "We really have to relearn what that is all about," he writes. "And I think you begin by trying to become human again. You stop thinking about people as statistical units and really try to figure out what they're all about—what turns them on and what turns them off. We've forgotten how to do this. Ask most interior designers to humanize an office environment and all they can come up with is plants."

❶ A flexible, adjustable desk is one of the elements in the Nelson Workspaces system designed to give the user of the furniture a sense of control of the territory. The Eyeshade lamp is manufactured by Koch & Lowy.

❷ The system uses the desk as a core, a basic building block, with plug-in enclosures of various shapes and sizes. Other accessories include personal planters, a book bulge, storage drawers, and a waste receptacle that also acts as a modesty panel. Steel is used for the exterior surfaces, and the surfaces surrounding the user are upholstered and soft

to the touch. The system is manufactured by Storwal International.

❸ The system offers skyline possibilities of variable heights and degrees of openness. The Venetian blind accessory allows the user to control views in and out.

❹ Nelson designed sorting modules for the mail room.

❺ Ten-foot- (3-m-) diameter nylon-covered umbrellas give a feeling of complete enclosure to the cylindrical conference spaces. Lighted internally, by lamps attached to the pole, they

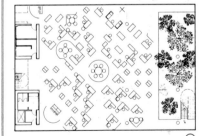

act as markers on large open floors. They seem remarkably soundproof to the people inside.

❻ and ❼ Nine-hundred work stations were installed in the AAL home office, set at a 45-degree angle to the building that architect John Carl Wanreke designed. The enormous

roof is skylighted; stretched fabric reduces glare. Brilliant batik banners coded with nature images identify work teams and departments below.

DEGW

Architects and space planners Duffy, Eley, Giffone, Worthington, (DEGW) of London and Mexico City specialize in office design. They have written extensively about its many aspects including the "fit" between organizational structure and office layout. They conceived an "inside-out" landscaped office, for Digital Equipment Corporation France to accommodate a particularly dynamic organization.

Digital, an international leader in the minicomputer field, is experiencing a phenomenal rate of growth. The French company, moving to a new headquarters building in Evry New Town, projected that their staff would grow from approximately 200 to 350 people between 1981 and 1984; a new member every week.

DEGW worked closely with Digital to develop an interior design and space planning concept which provided for expansion. The actual "fitting out" was the responsibility of the client, who specified the partition layout, services, and the previously agreed upon interior finishes. J. L. Duret was the architect for the building.

"The speed of growth places pressure both on the building manager and the ability of the organization to assimilate new personalities," says DEGW partner John Worthington. In addition, the management team was looking for a solution that would maximize communication and informal contacts in a company which was coping with a continuous influx of new recruits, as well as with the application of new technologies.

DEGW partner Francis Duffy has written, "…offices have special characteristics which make it easier and faster to learn crucial lessons about user requirements and satisfaction than in any other building type. Unlike hospitals, there is in offices an extremely simple relationship between each individual member or an organization and his own territory. The organization as a whole, and each departmental section within it can also see the limits of its organizational extension expressed in space." (*The Architectural Review*, June 1979)

In balancing corporate goals with individual aspirations at Digital, DEGW considered precedent. "France has a long tradition of providing enclosed offices, well-structured hierarchies, which are reflected in status symbols such as personal offices, and individual expression at the place of work," says Worthington. DEGW, from previous studies, had seen two trends appearing in office use: ambivalent staff reactions to open-office planning and increasing areas of ancillary activities such as meetings areas, equipment and reference space, and shared terminals.

DEGW proposed that the corporate guidelines for space allocations be rebudgeted. Rather than each grade of staff having an exact space standard, they suggested less individual space and more shared space. "Individuals, once again, are given enclosed spaces for contemplative or disruptive work. Interactive functions such as discussions, the storage and retrieval of information, and relaxation, occur on a

①

③

②

landscaped central boulevard. The layout reflects that professionals move between project environments, and very few staff members spend seven hours at their desk." The space plan was conceived so that the rear walls of offices could be easily moved to accommodate additional staff. To simplify space management, they established a simple rhythm of fixed walls to carry electrical and communication cables, define the location for fixed offices, and organize open areas.

The original offices reflected a style of individual concern for the workplace and a corporate style through an open-door policy, notice boards and informal meeting spaces around the copying and vending machines. The Evry building has continued the spirit of freshness and cooperation through the use of strong primary colors, straightforward signage and graphics, and glass walls for all the offices and meeting rooms.

"The success of the approach," says Worthington, "will only be assured by the test of time and the organization's ability to reflect the changing allocations of space in their style of work."

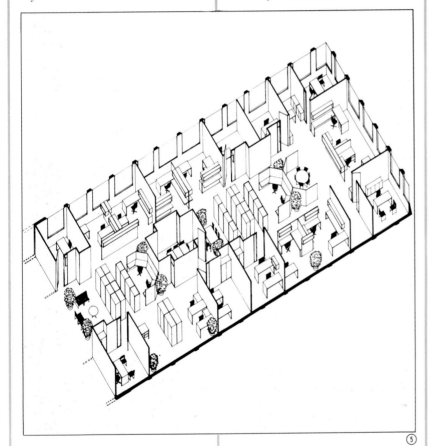

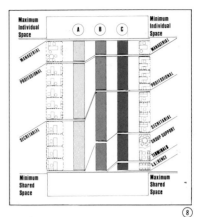

• Service Core • Primary Circulation	25%	BUILDING
• Amenity Space	10%	
• Ancillary Space	15%	SUPPORT
• Group Support	5%	
• Enclosed Office • Open Office	45%	WORKSPACE

❶ Individuals at Digital Equipment Corporation France were given enclosed spaces for contemplative or disruptive work. Interactive functions such as discussions, the storage and retrieval of information, and relaxation occur on a landscaped central boulevard.

❷ Chart illustrates how corporate goals and individual aspirations are often at odds. From previous studies DEGW concluded that staff reaction to open-office planning was ambivalent. Although open planning would improve team spirit, communications, equality, and effectiveness, the staff was concerned with loss of privacy, disruptions, and discomfort.

❸ To the outside world, the building exterior has been enlivened by kaleidoscopic murals.

❹ The use of strong primary colors, straightforward signage and graphics, and glazing to all offices and meeting rooms gives the Evry building a spirit of freshness and cooperation.

❺ To simplify space management, a simple rhythm of fixed walls was established, which defined the location for enclosed offices, organized the placing of groups in the open areas, and carried the electrical and communication cables.

❻ Flexible work stations were used to accommodate the company's growth, averaging about one new employee per week.

❼ and ❽ Charts showing that an increasing area of the office was being used for ancillary support activities such as meetings, references, and shared terminals.

Appendix

Programming Office Space

The Office Environment and Human Behavior

For a long time people have understood intuitively that the work environment affects human behavior. Perhaps the novelist, so attuned to living, expresses this most articulately, and with the most sensitivity. Dickens, Melville, Lewis—all have vividly described not only the workplaces of their respective eras but what those places did to the imaginary men and women they set down inside them. Virginia Woolf, on the other hand, wrote of how the lack of a workplace hampers creativity.

In recent years, the novelist's observations have been verified and elaborated upon by environmental psychologists. Well-versed in architecture, planning, interior design, anthropology, and sociology as well as psychology, environmental psychologists apply scientific methods to their study of workplaces so as to determine ways of improving them for the benefit of both employers and employees. They see the obvious: the need for fresh air, the need for adequate light, and so on. But their interdisciplinary training enables them to see beyond the surface as well, to factors so subtle that they elude mere intuition.

Today's offices are complicated places, and it takes a specially trained, finely tuned mind to unravel those complexities.

Increasingly, people are using the techniques of environmental psychology to understand and organize their offices. The increasing intricacy of organizations, along with lightning-quick advances in technology and the marketplace, have rendered the intuitive approach uneconomical and unreliable. Some more valid approach is essential. Workplaces are for people, and people's needs must be seen to, whether they themselves perceive those needs or not. Studies have shown that over a 40-year period of organizational life, operating costs are 6 percent and initial construction costs 2 percent of total costs, while personnel costs account for a whopping 92 percent.

The office environment must be at once efficient and satisfactory to employees. In seeing to this, the employer must be prepared to spend a certain amount of money; but it must be spent wisely, and only after careful analysis.

An office interior might be considered as no more than an assortment of inanimate objects—furniture, desks, lamps, and chairs. But those inanimate objects, mute and motionless as they are, have a curious way of influencing the course of human events. Take two desks, for instance. Put them too close together, and the typists who sit at them, once best friends, start going at each other tooth and nail.

Move the desks farther apart, though, and those two are bosom pals all over again—and what's more, they're both doing their jobs more efficiently. Or take one desk, and one typist, a mild-mannered fellow, who just happens to go about his work within earshot of an extremely noisy copying machine. After a month, he's ready for the insane asylum. Grinding sounds haunt his dreams. But then, move the desk away from that din and the man is typing away quickly and calmly.

While an office environment affects both efficiency and employee satisfaction, it will not do so unless it has been planned with workers' specific activities and needs in mind. Environmental psychologists use the following four methods to discover what these activities and needs are:

● Ask the employers and employees what they do and what they want. This can be done through questionnaires or personal interviews. Answers might then be interpreted by a computer to be structured in the most meaningful way.

● Observe what goes on during any typical workday, and also ask employers and employees to observe themselves.

● Consult a firm's records. Absenteeism and turnover rates provide important clues to what is going right in an office and what is going wrong.

● Consult existing research. Conclusions reached therein might prove applicable to the problems at hand.

In most cases, environmental psychologists use all four methods at once. A fifth method calls for employees to actually participate in the research gathering, analysis, and even in decision making. It has been shown that people are "expert" in their immediate areas of work. It is often beneficial to tap them as resources and get their feedback on ideas. What's more, when employees have a say in some change in their office environment, they feel more positive about their jobs, more committed to the new facilities in which they are to work, and more important as individuals whose opinions matter enough for designers, researchers and their employers to heed them.

Once enough data has been collected through these various methods, the actual physical environment can begin to take shape.

Organizational Structure and Office Layout

Why do organizations require new space? To expand, to contract, to lower the amount of rent they have to pay, or to establish a new image.

Moving to new quarters gives a company the opportunity to take a closer look at its organization in terms of both its practices and its goals. Filing systems, distribution of office supplies, mail distribution, copying operations, telephone systems, maintenance programs, and furniture can all be examined with an eye toward improvement. Office functions that used to take ten people to perform might reveal themselves as prime candidates for automation. Forms and stationery (notorious for their similarity to the most inscrutable hieroglyphics) might offer themselves up for drastic revision.

Along with all this, new spatial requirements might be recognized as well—ones that will best suit the organization's operational style, best reflect its structure and communication network, and best accommodate its plans for expansion.

Once that closer look has been taken, it is time to think about actual, physical changes—changes that can lead to increased efficiency and new economies in office operations. At this point, though, one might bear in mind the advice of Michael Saphier, space planner and office designer. In his book *Planning the New Office*, Saphier writes, "It is important to realize at the outset that there is no one answer that will solve all space problems for all companies. The human factor, the ingrained work habits of company personnel and their capacity for change, must be carefully weighed in considering alternative space concepts as they have been in considering possible changes in systems and procedures." If the physical environment and the organization don't "fit," if the office layout does not truly represent the way the office functions, then only inefficiencies, discomfort, and dissatisfaction will be the results.

In some instances, the sort of spatial layout an office calls for may be completely self-evident from the work that goes on there. For example, it makes sense for diamond dealers to occupy series of cellular, lockable offices where security is rigidly controlled. Here anonymity and confidentiality are of course strictly enforced, and any layout that did not account for this would be altogether inappropriate. Or consider the opposite extreme: a trader's room. Here many traders work together in a hectic operational center where eye contact and visibility are essential.

In other instances, it is the firm's tone that dictates the layout of its offices. Some organizations espouse an "open door" policy: the president wants to be available, so his office is at the head of the stairs leading up from the main lobby—and so on. Others believe in hierarchy and rigid, established lines of communication that have worked well in the past, which they wish to preserve in their new quarters.

In any event, a firm's philosophy of management will be expressed in office layout in terms of spatial concepts—or at least it should be. That layout might follow a *conventional plan*—that is, a series of cellular offices that vary in size to reflect the status of its occupants (this concept has also been referred to as the *structured plan* or the *closed plan*). Such a layout might include "bull pen" areas adjacent to enclosed private offices, as is the case in many office buildings in the United States. On the other hand, it might feature cellular offices lining both sides of a so-called double-loaded corridor, as is the case in Europe, where floor area is less abundant than in the United States. (It might be noted that today, European architects are taking American office construction into account in regard to their own buildings.)

The *open plan* is one alternative to this layout—a layout with no enclosed offices at all. Here the hierarchy of status is abandoned. Executives, for instance, are located near their departments and not necessarily near other executives. The result? Increased communication and improved work flow. Nevertheless, employees' views should be considered before switching to an open plan. As environmental psychologist Rob Kaminoff writes, in such situations, "while employees may feel that their managers are more accessible…they may also feel they are under the constant surveillance of their superiors who used to be tucked away on another floor."

The *modified plan* is a compromise between these two alternatives. Such a layout can accommodate both enclosed offices and open plan areas and offers tenants a choice between the two.

Whatever layout a company's organizational structure suggests, it is bound to determine the type of building that company rents or has designed as its headquarters. If conventional offices are contemplated, the perimeter of the building has to be designed to readily accept partitions. (In view of the popularity open plan layouts enjoyed in the 1970s, though, not all recently completed buildings have been designed with this possibility in mind.) Air conditioning and heating, too, have to be considered in terms of the layout. Individual rooms have more air-conditioning needs than a single open space. On the other hand, open plan offices require furniture that can create a sense of privacy and enclosure the building itself might not provide. In addition, adequate service—electric power and communication lines—must reach each work station because in open plan layouts there are no walls to distribute and conceal power and communication lines.

No matter what the layout, it is absolutely essential that work areas be in some way distinguished and separated from one another.

No layout exists that will suit any and all organizations. Organizations differ, and so must the layouts that reflect them. A firm must weigh the relative advantages of each spatial concept in light of its own operating styles. Furthermore, employees' opinions on these matters should be sought as well, along with their suggestions. Only careful consideration leads to the appropriate solution, and only careful planning will make that solution work in practice.

These are only two of the ways in which those seemingly innocent pieces of furniture can make life miserable for employees and disrupt the flow of office work to boot. Other problems could arise just as easily. Everyone wants to use the conference room at the same time of day. Several employees whose work requires complete privacy and concentration have taken to erecting barricades around their desks, or retreating to the coat closet with a stack of file folders, or yelling at their colleagues to shut up or else. Meanwhile, boxes of typing paper have been discovered in the mini-refrigerator: there was no place else to store them. Soon the situation slips into chaos, and it's all the furniture's fault. Had the office's design been more carefully thought out, these difficulties could have been circumvented. There would have been ample conference space, ample privacy, and ample storage space. Now, though, it is too late, and you find yourself living in World War III. Needless to say, nothing gets done.

Not only does the office environment affect efficiency; as environmental psychologist and architect Stephan Marc Klein has noted, it influences workers' moods as well. If an office space is attractive enough to make people feel good in it, chances are that they will work harder there. If it is a crumbling ruin, they will not. In such an office, employees soon stop giving their work the attention it warrants. Mistakes proliferate. A few dispirited souls begin to stay home sick—for a day, for two days, for a week at a time—rather than face the shambles that is the place where they work. Eventually they disappear altogether, and new ones must be sought and trained. Such dissatisfaction and the resulting decrease in productivity can be avoided through sensible design. Unfortunately, while sensible design might keep those workers satisfied, it might not necessarily make them more productive—a paradox out of which environmental psychologists have yet to find their way.

More than half of all office furniture sold in the United States are modular work stations and components. Modular work stations are used primarily in open-plan offices. As flexible systems, they eliminate fixed partitions. Open-plan offices call for new solutions for lighting, acoustics, and electrical distribution. At the same time, moving into open-plan offices from more conventional arrangements is a change both for the staff used to the open "bull pen" arrangement and those accustomed to enclosed, cellular offices.

Some furniture manufacturers have found it useful to provide information that describes their system and also outlines guidelines for design. The discussions about the new environment also help prepare for change.

The following articles are excerpts from brochures written by Haworth, Inc., a manufacturer in the United States, to explain their UniGroup system that incorporates TriAmbient lighting and TriCircuit Era-1 raceways. They discuss lighting, acoustics, and wiring in open offices in typical American speculative office buildings. Environmental elements such as floors, ceilings, and walls are not addressed here, nor are the equivalent problems of lighting, acoustics, and wiring in the cellular office.

Acoustics

The control of sound in the office environment is an integral part of interiors planning. To understand the means by which this control can be achieved, it is helpful to understand the nature and characteristics of sound.

The ear, like the eye, is a complex information gathering system. All too often we provide a crude acoustical and visual environment and rely on the marvelous adaptive mechanisms of the occupants to compensate. Negative attitudes frequently develop in such environments. The following two needs are basic to the effective functioning of the office organization.

The Need for Communica-

tion: Communication is the principal activity within an office. The listener must be able to hear and to understand the speaker in any conversation. Inadvertent listeners should be excluded, and both speaker and intended listener should have privacy from others.

To satisfy these requirements, the designer should establish **Zones of Communication**, areas within which people can hear and understand speech well and outside of which they cannot. In bull-pen office arrangements, such zones tend to include everyone, while in closed offices they extend only to the room boundaries. In managerial work stations in the open office, these zones should be limited to the work station perimeter, but in other areas where

people frequently work together, the zones may extend to several work stations. Thus the various zones will have different boundaries in one area than in another. This technique is called **Sound-scaping**, and will be discussed later.

The Need for Privacy: Whenever it is necessary to work alone, each person must be able to think independently, free from distracting, irrelevant, or inappropriate sounds. It is a common and serious design error to attempt to satisfy this need by making the office environment as quiet as possible. When this is done, all speech and activity sounds can be heard. The correct design goal is to create an environment that is free of distraction. For example, consider the acoustical environment on a crowded jetliner. It is possible to work virtually undisturbed with all those people around, yet it is a very noisy place in terms of sound level. When an office is made too quiet, other sounds cause distraction from the work task, which leads to a perceived loss of privacy—a major factor in complaints about the open office.

It may be necessary to limit the area in which private or confidential conversation can be understood. Outside that area is a zone of privacy, where speech may be audible but is unintelligible and conveys no information. Establishing this zone for each work station is a critical design element in making the open office work effectively.

Psychological Needs

There are two important psychological needs that relate directly to attitudes that affect performance; they relate less directly to function.

The Need for Community: The quest for privacy and status leads to the closed office; yet office doors are rarely closed. In the modern, interactive office environment, employees want privacy without isolation. Low level activity sounds of occupants create a sense of community and a dynamic work environment. Between **Zones of Privacy** and **Zones of Communication**, audible sounds which are low in level and not intelligible provide a pleasant background normally not present in closed offices.

The Need for Territory: Photographs, mementos, and desk lamps are manifestations of our need to establish territory. But often, such materials cover sound absorbant acoustical panels and reduce their effectiveness (suggesting the need for some hard-surfaced panels in work stations). Another aspect of this need for territory is that excessively loud sounds, such as those of copiers or loud telephone bells (as well as loud conversations), create significant loss of privacy, since they are interpreted as territorial intrusion. Such intrusions result in complaints and should be avoided.

In some cases, acoustical design of the office cannot control such sounds, and control of the source itself must be undertaken.

Some Fundamentals of Sound

In order to achieve good open office acoustics, it is first necessary to understand some of the fundamentals of sound transmission and measurement.

Sound Transmission: Sound is a simple form of mechanical energy, originating with a source, traveling via a path to a receiver (normally humans are the receivers of interest). Whenever sound is generated, it spreads out in all directions (like an expanding soap bubble), not just in the direction in which the source is facing. The sound level drops with increasing distance from the source, so distance is an important element in open office design.

As sound travels away from the source, it will strike some surfaces, such as panels or walls; some sound will be *transmitted* and some will be *reflected* from the surface.

If we place a sound-absorbing material on the side of the panel facing the source, some of the energy will be absorbed and a reduced amount will be reflected. Absorbent materials, by themselves, reflect little sound, but they also allow sound to pass through them. Hence, these materials should be backed with solid material to prevent transmission.

Sound will also bend or diffract over the top or around the sides of panels, permitting considerable sound energy to reach areas beyond.

To describe how effective various materials are in controlling these occurrences, we have several ratings that are in common use.

NRC (Noise Reduction Coefficient): This is a number between 0 and 1 which represents the fraction or percent of energy (striking the material) which is *absorbed* and not reflected. (Remember: The absorbens can absorb *only* the sound which reaches them; they can't reach out and "suck up" the sound.) An NRC rating of *0* means that no sound is absorbed by the material. A rating of *1* means that all of the sound is absorbed. The noise reduction coefficient is a construct, since it is based on the arithmetic average of the absorption of the material at several frequencies.

Almost 50 years ago, an industry association agreed upon using the arithmetic average of the absorption coefficients at the octaves centered on 250, 500, 1,000 and 2,000 Hz as a reasonable "average" effectiveness of acoustical tile for office noise reduction. When similar materials are compared, this average is useful. But when highly dissimilar materials are compared, or when the absorption at specific frequencies is important, the NRC rating can be very misleading.

STC (Sound Transmission Class): This is a one-number rating that describes the ability of a panel surface to *block* the transmission of sound through it. It is a construct, based upon a mathematical procedure which weights the performance of a panel throughout the frequency range. STC 0 means there is no drop in level through the panel; STC 50 means very little sound goes through.

In general, open office divider panels should provide not less than STC 23, and preferably somewhat higher values for a reasonable margin of safety.

Measurement of Sound: The measurement scale for sound levels is the uncommon term *deciBel* or *dB*. (Note, even the spelling is unique, with a capital letter in the middle of this word.)

This term refers to the logarithmic comparison of *ratios* between some measured value and a reference value (such as physical sound pressure or energy). It is *never* a unit, and deciBels must never be added or subtracted like units. For example, reducing a noise level from 100 dB to 90 dB is *not* a 10% drop, rather it is a 90% reduction in the energy level.

A drop in level of 20 dB between two locations is an enormous reduction in energy (100 to 1), but the ear hears it as about a 4 to 1 drop.

All you really need to know about deciBels are the levels of typical, commonplace sounds and activities. The table below lists some of these levels, so you can compare any situation to a typical condition.

Notice the table shows sound levels in dBA. This is because sound level meters hear a wider frequency range than we can, and they hear objectively, with no preference for frequency. Hence, we must bias them to hear as we do, by using a filter network and

Hearing

Hearing is the ear's response to sound. And, to provide the proper acoustical control in an office, we need to understand how people hear.

Humans have an enormous response range, from as low as 15 Hz to as high as 20,000 Hz in frequency, and almost a 100-

DeciBel LEVELS OF TYPICAL COMMON-PLACE SOUNDS AND ACTIVITIES

Apparent Loudness	Examples	dBA
Deafening	Jet aircraft	140
	Threshold of feeling	130
Very loud	Thunder	120
	Noisy industrial plant	100
	Loud street noise	90
Loud	Average street noise	70
	Average office/congested dept. store	60
Moderate	Moderate restaurant clatter	50
	School classroom/private office	40
Faint	Bedroom	30
	Rustling leaves	20
Very faint	Normal breathing	10
	Threshold of audibility	0

an "A-weighted" frequency response. This makes the meter respond more like humans in its measurement of loudness.

Normal speech between two persons takes place at a distance of about 3 to 3½ feet (0.9M to 1.1M), and produces a level of about 65 dBA at the listener's ear. This is so constant that people tend to adjust their voice effort or their physical separation to establish this level.

Levels below 30 dBA are considered very quiet; levels about 85 dBA are very loud, and speech is almost impossible. High levels, maintained for long periods, can produce permanent hearing loss. Above 120 dBA sound becomes painful.

million-to-1 range in sound pressure.

Our response is nonlinear, in that we are much more sensitive to frequencies from about 200 to 8,000 Hz than to low or very high frequencies.

The peak for male voice energy lies at about 350 Hz; for the female voice, about 1 octave higher, at about 700 Hz. However, the intelligibility of speech is carried in the frequency range of about 300 to 3,000 Hz. This means that the "rumble" of the male voice can be heard without interfering too much with speech intelligibility, but that the female voice tends to be more intelligible, since its energy is centered in the frequency range that counts.

Therefore, a good noise-reducing material must be effective from 250 Hz to 3,000 Hz if it is to work well in the office environment. This is where NRC ratings can be misleading. A material or panel may have a good NRC rating (.80 or better), but if the sound-absorbing characteristics do not perform at the frequency ranges required in the office, it will be a bad acoustical panel.

An optimum material should provide about 50% absorption at 250 Hz and rise rapidly to nearly 100% at about 500 Hz. Above 4,000 Hz, only "hissing" and similar sounds lie, and even ordinary air absorption can normally handle them.

Intelligibility and Audibility:

Theoretically, human hearing responds to sound pressure levels above the "threshold of hearing" (an incredibly low level—about two ten-thousandths of one-millionth of atmospheric pressure). So, for practical purposes, almost any sound is *audible.* What we are really concerned with is whether the sound carries any information (whether it is intelligible) or whether it interferes with what we are doing or with what we are trying to listen to (noise).

Intelligibility refers to the phenomenon of our hearing mechanism's ability to gather information from the available sounds. For example, as few as 15% of the words in sentences may make the meaning of the entire sentence clear to a listener. However, if this drops to fewer than 10%, intelligibility almost vanishes. In short, the brain is an incredible analyzing computer, able to fill in the gaps of almost 85% of missing words or syllables in contextual sentences; but it can't handle gaps of more than 90%. Laboratory test procedures have established "Articulation Indexes" based upon actual listeners' responses to "nonsense syllables." These indexes indicate the conditions under which "nor-

mal privacy" and "confidential privacy" may exist. "Normal privacy" includes the range from about 65% to 90% of speech in sentences being basically unintelligible, while "confidential privacy" includes conditions with more than 90% of speech in sentences being unintelligible.

Sounds may be "audible"—that is, they may stimulate the ear—without carrying any intelligibility or without being annoying. In the open office, limiting intelligibility to specified zones is the primary concern, but reducing other sounds to tolerable levels is also important. Noise is any unwanted sound, whatever its nature or level. Therefore, we want to control such unwanted sound so that it is not noticeable. There are two principle means of accomplishing this:

1. Reduce the amount of energy reaching the listener;
2. Raise the background level to where it "drowns" or "masks" the intruding sound.

Here's how it works.

In a very quiet location (under 30 dBA), we can hear low level sounds quite easily. A normal conversational voice, as far away as 200 feet (61 meters) in a non-reverberant space (such as out-of-doors with no wind), could still be heard and understood. In a very "soft" or nonreverberant office, even greater distances would be required. In most well-designed offices, the sound level falls off at about 4½ dB per *doubling* of distance from the source. So it is apparent that only unacceptably great distances between work stations would provide effective attenuation or reduction for most situations. Therefore, some form of barrier must be employed to further reduce the level of intruding sound.

An alternative, up to a point, would be to raise the steady "background" noise level of the area to a point where the intruding sound is no longer a significant

part of the acoustic energy affecting the listener's ear. Then, this intruding sound would no longer be "unwanted," since it would be unnoticed.

However, in the real world of office design, we must deal with what we can measure and control—background noise levels and sound reducing or attenuation materials. We can predict their performance reasonably well and plan for them to provide the privacy, intelligibility, and other acoustical characteristics desired.

Fortunately, all of the above can be handled in a simple, readily measured procedure—the *signal-to-noise ratio.* This means that wanted sound (the signal) must have some relative level to the unwanted sound (noise).

We have learned that intelligent sounds or signals can be detected whenever they exceed the background level. By using dB as a ratio, we can now add and subtract dB levels to get the desired *ratios.* When the signal level exceeds the background level by as little as 10 dB, high intelligibility exists; and 100% intelligibility occurs for connected sentences when the signal level is 15 dB above the background.

This suggests that normal speech (about 65 dBA at 3 feet [0.9 meter]) would be almost unintelligible beyond 3 feet (0.9 meter) *if* the background were at or above 65 dBA. However, few of us would want to work in such a steady background level—we would be forced to raise our voices in nearly every conversation.

From long experience and many tests, we know that most office workers will not tolerate levels much higher than 45 to 47 dBA of steady, neutral background if conversation, thought, and concentration are a significant part of their work.

Now, if we reduced the speech signal to 45 dBA or less by the time it reached those who did not want to (or should not) hear it, considerable privacy would result in an

acceptable 45 to 47 dBA background. This can be done by:

1. Distance—separating stations by some distance in a "soft," nonreverberant, highly absorptive environment.

2. Attenuation—providing barriers which prevent direct transmission between source and adjacent stations and by preventing reflections of sound from hard surfaces.

3. Masking—providing a steady, neutral background level at as high a level as will be accepted.

These constitute the "design rules" for good acoustics in the open office.

The Acoustical Design Rules

Since sound, in most situations, is transmitted from a *source* by many *paths* to a *listener,* it is important to evaluate and deal with *all three* elements in the open office.

It is usually difficult to do much about the sources. Machines may be quieted somewhat and telephone bells may be muffled; but the voice levels of workers can be quite resistant to any modification.

Most efforts must be focused on the paths—all of them, since each path operates essentially independently of the others. The situation is somewhat analogous to a bucket of water with several leaks—all of them must be stopped to prevent losing the water. So it is best to handle all acoustical elements in the design well; but it is better to handle all partially than to do some well and to neglect others entirely.

Control of the Source: The energy distribution pattern of the human voice is pretty well fixed and predictable. The equal energy curve shows energy levels at the rear of the head almost 10 dBA lower than directly in front. Little or nothing can be done to modify this, so it should be considered in any work station layout.

1. Loud talkers are poor candidates for the open office. Most people adjust their speech level to avoid excessive intrusion, but some do not. Office surveys can determine which talkers are considered by others to be loud—those whose normal speech may be as loud as 75 dBA at three feet (0.9 meter). Special provisions must be made for such persons.

2. Orientation of speakers is important. People can be understood much more easily when they face you. The sound of their voices may be as much as 10 dBA lower when they are facing away. If two people are not in direct communication, face them away from each other as much as possible.

When two people are conversing in one work station, try to orient them at right angles to a listener in an adjacent work station.

3. Office machines, such as copiers, should be located in areas that do *not* require a high degree of privacy (better yet, in a separate room or alcove).

Typewriters are usually located near those who use them, so they must be noise-controlled with devices like special typewriter covers and vibration pads. Typewriters should never be placed on panel-hung or wall-hung surfaces which transmit sound and vibration. Free-standing tables are advisable.

4. Building air supply noise must be kept low enough to avoid becoming a nuisance. With steady, invariant flow, it is even possible to use the sound as "masking"; but modern, variable-volume systems have variable noise levels, so they are rarely useful for this purpose.

Avoid placing work stations against the wall of mechanical equipment rooms. Corridors or noisy equipment, located along such walls, can be used as "buffers."

Avoid locating managerial work stations under main air duct junctions or similar normally noisy locations, such as large variable-volume boxes, etc.

5. Telephones are always a potential problem. Their bells should be muffled or replaced with buzzers or blinking lights. Try to place phones to encourage conversation while facing into an absorptive panel.

Control of the Paths: As we

discussed earlier, control of the paths by which sound travels from source to receiver is one of the principle acoustical options for the designer. Procedures and considerations for controlling these paths are detailed below:

1. *Ceiling Paths.* The ceiling is one of the most important sound transmission paths in the office. To avoid reflecting sound for great distances from the source, ceilings must have high absorptivity at *all* angles. A "random incidence" NRC of at least 80%, and good, uniform absorptivity from 250 Hz to at least 4,000 Hz are preferable.

Light fixtures or other large devices that replace the absorptive ceiling tile with sound-reflective surfaces seriously impair the ceiling's effectiveness. Such devices should be located to avoid reflecting sound between work stations, whenever possible; or, flat lenses can be replaced with special open, parabolic diffusers and the like.

The best control is to minimize ceiling lighting and use indirect ambient lighting.

2. *Distance.* Normally, the farther a listener is from a speaker, the less he will hear. However, cost usually limits the size of work stations and the distance between workers. Still, it is wise to attempt to maintain 8 to 12 feet (2.4 M to 3.6 M) between workers, if possible. The greater the need for privacy, the greater the distance required.

3. *Panels.* Traditionally, walls were used as sound and visual barriers between offices. Today, in the open office, panels of 80" (2 meters) or less in height are much more common. As we said earlier, some sound passes through the panels, some goes around or over them, and some is absorbed or reflected by the panel.

To provide maximum acoustical privacy, use good sound-absorbing panels with NRC ratings of at least 80% or better. And, to prevent sound from passing through the panels, they should have a minimum STC rating of 23.

Panel hinges or connections between panels must not leak sound. If you can see through, blow through, or stick a card through the hinge area, the panel effectiveness has been seriously impaired. Merely listening will demonstrate this.

Also, with carpeted floors (imperative in the open office), panels need not fit tightly to the floor, but the space at the bottom must be minimized—certainly less than 4" (100 mm), and perferably much less.

When using panels that display these characteristics, you can properly plan the acoustical controls desired for each area or office. Keep in mind that not all offices or work areas require or want acoustical privacy. This is where the "zones of communication" must be considered. You must know the needs of the people within each area or office, and the panel layout and acoustics should meet those needs. For example, when several people work together and maintain constant verbal communication with one another, you would not want 80" (2 meters) high acoustical panels separating them. Instead, panels of 42" (1 meter) or 48" (1.2 M) height might be sufficient. Then enclose the entire work area with 80" (2 meters) acoustical panels to absorb the sound before it can travel into adjoining work stations. In this example, the zone of communication extends to several work stations.

In a managerial work station, these zones should be limited to the work station perimeter. To provide for maximum acoustical privacy in these areas, you should consider the following:

a. Increase the panel height. Height significantly improves barrier effectiveness. Panels 48" (1.2 M) or less in height are almost useless as sound barriers. In practice, it has been found that 60" (1.5 M) is a practical minimum, noticeably improving with every inch-or-more increase above that.

b. Increase the panel width. Sound will diffract around the end of panels as well as over the top. In general, the panel width should be twice the panel height to make it an effective barrier.

c. Move adjacent workers closer to the panel. The closer both speaker and listener are to a good acoustical panel, the more privacy each will have. By placing absorptive panels directly in the path of the speaker's voice and moving the speaker close to the panel, the sound is absorbed before it has a chance to "spread out."

d. Put components on panels between work stations. Components make the panel thicker, increasing the angle between speaker and listener on opposite sides of the panel, and have the effect of increasing the effective height of the panel.

4. *Walls.* Reflective walls, like nonabsorptive panels, can create inadvertent communication paths, even at distances of 20 feet (6 meters) or more. Whenever such surfaces are located or oriented so they reflect sound between work stations, they should be covered with an absorptive, acoustical surface.

a. Work stations near walls should have their panels tight against the walls. Even a small gap is a serious "sound leak," comparable to open connections between panels.

b. Work stations near windows, and requiring light from the windows, should have glass side panels to keep the sound within the work station but not block the light.

c. Use windowed wall areas as aisles. Avoid acoustical problems created by windows by converting exterior exposures to walkways, and use absorptive work station panels to separate workers from both windows and aisles.

Heavy draperies at windows can help *if* always closed; but they are usually retracted to the point of uselessness.

5. *Floors.* Open office floors must be carpeted to absorb sound and to minimize foot and chair noise. Good, wear-resistant carpets, with as deep a pile as feasible, are usually acceptable. They tend to provide an NRC of 20% to 40%, with most of their absorption above 1,000 Hz. Since carpet covers such a large area, and furniture and panels tend to block and scatter sound reflections from the carpet, it need not be as absorptive as the panels or ceilings.

Control at the Listener's Position:

After the sound has left the source and has been attenuated on its several paths to the listener, there will be a residual level that may still be audible and often intelligible. As we noted earlier, the ability to hear and understand speech is dependent on the loudness of the received sound relative to the background level. Thus, another design variable is control of the background sound level.

This process is variously called "acoustic perfume," "white sound," or "masking." *Masking* is the most accurate term, since it correctly describes what is happening—the introduction of a frequency-controlled, innocuous, random sound which masks out undesirable signals. However, like perfume, a little goes a long way.

Masking does not *eliminate* sound or reduce noise; rather, it *increases* the sound energy level in the space. It must never be used when quieting is the objective or when the existing sound level is already too high. Its sole purpose is to *raise* a too-quiet background sufficiently to cover or mask little, annoying activity sounds or to cover up speech sounds which should not be heard.

The desired background sound level can be created by the following:

1. Fixed volume ventilation systems have been used in the past by adjusting the diffusers to produce the spectrum and level desired in the space below. This is difficult and not readily controlled. With variable volume systems it is not practical.

2. Electronic "pink noise" generating systems, using speakers in or above the ceiling, provide a carefully controlled background sound. Individual masking units, located only where required, are also used in some installations, but are not recommended because their presence is noticeable, and masking should be unnoticed.

The design and adjustment of a masking system, tailored for the specific installation, is a complex job, usually requiring the services of an experienced and competent consultant. Otherwise, the system may cause more problems than it solves.

How Much Control is Possible?

There are two GSA (General Services Administration) test procedures which measure, to some degree, the effect of each element in the control of paths in open offices. However, the "NIC" (Noise Isolation Class) which results from these procedures gives only the contribution of each element in a highly artificial, almost completely absorptive environment. The resulting numbers are not particularly helpful to anyone except very experienced consultants.

A simple, quick test method exists to provide meaningful data for the *entire* office in its acutal environment.

A calibrated sound source is placed at the normal head location of a worker in one station, and a sound level of dBA is established and measured in a prescribed way. Then a sound level meter is placed with its microphone where the listener's ears would be in an adjacent work station. The difference in dBA level gives a pretty good idea of the privacy to be expected.

Differences of 20 dBA or higher (they rarely exceed 22 dBA) are good, and are about as high as can be expected from even very good components in a well-planned layout. Differences as low as 14 dBA have been measured in poor arrangements or in those with poorly designed elements.

This means that only if the background level is at least 45 dBA can any significant degree of privacy be provided, because the "signal-to-noise" ratio necessary can be provided only with an adequate background level.

The Design Process

A good design is successful if it integrates the various acoustical factors mentioned at each and every work station. Being successful is providing the proper balance between cost and performance. Design variations are great and very specific. However, we would like to provide some general guidelines for use by the designer during the initial stages of an open office layout.

1. Decide whether acoustical considerations are important to the project or not. If they are, plan to use sound absorptive panels with high STC and high NRC, a ceiling with high NRC and a masking sound system.

2. Distribute occupants as uniformly throughout the space as possible.

3. Avoid work station openings facing window walls or other work station openings.

4. Consider the entire office environment, floor, walls and ceiling, as being composed of mirrors. If you can visualize seeing the reflection of another occupant from any work station, the point at which the reflected image might occur should be absorptive. This is particularly true of walls.

5. Place potentially noisy equipment near the people who will benefit most by its use, and, if necessary, into a very absorptive room.

6. Consider the need for confidential communications and plan to accommodate them in closed rooms.

7. Consider the use of indirect, ambient lighting as an important acoustical factor, as well as an important energy and lighting factor.

8. Have an acoustical consultant analyze the system layout to determine the Articulation Index between each work station pair and to isolate any weak points in the design.

Electricity

Today's technological advancements in automated office equipment have demanded increased power and communications in open plan office furniture. To understand fully the problems encountered and the solutions available, it is necessary to understand the basic methods of power and communications distribution.

Energy Distribution Needs

The availability of flexible and sufficient access to electrical power and communications service is an increasing need for users of modern, state-of-the-art work environments. Conventional energy distribution techniques in most buildings provide little consistency or compatibility with interior requirements.

The Need for Access: Conventional energy distribution systems lack the capacity to supply economically enough receptacle outlets to meet the expanded use of electronic devices and appliances used in the office today. Typically, work stations exhibit a low requirement for amperage but demand numerous receptacles (outlets). Work stations generally require from 4 to 12 outlets depending on the demands of the work being performed. To satisify these requirements, the designer must establish branch circuits with sufficient access to receptacles (outlets) to meet the need of each work station.

The Need for Flexibility: In order to achieve flexibility with conventional energy distribution systems, excessive use of extension cords has developed. This can cause serious hazards, including circuit overloads and the possibility of physical harm to the occupants from extension cords and receptacles lying in foot traffic paths. These situations are typical of conventional wiring methods that locate receptacles in the wrong places.

Unfortunately, services for electrical and communications distribution are either already installed or arranged for through methods that are largely out of the designer's control. To meet the needs for flexibility and access to electrical and communications service, the designer can use an open office furniture system that offers the user maximum flexibility and access to branch circuits.

Conventional Distribution Systems

Knowledge of conventional electrical and communication systems is an important first step in understanding the interfacing of open office design with these systems. To aid in this, the basic conventional distribution systems are presented here with fundamental elements that affect the interface with open office electrical and communications distribution systems.

Wall and Column Receptacles (Outlets): The energy distribution method most commonly used in the U.S.A. involves the location of power receptacles (outlets) in fixed walls and columns. In this method of wiring, wire is fed through conduit in walls to junction boxes attached to the wall structure. Then electrical receptacle (outlet) assemblies and telephone cables are added and the junction boxes are finished with cover plates for internal wiring protection and to cover the rough hole around the junction box. Approaches of this type are common in smaller office areas where work stations are adjacent to walls and columns. Distribution systems such as this are also abundant in most older structures and in new buildings with limited construction budgets.

Work station planning, using wall and column receptacles (outlets), must be done so as to provide local receptacles (outlets) for power. Work station designs of this type are best accommodated in buildings containing many columns, with work stations that radiate out from the columns. For areas with widely spaced columns and fixed walls that enclose very large spaces, the use of supplemental energy distribution techniques can be combined with this method to deliver energy to isolated areas and keep cost down.

Changing the location of wall or column junction boxes is difficult and expensive, since new holes in walls for junction boxes will have to be cut. To prolong the life of the primary power system, wall junction boxes should be carefully spaced.

Plenum Delivery: Electrical and communications distribution through the plenum, the open area between a suspended ceiling and the floor above, is also commonly used. Electrical wiring is routed through the plenum using standard conduit. Where plenums are used as part of the ventilation system, fire codes sometimes require communications cables to also be enclosed in conduit. Delivery from the plenum requires that electrical and communications cables be routed from the ceiling to the work stations by poles attached to the ceiling structure or to the furniture system.

With plenum delivery, there are no absolute rules on the spacing of power entries. However, the establishment of a conduit grid in the plenum with junction boxes at each intersection with flexible metal conduit attached offers the ability to make changes without expensive rewiring.

The use of too many power poles can become distracting and ugly. The use of 3-circuit, 3-phase power can reduce the number of power poles required to supply work station needs.

Overhead delivery relieves many of the constraints on work station position or configuration.

However, ceiling design can be a significant factor in layout plans. Light fixtures in coffered ceilings can dictate placements of power and requirements.

Floor Grid Systems: There are several methods of distributing power and communications wiring through the floor structure of a building. The most commonly used in smaller buildings is a system of steel tubes or ducts placed on 5' or 6' (1.5m or 1.8m) intervals. In larger multi-level buildings wiring may be run within cellular steel decks or concrete floors for convenient access to floor and ceiling outlets. The ceiling method offers the most raceway potential. Active cells are typically chosen to be 4' to 6' (1.2m to 1.8m) apart, although any of the cells can be

designated to carry wires.

Wires are supplied to the grid systems by conduit or feeder trenches connected to the main supply area and running at right angles to the cells or ducts. Feeder trenches have removable covers for the laying in of power and communications cables. Once the cables are in the feeder trenches they are fed through the cells or ducts to a termination point. At the termination point, a hole is drilled into the raceway through the concrete floor, allowing the connection of wires to a service fixture. The service fixtures are typically mounted in boxes or "monuments," floor outlet boxes, fastened to the floor.

Raised Floors: Raised floors are generally used in computer

rooms to conceal high density wiring and are often referred to as computer-room floors. Raised floors vary in load capacity from computer-room heavy to general construction weight, and the cost varies respectively. Raised floor panels, set on pedestals mounted to the building's floor, create an unrestricted space between the floor panels and the building's floor. The height of the access space below the floor panels can vary from about 4 inches to 3 feet (100mm to 900mm) and the pedestals are often height-adjustable for leveling. Though an expensive alternative to attaining electrical and communications objectives for open plan systems, raised floors can offer an economical solution to renovating an older building. By installing the mechan-

Glossary of Terms

Access Points— *Points within the electrical and communication distribution system that allow service access. This includes junction boxes, special receptacle connections, and raceway or duct openings.*

Ampere (Amp)— *A unit used to measure the strength of current.*

Circuit— *A complete electrical current path required to operate electrically powered devices.*

Circuit Breaker— *A switch that controls application of power to a building's power distribution system. It can automatically shut all power off should current in excess of its rated value be drawn.*

Conductor— *Wire used to carry electrical current to the point of use.*

Conduit— *Metal tubes that contain and protect electrical and communications wires.*

Flexible Metal Conduit— *Flexible metal tubes that contain and protect electrical and communications wires.*

Floor Monument (Floor Outlet)— *A floor-attached receptacle (outlet) used with power distribution systems built into floor structures or laid under carpet.*

Grounding— *A safety precaution accomplished by connecting receptacles (outlets) to earth ground or other conducting body. This is*

done to route any hazardous energy conditions to a location where they won't do any harm.

Listed by Underwriters Laboratories— *Indicates that equipment has been tested and meets minimum standards of safety established by Underwriters Laboratories. (U.S.A. only)*

Modular Relocatable Cables— *Flexible cables with special connector ends that allow quick circuit disconnection and reconfiguration.*

Single Phase Power— *A power structure that supplies one circuit.*

Straight Span Connector— *Connector used to span non-powered panels to continue power along a straight panel run.*

Three Phase Power— *A power structure that provides three independent sources.*

Under-Carpet Flat Wiring— *Electrical wire that is flat to allow routing under carpet squares. It is about 0.03" (0.008mm) thick and the width varies with the number of circuits it can carry (from one to three).*

Volt— *The force which produces current flow in an electrical circuit.*

Watt— *The measure of electrical power that varies in direct proportion to voltage and current used.*

ical systems (plumbing, ventilation, etc.) and electrical and communications cables over an old floor, and then placing a raised floor over everything, you can have maximum flexibility with minimum installation cost.

There are no special restrictions on access point spacing. However, to minimize cable confusion beneath the floor, a wiring grid system similar to that suggested for plenum wiring should be established.

Supplemental Energy Distributions

There are several systems of supplemental electrical and communications distribution. Many are just methods of bringing power and communications to where it is most needed and are not good systems of distribution. Modular relocatable cables and under-carpet flat wiring are two systems that, when utilized with the conventional distribution methods already discussed, provide more flexibility to open office designs.

Modular Relocatable Cables: Modular relocatable cables are a system of electrical and communication components (receptable assemblies, junction boxes, flexible metal conduit, etc.) prewired with either single- or dual-circuit capabilities. Each component or cable is fitted with special couplers to permit the assembly of branch circuits by simply plugging the components together.

Modular cables are incorporated into the plenum or beneath a raised floor to form flexible branch circuits that easily accommodate changing requirements.

Under-Carpet Flat Wiring: The newest development in elec-

trical and communications distribution in the U.S.A. is flat wiring. Flat wiring consists of three, four, or five flat conductors for distributing power to one-, two-, or three-circuit electrical systems. These flat conductors are placed edge to edge and separated and enclosed by insulating material. A bottom plastic shield attached to the cable provides protection against physical damage when the cable is installed on the floor. A metallic top shield is connected to ground and provides electrical and safety protection against physical damage. After the cable is laid, a steel tape covers the entire system to provide mechanical protection. The entire assembly is only 30/1000 of an inch (0.008mm) thick, about as thick as a credit card. However, at corners or junctions where cables are spliced together, the system can become as thick as 0.09" (0.023mm) causing a noticeable mound in the carpet surface.

Hardware to enable the connection of flat wiring to conventional electrical or communication cables is available from the manufacturer of the flat wiring. Codes require carpet tiles for inspection and convenient cable access.

Flat wiring can best be used to supply power and communications from walls or columns to island work stations. With pre-wired open office furniture systems power can be brought directly into the panels from the walls or columns, not requiring flat wire. However, if more power is available, it can be extended from one group of work stations to another unattached group by the use of flat wire.

In new construction, flat wiring can be used in place of under-floor duct or cell systems and save on the overall construction cost of the building. But to use flat wiring with an existing floor grid system would add extra cost to the job because of the increased cost of carpet tiles over broadloom carpet.

Planning Summary

A successful design is one that utilizes the full potential of the open office system, balancing the cost and performance required by the user.

The following guidelines are used by the designer during initial stages of an open office layout.
1. Decide whether electrical and communications distribution are important to the project or not.
2. Determine special electrical or communications needs.
3. Determine the type of electrical service; floor grid, plenum or walls and columns, and whether it is single-, dual-, or three-phase.
4. Provide sufficient number of receptacles (outlets) per circuit and the proper loading of each circuit.

Lighting

The use of indirect ambient lighting has rapidly become an integral part of interiors planning. Open plan systems have brought flexibility to the office and new requirements for lighting. This planning information explains lighting problems in the open office.

To understand and plan for lighting, it is necessary first to describe the task. A visual task is defined in terms of *size, contrast, brightness* and *color*. In addition, it is necessary to consider *time*.

If the size of print, for example, is large and clear, less light will be required. If the task consists of black printing on a white background, the contrast is high and, again, less light is needed. Brightness relates to the amount of light reflected off the task background and may require more or less light, depending on the task material. The color of the task is not usually a problem in offices, but could be, for example, where fabric samples must be matched.

The easiest office task would be reading a white sheet of paper with black printing for a short period of time. More difficult tasks would be reading pencil copy on yellow paper (low contrast) or using an adding machine or typewriter for longer periods of time.

Effects of Surroundings: How we see a task is greatly affected by the surroundings. There are several terms and conditions which relate to lighting.

These must be recognized and identified before you can plan a lighting layout properly.

Disabling Glare: This occurs when a person has a direct line of view to a bright object such as a window or light fixture. The eye must constantly adjust from the task to the higher brightness, resulting in eye fatigue.

Veiling Reflections: Veiling reflections are caused by regular reflections from a bright source (windows or light fixtures) being superimposed on the task. The result is partial or total obscuring of detail because of reduced contrast. For example, try reading glossy magazine stock near a light source.

Shadows: Shadows, created by obstructions between the light source and the task, are bad for visibility. Contrast is drastically reduced. This is a major problem when writing or drawing, especially with pencil on low brightness paper.

Surface Brightness: Surface brightness, also called luminance, is the amount of light reflected off a surface. The unit measurement of this light is called *footlamberts* (lamberts). When surfaces of drastically high and low brightness are present in a work station, the eyes are constantly adjusting to differing brightnesses. If the changes are major and happen often, eyes become tired and the ability to work is reduced.

Lamp Effects on Color and Visibility: There are three ways in which light sources affect color and visibility: the amount of illumination, color rendering, and the color temperature (warm to cool). Select your colors so you're not surprised when the job is installed.

Output vs. Color: The amount of light in a space affects the way

color is seen. Dark colors become almost black when little light is present. Lighter colors also change when the light levels are raised or lowered.

Color Rendering Index: The color rendering properties (called color rendering index or C.R.I.) of a lamp have great impact on colors. The chart below gives the obvious changes in several colors under each type of source. Yellow is not included, as it changes very little under various sources. The chart also shows the color temperature in Kelvin degrees and relates how efficiently various lamps produce light = lumens ÷ lamp wattage. Incandescent lamps, for example, have the highest C.R.I. of any source but are the least efficient and don't render blues and greens well. When choosing a nonstandard source, always test it with the color specified before ordering.

Temperature: Kelvin temperature (or color temperature) also has some effect on apparent color. From long experience and many tests we know that the environment can be affected adversely if the color temperature is too high or too low. Also, the apparent color of the light has a psychological effect on people. As the illumination intensity increases, the color temperature should be increased, and in office areas which vary from 25 to 100 footcandles (270 to 1076 lux), the color temperature should be at least 3,000° K. The cooler the color appears, the higher the Kelvin temperature.

Some Fundamentals of Lighting

In order to achieve good lighting, it is first necessary to understand some of the fundamentals of lighting quality and measurement.

Quantity of Light:

It is important today that lighting be energy efficient, flexible, and of high quality. With the low cost of energy in the past, and bull pen offices, lighting levels were kept high for the entire office. This was wasteful and, in most cases, very poor quality light because of disabling glare, shadows and veiling reflections, depending on the positioning of the desks. And for most tasks, the light was too bright.

To be energy efficient, lighting must be flexible so it can be placed where it is needed. The charts below show the recommended level of illumination for each area and for each type of task. The levels of illumination in the charts are expressed in *footcandles* (fc) (lux), which are units of direct illumination on a surface one square foot (square meter) in area and on which there is uniformly distributed light. This unit of measurement is best used for general lighting levels. Where lighting for a specific task area—task lighting— is important, lighting levels should be expressed in E.S.I. footcandles (lux).

Quality of Light:

E.S.I. (equivalent sphere illumination) footcandles (lux) relate to the quality of task visibility rather than just the quantity of light and should only be used to express footcandle (lux) levels of task lighting. A very simplified calculation would read: E.S.I. fc (lux) = Standard fc (lux), minus direct glare, minus veiling reflections.

Maintained Footcandle (Lux) Levels:

Another consideration when determining proper illumination over a period of time is the *light loss factor*. There are many different types of light loss factors, but the two most important ones are called lamp lumen depreciation (LLD) and luminaire dirt depreciation (LDD).

Lamp Lumen Depreciation:

LLD refers to the fact that as lamps burn for many thousands of hours their light output diminishes. This difference is noted in lamp manufacturers' catalogs as initial lumens and mean lumens respectively. For example, the difference between initial output and mean output in a metal halide lamp is a 31% decrease, in a 40W fluorescent lamp a 12% decrease occurs, and in a 30W fluorescent lamp, a 15% decrease.

Luminaire Dirt Depreciation:

LDD is based on the fact that dirt and dust obviously collect on any surface. As dirt and dust collect on the luminaire, light output is reduced. Cleaning the luminaire reduces this problem.

The combination of lamp lumen depreciation (LLD) and luminaire dirt depreciation (LLD) results in the light loss factor. This factor is also determined through use of a formula: light loss factor (LLF) = LLD × LDD.

Light loss factors for lamp/ luminaire combinations that are generally true regardless of manufacturer are as follows:

Metal halide indirect fixtures (horizontal lamp)_____57%

40W fluorescent indirect fixtures _____72%

30W fluorescent indirect fixtures _____70%

The above LLF's are based on the following:

1. Group relamp all H.I.D. fixtures every three years @ 3,000 hrs/ yr.

2. Group relamp all fluorescent fixtures every six years @ 3,000 hrs/yr.

LIGHT LOSS FACTORS

Time	H.I.D.	40W Fluorescent	30W Fluorescent
6 months	66%	85%	82%
1 year	64%	82%	80%
18 months	62%	79%	76%
2 years	60%	77%	74%
30 months	58%	74%	71%
3 years*	57%	72%	70%

*Recommended as minimum requirement

COLOR RENDERING PROPERTIES

Lamp	Color Temp. °K	Efficacy (lumens/watt)	C.R.I.	Apparent Color of the Light	Blue	Green	Red
40W (30W) Cool White Fluorescent	4370	63 (50)	67	Slight blue	Slightly grays or darkens	Grays, except blue-greens	Grays and darkens
40W (30W) Cool White Deluxe Fluorescent	4050	52 (35)	85	None	Lightens, cools, clearer	Clear, light	Clear, vibrant
250W Metal Halide Coated	3800	65	70	None	Cools, brightens	Cools, brightens	Clear vibrant
40W (30W) Warm White Fluorescent	3105	64 (51)	55	Slight yellow	Clear, rich	Light green bright dark green-warmed	Light red-bright dark red-browns
100W Incandescent	2854	17	97	Light orange	Dulls, darkens	Darkens, brownish hue	Vibrant
250W High Pressure Sodium	2100	97	23	Golden	Grays, darkens	Yellows	Browns

3. Clean all luminaires every three years.

If the lamps and luminaires are cleaned more often, the light loss factors are corrected as in the chart below. If an office environment is especially dirty, clean every 12 to 18 months.

The Design Process

To insure that your finished project is properly illuminated, a design procedure which coordinates the development of the space plan, electrical requirements, color scheme and lighting is required.

The Space: Since ambient lighting is reflected off the ceiling, the ceiling material is an important consideration. Ceiling material reflectance values should be at least 75% or better and a diffuse surface is required, as a specular (smooth and shiny) surface will mirror the image of the light fixture.

Plan each work station to meet the task requirements of the occupant. Then go back through the plan, making sure no primary or secondary work surface faces a window. These work surfaces must be oriented perpendicular to or facing away from a window wall to avoid direct glare.

The Color Scheme: The color chosen for each individual surface has an effect on the brightness of that particular surface. Obviously, light colors reflect more light and dark colors less—the brightness of any surface is directly related to the amount of light striking that surface. The equation is:

Brightness footlamberts (lamberts) = amount of light striking surface footcandles (lux) × the reflectance value of the color.

A good rule of thumb for the limit of a brightness ratio is:

Task to work surround limit 1 to ¼ brightness ratio;

Task to work station limit 1 to ⅛ brightness ratio.

In other words, the brightness of the work surround should not be less than a quarter the brightness of the task. For instance, if you have a task which has a reflectance of 80% (example: a sheet of paper without a lot of printing on it), the work surface and immediately adjacent panels should have a reflectance value of 20% or greater.

A task light mounted over a work surface will provide satisfac-

tory results to keep brightness ratios within their limits if the work surface, back and side panels have a reflectance greater than 20%. Where no task light exists, the brightness of panels around the work surface become important considerations. A vertical panel will normally receive about half the illumination received by horizontal work surfaces. A vertical panel, with no overhanging components, that is adjacent to a work surface where no task light is present must have a higher reflectance (30% to 40%) to meet the brightness ratio limit. If there is an overhanging component on the panel without a task light, the reflectance value is raised (40% to 60%).

The Positioning of Fixtures

There are four types of illumination which you should consider in order to create a comfortable working environment:

1. Task Lighting

2. Vertical Surface Illumination

3. Accent Lighting

4. Ambient Illumination

Once you have the color scheme and work station layouts deter-

mined, you can start positioning the light fixtures.

Task Lighting: Go through your layout and place task lights under the components which overhang work surfaces. Also place fluorescent ambient fixtures with down-lights on adjacent panels.

When task tables or desks are located where task lights can't be mounted, it becomes necessary to use ambient fixtures to increase the lighting to appropriate levels for the task. Footcandle (lux) levels are accumulative in that where the light from one fixture overlaps the light from another fixture, the footcandle (lux) levels can be added together to achieve the level desired. Free-standing H.I.D. fixtures can also be placed close to the task table to achieve task lighting.

Where a free-standing desk is used in the middle of a work station, the walls would be considered as remote panels for reflectance values.

Vertical Surface Illumination: Vertical surface illumination requirements not accommodated in the previous step should now be considered. Be sure to balance any daylight present in a work station either with light fabrics or by use of the down-light component of an appropriate fluorescent ambient unit. Also, add vertical surface illumination on large areas of panels where

GENERAL (AMBIENT) LIGHTING LEVEL REQUIREMENTS*

	footcandles	lux
Work station, nontask areas	25 to 30	270 to 323
Circulation (corridor) areas	10 to 20	108 to 215
Conference rooms, nontask areas	25 to 30	270 to 323
Lounge and waiting areas	25 to 30	270 to 323
Filing areas	30 to 40	323 to 430

*Now under debate

TASK LIGHTING LEVEL REQUIREMENTS*

		footcandles	lux
Reading:	Simple (high contrast) copy	50	538
	Difficult (low contrast) copy	70	753
Writing:	Short periods of time	50	538
	Long periods of time	70	753
Typing:	From good quality originals	50	538
	From poor quality originals	70	753
	Accounting areas	100	1076
	Drafting boards	100	1076
	CRT screens (display terminals)	50	538

*Now under debate

reflectance value is lower than 20% and in locations remote from the windows.

Accent Lighting: Add accent lighting, as desired, for the chalkboards, tack boards, and display shelves. If plants are to be accented with the down-light component of one of the fluorescent ambient units, determine their positioning and place the units in close proximity to them.

Planning Summary

For quick review, the following steps represent the complete planning and design process. Remember to follow each step in its proper progression and to complete and determine the requirements of the respective steps.

Also, familiarize yourself again with the general lighting information presented.

1. Determine special lighting and electrical needs.

2. Plan your space and double check.

3. Develop the color scheme and check reflectance data.

4. Place task lighting and determine ambients' task potential.

5. Provide vertical surface illumination and balance daylight.

6. Add accent lighting and consider plants.

7. Finish by accommodating ambient illuminating needs.

Glossary of Terms

Accent Lighting—*Directional lighting to emphasize a particular object or draw attention to a part of the field of view.*

Ambient Lighting—*Lighting designed to provide a uniform level of illumination throughout an area, exclusive of any provision for special task requirements.*

Candlepower—*A basic unit for measuring light output from a source in a given direction. For example, a typical wax candle has a candlepower of one candela when viewed from any side. Candela is the unit of measurement for candlepower.*

Coefficient of Utilization—*The ratio of the amount of light (lumens) from a fixture received on the work-plane to the lumens emitted by the fixture's lamps alone.*

Color Rendering—*A general expression for the effect of the light source on the color appearance of objects.*

Diffused Lighting—*Light that is not predominantly incident from any particular direction.*

Direct Glare—*Glare resulting from high brightnesses in the field of view or from reflecting areas of high brightness; i.e., windows or lighting fixtures.*

Direct Lighting—*Lighting by fixtures distributing 90% to 100% of the emitted light downwards to the work-plane.*

Disabling Glare—*Glare resulting in reduced visual performance and visibility. It is often accompanied by discomfort.*

Efficacy—*The quotient of the total amount of light (lumens) emitted by the total lamp input. It is expressed in lumens per watt (lm/W).*

Efficiency—*Fixture efficiency is the ratio of light (lumens) emitted by a fixture to that emitted by the lamp or lamps therein.*

Equivalent Sphere Illumination—*The level of sphere illumination (totally diffuse with no glare) which would produce task visibility equivalent to that produced by a specific lighting environment. It denotes the quality, as a ratio of the quantity, of light reaching the work-plane.*

Footcandle (lux)—*The unit of direct illumination on a surface one square foot (square meter) in area on which there is uniformly distributed light.*

Footlambert (lambert)—*A unit of luminance equal to $1/\pi$ candela per square foot (square centimeter) or to the uniform luminance of a perfectly diffuse surface emitting or reflecting light at the rate of one lumen per square foot (square centimeter) or to the average luminance of any surface emitting or reflecting light at that rate.*

Lamp—*A generic term for a man-made source of light.*

Light Loss Factor (LLF)—*A factor used in calculating the level of illumination after a given period of time under given conditions. Equals lamp lumen depreciation multiplied by the luminaire dirt depreciation factor.*

Lumen—*The unit of luminous flux (light output).*

Luminaire—*Another name for a lighting fixture. It is the complete unit including lamps, housing, reflector, louvers (if any), etc.*

Reflectance of a Surface—*The ratio of the reflected flux (light) to the incident flux.*

Reflector—*A device used to redirect the light from a source by the process of reflection.*

Task Lighting—*Lighting which provides illumination for a specific task area.*

Visual Surround—*Includes all portions of the visual field except the visual task.*

Useful Addresses

Office design is a complex field encompassing real estate, management, organizational studies, office technology, and environmental psychology as well as architecture and interior design. The following list is a resource guide to some sources of information available in these diverse fields. Included is a list of associations, office furniture sources, manufacturers and suppliers, building products, equipment, and magazines.

Associations: United States

ACOUSTICAL SOCIETY OF AMERICA
335 East 45th Street
New York, New York 10017

ADMINISTRATIVE MANAGEMENT SOCIETY
Maryland Road
Willow Grow, Pennsylvania 19090

Will supply information on any aspects of office management, systems, and procedures.

AMERICAN INSTITUTE OF ARCHITECTS
1735 New York Avenue, N.W.
Washington, D.C. 20006

AMERICAN INSTITUTE OF MANAGEMENT
125 East 38th Street
New York, New York 10016

AMERICAN MANAGEMENT ASSOCIATION
135 West 50th Street
New York, New York 10020

In addition to conducting seminars on all subjects related to office planning, the association publishes books and other literature.

AMERICAN SOCIETY OF CIVIL ENGINEERS
345 East 47th Street
New York, New York 10017

Electrical, electronic, air conditioning, and illuminating engineering, among others.

AMERICAN SOCIETY FOR INDUSTRIAL SECURITY
2000 K Street, N.W.
Washington, D.C. 20006

AMERICAN SOCIETY OF INTERIOR DESIGNERS
730 Fifth Avenue
New York, New York 10019

ART DEALERS ASSOCIATION OF AMERICA
575 Madison Avenue
New York, New York 10022

ASSOCIATION OF RECORDS MANAGERS AND ADMINISTRATION
P.O. Box 281
Bradford, Rhode Island 02808

AUDIO ENGINEERING SOCIETY
60 East 42nd Street
New York, New York 10017

BIFMA (THE BUSINESS AND INSTITUTIONAL FURNITURE MANUFACTURERS ASSOCIATION)
2335 Burton, S.E.
Grand Rapids, Michigan 49506
Tel.: 616-452-9292

BUILDING OWNERS AND MANAGERS ASSOCIATION
1221 Massachusetts Avenue, N.W.
Washington, D.C. 20005

CARPET AND RUG INSTITUTE
P.O. Box 2048
Dalton, Georgia 30720

CERAMIC TILE INSTITUTE
700 North Virgil Street
Los Angeles, California 90029
Tel.: 213-660-1911

DESIGN MANAGEMENT INSTITUTE
Massachusetts College of Art
50 Milk Street, 15th Floor
Boston, Massachusetts 02109

ENVIRONMENTAL DESIGN RESEARCH ASSOCIATION, INC.
L'Enfant Plaza Station
P.O. Box 23129
Washington, D.C. 20024

An interdisciplinary group of environmental psychologists, architects, geographers, and social scientists interested in the behavioral basis of design.

FACILITIES MANAGEMENT INSTITUTE
3971 South Research Park Drive
Ann Arbor, Michigan 48104
Tel.: 313-994-0200

Teaches courses, conducts research, consults, publishes, and maintains an information clearinghouse to develop facilities management practices. A division of Herman Miller Research Corp.

ILLUMINATING ENGINEERING SOCIETY
345 East 47th Street
New York, New York 10017

INDUSTRIAL DESIGNERS
SOCIETY OF AMERICA
1750 Old Meadow Road
McLean, Virginia 22101

Information on design for the
handicapped.

INSTITUTE OF BUSINESS
DESIGNERS
1155 Merchandise Mart
Chicago, Illinois 60654
Tel.: 312-467-1950

INSTITUTE OF ELECTRICAL
AND ELECTRONICS
ENGINEERS
345 East 47th Street
New York, New York 10017

INSTITUTE OF MANAGEMENT
CONSULTANTS
347 Madison Avenue
New York, New York 10017

INSTITUTE FOR
PROFESSIONAL EDUCATION
1901 North Fort Myer Drive
Arlington, Virginia 22209

Information on word processing,
microfilming, and data processing.

INTERIOR PLANTSCAPE
ASSOCIATION
11800 Sunrise Valley Drive
Reston, Virginia 22091
Tel.: 703-476-8550

INTERNATIONAL
AUDIOVISUAL SOCIETY
P.O. Box 54
Cullowhee, North Carolina 28723

NATIONAL COUNCIL OF
ACOUSTICAL CONSULTANTS
8811 Colesville Road
Silver Spring, Maryland 20910

NATIONAL FIRE PREVENTION
ASSOCIATION
470 Atlantic Avenue
Boston, Massachusetts 02110

NATIONAL RECORDS
MANAGEMENT COUNCIL
60 East 42nd Street
New York, New York 10017

SOCIETY OF PROFESSIONAL
MANAGEMENT CONSULTANTS
205 West 89th Street
New York, New York 10024

TILE COUNCIL OF
AMERICA, INC.
P.O. Box 2222
Princeton, New Jersey 08540
Tel.: 201-921-7050

WOMEN'S OCCUPATIONAL
HEALTH RESOURCE CENTER
Columbia University School of
    Public Health
60 Haven Avenue B-1
New York, New York 10032
Tel.: 212-694-3464

Associations: United Kingdom

BRITISH INSTITUTE OF
INTERIOR DESIGN
22–24 South Street
Ilkeston, Derbyshire
Tel.: 0602-329781

FURNITURE INDUSTRY
RESEARCH ASSOCIATION
Maxwell Road
Stevenage, Hertfordshire
Tel.: 0438-3433

Research, information service,
advisory services, furniture testing, management, methods of
production engineering, statistics,
marketing consultancy, education
and training.

OFFICE MACHINES AND
EQUIPMENT FEDERATION
16 Wood Street
Kingston-upon-Thames KT1 1VE
Tel.: 549-7699

Furniture and office equipment,
office supplies, communications
and allied products. Publishes the
magazine *Office Pride*.

BRITISH FURNITURE
MANUFACTURERS'
FEDERATED ASSOCIATIONS
30 Harcourt Street
London W1H 2AA
Tel.: 724-0854

Information service, equipment
data, exhibitions and shows, ex-
portation, meetings, education
and training, collection of statistics.

SIAD (SOCIETY OF INDUSTRIAL
ARTISTS AND DESIGNERS)
12 Carlton House Terrace
London SW1
Tel.: 839-4453

Promotes the understanding and
use of good design. Specialist
panels carry out research on
technological and economic developments. Furniture and Commercial and Industrial Interior
Design are categories within the
SIAD. The SIAD publishes the
journal *The Designer* and orga-
nizes conferences and awards. It
publishes literature on fees, professional conduct, and copyright
and runs a designer index, an
information service, and a library.

THE DESIGN COUNCIL
28 Haymarket
London SW1Y 4SU
Tel.: 839-8000

A grant-sided body whose aim is
to promote the improvement of
design in the products of British
industry. The main activities are
design advisory service; designer
selection service; Design Council
awards; design index (7,000 products, including office furniture);
Design magazine and *Engineering*
magazine; Design Council books;
design education; marketing ser-

vices (including buyers guides and
directories of British manufacturers); and design centers in London and Glasgow.

RIBA (ROYAL INSTITUTE OF
BRITISH ARCHITECTS)
66 Portland Place
London W1
Tel.: 580–5533

Directory of architects (for example, those specializing in office
planning and design); information
service; research; study groups;
conferences; library; education
and training; competitions; export
promotion; publications; and the
RIBA Journal.

Associations: Australia, Japan, New Zealand, South Africa

BRANZ (BUILDING RESEARCH
ASSOCIATION OF NEW
ZEALAND)
P.O. Box 9375
Wellington

DESIGN INSTITUTE SOUTH
AFRICAN BUREAU OF
STANDARDS
H5 22 Forum Building
Stuben Street
Private Bag X191
Pretoria 0001
Transvaal

IDCA (INDUSTRIAL DESIGN
COUNCIL OF AUSTRALIA)
The National Secretariat
114 Williams Street
Melbourne, Victoria 3000
Tel.: 601624

IDEA (INDUSTRIAL DESIGN
INSTITUTE OF AUSTRALIA)
21 Burwood Road, 2nd Floor
Hawthorn, Victoria 3122
Tel.: 8191311

INSTITUTE OF SOUTH AFRICAN
ARCHITECTS and SOUTH
AFRICAN COUNCIL FOR
ARCHITECTS
P.O. Box 31756
Braamfomtein, 2017
Tel.: 724-9241

JAPAN ARCHITECTS
ASSOCIATION
Kenchiku-ka Kaikan
Shibuya-ku
2–3–16 Jingumae
Tokyo

NEW ZEALAND INDUSTRIAL
DESIGN COUNCIL
70 Ghuzmee Street
Wellington
(Postal Private Bag Tearo)
Tel.: 847-612

NEW ZEALAND INSTITUTE OF
ARCHITECTS
Maritime Branch
2–10 Custom House K
Wellington
Tel.: 735-346

NEW ZEALAND SOCIETY OF
INDUSTRIAL DESIGNERS
P.O. Box 3432
Auckland

ROYAL AUSTRALIAN
INSTITUTE OF ARCHITECTS
2A Mugga Way
Redhill, Act 2603
also at P.O. Box 373
Manuka, Act 2603

SOCIETY OF INDUSTRIAL
ARTISTS AND DESIGNERS OF
SOUTH AFRICA
National Council
P.O. Box 23394
Jobert Park 2044
Transvaal
Tel.: 838-5013

Office Furniture: United States and Canada

AIRBORNE/ARCONAS
CORPORATION
580 Orwell Street
Mississauga, Ontario,
Canada L5A 3V7
Tel.: 416-272-0727

ALL-STEEL, INC.
P.O. Box 871, Route 31 and
   Ashland Avenue
Aurora, Illinois 60507
Tel.: 312-859-2600

ALMA DESK COMPANY
P.O. Box 2250
High Point, North Carolina 27261
Tel.: 919-885-4101

AMERICAN DESK
P.O. Box 429 or 49 and West
   Avenue G
Temple, Texas 76501
Tel.: 817-773-1776

AMERICAN SEATING COMPANY
902 Broadway Avenue, N.W.
Grand Rapids, Michigan 49504
Tel.: 616-456-0600

ART STEEL COMPANY, INC.
170 West 233rd Street
Bronx, New York 10463
Tel.: 212-548-5000

ATELIER INTERNATIONAL,
LTD.
595 Madison Avenue
New York, New York 10022
Tel.: 212-644-0400

AXIOM DESIGN
728 Montgomery Street
San Francisco, California 94111
Tel.: 415-788-5020

B & B AMERICA
745 Fifth Avenue
New York, New York 10151
Tel.: 212-752-5234

BAKER FURNITURE,
CONTRACT DIVISION
Number 917 Merchandise Mart
Chicago, Illinois 60654
Tel.: 312-329-9410

BRICKEL ASSOCIATES, INC.
515 Madison Avenue
New York, New York 10022
Tel.: 212-688-2233

BRUETON INDUSTRIES, INC.
227–02 145 Road
Springfield Gardens, New York
   11413
Tel.: 212-527-3000

C I DESIGNS
574 Boston Avenue
Medford, Massachusetts 02155
Tel.: 617-391-7800

CASA BELLA IMPORTS, INC.
3750 Biscayne Boulevard
Miami, Florida 33137
Tel.: 305-573-0800

CASTELLI FURNITURE, INC.
950 Third Avenue, 9th Floor
New York, New York 10022
Tel.: 212-751-2050

CONDI FURNITURE
MANUFACTURING
1965 East Vista Bella Way
Compton, California 90220
Tel.: 213-774-8300

DAVID-EDWARD, LTD.
3501 Marmenco Court
Baltimore, Maryland 21230
Tel.: 301-789-0700

DUNBAR FURNITURE
CORPORATION
601 South Fulton Street
Berne, Indiana 46711
Tel.: 219-589-2111

FACIT
66 Field Point Road
Greenwich, Connecticut 06830
Tel.: 203-622-9150

GF BUSINESS EQUIPMENT, INC.
229 East Dennick Avenue
Youngstown, Ohio 44501
Tel.: 216-746-7271

HALLER SYSTEMS, INC.
8687 Melrose Avenue Number 257
Los Angeles, California 90069
Tel.: 213-854-1109

HARDWOOD HOUSE, INC.
569 Lyell Avenue
Rochester, New York 14606
Tel.: 716-254-0600

HARTER CORPORATION
910 Prairie Avenue
Sturgis, Michigan 49091
Tel.: 616-651-3201

E.F. HAUSERMAN COMPANY
5711 Grant Avenue
Cleveland, Ohio 44105
Tel.: 216-883-1400; 800-321-8698

HAWORTH, INC.
One Haworth Center
Holland, Michigan 49423
Tel.: 616-392-5961; 800-632-3892

HELIKON FURNITURE
COMPANY, INC.
607 Norwich Avenue
Taftville, Connecticut 06380
Tel.: 203-886-2301

ICF, INC. (INTERNATIONAL
CONTRACT FURNISHERS)
305 East 63rd Street
New York, New York 10021
Tel.: 212-750-0900

JG FURNITURE SYSTEMS,
A DIVISION OF BURLINGTON
INDUSTRIES
121 Park Avenue
Quakertown, Pennsylvania 18951
Tel.: 215-536-7343

JSI (JASPER SEATING COMPANY)
932 Mill Street
Jasper, Indiana 47546
Tel.: 812-482-3204

KITTINGER COMPANY
1893 Elmwood Avenue
Buffalo, New York 14207
Tel.: 716-876-1000

KNOLL INTERNATIONAL
The Knoll Building
655 Madison Avenue
New York, New York 10021
Tel.: 212-826-2400; 800-223-1354

KREUGER
1330 Bellevue Street
P.O. Box 8100
Green Bay, Wisconsin 54308

LEHIGH-LEOPOLD FURNITURE
2825 Mount Pleasant Street
Burlington, Iowa 52601
Tel.: 319-753-2271; 800-553-2371

MERIDIAN, INC.
6830 Grand Haven Road
Spring Lake, Michigan 49456
Tel.: 616-842-1852

MILLER, HERMAN, INC.
8500 Byron Road
Zeeland, Michigan 49464
Tel.: 616-772-3300

MODERN MODE, INC.
6425 San Leandro Street
Oakland, California 94621
Tel.: 415-568-6650

NKR
1590 Matheson Boulevard
Mississauga, Ontario
Canada L4W 1JI

PACE COLLECTION, INC.
11–11 34th Avenue
Long Island City, New York 11106
Tel.: 212-721-8201

PROBBER, HARVEY, INC.
44 Probber Lane
Fall River, Massachusetts 02726
Tel.: 617-674-3591

ROSE JOHNSON
1111 Godfrey Avenue, S.W.
Grand Rapids, Michigan 49503
Tel.: 616-245-2103

SHAW WALKER COMPANY
P.O. Box 209
Muskegon, Michigan 49443
Tel.: 616-722-7211

STEELCASE, INC.
1120 36th Street, S.E.
Grand Rapids, Michigan 49501
Tel.: 616-247-2710

STENDIG, INC.
410 East 62nd Street
New York, New York 10021
Tel.: 212-838-6050

STORWAL INTERNATIONAL, INC.
901 Merchandise Mart
Number 901
Chicago, Illinois 60654
Tel.: 312-822-9240

STOW/DAVIS
25 Summer Avenue
Grands Rapids, Michigan 49504
Tel.: 616-456-9681

STUART, JOHN, INC./JOHN WIDDICOMB COMPANY
979 Third Avenue
New York, New York 10022
Tel.: 212-421-1200

SUNAR, LTD.
18 Marshall Street
Norwalk, Connecticut 06854
Tel.: 203-866-3100

THONET INDUSTRIES
491 East Princess Street
P.O. Box 1587
York, Pennsylvania 17405
Tel.: 717-845-6666

VECTA CONTRACT, INC.
1800 South Great Southwest Parkway
Grand Prairie, Texas 75051
Tel.: 214-641-2860

WESTINGHOUSE ELECTRIC CORPORATION, ARCHITECTURAL SYSTEMS DIVISION
4300 36th Street, S.E.
Grand Rapids, Michigan 49508
Tel.: 616-949-1050

JOHN WIDDICOMB
205 East 58th Street
New York, New York 10028

WOOD AND HOGAN
305 East 63rd Street
New York, New York 10021
Tel.: 212-355-1335

XCEPTION DESIGN, LTD.
2875 Industrial Boulevard
Laval, Quebec,
Canada H7L 3V8
Tel.: 514-668-0710

ZOGRAPHOS DESIGNS, LTD.
150 East 58th Street
New York, New York 10022
Tel.: 212-421-6650

FURNITURE FAIRS

Large trade fairs, in addition to exhibiting furniture, usually have a series of conferences, some of which address office design.

NEOCON is held annually in the Merchandise Mart in Chicago in June; IBS Birmingham (biennially October); SICOB Paris (September); Cologne Furniture Fair (biennially for office furniture); Milan (September).

Office Furniture: United Kingdom

ANTOCKS LAIRN, LTD.
Lancaster Road
Cressex
High Wycombe, Buckinghamshire HP12 4HZ
Tel.: 0494-24912

APEX STEEL FURNITURE COMPANY
225 Selbourne Road
Luton, Bedfordshire LU4 8NP

ARAM DESIGNS, LTD.
3 Kean Street
Covent Garden
London WC2B 4AT
Tel.: 240-3933

ARENSON INTERNATIONAL
Lincoln House
Colney Street
St. Albans AL2 2DX

CADO FURNITURE(UK), LTD.
54 Portman Square
London W1H 9PR
Tel.: 486-4931

CARSON OFFICE FURNITURE, LTD.
1 Beeston Place
London SW1W 0JJ
Tel.: 828-2087

CLICK SYSTEMS, LTD.
Low Moor Road
Kirkby-in-Ashfield
Nottingham NG17 7LH
Tel.: 0623-754012

COLLINS AND HAYES, LTD.
Ponswood
Hastings, Sussex TN34 1XF
Tel.: 0424-430186

CONTINENTAL COMFORT
15 Station Road
Longfield, Kent DA3 7QD
Tel.: 04747-5067

DP OFFICE CONCEPTS, LTD.
Hanover Buildings
Rose Street
Edinburgh EH2 2YQ
Tel.: 031-226-4927

DU-AL FURNITURE, LTD.
Du-al House
Byron Road
Harrow, Middlesex HA1 1LY

DESKING SYSTEMS
Valley Works
Lane End Road
Sands Industrial Estate
High Wycombe, Buckinghamshire

DISCOVERY SYSTEMS
Giltspur House
6 Giltspur House
London EC1A 9DE
Tel.: 248-3091

DODSON BULL
INTERIORS,
LTD.
The Barbican Trade Centre
100 Aldergate Street
London EC2
Tel.: 628-7020

ENVIROPLAN
Falconer Road
Haverhill, Suffolk CB9 7XU
Tel.: 0440-705349

ERGONOM INTERNATIONAL
38 Warren Street
London W1P 6JN
Tel.: 387-8001

EVERTAUT, LTD.
P.O. Box 33
Darwen, Lancashire BB3 2PW

FACIT OFFICE FURNITURE
DIVISION
3–4 Little Portland Street
London W1N 5AG
Tel.: 636-1164

FLEXIFORM
67 Wellington Street
Leeds LS1 1JL
Tel.: 0532-441026

FORM INTERNATIONAL, LTD.
Whittington House
19–30 Alfred Place
London WC1E 7EA
Tel.: 580-2080

GIROFLEX, LTD.
6 Giltspur Street
London EC1
Tel.: 236-0653

GRANT WESTFIELD, LTD.
Westfield Road
Edinburgh EH11 2QF

W. HANDS AND SONS
36 Dashwood Avenue
High Wycombe, Buckinghamshire
   HP12 3DX
Tel.: 0494-24222

HARTLAND BENTHEIM DESIGN
CONSULTANCY, LTD.
120 Kings Road
London SW3 4TR
Tel.: 581-4851/2

G.A. HARVEY OFFICE
FURNITURE
17–19 Redcross Way
London SE1 1TB
Tel.: 858-3232

HAUSERMAN, LTD.
Allen House
1 Westmead Road
Sutton, Surrey SM1 4JA
Tel.: 01-643-0835

PETER HAXWORTH AND
COMPANY, LTD.
17 Islip Road
Oxford OX2 7SN
Tel.: 0865-511831

HEAL CONTRACTS, LTD.
196 Tottenham Court Road
London W1A 1BJ
Tel.: 637-5232

HILLE INTERNATIONAL, LTD.
132 St. Albans Road
Watford, Hertfordshire
   WD2 4AG
Tel.: 92-42241

GEOFF HOLLINGTON
ASSOCIATES
74a Belsize Lane
London NW3 5BJ
Tel.: 431-2211

HOSTESS FURNITURE, LTD.
Vulcan Road
Bilston, West Midlands WV14 7JR
Tel.: 0902-43681

INTEGRATED FURNITURE
SYSTEMS, LTD.
44 Cathedral Place
London EC4M 7NQ
Tel.: 248-0712

INTERCRAFT
Berkeley Square House
Berkeley Square
London W1
Tel.: 493-1725

INTERSPACE, LTD.
Rosemont Road
London NW3
Tel.: 794-0333

ISOPLAN, LTD.
Icknield Way
Tring, Hertfordshire HP23 4JX
Tel.: 044-282-4111

KARTELL DIVISION
WCB Plastics, Ltd.
Road One
Industrial Estate
Winsford, Cheshire CW7 3RA
Tel.: 060-65-3921

LINVAR, LTD.
Barkby Road
Leicester LE4 7LL
Tel.: 0533-769181

LUCAS FURNITURE SYSTEMS
616 Wick Lane
London E3 2JJ
Tel.: 980-3232

N.S. MACFARLANE
(FURNITURE), LTD.
557 Sauchiehall Street
Glasgow G3 7PQ
Tel.: 041-221-7876

MAGPIE FURNITURE, LTD.
Four Marks
Alton, Hampshire
Tel.: 0420-63536

M. MARGOLIS, LTD.
341 Euston Road
London NW1
Tel.: 387-3188

MEDFURN
Elsley House
24–30 Great Titchfield Street
London W1P 7AD
Tel.: 580-9432

MINES AND WEST OF
DOWNLEY, LTD.
Downley
High Wycombe, Buckinghamshire
   HP13 5TX
Tel.: 0494-34411

MARTIN NEIL DESIGNS, LTD.
15 Dock Street
London E1 8JW
Tel.: 481-3034

HERMAN MILLER
149 Tottenham Court Road
London W1P OJA

OFFICE CONTRACTS
324 Kennington Park Road
London SE11

OMK DESIGN, LTD.
16–17 Lower Square
Isleworth
London TW7 6BW
Tel.: 650-6443/7

OPEN-PLAN
The Fairway
Bush Fair
Harlow, Essex CM18 6NJ
Tel.: 0279-418211

ORGA-TECH, LTD.
42 Gorst Road
London NW10 6LD
Tel.: 965-5611

PEARL DOT FURNITURE
WORKSHOPS
2 Roman Way
London N7
Tel.: 609-3169

PEL, LTD.
Oldbury
Warley, West Midlands B69 4HN
Tel.: 021-552-3377

PIEFF OFFICE FURNITURE,
LTD.
Portersfield
Cradley Heath
Warley, West Midlands B64 7BQ

PLUMB CONTRACTS, LTD.
West Orchard House
Bishop Street
Coventry CV1 1HS
Tel.: 0203-21433

PRIMO FURNITURE, LTD.
443–445 Holloway Road
London N7 6LW
Tel.: 263-3131

PROJECT OFFICE FURNITURE,
LTD.
Hamlet Green
Haverhill, Suffolk CB9 8QJ
Tel.: 0440-705411

RACE FURNITURE
New Road
Sheerness, Kent
Tel.: 07956-2311

RAMCHESTER, LTD.
68 Rochester Row
London SW1P 1JU
Tel.: 828-7565/6

JENS RISOM DESIGN, LTD.
141–143 Drury Lane
London WC2B 5TB
Tel.: 836-0713

GORDON RUSSELL, LTD.
Broadway
Worcestershire WR12 7AD
Tel.: 0836-853345/858211

SCANDIA
Darton Park
Dorton, Aylesbury HP18 9NR

SCOTT HOWARD ASSOCIATES,
LTD.
2 Manvers Street
Bath, Avon BA1 1JQ
Tel.: 0225-65911/2

SEID INTERNATIONAL (UK),
LTD.
49 Church Street
Barnsley, Yorkshire S70 2AH
Tel.: 0226-44000

SOLUTIONS INTERIOR DESIGN,
LTD.
27 John Adam Street
London WC2N 6HX
Tel.: 930-5285

SPECTRUM ARCHITECTURAL
IMPORTS, LTD.
53 Endell Street
London WC2
Tel.: 836-1104

STEELCASE STRAFOR (UK),
LTD.
50–54 Southampton Row
London WC1B 4AR
Tel.: 405-4474/8

STITCH FURNITURE
Unit 32
Nechells House
Richard Street
Birmingham B7 4AA
Tel.: 021-359-2038

TAN-SAD CHAIR COMPANY
(1931), LTD.
Lodge Causeway
Fishponds, Bristol BS16 3JU

TURNEVILLE SMITH AND SON,
LTD.
16–17 Hay Hill
Berkeley Square
London W1
Tel.: 499-1638

TWINLOCK, LTD.
36 Croydon Road
Beckenham, Kent BR3 4BH
Tel.: 658-3927/8

UNIT 4 CONTRACTS, LTD.
17–19 Neal Street
London WC2H 9PU
Tel.: 836-6753

VICKERS FURNITURE
P.O. Box 10
Dartford, Kent DA1 1NY

VOKO (UK), LTD.
11–14 Grafton Street
London W1X 3LA
Tel.: 629-5383

WILKINSON FURNITURE, LTD.
Monkhill
Pontefract, West Yorkshire
    WF8 2NS
Tel.: 0977-71191

WILLIAM VERE, LTD.
Chapel Lane
Sands
High Wycombe, Buckingham
    HP12 4BG
Tel.: 0494-22361

WILLIS COMPUTER SUPPLIES,
LTD.
P.O. Box 10
South Mill Road
Bishops Stortford, Hertfordshire

WILTSHIER CONTRACT
FURNISHING, LTD.
11 King Street
London WC2
Tel.: 836-9123

WOLFF AND ALEXANDER, LTD.
16 John Dalton Street
Manchester M2 6HT
Tel.: 061-832-5074

Office Furniture: West Germany

BEHR
Peter Müller
4310 Rheinfelden
Postfach 172
Tel.: 0049-7623/40909

BÜROSYSTEM UNKE
Industriestrasse 23
D-8904 Friedberg-Derching
Tel.: 821-78222

COMFORTO
Bergstrasse 1
D-4730 Ahlen
Tel.: 023-82/6631

FLEXFORM
Alteco
Kunstgewerbe GmbH
8021 Hohenscheftlarn
Tel.: 081/784198

FLÖTOTTO
EINRICHTUNGSSYSTEME
Postfach 6004
4830 Gütersloh 16
Tel.: 05209/591-0

AUGUST FROSCHER GmbH
AND COMPANY KG
Postfach 20
Bahnhofstrasse
7141 Steinheim
Tel.: 071-44/6051

GEBR. LÜBKE GmbH AND
COMPANY KG
Postfach 1660/3811
4840 Rheda-Wiedenbrück

GIRSBERGER
SITZMÖBELFABRIKEN
D-7833 Endingen
Tel.: 0-76-42-7081

INTER-PROFIL
Heumarkt 14
Cologne

KLÖBER GMBH AND COMPANY
Postfach 1320
7770 Uberlingen/Bodensee

KNOLL INTERNATIONAL
Simmenstrasse 1
7141 Murr/Murr

KÖNIG AND NEURATH
6367 Karben 1
Frankfurt/Main
Tel.: 06039/7081

ALEX LINDER GmbH
Siemensstrasse
D–7443
Frickenhausen bei Nürtingen
Tel.: 7022–4011

MERO
Postfach 6169
Steinachstrasse 5
D 8700 Wurzburg

NESTLER GmbH
Postfach 1920
7630 Lahr
Schwartzwald

PFALZ MOBEL
Postfach 1460
6908 Wiesloch

PLANMÖBEL EGGERSMANN
KG
Königsbergerstrasse 2
D–4992 Espelkamp
Tel.: 5772-4061

POHLSCHRÖDER GmbH AND
COMPANY KG
Postfach 689/690
Abt.M W 4600 Dortmund 1

RÖDER GmbH,
SITZMÖBELWERKE
Rontgenstrasse 10-16
6000 Frankfurt 60

ROSENTHAL
Postfach 1520
D-8672 Selb/Bayern
Tel.: 09287-721

RTR BÜROMÖBELFABRIK
RICHARD TRITSCH GmbH AND
COMPANY KG
Raventallerstrasse 49
D-7750 Rastatt
Tel.: 7222-34011

V. SCHÄRER SÖHNE AG
3110 Munsingen
Tel.: 031-92-1437

VITRA GmbH
Postfach 1240
D-7858 Weil am Rhein

VOKO
Postfach 6540
63 Gieben 1

WILDE & SPIETH
Zepplinstrasse
D-7300 Esslingen

Office Furniture: Italy

ARFLEX
20051 Limbiate (Milan)
Via Monte Rosa 27
Tel.: 02-9961241

U.S.A. under license:
Beyleriam, Ltd.
305 East 63rd Street
New York, New York

ARTEMIDE
Via Brughiera
20010 Pregnan Milanese
Milan
Tel.: 02-9391255

BELLOTTI SpA
20121 Milan
Via Legnano 8
Tel.: 02-3452246

BRUNATI SpA
20036 Meda (Milan)
Via Piave 24
Tel.: 0362-72743/5

CANTIERI CARUGATI
22070 Rovello Porro (Como)
Via Dante 13
Tel.: 02-9602800

CAPPELLINI
22060 Carugo (Como)
Via Cavour 7
Tel.: 031-761717

CASSINA SpA
20036 Meda (Milan)
Via L Busnelli 1
Tel.: 0362-70581

CASTELLI
Bologna 40128
Via Torreggiani 1

CITTERIO SpA
22040 Sirone (Como)
Tel.: 031-850142

COM (COOPERATIVA OPERAI
METALLURGICI)
Via Castelfranco 17
40017 San Giovanni
Persiceto
Bologna
Tel.: 051-821130

CONFORTI SA
37100 Verona
Via A Saffi 2
Tel.: 045-25692

COSTI AND C SpA
20135 Milan
Via Trebbia 22
Tel.: 02-585158/585295

FACOMET
20139 Milano
Via Ripamonti 89

FANTONI ARREDAMENTI SpA
Osoppo (Udine)
Tel.: 0432-986061

FARAM SpA
31040 Giavera Del Montello (TV)
Tel.: 0422-876211

FLEXFORM
Via Einaudi 23/25
20036 Meda (Milan)
Tel.: 0362-74426

ICF DE PADOVA
20090 Vimodrone (Milan)
Strada Padana Superiore 280
Tel.: 02-2500841/4

JOINT
Via Legnano 4
Milan 20121
Tel.: 02-878151

They are the stockists of the Metro
System in Italy.

KARTELL
Viale delle Industrie
20082 Noviglio (Milan)
Tel.: 02-9054065

KNOLL INTERNATIONAL
Via Flaminia 147
06034 Foligno (Perugia)

MARCATRE SpA
20020 Misinto (Milan)
Via Sant'Andrea 3
Tel.: 02-9648451

MIM-GERES SpA
20122 Milan
Via Durini 24
Tel.: 02-5456016

OCM Srl
20075 Lodi (Milan)
Via Landriani 10
Tel.: 0371-63782

OLIVETTI SYNTHESIS
54100 Massa
Via Aurelia Ovest 65
Tel.: 0585-47811

OSCAM SpA
Solaro (Milan)
Via Varese 175
Tel.: 02-9691166

PLANULA SpA
51031 Agliana (Pistoia)
Tel.: 0574-710581-5

ROBOTS
Via Caldara 34
Milan
Tel.: 02-592928

SACEA SpA
Via Ronchi 43
20025 Legnano (Milan)
Tel.: 0331-545383

SAGSA
Via Ripa Ticinese 111
Milan
Tel.: 02-8397738

SAPORITI ITALIA
21010 Besnate
Varese
Tel.: 0331-274198

SKIPPER SpA
20121 Milan
Via S Spirito 14
Tel.: 02-705691

TECNO
Via Bigle 22
Milan 20121
Tel.: 02-790341-4

UNIFOR EMME 3 SpA
22078 Turate (Como)
Via Isonzo 1

ZANOTTA
Via Vittorio Veneto 57
20054 Nova Milanese
Milan
Tel.: 0362-902813

ZETA SpA
20050 Verano Brianza (Milan)
Via XXIV Maggio 8
Tel.: 02-9689681-3

Office Furniture: Sweden

AB CURT ENSTRÖM
P.O. Box 57
S 16391 Spånga
Tel.: 8-36-29-20

FACIT
Luxbacken 1
L.Essingen
S 105 45 Stockholm
Tel.: 8-738-6000

AB BRUNO HERBST
Ekbacksvägen 2–4
S 161 30 Bromma
Tel.: 8-252600

A. KLAESSONS MÖBEL FABRIK
S710 10 Fjugesta

NKR DESIGN AB
Jönköping
Tel.: 036-14-2300

Office Furniture: Finland

ARTEK
Keskuskatu 3
00100 Helsinki 10
Tel.: 90-177533

AVARTE OY
Telakakatu 3
SF-60150 Helsinki 15
Tel.: 90-171-727

HEIMI OY
Eerikin Katu 11
SF-00100 Helsinki 10
Tel.: 90-648-701

LAHDEN PUUTYÖ OY
P.O. Box 117
15101 Lahti 10
Tel.: 918-335111

MARTELA OY
Kornetintie 6
00380 Helsinki 38
Tel.: 90-556311

SYSTEM OY
Aleksiskivenkatu 3
SF-00500 Helsinki 50

VIVERO OY
Munkkisaavenkatu 12
SF-00150 Helsinki 15

Office Furniture: Denmark

CADO THE ROYAL SYSTEM A/S
H. C. Andersens Boulevard 6
1553 Copenhagen V
Tel.: 01045-1111122

FRITZ HANSEN EFT A-S
DK-3450 Allerød
Tel.: 03-27-2300

E. KOLD CHRISTENSEN ApS
131 Rygards Alle
DK-2900 Hellerup

LABOFA
Smidstrupvej 11
DK-4230
Skaelfkoer
Tel.: 01045-3594800

PAUSTIAN
Vesterbrogade 67-1260
Copenhagen

PETER HIORT-LORENZEN
Lille Strandstraede 7
1254 Copenhagen K
Tel.: 01-12-17-14

Office Furniture: Switzerland

KNOLL INTERNATIONAL AG
Bernerstrasse Nord 208
CH-8064 Zurich

SAIMU
CP 39 Pazzallo
Noranco
(for Olivetti Synthesis)

STOLLGIROFLEX, LTD.
Hauptstrasse
5322 Koblenz
Tel.: 56 461115

KARL ZÜND AND COMPANY AG
Sitzmobelfabrik
CH-9445 Rebstein SG
Tel.: 004171/771392

Office Furniture: Holland

INTERHORST
Plantage Middenlaan 20
NL-1018 DE
Amsterdam
Tel.: 20-262 353

KREYMBORG b v
De Lairessestraet 125
Amsterdam

HANS W. WILLEMSE
Bosrand 15
3881 G S
Putten
Tel.: 0341-1192

Office Furniture: France

AIRBORNE
3 Rue de Grenelle
75006 Paris
Tel.: 222-23-50

ARFLEX FRANCE SA
162 Boulevard Voltaire
Paris XI

ARTIFORT FRANCE
221 Rue Benoit Franchon
78500 Sartrouville
Tel.: 915-17-72

ATAL
7 Rue Mariotte
75017 Paris
Tel.: 261-80-00

BRM
Boulevard de Thouars BP 67
79300 Bressuire
Tel.: 49-74-14-00

CASTELLI SA
13 Boulevard Ney
75018 Paris
Tel.: 200–32–00

CENTRE RONEO
37 Avenue de Friedland
75008 Paris
Tel.: 563-48-76

EBC (L'EQUIPEMENT DU
BUREAU CONTEMPORAIN)
10 Avenue du Genéral de Gaulle
93116 Rosny-sous-Bois
Tel.: 1-528-12-90

FACIT DM
308 Rue du Président S Allende
92700 Colombes
Tel.: 780-71-17

FANTONI MEUBLES ET
FONCTION
135 Boulevard Raspail
Paris

FARAM
4 Avenue de Friedland
75008 Paris
Tel.: 561-07-38

FORUM DIFFUSION
16 Rue Franklin
75016 Paris
Tel.: 647-90-10

FRÖSCHER SITFORM SARL
3 bis Rue Julien-Poupinet
BP 12
78150 Le Chesnay
Tel.: 3-955-24-09

GIROFLEX SARL
34 Boulevard de Grenelle
75015 Paris
Tel.: 577-29-19-46

GROSFILLEX EQUIPEMENTS
COLLECTIFS
Arbent
01107 Oyonnax
Tel.: 74-77-68-22

INTERBURO INTERNATIONAL
(SEID INTERNATIONAL)
153 Rue du Faubourg
  St.-Honoré
75008 Paris
Tel.: 562-22-40

INTERFORM
162 Boulevard Voltaire
75011 Paris
Tel.: 371-12-11

KNOLL INTERNATIONAL
  FRANCE
268 Boulevard St.–Germain
75007 Paris

LABOFA
Sainte Bibliothèques Reska
8 bis Rue des Taillandiers
75011 Paris
Tel.: 805-82-90

LITTON MOBILIER DE BUREAU
7 Rue Mariotte
75017 Paris
Tel.: 261-80-00

MD ENTREPRISES
85 Rue du Bac
75007 Paris
Tel.: 544-38-84

MOBILIER INTERNATIONAL
162 Boulevard Voltaire
75011 Paris
Tel.: 371-12-11

MULLCA
101 Avenue de Bobigny
93130 Noisy-Le-Sec
Tel.: 843-00-44

NELCO
20 Avenue du Président Allende
Zone Industrielle Ile Mozinor
Porte 22
93100 Montreuil
Tel.: 857-33-48

ORDO
253 Route de Nantes
85600 Montaigu
Tel.: 51-94-01-02

PERVAU
56 bis Rue National
75013 Paris
Tel.: 586-17-50

PLANSYSTEM
10 Rue St.-Senoch
75017 Paris
Tel.: 227-31-63

SCHLAPP-MÖBEL FRANCE
11 Villa Collet
75014 Paris
Tel.: 542-70-05/68–07

SPEITH FRANCE
24–28 Rue des Grands Champs
75020 Paris
Tel.: 373-25-57-374/75–26

STAFOR
134 Boulevard Haussmann
Paris
Tel.: 562-72-8

STEINER
18 Boulevard Maréchal-Foch
BP 59
93162 Noisy-Le-Grand
Tel.: 304-96-25

SYNTHESIS FRANCE
85 Rue de Landy
93300 Aubervilliers
Tel.: 1-833-32-62

TEDA
24 Rue Juge
75015 Paris
Tel.: 579-95-76

UNIFOR SA
6 Rue des Saints Pères
75007 Paris
Tel.: 260-76-22

UNIMOB
31 Rue d'Alençon
92400 Courbevoie

WESTINGHOUSE ELECTRIC
FRANCE SA
Tour Gan Cedex 13
92082 Paris La Défense
Tel.: 776-44-21

LE GUIDE DU MOBILIER DE
BUREAU (50 manufacturers in
one catalogue)—Available from:
SOCIP
4 Rue des Épinettes
75017 Paris

Manufacturers and Suppliers: United States

APCO GRAPHICS, INC.
Robin E. Williams, Dept. AC1
388 Grant Street, S.E.
Atlanta, Georgia 30312
Tel.: 404-688-9000

(Signage)

ARCHITECTURAL GRAPHIC
SYSTEMS, INC.
550 Bryant Street
San Francisco, California 94107
Tel.: 415-391-0449

(Signage)

ARCHITECTURAL
SUPPLEMENTS, INC.
150 East 58th Street
New York, New York 10022
Tel.: 212-758-0926

(Lighting and accessories)

ARTEMIDE, INC.
150 East 58th Street
New York, New York 10155
Tel.: 212-980-0710

(Lighting)

BEYLERIAN, LTD.
11 East 26th Street
New York, New York 10010
Tel.: 212-684-6650

(Accessories)

ELDON OFFICE PRODUCTS
1130 East 230th Street
Carson, California 90745
Tel.: 213-518-1600

(Accessories)

FORTUNY, INC.
509 Madison Avenue
New York, New York 10022
Tel.: 212-753-7153

(Accessories)

FULLER OFFICE FURNITURE
CORPORATION
10–16 44th Drive
Long Island City, New York 11101
Tel.: 212-688-2243

(Accessories)

HARRY GITLIN INC.
305 East 60th Street
New York, New York 10022
Tel.: 212-751-7130

(Lighting)

HABITAT, INC.
150 East 58th Street
New York, New York 10022
Tel.: 203-792-7400

(Lighting)

HALO LIGHTING, DIVISION
MCGRAW-EDISON COMPANY
400 Busse Road
Elk Grove, Illinois 60007
Tel.: 312-956-8400

(Lighting)

KLIEGL BROTHERS
32–32 48th Avenue
Long Island City, New York 11101
Tel.: 212-786-7474

(Lighting)

LIGHTING ASSOCIATES, INC.
305 East 63rd Street
New York, New York 10021
Tel.: 212-751-0575

(Lighting)

LIGHTOLIER, INC.
346 Claremont Avenue
Jersey City, New Jersey 07305
Tel.: 201-333-5120

(Lighting)

LUXO LAMP CORPORATION
Monument Park
Port Chester, New York 10573
Tel.: 914-937-4433

(Desk lamps)

MCDONALD PRODUCTS
2685 Walden Avenue
Buffalo, New York 14225
Tel.: 716-684-7200

(Accessories)

MCPHILBEN/OMEGA
LIGHTING COMPANY
270 Long Island Expressway
Melville, New York 11746
Tel.: 516-293-8500

(Lighting)

METCOR MANUFACTURING
749 South Kohler Street
Los Angeles, California 90021
Tel.: 213-627-0731

(Accessories)

NESSEN LAMPS, INC.
3200 Jerome Avenue
Bronx, New York 10468
Tel.: 212-295-0220

(Lighting)

OMEGA LIGHTING COMPANY
270 Long Island Expressway
Melville, New York 11747
Tel.: 516-293-8500

(Lighting)

PETER PEPPER PRODUCTS,
INC.
17929 South Susana Road
Compton, California 90221
Tel.: 213-979-0815

(Accessories)

RUBBERMAID COMMERCIAL
PRODUCTS, INC.
3124 Valley Avenue
Winchester, Virginia 22601
Tel.: 703-667-8700

(Accessories)

SMITH METAL ARTS COMPANY,
INC.
1721 Elmwood Avenue
Buffalo, New York 14207

(Accessories)

SMOKADOR, INC.
470 West First Avenue
Roselle, New Jersey 07203
Tel.: 201-241-5300

(Accessories)

TSAO DESIGNS, INC.
31 Grove Street
New Canaan, Connecticut 06840
Tel.: 203-966-9559

(Accessories)

Building Products: United States and Canada

ALCAN ALUMINUM
CORPORATION
100 Erieview Place
Cleveland, Ohio 44114
Tel.: 216-523-6800

(Ceilings)

ALLIED CORPORATION
Allied Fibers and Plastics
Company
1411 Broadway
New York, New York 10018

(Carpet fibers)

AMERICAN OLEAN TILE
COMPANY
1000 Cannon Avenue
Lansdale, Pennsylvania 19446
Tel.: 215-855-1111

(Tile)

AMTICO FLOORING, DIVISION
OF AMERICAN BILTRITE, INC.
3131 Princeton Pike Park
Lawrenceville, New Jersey 08648
Tel.: 609-896-3000

(Resilient flooring)

ARMSTRONG WORLD
INDUSTRIES, INC.
P.O. Box 3001
Lancaster, Pennsylvania 17601
Tel.: 717-397-0611

(Ceilings and flooring)

BADISCHE CORPORATION
P.O. Box Drawer D
Williamsburg, Virginia 23185
Tel.: 804-887-6573

(Carpet fibers)

BALI BLINDS-MARATHON
CAREY-MCFALL COMPANY
Loyalsock Avenue
Montoursville, Pennsylvania
17754
Tel.: 717-368-8666

(Window coverings)

BIGELOW SANFORD, INC.
P.O. Box 3089
Greenville, South Carolina 29602
Tel.: 803-299-2000

(Carpeting)

BLOOMSBURG CARPET
INDUSTRIES
919 Third Avenue
New York, New York 10022
Tel.: 212-688-7447

(Carpeting)

BRAND-REX
Telecommunications Division
P.O. Box 498
Willimantic, Connecticut 06226
Tel.: 203-423-7783

(Undercarpet telephone cable)

COLLINS AND AIKMAN
CORPORATION COMMERCIAL
FLOOR SYSTEMS
210 Madison Avenue
New York, New York 10016
Tel.: 212-578-1217

(Carpeting)

CORK PRODUCTS COMPANY,
INC.
250 Park Avenue South
New York, New York 10003
Tel.: 212-254-6477

(Flooring)

DESIGNED WOOD FLOORING
CENTER, INC.
940 Third Avenue
New York, New York 10022
Tel.: 212-421-6170

(Flooring)

DESIGN TEX FABRICS, INC.
56–08 37th Avenue
Woodside, New York 11377
Tel.: 212-335-9000

(Fabrics)

DOMESTIC MARBLE AND
STONE
41 East 42nd Street
New York, New York 10017
Tel.: 212-557-1980

(Marble)

EDWARD FIELDS, INC.
232 East 59th Street, 2nd Floor
New York, New York 10022
Tel.: 212-759-2200

(Carpeting)

FORMS AND SURFACES
P.O. Box 5215
Santa Barbara, California 93108
Tel.: 805-969-4767

(Hardware)

FRANCISCAN CERAMIC TILE
2901 Los Feliz Boulevard
Los Angeles, California 90039
Tel.: 213-663-3361

(Flooring)

GENERAL TIRE AND RUBBER
COMPANY/GTR
WALLCOVERING COMPANY
401 Hackensack Avenue,
    Suite 704
Hackensack, New Jersey 07601
Tel.: 201-489-0100

(Wallcovering)

GRANT HARDWARE COMPANY,
A DIVISION OF GRANT
INDUSTRIES, INC.
33A High Street
West Nyack, New York
    10994–9967
Tel.: 914-358-4400

(Window covering)

GRETCHEN BELLINGER, INC.
979 Third Avenue, 5th Floor
New York, New York 10022
Tel.: 212-688-2850

(Fabrics)

HOBOKEN WOOD FLOORING
CORPORATION
100 Willow Street
East Rutherford, New Jersey
    07073
Tel.: 201-933-9700

(Wood flooring)

HUNTER DOUGLAS, INC.
ARCHITECTURAL BUILDING
PRODUCTS DIVISION
P.O. Box 650
Durham, North Carolina 27702
Tel.: 800-334-8569

(Window coverings)

INTEGRATED CEILINGS, INC.
2231 Colby Avenue
Los Angeles, California 90064
Tel.: 213-272-1136

(Ceilings)

ITALIAN TILE CENTER
499 Park Avenue
New York, New York 10022
Tel.: 212-980-8866

(Flooring)

JASON INDUSTRIAL, INC.
340 Kaplan Drive, Box 507
Fairfield, New Jersey 07006
Tel.: 201-227-4904

(Flooring)

KENTILE FLOORS, INC.
58 Second Avenue
Brooklyn, New York 11215
Tel.: 212-768-9500

(Flooring)

BORIS KROLL FABRICS, INC.
979 Third Avenue, 2nd Floor
New York, New York 10022
Tel.: 212-755-6200

(Fabrics)

LARSEN, JACK LENOR, INC.
41 East 11th Street
New York, New York 10003
Tel.: 212-674-3993

(Fabrics and carpeting)

LEES CARPETS
Valley Forge Corporate Center
King of Prussia, Pennsylvania
    19406
Tel.: 215-666-7770

(Carpeting)

LEVOLOR LORENTZEN, INC.
1280 Wall Street West
Lyndhurst, New Jersey 07071
Tel.: 201-460-8400; (Illinois)
    800-322-4400; 800-447-4700

(Window coverings)

LOUVERDRAPE, INC.
1100 Colorado Avenue
Santa Monica, California 90401
Tel.: 213-450-6100; 800-421-6666

(Window coverings)

MARBLE TECHNICS, LTD.
40 East 58th Street
New York, New York 10022
Tel.: 212-750-9189

(Marble floors and walls)

MECHO SHADE CORPORATION
42–03 35th Street
Long Island City, New York 11101
Tel.: 212-729-2020

(Window coverings)

MOHAWK CARPET
57 Lyon Street
Amsterdam, New York 12010
Tel.: 518-841-2211

(Carpeting)

MONDO RUBBER (CANADA),
LTD.
2655 Francis-Hughes
Chomedey
Laval, Quebec
Canada H7L 3S8
Tel.: 514-668-7600

(Resilient flooring)

MONSANTO TEXTILES
COMPANY (S.E.F.)
1114 Avenue of the Americas
New York, New York 10036
Tel.: 212-764-5000

(Carpeting)

W.F. NORMAN CORPORATION
P.O. Box 323
Nevada, Missouri 64772
Tel.: 417-667-5552; 800-641-4038

(Ceilings)

OHLINE CORPORATION
1930 West 139th Street
Gardena, California 90249
Tel.: 213-327-4630

(Window coverings)

OSTERMANN AND SCHEIWE
U.S.A.
P.O. Box 668
Spanaway, Washington
Tel.: 206-847-1951

(Walls and ceilings)

OWINGS-CORNING
FIBERGLASS CORPORATION
Fiberglass Tower
Toledo, Ohio 43659
Tel.: 419-248-8182

(Acoustical partitions)

PPG INDUSTRIES, INC.
One Gateway Center
Pittsburgh, Pennsylvania 15222
Tel.: 412-434-3892

(Glass and glass block)

PYROLITE SYSTEMS, INC.
500 Jericho Turnpike
Mineola, New York

(Door hardware)

REPUBLIC STEEL INDUSTRIES
PRODUCTS DIVISION
1038 Belden Avenue, N.E.
Canton, Ohio 44705
Tel.: 216-438-5200; 800-321-0216

(Shelving)

H.H. ROBERTSON COMPANY
400 Holiday Drive
Pittsburgh, Pennsylvania 15220
Tel.: 412-928-7500

(Underfloor ducting)

SCHLAGE LOCK COMPANY
(PART OF WORLDWIDE
INGERSOLL-RAND)
2401 Bayshore Boulevard
San Francisco, California 94134
Tel.: 415-467-1100

(Hardware)

ISABEL SCOTT FABRICS
CORPORATION
245 Newtown Road
Plainview, New York 11803
Tel.: 516-249-3100

(Fabrics)

SIMPLEX CEILING
CORPORATION
50 Harrison Street
Hoboken, New Jersey 07030
Tel.: 212-349-1890

(Ceilings)

STANLEY HARDWARE
DIVISION
195 Lake Street
New Britain, Connecticut 06050
Tel.: 203-225-5111

(Hardware)

SUPREME EQUIPMENT AND
SYSTEMS CORPORATION
170 53rd Street
Brooklyn, New York 11232
Tel.: 212-492-7777

(Files)

THOMAS AND BETTS
920 Route 202
Raritan, New Jersey 08869
Tel.: 201-685-1600

(Wiring)

UNITED STATES GYPSUM
COMPANY
101 South Wacker Drive
Chicago, Illinois 60606
Tel.: 312-321-3865

(Walls and ceilings)

WELLCO CARPET
CORPORATION
P.O. Box 281
Calhoun, Georgia 30701
Tel.: 404-629-7301

(Carpeting)

WOLF-GORDON
WALLCOVERING (W-G VINYLS,
INC.)
132 West 21st Street
New York, New York 10011
Tel.: 212-255-3300

(Wall coverings)

Equipment: United States

BELL AND HOWELL
Automated Systems Division
280 Riley Street
Zeeland, Michigan 49464

(Equipment)

IBM
Armonk, New York 10504

(Equipment)

MOTOROLA, INC.
Communications Group
1301 East Algonquin Road
Schaumberg, Illinois
Tel.: 312-397-1000

(Equipment)

OLIVETTI CORPORATION OF
AMERICA
155 White Plains Road
Tarrytown, New York 10591
Tel.: 914-631-8100

(Equipment)

SONY CORPORATION
9 West 57th Street
New York, New York 10019

(Equipment)

TELSTAR COMMUNICATIONS
130 Buena Vista Avenue
Yonkers, New York 10701

(Communications)

WANG LABORATORIES, INC.
One Industrial Avenue
Lowell, Massachusetts 01851
Tel.: 617-459-5000

(Office equipment)

Magazines: United States and United Kingdom

Administrative Management
51 Madison Avenue
New York, New York 10010

Articles on planning, design, systems and procedures, comparative analysis of office equipment, etc.

The Architect's Journal
9 Queen Anne's Gate
London SW1H 9BY

The November 11 and November 18, 1981, issues were a comprehensive review of office design.

Architectural Record
1221 Avenue of the Americas
New York, New York 10020

The Architectural Review
The Architectural Press, Ltd.
9 Queen Anne's Gate
London SW1H 9BY
Tel.: 01-22-4333

Audio Video
380 Madison Avenue
New York, New York 10017

Building Operating Management
Box 694
407 East Michigan Street
Milwaukee, Wisconsin 53201

Building Owner and Manager
1221 Massachusetts Avenue, N.W.
Washington, D.C. 20005

Buildings
427 Sixth Avenue, S.E.
Cedar Rapids, Iowa 52406

Business Systems & Equipment
Maclean Hunter, Ltd.
76 Oxford Street
London W1
Tel.: 637-7511-8

Communications
1900 West Yale
Englewood, Colorado 80110

Contract
1515 Broadway
New York, New York 10036

Articles on office planning, furniture, furnishings, space concepts, etc.; also publishes an annual directory of sources of furniture and furnishings.

Corporate Design
850 Third Avenue
New York, New York 10022
Tel.: 212-593-2100

Engineering News Record
1221 Avenue of the Americas
New York, New York 10020

Facilities Design and Management
1515 Broadway
New York, New York 10036
Tel.: 212-869-1300

Food & Equipment Product News
347 Madison Avenue
New York, New York 10017

Industrial Design
1 Astor Plaza
New York, New York 10036

Information on design for the handicapped, office products, and ergonomics.

Information & Records Management
250 Fulton Avenue
Hempstead, New York 11550

Interior Design
850 Third Avenue
New York, New York 10022
Also publishes an annual directory of sources of furniture and furnishings.

Interiors
1515 Broadway
New York, New York 10036
Tel.: 212-764-7300
Reports about office design every month. The June 1981 issue was a special issue devoted to "The Office of the Future: a report of the *Interiors*/Design Management Institute Conference"; "Managing Corporate Office Design" was in the April 1982 issue.

Journal of Systems Management
24587 Bagley Road
Cleveland, Ohio 44138

Management World
Maryland Road
Willow Grove, Pennsylvania 19090

Modern Office Procedures
614 Superior Avenue West
Cleveland, Ohio 44113

The Office
1200 Summer Street
Stamford, Connecticut 06904

Office Equipment Index
Maclaren Group
Davis House
69–77 High Street
Croydon CR9 1QH
Tel.: 688-7788

Office Equipment News
Business Publications, Ltd.
109–119 Waterloo Road
London SE1 8UL
Tel.: 928-3388

Office Product News
645 Stewart Avenue
Garden City, New York 11530

Office Systems
IPC Electrical-Electronics Press, Ltd.
Quadrant House
The Quadrant
Surrey SM2 5AS
Tel.: 661-3500

Progressive Architecture
600 Summer Street
Stamford, Connecticut 06904

Reproductions Review & Methods
401 North Broad Street
Philadelphia, Pennsylvania 19108

Security Management
2000 K Street, N.W.
Washington, D.C. 20006

Telecommunications
610 Washington Street
Dedham, Massachusetts 02026

Word Processing World
51 Madison Avenue
New York, New York 10010

Several magazines have had special issues devoted to office design: *Domus* (December 1979); *Technique et Architecture* (May 1981); *Bauwelt* (January 1977); *Interiors* (June 1981, the automated office); and *The Architect's Journal* (November 11 and 18, 1981).

Bibliography

Altman, Mary Ann. "Revisiting Law Office Layout and Design." *American Bar Association Journal,* Vol. 65, November 1979.

Benjamin, I.A., and S. Davis. "Flammability Testing for Carpet." NBSIR 78–1436, Washington, D.C., U.S. Department of Commerce, 1978.

Bradford, Peter, producer; Barbara Prete, ed. *Chair: The Current State of the Art with the Who, the Why, and the What of It.* New York: Thomas Y. Crowell, 1978.

Brief, Michael E. "Interior Plantscaping: What the Designer Needs to Know." *Designer West,* Vol. 28, No. 10, August 1981.

Caplan, Ralph. *The Design of Herman Miller.* New York: Whitney Library of Design, 1976.

The Carpet and Rug Institute. *Carpet Specifier's Handbook.* Dalton, Georgia 1980.

Center for Fire Research, Institute for Applied Technology, National Bureau of Standards, Washington, D.C. 20234

Consumers Guide, editors of. *Decorating Your Office for Success.* New York: Harper and Row, 1979.

Cowan, Peter, director, and David Fine, John Ireland, Clive Jordan, Dilys Mercer, and Angela Sears of the Joint Unit for Planning Research, University College of London and the London School of Economics. *The Office: A Facet of Urban Growth*. New York: American Elsevier Publishing Co., Inc., 1969.

Delgado, Alan. *The Enormous File*. London: John Murray, 1980.

Duffy, Francis, et al. *Planning Office Space*. New York: Nichols Publishing Co., 1976.

Duffy, Francis. "Interior Design: Future of Office Planning." *The Architectural Review*, June 1979.

———. "Paper Factory or Room with a View?" *Architectural Journal*, September 1979.

Floor Covering Weekly. *Handbook of Contract Floor Coverings*. New York: Bart Publications Inc., 1981.

Fracchia, Charles A. *So This is Where You Work?* New York: A Studio Book, The Viking Press, 1979.

Friedman-Weiss, Jeffrey. *Working Places*. New York: St. Martin's Press, 1980.

Galloway, Lee. *Organizing the Stenographic Department*. New York: Ronald Press, 1924.

Gorb, Peter, ed. *Living by Design*. London: Lund Humphries, 1979.

Haines Lundberg Waehler. *Analysis of Office Furniture Systems*. New York, 1981.

An inhouse workbook used by the Interiors Division.

Hall, Edward T. *The Hidden Dimension*. Garden City, New York: Anchor Books, Doubleday and Co., Inc. 1966

Hayward, J.F. *English Desks and Bureaux*. London: Victoria & Albert Museum, Her Majesty's Stationery Office, 1968.

Hewes, Jeremy Joan. *Workstead: Living and Working in the Same Place*. New York: Dolphin Books, Doubleday and Co., Inc., 1981.

Hicks, David. *Living With Design*. New York: William Morrow and Co., Inc., 1979.

Joiner, Duncan. "Social Ritual and Architectural Space." In *Environmental Psychology, 2d ed.—People and Their Physical Settings*. Harold M. Proshansky, William H. Ittelson, and Leanne Rivlin, eds. New York: Holt, Rinehart and Winston, 1970.

Kramer, Sieverts and Partners. *Open Plan Offices*. London: McGraw-Hill Book Co. (UK) Ltd., 1977.

Leffingwell, William Henry. *Office Management: Principles and Practices*. Chicago: A.W. Shaw Co., 1925.

Malkin, Jain. *The Design of Medical and Dental Facilities*. New York: Van Nostrand Reinhold Co., 1982.

Management Conference. *Improving Office Environment*. Elmhurst, Illinois: Business Press, 1969.

Manning, Peter, ed. for the Pilkington Research Unit. *Office Design: A Study of Environment*. University of Liverpool, Department of Building Science, reprinted 1966.

Mills, C. Wright. *White Collar*. New York: Oxford University Press, 1951, reprinted 1976.

Mills, Edward David. *The Changing Workplace: Modern Technology and the Working Environment*. London: George Godwin, Ltd., 1972.

Mogulescu, Maurice. *Profit Through Design*. Amacom, 1970.

Moskowitz, Milton; Michael Katz; and Robert Levering. *Everybody's Business*. San Francisco: Harper and Row, 1980.

Mumford, Lewis. *The Culture of Cities*. London: Routledge, 1938.

Osborn, Alex F., and Robert E. Ramsay. *The Optimism Book for Offices*. Jamestown, New York: Art Metal Construction, Inc., 1918.

Palmer, Alvin E., and M. Susan Lewis. *Planning the Office Landscape*. New York: McGraw-Hill Book Co., 1977.

Parsons, H. McIlvaine. "Work Environments." In *Human Behavior and Environmental Advances in Theory and Research*, Vol. I, Irwin Altman and Joachim F. Wohlwill, eds. New York: Plenum Press, 1976.

Pentagram. *Living By Design*. London: Lund Humphries; New York: Whitney Library of Design, 1979.

Pevsner, Nikolaus. *A History of Building Types*. Princeton, New Jersey: Princeton University Press, 1976.

———. *The Sources of Modern Architecture and Design*. New York: Frederick A. Prager, 1968.

Pile, John F. *Interiors 3rd Book of Offices*. New York: Whitney Library of Design, 1976.

———. *Open Office Planning*. New York: Whitney Library of Design, 1978.

Prete, Barbara, ed.; Peter Bradford, producer. *Chair: The Current State of the Art with the Who, the Why, and the What of It*. New York: Thomas Y. Crowell, 1978.

Price, Judith. *Executive Style*. New York: The Linden Press, Simon and Schuster, 1980.

Propst, Robert. *The Office—A Facility Based on Change*. Zeeland, Michigan: Herman Miller, Inc., 1968.

Salmon, Geoffrey. *The Working Office*. London: Design Council, 1979.

Saphier, Michael. *Office Planning and Design*. New York: McGraw-Hill Book Co., 1969.

———. *Planning the New Office*. New York: McGraw-Hill Book Co., 1978.

Schultze, Earl, and Walter Simmons. *Offices in the Sky*. Indianapolis: Bobbs Merrill, 1959.

Shoshkes, Lila. *Space Planning*. New York: Architectural Record Books, 1976.

"The Steelcase National Study of Office Environments: Do They Work?" Conducted by Louis Harris & Associates, Inc., 1978.

Steele, Fred I. *Physical Settings and Organization Development*. Reading, Massachusetts: Addison-Wesley Publishing Co., 1973.

Stein, Richard G. *Architecture and Energy*. Garden City, New York: Anchor Press, Doubleday and Co., 1978.

Toffler, Alvin. *The Third Wave*. New York: William Morrow and Co., Inc., 1980.

Von Jürgen, Joedicke. *Office and Administration Buildings*. Stuttgart: Karl Kramer Verlaf, 1975.

Whiton, Sherrill. *Interior Design and Decoration* (4th ed.). Philadelphia: J.B. Lippincott Co., 1974.

Index

A

Accessories, office, 116
Acoustic consultants, getting help from, 240. *See also* Design professionals, getting help from
Acoustic panels, 66–67
Acoustic plaster, 68
Acoustic tiles, 66–67, 68
Action Office, furniture system, 36, 98
Advertising agencies, office needs of, 188–189
Aluminium-panel ceilings, 67–68
Ambient lighting. *See* Lighting, ambient
Architects, office needs of, 190
Art, in the office, 122
Asphalt tiles, as a flooring material, 87
Automation, of office. *See* Technology, office automation and

B

Bearing walls, 74
Beepers, 230
Bennett, Ward, work of, 48
Best Products Building, 170
Board rooms, 134–135
Building leases, 238–239
    continuing rights, 239
    rent commencement, 239
    work letter, 238–239

C

Carpets, 82–85
    cost of, in general, 82
    factors to consider when selecting, 82–84
    flammability of, 85
    installation of, 84
    the open office and, 82
    preventive maintenance of, 85
    wear and tear of, 84–85
    See also Flooring materials
Carpet tiles, 84–85. *See also* Flooring materials
Casement cloths, 92
Cathode ray terminal (CRT). *See* Video display terminal (VDT)
Ceilings, 66–69
    aluminium panel, 67–68
    coffered, 68
    exposed, 68–69
    gypsum board, 68
    plaster, 68
    suspended, 66, 67
    wood, 68
Central Beheer Building, 15, 40, 172–173
Ceramic tiles, as a flooring material, 88
Chairs. *See* Desk chairs; Lounge chairs; Sofas; Visitors' chairs
Clerestory windows, 78, 202
Clerical areas, 142
Coat closets, 144
Coffered ceilings, 68
Commercial offices, earliest, 10
Company image, designing for, 236–237
Condominium office buildings, 43
Conference rooms, 148, 190, 249
Conran, Terence, work of, 62
Consulates, office needs of, 192

Conversions
    of a ferryboat, 176
    of townhouses, 182
    of a Victorian mansion, 178
Convertible offices, at home, 214–216
Cork
    as a flooring material, 82, 87
    as a wallcovering, 76
Corridors, 144
Credenzas, 104
Curtain walls, 74

D

Daroff, Karen, and the Smithkline Building, 246–247
Demountable partitions, 77
Dentists, office needs of, 194–195
Design development, 240
Designers
    getting help from, 238–239, 240
    office needs of, 189
Design professionals, getting help from, 238–241
    acoustic consultants, 240
    designers, 238–239, 240
    lighting consultants, 240
    management consultants, 239
    mechanical engineers, 240
    structural engineers, 240
Desk chairs, 106–107
Desks
    W.H. Leffingwell on, 98
    Robert Propst on, 36, 98
    See also Partner's desks; Pedestal desks; Table desks
Doctors, office needs of, 196–197
Doors, 96–97. *See also* Entrance doors
Downlights, 72
Draperies, 92–93
Drapery pockets, 68, 92
Drywall construction, 74
Duffy, Eley, Giffone, Worthington (DEGW), work of, 250–251

E

Employee cafeterias, 138
Electronic background music. *See* White noise
Electronic mail, 38
Electronic pagers, 230

Electronics
    at home, 222
    and office design, 114
    See also Technology
Energy conservation project, Enerplex, 42–43
Entrance doors, 126
Ergonomics, 24, 40, 106, 114
Executive bars, 140
Executive baths, 140
Executive dining rooms, 136
Executive secretary areas, 132
Executive suites, 130
Exposed ceilings, 68–69
Eye strain, strategies for reducing, 70

F

Fabric, as a wallcovering, 50, 76
Famous people, offices of, 30, 32
Fashion designers, 198
Filing, 150
Film, offices in, 28
Flooring materials, 82–89
    asphalt tiles, 87
    carpets, 82–85
    ceramic tiles, 88
    cork, 82, 87
    cost of, in general, 82
    glazed tiles, 88
    leather, 87
    linoleum, 87
    masonry, 82, 88–89
    paver tiles, 88
    quarry tiles, 88
    reinforced vinyl tiles, 82, 86–87
    vinyl, 82, 87
    wood, 82, 88
    See also Resilient flooring
Floors. *See* Flooring materials
Fluorescent lighting, 70, 72, 73
Ford Foundation Building, 168
Forster Associates, and the Willis Faber & Dumas Building, 174
Free-standing walls, 80

G

Glass, as a wall finish, 78–79
Glass blocks, as walls, 55, 78–79
Glazed tiles, as flooring, 88
Government offices, earliest, 10
Gwathmey/Siegel and Associates, work of, 54–55
Gypsum-board ceiling, 68
   panels, for walls, 74

H

Hardy Holzman Pfeiffer Associates, and the Best Products Building, 170
Heating, cost of, 42
Hertzberger, Herman, and the Central Beheer Building, 172–173
Hicks, David, work of, 60
Home
   convertible office at, 214–216
   office electronics at, 222
   separate office at, 218–220
   working at, pros and cons, 210–212
High-intensity discharge lighting, 73
Horizontal blinds. *See* Venetian blinds
Humanizing the office, 40–41, 44, 248–249

I

Image, of company, designing for, 236–237
Incandescent lighting, 72, 73
Industrial Revolution
   expansion of offices during, 12
   insurance companies and, 14
Intelligent processor, 38
Interiors
   art deco, 58, 59
   cost of, 43
   systematization of, 26–27
   types of, 20
Interior walls. *See* Partitions

K

Kitchen areas, 152

L

Lamps, 118
La Porte, Doris, work of, 52
Lawyers, office needs of, 200–202
Leases. *See* Building leases
Leather, as a flooring material, 87
Leffingwell, W.H.
   on desks, 98
   Office Management, Principles and Practices, 24
Libraries, 146, 202
Lighting, 70–73
   ambient, 43, 67, 72, 162
   cost of, 42, 70, 73
   downlights, 72
   fluorescent, 70, 72, 73
   high-intensity discharge, 73
   incandescent, 72, 73
   task, 43, 67, 72, 73, 104, 162
   track, 72–73
   veiling reflection and, 70
Lighting consultants, getting help from, 240. *See also* Design professionals, getting help from
Lighting recess, 68
Linoleum, 87
Lounge chairs, 110, 111

M

Machines, office, spaces for, 156
Mail rooms, 154
Management, of office. *See* Office management, introduction of
Management consultants, getting help from, 239. *See also* Design professionals, getting help from
Masonry floors, 82, 88–89
Mechanical engineers, getting help from, 240. *See also* Design professionals, getting help from
Mirrors, as a wall finish, 77
Mock-ups, 240, 244, 247
Modern offices, evolution of, 14–15
Moving offices, 224, 226–228

N

Nelson, George, and the Aid Association to Lutherans Building, 248–249

O

The Office: A Facility Based on Change (Propst), 98
Office management, introduction of, 24–25
Office Management, Principles and Practices (Leffingwell), 24
Open office, the
   carpeting and, 82
   demountable partitions and, 77
   design considerations for, 164–165
   history of, 36–37
   S. C. Johnson & Son Building, 166–167
   Quickborner Team and, 36, 234
   space planning for, 234, 247
   systems available for, 160–162
   walls and, 74
Open-plan office. *See* Open office, the
Operational areas, 142

P

Paint, as a wall finish, 74–75
Partitions, 74, 75, 78
Partner's desks, 102
Paver tiles, as flooring, 88
Pedestal desks, 100
Pentagram, work of, 58–59, 180
Pink noise, 162
Planning office space. *See* Space planning
Planning the New Office (Saphier), 238
Plants, in the office, 120–121, 168
Plaster ceilings, 68
Platner, Warren, work of, 242–243

Plenums, 66, 67, 68
Portable offices, 230
Portable telephones, 230
Post-occupancy evaluations, 240
Preliminary design, 239–240
Producers, office needs of, 204
Productivity, and the office environment, 40–41
Professional offices, earliest, 10
Propst, Robert, 36, 98, 99
   Action Office, furniture system of, 36, 98
   The Office: A Facility Based on Change, 98
Publishers, office needs of, 200

Q

Quarry tiles, as flooring, 88
Quickborner Team, 24, 41, 36, 234

R

Reception areas, 128–129, 198, 202, 247
Reflected ceiling plan, 66
Reinforced vinyl tiles, as a flooring material, 82, 86–87
Resilient flooring, 86–87. *See also* Flooring materials
Reveals, 68
Roche, Dinkeloo & Associates
   and the Ford Foundation Building, 168
   and the Union Carbide Building, 244–245
Rubber, as flooring, 82, 87

S

Saladino Associates, work of, 56
Saphier, Michael, *Planning the New Office*, 238
Screening rooms, in advertising agencies, 188
Shades, 92
Shoskes, Lila, *Space Planning*, 26
Shutters, 93
Silicon chips, 34
Skylights, 69, 242–243
Skyscrapers, 16–17

Smithkline Building, 246–247
Sofas, 110
Space planning, 26–27
  concept of, 26–27
  in design of law offices, 200
  general considerations, 234–235
  the open office and, 234, 247
  technology and, 234
Space Planning, (Shoskes), 26
Stairs, 158
Stone, as a flooring material. *See* Masonry floors
Storage
  in the convertible office at home, 214
  of data, in general 150
  of files in law offices, 202
Structural engineers, getting help from, 240. *See also* Design professionals, getting help from
Suspended ceilings, 66, 67

T

Table desks, 98–99
Task lighting, *See* Lighting, task
Technology
  automation and, 38–39, 234
  carpet fibers and, 83
  history of, in office, 22
  recent developments, 34, 230
  space planning and, 234
  telephones and, 112, 230
Telephones, 112–113
  portable, 230
Tempered glass, 78
Tiles, as a flooring material. *See* Flooring materials
Track lighting, 72–73
Traders, office needs of, 208

U

Unilever House, 58–59
Union Carbide Building, 26, 27, 244–245

V

Veiling reflection, 70
Venetian blinds, 91

Vertical blinds, 92
Video conferences, 38, 39
Video display terminal (VDT), 38, 40, 70, 114, 222
Vignelli Associates, work of 50–51
Vinyl
  as a flooring material, 82, 87
  as a wallcovering, 76
Visitors' chairs, 108
Visual display unit (VDU). *See* Video display terminal (VDT)
Voice-activated computer, 39, 114
Voice mail, 230

W

Waffles, 69
Waiting rooms, 194, 195, 196
Wallcoverings, 75–76. *See also* Walls
Wallpaper, 76
Walls, 74–80
  construction of, 74
  demountable partitions, 77
  free-standing, 80
  with glass, 78–79
  glass-block, 55, 78–79
  mirror, as a finish material, 77
  the open office and, 74
  paint, as a finish for, 74–75
  sound isolation and, 74
  wood, 76–77
  See also Wallcoverings
Walter Landor and Associates, ferryboat conversion, 176
White noise, 41, 162
Willis Faber & Dumas Building, 174
Window coverings, 90–93
  draperies, 92–93
  shades, 92
  shutters, 93
  Venetian blinds, 91
  vertical blinds, 91–92
Windows, 90–95
  clerestory, 78, 202
  coverings for, 90–93
  in doctors' offices, 197
Wire glass, 78
Wood
  ceilings, 68
  floors, 82, 88
  walls, 76–77
Word processors, 34, 200
Wright, Frank Lloyd, and the S. C. Johnson & Son Building, 166–167

Picture Credits

20/21
1, 2, 5. The Prudential Insurance Co.;
3. National Monuments Record, London, ©Batsford;
4. The Walker Art Center.

22/23
1, 3. The Prudential Insurance Co.;
2. The Continental Corporation;
4, 5. The Library of Congress.

24/25
1–3, 5. The New York Public Library;
4. ©The Design Council, London.

26/27
1. The Prudential Insurance Co.;
2. Ezra Stoller ©ESTO.

28/29
1–5. The Museum of Modern Art, N.Y.

30/31
1, 3. Richard Bryant;
2. MPBW, London;
4. Crown Copyright, London;
5. Ezra Stoller ©ESTO.

32/33
1. Victoria and Albert Museum, London;
2. The Metropolitan Museum of Art, New York;
3. Felix Mann, Eastman House, Rochester, N.Y.;
4. The Library of Congress;
5. ©ESTO.

34/35
1, 2, 5. IBM;
3. Xerox Corporation;
4. Steelcase, Inc.

36/37
1, 3, 4. The Quickborner Team;
2. Ezra Stoller ©ESTO;
5. Philip Sayer ©The Design Council.

38/39
1. Herman Miller, Inc.;
2. ©Pentagram;
3. Mark Ross.

40/41
1. The E.F. Hauserman Co.
2. Norman McGrath;
3. Kenneth Gilliam;
4. Louis Reens;
5. Ezra Stoller ©ESTO;
6. Derek Balmer.

42/43
1. Wolfgang Hoyt ©ESTO;
2. Donovan and Green;
3. Rock Townsend;
4. Gensler & Associates.

44/45
1. David Leach;
2. Jaime Ardiles-Arce;
3, 5. Ken Kirkwood;
4. ©David Hicks;
6. Environetics, Inc.

48/49
1. Bob Winchell;
2, 3. Jaime Ardiles-Arce;
4. John Hill;
5. Peter Aaron ©ESTO.

50/51
1, 2, 4, 5. Nini Mulas;
3, 6, 7. Luca Vignelli.

52/53
1–6. Jaime Ardiles-Arce.

54/55
1–6. Otto Baitz.

56/57
1–4. Jaime Ardiles-Arce.

58/59
1–7.©Pentagram.

60/61
1–5. Ken Kirkwood.

62/63
1–7. Ken Kirkwood.

66/67
1. Armstrong World Industries;
2. Norman McGrath.

68/69
1. David Leach;
2. Ezra Stoller ©ESTO;
3. Jaime Ardiles-Arce;
4. Peter Aaron ©ESTO;
5. Jessica Strang.

70/71
1. ©Trickett Associates;
2. Ezra Stoller ©ESTO;
3. Bernard Liebman;
4. Norman McGrath;
5. Elliot Fine.

72/73
1. Ken Kirkwood;
2, 4. Mark Ross;
3. Jaime Ardiles-Arce.

74/75
1. Jaime Ardiles-Arce;
2. Elliot Fine;
3. Norman McGrath.

76/77
1. Bernard Liebman;
2. Richard Bryant;
3. Norman McGrath.

78/79
1. Jaime Ardiles-Arce;
2, 3. Mark Ross;
4. Louis Reens.

80/81
1. Mark Ross;
2. ©Trickett Associates;
3, 4. Norman McGrath;
5. Jaime Ardiles-Arce;
6. Richard Bryant.

82/83
1. Tom Crane;
2. Jaime Ardiles-Arce;
3. Ezra Stoller ©ESTO.

84/85
1, 4. Interface Flooring Systems;
2. Norman McGrath;
3. Richard Bryant.

86/87
1. Norman McGrath;
2. Jaime Ardiles-Arce.

88/89
1, 4. Designed Wood Flooring Center;
2. The Italian Tile Center;
3. Norman McGrath.

90/91
1. Jessica Strang;
2, 3. Ezra Stoller ©ESTO;
4. Jaime Ardiles-Arce;
5. Norman McGrath;
6. Hunter Douglas, Inc.

92/93
1. Norman McGrath;
2. Flötotto;
3. C. Kottal, Levolor Lorentzen, Inc.;
4. Tom Crane;
5, 6. Jaime Ardiles-Arce.

94/95
1, 4. Jaime Ardiles-Arce;
2. Mark Ross;
3. Bernard Liebman;
5. Ken Kirkwood.

96/97
1, 2, 5. Norman McGrath;
3. David Frazier;
4. Philip Sayer ©The Design Council, London;
6. Jaime Ardiles-Arce.

98/99
1. Alexander Georges;
2. Rosenthal;
3. Sunar;
4. Olivetti;
5. Nini Mulas;
6. Robert Giard.

100/101
1, 3. Knoll International;
2. Brickell Associates;
4. Sunar;
5. John Widdicomb, Inc.;
6. Herman Miller, Inc.

102/103
1, 3, 4. Jaime Ardiles-Arce;
2. The Desk Shop, Oxford, England.

104/105
1. ©ESTO;
2. David Frazier;
3. Jaime Ardiles-Arce;
4, 5. Norman McGrath.

106/107
1. Brickel Associates;
2. Herman Miller, Inc.;
3. Atelier International;
4. Harter Corporation;
5. Vivero;
6. Stendig, Inc.;
7. Pledge;
8. Knoll International;
9. Krueger;
10. Stow/Davis;
11. Vecta Contract;
12. Steelcase, Inc.

108/109
1. Jaime Ardiles-Arce;
2. ©David Hicks;
3. Tom Crane;
4. ©Conran.

110/111
1, 3. Jaime Ardiles-Arce;
2. Laura Ashley;
4. David Leach.

112/113
1, 6. Jaime Ardiles-Arce;
2, 4. Norman McGrath;
3. Jon Naar ©1982;
5. Herman Miller, Inc.

114/115
1, 2. Jaime Ardiles-Arce;
3. Stendig, Inc.;
4. ©ESTO.

116/117
1. Frank Ritter;
2, 3. dePolo/Dunbar;
4. Jaime Ardiles-Arce;
5. Luca Vignelli;
6. Hunter Douglas, Inc.

118/119
1. Artimede;
2. Jaime Ardiles-Arce;
3. David Frazier;
4. Norman McGrath.

120/121
1. Mark Ross;
2. Tim Street Porter;
3. ©Trickett Associates;
4. ©Hertzberger.

122/123
1. Richard Bryant;
2. Tim Street Porter;
3. Mario Bellini;
4. Mark Ross;
5. Ezra Stoller ©ESTO.

126/127
1, 6. Jaime Ardiles-Arce;
2, 3, 5. Norman McGrath;
4. Tim Street Porter.

128/129
1. Ken Kirkwood;
2. Roger Bester;
3, 6. Jaime Ardiles-Arce;
4. Norman McGrath;
5. Richard Bryant, DEGW.

130/131
1, 2. Norman McGrath;
3. Mark Ross;
4. Jaime Ardiles-Arce;
5. The Space Design Group.

132/133
1. Norman McGrath;
2. Jeremiah Bragstad;
3. Jaime Ardiles-Arce;
4, 5. Tom Crane.

134/135
1, 2. Bernard Liebman;
3. Nini Mulas;
4. ©The Design Council, London;
5. Richard Bryant;
6, 7. Ezra Stoller ©ESTO.

136/137
1, 4, 5. Norman McGrath;
2. Tom Crane;
3. Luca Vignelli.

138/139
1. ©The Design Council, London;
2. Mark Ross;
3. Ronald Livieri, KRJD & A;
4, 5. Norman McGrath.

140/141
1, 6. Jaime Ardiles-Arce;
2. Mark Ross;
3. Ken Kirkwood;
4. Norman McGrath;
5. Jessica Strang;
7. Ezra Stoller ©ESTO.

142/143
1. Kenneth Gilliam;
2. Jessica Strang;
3, 4. Tom Crane;
5. Mark Ross;
6. Ronald Livieri, KRJD & A.

144/145
1. Bernard Liebman;
2–4. Norman McGrath;
5. Louis Reens;
6. Mark Ross;
7. Jessica Strang.

146/147
1, 3. Jaime Ardiles-Arce;
2. Norman McGrath;
4. Ezra Stoller ©ESTO.

148/149
1. Tom Crane;
2. John Franklin and Kennedy Sumner;
3. Ken Kirkwood;
4. Norman McGrath;
5. Ronald Livieri, KRJD & A;
6. Jaime Ardiles-Arce.

150/151
1, 6. Steelcase, Inc.;
2. Norman McGrath;
3. Ken Kirkwood;
4. Jaime Ardiles-Arce;
5. Supreme Equipment & Storage Systems Corp.;
7. Jessica Strang;
8. Haller Systems Inc.

152/153
1. Trickett Associates;
2. Tom Crane;
3. Bernard Liebman;
4, 5. Richard Bryant;
6. ©Trickett Associates;
7. Jon Naar ©1982.

154/155
1. Bell & Howell;
2. Jaime Ardiles-Arce;
3. Jeremiah Bragstead;
4. Herman Miller, Inc.;
5. David Hirsch.

156/157
1. Mark Ross;
2, 3. Norman McGrath;
4. Jaime Ardiles-Arce;
5. National Photo (Persbureau B.V.).

158/159
1, 4. Norman McGrath;
2. Jaime Ardiles-Arce;
3. David Hirsch;
5. Karl Rosenberg;
6. Mark Ross.

160/161
1. Haller Systems, Inc.;
2. Sunar;
3. Jaime Ardiles-Arce;
4. Flostotto.

162/163
1–5. Atelier International;
6. Herman Miller, Inc.

164/165
1. Hedrich-Blessing;
2. Sunar;
3. Jerry Bragstad.

166/167
1, 8, 9. S.C. Johnson and Son;
2, 4. John Pile;
3, 5–7. Yasuto Tanaka.

168/169
1, 3–5. Ezra Stoller ©ESTO;
2. Ronald Livieri, KRJD & A;
6. Norman McGrath.

170/171
1–6. Norman McGrath.

172/173
1, 5–8. ©Hertzberger;
2–4, 9. Abby Suckle.

174/175
1, 3–6. Ken Kirkwood;
2. Phil Sayer ©The Design Council.

176/177
1–3, 5, 6. Landor Associates;
4. Mark Kauffman.

178/179
1–6. Mark Kauffman.

180/181
1–7. ©Pentagram.

182/183
1–6. Richard Bryant.

184/185
1, 2. Ken Kirkwood;
3, 4. Tim Street Porter;
5. Architectural Association Library, London;
6. Serena Vergano;
7, 8. Mario Bellini.

188/189
1. Peter Vitale;
2, 3. Bernard Liebman;
4, 5. ©Pentagram;
6. Richard Bryant.

190/191
1. Peter Aaron ©ESTO;
2. Norman McGrath;
3. Jaime Ardiles-Arce;
4. Ken Kirkwood;
5. Mark Ross.

192/193
1, 5. Norman McGrath;
2–4. ©Pentagram.

194/195
1, 2, 4, 6, 7. Michael Denny;
3, 5. Mark Kauffman.

196/197
1, 2, 5, 6. Norman McGrath;
3, 4. Maris Photo.

198/199
1. Jaime Ardiles-Arce;
2, 3. Norman McGrath.

200/201
1. Gensler & Associates;
2–4. Jaime Ardiles-Arce.

202/203
1–5. Jaime Ardiles-Arce.

204/205
1–6. Jaime Ardiles-Arce.

206/207
1, 2. Robert Mayers;
3. Oxford University Press;
4. Norman McGrath;
5. The Design Council;
6. Ezra Stoller ©ESTO.

208/209
1–7. ©Pentagram.

210/211
1–3. Les Carron.

212/213
1. E. Stoecklein;
2–6. Norman McGrath.

214/215
1–5. International Contract Furnishings, Inc.

216/217
1. Oliver Gregory;
2. David Frazier;
3. Norman McGrath;
4, 5. Peter Vitale;
6–8. Ken Kirkwood.

218/219
1, 2. Derry Moore;
3, 4. Johnson Burgee;
5. Paul Warchol ©ESTO.

220/221
1. David Leach;
2, 3. William Ellis;
4, 5. Ken Kirkwood.

222/223
1. Chris Callis;
2. Peter Aaron ©ESTO.

224/225
1, 2. ©The Design Council;
3–5. Phil Sayer ©The Design Council.

226/227
1. Cees Van der Meulen;
2, 3. National Photo (Persbureau B.V.).

228/229
1–4. Douglas Barnard, Inc.;
5. Jaime Ardiles-Arce.

230/231
1–3. Motorola, Inc.;
4. The Sony Corporation;
5. Beth Galton;
6. The Sony Corporation.

234/235
1. ©Trickett Associates;
2. The E.F. Hauserman Company;
3. Neville Lewis Assoc.;
4. Mark Ross;
5. Haller Systems Inc.

236/237
1, 6. Norman McGrath;
2. ©Rock Townsend;
3. Roger Bester;
4. Tom Crane;
5. ©David Hicks.

238/239
1. Arsene/Lambros Design;
2. Skidmore, Owings and Merrill;
3. dePolo/Dunbar.

240/241
1, 2. Ken Kirkwood;
3. Gil Amiaga.

242/243
1–5, 7. Ezra Stoller ©ESTO;
6. Platner Associates.

244/245
1–8. Ronald Livieri, KRJD & A.

246/247
1, 4, 6–7. Norman McGrath;
2, 3, 5. Tom Crane;
8. Daroff Design Inc.

248/249
1–7. George Nelson and Associates.

250/251
1, 3, 4, 6. Richard Bryant;
2, 5, 7, 8. DEGW.

The Office Book is really about working. In the process of writing it, I had the opportunity to work with many people—architects, designers, and those from other fields. Their generosity with time, expertise, and information made writing The Office Book a gratifying and exciting experience. I gratefully acknowledge their help and salute their devotion to excellence in their work.

Acknowledgements

Creative Perspectives; Steven Kiviat and Nancy Reedy of Atelier International; Justin Lamb for the use of his library; Landor Associates; Jain Malkin; Florence Mayers; Bob Mayers and John Schiff; James Rappoport; Karl Rosenberg; Arlene Rudicoff at Karl Ruff Associates; William Kent Schoenfisch, Michael Schwarting of Design Collaborative; Edith Siroto; Abby Suckle; John Sullivan of I.M. Pei; Henry

Bernstein typed the manuscript and contributed moral support.

The photographs in this book convey as much information as the text. I was fortunate to be able to include so many beautiful photographs, and I'd like to thank the individuals and firms that supplied them. I'm especially grateful to Jaime Ardiles-Arce, Norman McGrath, Mark Ross, and Ezra Stoller for access to their files and to Ken Kirkwood for his commissioned work.

Transforming manuscript and transparencies into a book, the realm of publishing, was a new world for me. I'd like to thank the people who helped me through it. Michael and Eileen Friedman offered constant support after having suggested I undertake this project. Agent Charlotte Sheedy advised me along the way. Martina D'Alton, officially a picture researcher, also researched the history section and helped structure the book. Sylvia Katz supplied photographs and supervised photography in the U.K. and Europe with long-distance good cheer. Contributing editors Pamela Ferguson, Richard Horn, and Kathy Matthews helped shape the manuscript. Melissa Sutphen helped with the captions. Editor John Smallwood always kept the end in sight; special thanks to project editor Linda Sunshine, who got us there, with grace. Consulting editors Francis Duffy and John Pile made valuable suggestions about the text and photographs. They also helped sort out errors and omissions. Those that remain are my own.

Special thanks to Larry Kazal and M & Co. His design for The Office Book communicates the ideas that everyone worked so hard to convey and makes its own statement about the power of design.

New York, New York
1982

To the architects and designers of "Designer's Choice," I offer admiration and special thanks for sharing their ideas: Ward Bennett, Terence Conran, Karen Daroff, Francis Duffy, Charles Gwathmey, David Hicks, Peter Harrison of Pentagram, George Nelson, Doris La Porte, Warren Platner, Kevin Roche, John Saladino, Robert Siegel, Lella Vignelli, and John Worthington.

I'd like to thank the many colleagues and friends who supplied advice and support: Marvin Affrime, David Bjerklie, and Jules Lasky of The Space Design Group; Raul de Armas and Debby Curtain of Skidmore, Owings and Merrill; David Arnold; Giles Aureli; Fred Bach of the Quickborner Team; Douglas Barnard, ASID; Laura Diffenderfer for sharing her expert knowledge of the carpet industry; M. Arthur Gensler and Associates; Nancye Green and Jane Zash of Donovan and Green; Jordan Gruzen; Klaus Herdeg; Pat Hopp of Herman Miller, Inc.; Lynn and Richard Orbach of

Smith-Miller of Rubin and Smith-Miller; John Thomas for his tour of the "Back Room"; Frieda Wenger; and Charles Winecoff. Special thanks to Valentine Lehr of Lehr Associates for his help with metric equivalents in the Appendix. For sharing information about their professions and work environments, I'd like to thank Shirley Chernela; Nan Dillon; Richard Golub; Dr. Albert Graf; Ken Iscol; Frederick Kahn, D.D.S.; Barry Klingman; Adam Moss; Joel Marsh; and Arthur Sachs of the Arthur Sachs Insurance Agency. Special thanks to Jim Henson of Henson Associates. To the countless others who helped me in this vast project, I am very grateful.

Architect and environmental psychologist Stephan Marc Klein, my partner, deserves special mention. He helped conceptualize and inform The Office Book from its inception. Rob Kaminoff, Yona Nelson-Shulman, and Rich Wener, our CONTEXT co-directors, made valuable contributions. Karen Graham and Richard Kaselow also offered suggestions. Marsha